CAPTIVE CITY

CAPTIVE CITY

CAPTIVE CITY

by

OVID DEMARIS

LYLE STUART, INC.
new york

To Inez

AUTHOR'S FOREWORD

One of the problems in writing a book of this nature is that the contemporary sometimes ripens into history long before it reaches the reader. People have a way of dying or losing elections or just fading into the morass of the city, never to return. But what's in a name? It is all one in the end. The only lasting reality is the System, Democratic or Republican, it is always there, always the same. And that is the real story of Chicago.

Many have contributed to the making of this book. For reasons entirely proper, some would prefer to remain anonymous. I honor their wish and offer my warmest thanks. I am equally grateful to the others: Vinton W. Bacon, John H. Bickley, Giacomo J. Bologna, Harry R. Booth, Ray Brennan, W.J. Devereux, Julius Draznin, William J. Duffy, Paul E. Kamerick, the late Joseph Morris, Richard Patch, Virgil W. Peterson, M.B. Phillips, Thomas R. Sheridan, Paul Simon, Charles Siragusa, Ted Smart, Charles Voll, Charles G. Ward, Lloyd Wendt, Orlando W. Wilson, Joseph I. Woods, and Laura Lynn Tucker, who contributed the library of her father, the late Rev. Elmer Lynn Williams. I especially wish to thank my wife Inez for her valuable assistance in research and in the preparation of the final manuscript.

TABLE OF CONTENTS

Author's Foreword   vii

Book One: THE OMNISCIENT OUTFIT   1

Book Two: THE CLOUT MACHINE   93

Book Three: THE LAWLESS LAW   233

Appendix: THE ANTISOCIAL REGISTER   321

Index   355

BOOK ONE
THE OMNISCIENT OUTFIT

Who is responsible for the powerful Chicago rackets which have blighted business, looted the treasuries of labor unions, padded public contracts, made puppets of policemen, cowed courts, maimed and murdered with impunity? It is not a dark mystery which cannot be solved. Yet exasperated citizens are repeatedly asking why are not these rackets smashed and the racketeers put in jail? The answer is that racketeers are useful to certain men favorably situated in business, in politics, and even in some of the professions and to a portion of the press. It is only when the racketeer becomes too strong and gets out of hand that the cry is raised by privileged persons that the racketeer must go.

—LIGHTNIN' (June 1940)

In the modern criminal underworld we face a nationwide, highly organized, and highly effective internal enemy.

—JOHN F. KENNEDY

1

From the moment of its incorporation as a city in 1837, Chicago has been systematically seduced, looted and pilloried by an aeonian horde of venal politicians, mercenary businessmen and sadistic gangsters. Nothing has changed in more than 130 years. The same illustrious triumvirate performs the same heinous disservices and the same dedicated newspapers bleat the same inanities. If there has been any change at all, it has been within the triumvirate itself.

In the beginning, the dominant member was the business tycoon, the ruthless entrepreneur out to make a quick financial killing, whether it be in land speculation, railroads, hotels, meat packing or public utilities. Pirates like Potter Palmer, Philip Armour, George Pullman, Charles T. Yerkes and Samuel Insull fed the city with one hand and bled it dry with the other. Then, around the turn of the century, with the population explosion out of control, the politician gained the upper hand over his partners in the coalition. It remained for the gangster to complete the circle in 1933 following the murder of Mayor Cermak. Today it is nearly impossible to differentiate among the partners—the businessman is a politician, the politician is a gangster, and the gangster is a businessman.

This, then, is the story of this revolving triumvirate, and of the people who support its crimes and applaud its circuses.

Since it has been impossible to penetrate the mysterious upper echelon of the Mafia, the criminal nexus of organized crime, police like to think of it in terms of a corporate structure. In this scheme, Tony Accardo* becomes chairman of the board, the old man who was kicked upstairs after thirteen years of exemplary leadership. Gathered around him at the board table are such venerable directors as Paul "The Waiter" Ricca,* Anthony Pinelli,* James DeGeorge,* Frank LaPorte* and Phillip Bacino.* There are others, of course, who have managed to infiltrate the real corporate structure and who live unimpeachable private lives in quiet luxury, give generously to charities, and direct their criminal activities through trusted emissaries.

* See Appendix for biographies.

3

As president of the corporation, Sam Giancana* is the chief executive, the boss of all bosses, the man responsible for the day-to-day success of the operation. Under him are vice presidents, department heads, district supervisors and straw bosses. This executive staff of approximately a thousand men commands a force conservatively estimated at over fifty thousand—about one percent of the population of Cook County—consisting of burglars, hijackers, fences, counterfeiters, moonshiners, panderers, prostitutes, B-girls, cabdrivers, bartenders, extortioners, narcotics peddlers, juicemen, collectors, torturers, assassins, kinky cops,† venal judges and politicians, union and business fronts, plus an array of gamblers including bookies, steerers and policy runners. The annual "revenue" in Cook County is estimated at more than $2 billion, a figure arrived at by local authorities and newspapers—federal sources place the gambling take alone at more than $1 billion.

In terms of leadership, this makes Giancana the most powerful archcriminal in the world. Where New York rackets are divided among six separate organizations (five boroughs and New Jersey), Giancana is the ostensible ruler of a single syndicate with interests extending as far west as Hawaii. His immediate perimeter stretches from Cleveland to Kansas City, from Hot Springs to New Orleans. Trusted lieutenants operate lucrative rackets in Florida, the West Indies, Arizona, Nevada and California.

Although the corporate structure analogy helps to simplify an otherwise baffling conspiracy of inexplicable loyalties and alliances, there is much that still remains obscure. Even the FBI, which likes to keep things neat and orderly, has failed to arrive at a definitive picture. "The reason why the real Mafia cannot be fought efficiently," Luigi Barzini observed in *The Italians,* "is that it is many things at the same time but not one tight well-run organization. It is a many-headed dragon which can continue to live for a long time with no head at all. . . . In order for a [single international organization] to exist and function it would have to be disciplined and centralized. It would be dangerous but easy to discover, penetrate, and destroy."

Historically, raids, arrests and even imprisonment of bosses have had little effect in curbing the ever-expanding growth of organized crime in America. This has been particularly true in Chicago where

* See Appendix.
† *Kinky* is Chicagoese for crooked, corrupt, venal; in the pay of the Syndicate.

4

organized crime has enjoyed a greater degree of discipline and centralization.

Known variously as the Outfit, the Boys, Capone mob, Syndicate, Invisible Government, the Mob, Cosa Nostra, Mafia and the Italian Organization, the Chicago branch of the crime cartel is the most politically insulated and police-pampered "family" this side of Sicily. As a tribute to its solidarity, only three men have worn the diadem of "Enforcer" (the Outfit's term for president) in the thirty-five years since prison doors closed behind Al Capone, and none were murdered: Frank Nitti committed suicide in 1943 on the day he was indicted by a federal grand jury in New York City in the Browne-Bioff multimillion-dollar movie extortion case, and his successor, Accardo, willingly abdicated in favor of Giancana in 1956 when the Internal Revenue Service became annoyingly curious about his sources of income.

As a consequence of this investigation, Accardo was convicted of income tax evasion. However, the case was reversed by the United States Circuit Court of Appeals, sitting in Chicago, because of "prejudicial" newspaper publicity during the trial. After forty years in his chosen profession, Accardo could still boast he had never spent a night in jail. He came close to it once, but was saved when a municipal court judge got out of bed to release him on his own personal recognizance.

His heir has fared less successfully in that area. Gilormo Giangono, baptised Momo Salvatore Giangono, alias Sam Giancana (and a score of other aliases), served his apprenticeship with a notorious West Side teen-age mob known as the "42 Gang," which took in recruits as young as nine years of age. Other contemporary members included Sam Battaglia,* Felix "Milwaukee Phil" Alderisio,* Marshall Caifano,* Sam DeStefano,* Charles Nicoletti,* Albert Frabotta,* Fiore Buccieri,* Frank Caruso,* William Aloisio,* William Daddano,* Joseph "Joey Caesar" DiVarco,* Leonard Gianola,* Vincent Inserro* and Rocco Potenza,* most of the key figures who later formed the nucleus of Giancana's band of "Youngbloods," a new generation of gangsters that came to power in the mid-1950s.

Born on May 24, 1908, Giancana served his first jail term at the age of seventeen—thirty days in the Bridewell for auto theft. His subsequent police record indicates thirteen arrests in 1926, fifteen in 1927 and twenty-two in 1928. At least a fifth of these arrests resulted

* See Appendix.

5

in felony indictments, but not a single case reached the trial stage. In each instance, "sympathetic" judges dismissed the charges, employing every trick in the legal grab bag. Before he was twenty, Giancana had been arrested three times on suspicion of murder. In the one murder case in which he was indicted (and released on bail), the prosecution witness was "coincidentally" murdered before the trial. This is a fairly common local phenomenon.

After picking up eight arrests in the first three months of 1929, there followed a court-imposed respite when he was sentenced to one to five years in the state penitentiary for burglary. Released from Joliet before Christmas 1932, he promptly returned to his métier undaunted by the fact that his boyhood hero, Al Capone, was in the Atlanta penitentiary. Soon police in the old Maxwell Street District were crediting him with being the fastest "wheelman" on the West Side, an honor that was later to earn him a job as Accardo's chauffeur and bodyguard. Meanwhile, when not out on jobs, he chauffeured for "Machine Gun" Jack McGurn (nee Jack Demore), a Syndicate assassin and a prime suspect along with Accardo in the St. Valentine's Day Massacre.

Giancana's climb through the ranks of burglars, gamblers, pimps, bootleggers, extortioners, dope pushers and murderers was not quite as swift as Accardo's, who was only two years his senior, but it was good enough to impress the boys of the old 42 Gang. Policemen and politicians were likewise impressed. As his career accelerated in the next seven years (1932–1939), he picked up only five arrests, all of them in the first two years. The Giancana faction of the Syndicate was fast becoming a reality when suddenly he found himself facing a federal rap for operating a large whisky still on a Garden Prairie farm.

If ever a prison term was a blessing in disguise, it was the three years of the four-year sentence that Giancana served in Terre Haute. It was there that he met Edward Jones, then a South Side policy king serving time for income tax evasion. The Negro gambler told Giancana that he and his brother, George, reaped so much money from their policy wheels that they had to spread the cash to 25 banks. It was a shocking revelation, particularly since Giancana had previously dismissed policy as just a nickel and dime racket.

Released from Terre Haute in 1942, again in time for Christmas, Giancana imparted his new intelligence to Accardo, who advised caution since the Outfit already was getting intense heat from the federal government in the Browne-Bioff fiasco. At first Giancana and

6

his band of Youngbloods tried to muscle in with threats and shake-downs. One of the gimmicks employed was a proposal that the Outfit could keep the policy business from getting into the newspapers. When this oblique approach failed, some of the smaller policy operators were routed by a series of beatings and bombings.

Shortly after his release from Terre Haute in 1946, Jones was kidnaped and held captive in the basement of a new home Giancana had purchased through attorney Anthony V. Champagne—it is Gian-cana's present Oak Park residence. After being ransomed by his family for $100,000, Jones and his brother fled to Mexico. Their top lieutenant, Theodore P. Roe, was left behind to fight the Syndicate at a recompense commensurate with the risk—according to his income tax returns, his cut netted him more than a million dollars a year. He managed to survive for six years. In June 1951, when three of Giancana's Youngbloods curbed his automobile in an attempt to kidnap him, a gun battle broke out and Leonard Caifano, a brother of Marshall Caifano, was killed. A year later Roe was eliminated by a shotgun blast. The rest of the policy kings meekly fell in line, and the Outfit added policy to its already long list of lucrative rackets.

Giancana, who was described by one police official as "a snarling, sarcastic, ill-mannered, ill-tempered, sadistic psychopath," was sud-denly one of the most popular "items" in the local press, being re-ferred to as "a new and heavy power in the Syndicate and a right-hand man of Accardo." In 1948 he was "in charge of the rough stuff department for Tony Accardo." In 1950 he was "one of the principal Chicago area hoodlums and is considered a 'general overseer' of illegal gambling in Chicago." In 1951 he was spending "considerable time in Florida but never at the same time as Tony Accardo as one or the other is always around the local area to make sure that business is conducted as usual." In 1952 he had "gambling interests in Cuba" and was a "big man in the shrimp industry." In 1952 he was attending a "meeting between Sheriff Kelly of Miami and Murray Humphreys, Jake Guzik, Gus Alex* and Tony Accardo at Miami." In 1953 he and Accardo and Guzik were holding conferences in Reno and Las Vegas with other kingpins of the national syndicate. In 1954 Judges John A. Sbarbaro and Joseph A. Pope attended the wake of Giancana's wife, Angeline, along with politicians and hood-lums. In 1955 he accompanied Accardo, Humphreys, Joey Glimco* and John Lardino* to the wake of Louis "Little New York" Cam-pagna. In 1956 he was proclaimed "Enforcer" during a dinner party

* See Appendix.

at the Tam O'Shanter Country Club. The coronation ceremony was deceptively simple: Accardo merely placed a hand on Giancana's shoulder and said, "I want you to meet my good friend, Sam Giancana."

To judge from the complexity and duplicity inherent in the operation of this multibillion-dollar criminal colossus, one would assume that the chief executive would be a man of extraordinary brilliance, an evil genius. Actually Giancana was a sixth-grade dropout at the age of fourteen; his lack of education was reflected in a psychological evaluation performed at Terre Haute in 1940. The tests indicated he was still the equivalent of a sixth grader in knowledge, with a general IQ of 71 verbal and 93 nonverbal, with poor accuracy and good speed. Drafted by the U.S. Army in 1943, he was rejected as "a constitutional psychopath" with an "inadequate personality and strong anti-social trends."

The only indictment brought against Giancana in the two decades that followed his release from Terre Haute was in 1951 on charges of conspiracy in the operation of a handbook gambling establishment known as the "Wagon Wheel." The indictment was quashed by Judge Wilbert F. Crowley on the grounds that the federal laws relied upon for the conspiracy count were obsolete. Following the gang-type murder of banker Leon Marcus in 1957, Giancana was served with a six-year-old capias on the gambling conspiracy indictment and questioned about his business involvement with Marcus. Judge Crowley promptly released him on a writ of habeas corpus, and later at a bench trial, Crowley found him not guilty.

By 1963 the bald, beady-eyed, silk-suited gangster had become a full-fledged girl-chasing international playboy. He was calling Frank Sinatra "pal" and Phyllis McGuire, the tall centerpiece of the singing trio, "sweetheart"—it was an inspiring tabloid romance: the next-doorsy girl and the king of crime. He drove a pink Cadillac and presented admirers with expensive gifts, including Cadillacs. He spent about one week out of each month in Chicago. The rest of the time he mixed business with pleasure as he junketed through the United States, Mexico, South America, Hawaii and Europe.

Money, power, wine, women and an international press finally went to his head. In the summer of 1963 he challenged the FBI. In federal court in Chicago, he charged them with harassing him by keeping his house under constant surveillance and by dogging his

8

footsteps even on the golf course. In fact, when G-men teed off behind him his game often soared to 115, some twenty-odd strokes above his normal score. Federal Judge Richard B. Austin, a former Chicago politician and himself a golfer, could not have agreed more. He granted an injunction limiting surveillance to a single FBI automobile, parked at least a block away from Giancana's home or a block behind when following his car. He further stipulated that a disinterested foursome must play between him and the G-men whenever he went to a golf course. Then, adding insult to injury, Austin fined the Chicago FBI chief $500 for refusing to testify about the Bureau's surveillance techniques, a refusal based on specific orders from Attorney General Robert F. Kennedy. "I know there are some not interested in civil rights and not concerned with privacy who will in the future approve of this type of harassment," Austin stated in his opinion. "I cannot give my sanction."

Although the ruling was hailed in some quarters as an admirable example of democracy in action, the United States Circuit Court of Appeals reminded Austin of a basic principle of law: "Defendants in this case [the FBI] are part of the executive department of the United States and they are not subject to supervision or direction by the courts as to how they shall perform the duties imposed by law upon them. . . . This would be an unwarranted interference and intrusion upon the discretion vested in this case. . . . For these reasons the preliminary injunction . . . shall be stayed pending further review thereof by this court."

A year later, the appeals court vacated the injunction but upheld the fine against the FBI chief. Giancana's attorney, George N. Leighton (now a criminal court judge), failed to convince the court that the plaintiff had suffered damages in excess of $10,000, a requisite in federal actions. "His freedom," cried Leighton, "is worth a billion dollars."

But at the moment Leighton would have been hard pressed to find any takers at a fraction of the price. Few of the Syndicate bosses appreciated the gratuitous publicity. In his arrogance, Giancana had committed the fatal *faux pas* of his career. By publicly challenging the FBI, he had placed J. Edgar Hoover in an untenable position. The results were predictably disastrous.

On January 12, 1965, some three months after Joseph "Joe Bananas" Bonanno was "kidnaped" at gunpoint on Park Avenue in New York City, Giancana flew to a New York meeting of the Mafia's national commission, allegedly to select a successor to Bonanno's

9

underworld family. Also a member of the commission, Bonanno had bossed rackets in Brooklyn and Tucson, and had been among the Mafia elite snared at the 1957 Apalachin convention.

Giancana's attempt to sneak in and out of New York City failed dismally. Traveling under the alias of Sam Volpe, he was on his way up the boarding ramp of a Chicago-bound jet when G-men presented him with a subpoena to appear before a New York City federal grand jury the next morning. Giancana made six appearances before the grand jury which was investigating the disappearance of Bonanno. Meanwhile, the Chicago press, hating anyone to steal its gangster thunder, was hinting that Bonanno's death sentence had originated in their city. (On May 17, 1966, nineteen months after this mysterious disappearance, Bonanno surrendered to federal authorities in New York City.)

2

Chicago gangsters receive the kind of publicity Hollywood stars dream about. A typical example was the 1965 federal grand jury investigation of Giancana in Chicago which literally produced thousands of stories. Every conceivable angle—and many not so conceivable—was covered in news stories, features, articles, erudite analyses, historical essays, gossip columns, boxes, photo captions, cartoons, letters to the editor and editorials. Measured in terms of advertising space, the coverage would have cost millions of dollars.

At a press conference on May 13, the day before the probe opened, United States Attorney General Nicholas B. Katzenbach promised that "some important crime syndicate leaders" will be convicted in Chicago "in the next year or two." "Katzenbach," said Chicago's *American,* "made it clear as a gang chief's diamond ring that somebody is chattering like a chipmunk."

"We often go a long time, then we get a break and somebody starts talking," Katzenbach said. "We're arriving at that situation in Chicago. I strongly support a law to broaden immunity. It is important to be able to get people to talk. It is indispensable in investigation of the crime syndicate."

Naturally, the announcement precipitated a spate of speculation in the press. After consulting with "a top justice department official in Washington," the *American* concluded that "the tottering kingpin of the Chicago crime syndicate [was] in real danger of being indicted" since his "appearance Friday before the grand jury is not mere

10

harassment." In the words of the Washington official: "We have something on him, and we're going to confront him with it. I hope we can make it stick."

The Chicago *Daily News* was already contemplating a change in command. "Sam Battaglia, according to some reports, is in line to succeed Giancana." Next came a few encouraging words about the impending heir: "Battaglia gave the FBI man a more spirited contest, however, racing his expensive auto up to 90 miles per hour Monday on the Northwest Tollway before pulling over to the shoulder. [He was] believed to have been heading for the seclusion of his [200-acre] race horse breeding farm near Pingree Grove, a hamlet about 10 miles west of Elgin in Kane County." (Giancana had been subpoenaed while furtively stepping out of an outdoor phone booth in Forest Park.)

On the first day of the probe, the big story was a detailed chronicling of the latest sartorial elegance in hoodlum fashions. Giancana, first on the scene, was credited with setting the style pace when he breezed through the lobby of the Federal Building in a narrow-brim fedora identified as similar to the type worn by Rex Harrison in *My Fair Lady,* a blue-gray silk suit, narrow gray tie, white shirt, pointed black shoes, diamond ring, manicured nails, deep tan, dark glasses and a "pleasant expression." His retinue was similarly attired with slight variations in the color scheme. When the gangster chief left the courthouse, one of his attorneys angrily reprimanded reporters: "Haven't you guys any ethics? Why don't you leave him alone? Some professions have no ethics."

Specifically, the government sought indictments in five major areas: (1) Income tax violations based on gifts, including jewelry, automobiles and international travel, he showered on at least five women (his reported income was $65,000 to $80,000 a year—tax experts estimated his personal income at well over a million a year); (2) violations of ITAR (Interstate Travel in Aid of Racketeering), particularly as to the Outfit's gambling enterprises in Las Vegas, Hot Springs, Miami, St. Louis and New Orleans; (3) infiltration of legitimate business, including large hotel and motel chains, and the Cal-Neva Lodge in Nevada; (4) vote fraud and political corruption in Chicago, the Illinois state legislature and the United States Congress, (5) narcotics traffic, which as a Mafia don he directed on an international scale along with members of the commission.

The political aspect of the probe was evident from the list of witnesses subpoenaed to testify: Anthony Tisci, secretary to Con-

11

gressman Frank Annunzio; Benjamin "Buddy" Jacobson and Pat Marcy, political clouters* in the First Ward Democratic organization; John D'Arco, First Ward Democratic committeeman and former alderman; Richard Cain, former chief investigator of the Sheriff's police, convicted of conspiring to commit perjury in a quarter-million-dollar drug hijacking case; and Murray "The Camel" Humphreys, whose frequent visits to Washington had long aroused the curiosity of FBI agents.

Over the weekend, Giancana's attorneys obtained a court order to bar the press from the fifteenth floor where the grand jury convened. In issuing the ban, U.S. District Judge Joseph Sam Perry noted that "Sometimes you need protection. . . . Our rules allow us to protect the courtrooms. I will extend the rule to the grand jury. I believe that to be fitting."

The ruling was invoked two days before Phyllis McGuire made her premier appearance. On that day, seasoned crime reporters prattled like society columnists.

"You fellows have been writing bad stories about me and Sam," Phyllis chided them. "It makes me look terrible because I'm not a single—I'm part of a trio. If it was only me, maybe it wouldn't be so bad. But my sisters and my parents are heartbroken about this."

In her syndicated column, Dorothy Kilgallen recalled a conversation with Phyllis that had taken place a few days before Christmas of 1963. "I'm going to give him up," Phyllis had vowed. "It's terribly unfair, but I promise you it's true. Look at me and see if you can't tell by my eyes that I'm not lying. I'm not going to see Sam again."

The daily newspaper hints that Giancana's pals were "blowing the whistle" never materialized. The only breakthrough was between the grand jury and the press. "Federal investigators, attorneys and agents have been noticeably upset by information leaks on the names of those subpoenaed by the federal grand jury this week," the *Daily News* noted. "They make it clear also that they are not staging the current massive show of criminal talent just to give hoodlums a chance to clown around in public."

Later, when federal attorneys announced (*without revealing identities*) that nearly a hundred persons had been subpoenaed by the grand jury, the *American* scooped the opposition with a story headlined: GRAND JURY FISHES WITHOUT BIG TUNA—"Picture poor Anthony J. Accardo, sitting dolefully in his rocking chair in that $160,000 ranch house at 1407 N. Ashland Ave., River Forest,

* In Chicago's unique vernacular, "clout" means political influence, the power to fix things.

12

paging thru his memory book and sighing, 'They haven't called me.'
. . . Imagine what happens to a man's status in his society when the
newspapers don't even report he's been taking the 5th amendment
again. A few years ago Accardo was . . . considered the chief
gangster in all Chicagoland. Name-droppers dropped his name along
Rush street. . . . If there has been any speculation that Accardo has
been elevated to the rank of gang boss emeritus, the current grand
jury snub just about ends it. Or does it??? Maybe Mr. Accardo has
gone back to Acapulco—he sometimes does this time of year—and is
thumbing his nose at the whole works."

(Once while "thumbing his nose" at a Civil Service Commission
inquiry into the behavior of Police Lieutenant Anthony DeGrazio,
who had accompanied Accardo on a European junket, the gang
chieftain hid out in the Pacific Palisades [California] home of Howard
J. Beck. A motion picture producer, Beck later admitted that he had
known Accardo for fifteen years and had no knowledge of his criminal
background. One of the films produced by Beck was *Brotherhood of
Evil*—a hard-hitting book on the Mafia, but an innocuous movie.)

On May 27, 1965, at his third appearance before the federal grand
jury, Giancana again invoked the Fifth Amendment. This time, however, federal prosecutors had a surprise for him. The long investigation by the FBI had convinced the government that the gang boss was
too well-insulated from the actual operation of Syndicate rackets to
be implicated in any indictable violations. The immediate aim of the
probe was to get lower rank hoodlums to talk. When this failed, the
government reversed its strategy. They granted Giancana immunity
from prosecution. The move was based on the immunity provisions of
the Federal Communications Commission Act, an act which outlaws
the use of telephone and telegraph to plot crime or to move the
proceeds of illicit activity. Once granted immunity, Giancana could
no longer claim his constitutional privilege against self-incrimination.
He would be forced to either answer all questions posed to him by
prosecutors and members of the grand jury or go to jail for contempt
of court. The chances of successfully lying his way through the
interrogation were beyond a reasonable probability.

The rules of the new game were explained to Giancana and his six
attorneys by Chief U.S. District Judge William J. Campbell: "If I find
that the jury has correctly applied provisions of the immunity statutes
and if the witness should persist in his refusal to testify, the precedent
in this district has been not to impose sentence for contempt, but to

13

commit the witness to the custody of the United States marshal, there to remain until he obeys the order of the court." Under the law, this meant for the remaining term of the grand jury, which in this instance still had a year of life before it expired in June 1966. In defining immunity, Judge Campbell said, "Where immunity is applied by a jury, I interpret it to extend to any and all crimes, state or federal, that may possibly arise, directly or indirectly, from any testimony the witness may give."

The government's maneuver threw Giancana's legal arsenal into a forensic tailspin. Granted a three-day postponement to prepare arguments on the motion, the six attorneys—Thomas A. Wadden, Robert L. Weinberg, Edward Bennett Williams, Anthony V. Champagne, Judy Richards and Richard E. Gorman—went into an emergency huddle.

In a Forest Park cocktail lounge that evening, Giancana gulped down Scotch highballs and spat out obscenities. Accompanied by a "dumpy" blonde and Dominic Blasi,* his chauffeur-bodyguard, Giancana bought a drink for the house before launching into a protracted tirade against Phyllis, reporters, photographers, prosecutors, FBI agents and sundry other recent irritations.

When the grand jury reconvened on June 1, Judge Campbell ruled that it had correctly applied the immunity provisions and instructed Giancana to answer all questions. When he again invoked the Fifth Amendment, Judge Campbell adjudged him in "direct and continuing contempt of this court."

A defense motion for a stay of execution of the order pending an appeal was denied. "This offense is neither bailable nor appealable," Campbell said. "He doesn't have to be confined at all if he obeys the order of the court." Then turning to Giancana, he said: "You have the key to your own cell. When you decide to obey the lawful order of this court, notify the United States marshal and he will bring you before this court."

A few hours later, Giancana was booked into the Cook County Jail for his first night in a cell in twenty-three years. An emergency petition was filed with the United States Court of Appeals within hours of his confinement asking for a hearing on the very next morning. Giancana's plea for freedom was rejected, without comment, twice in two weeks—first by the appeals court and then by Justice Tom C. Clark, acting on behalf of the United States Supreme Court, which was then in summer recess.

* See Appendix.

14

Meanwhile, the anxious populace was being bombarded by lengthy hourly bulletins on the habits, mood, menu, weight, ailments, general appearance, visitors, television and reading preferences, methods of washing underwear, sleeping positions and witty quips of the jail's most renowned inmate.

Finally, United States Marshal Joseph Tierney imposed a ban on all publicity. "I'm most unhappy about jail guards acting as press agents, and holding press conferences," he said. "We can't have a public relations setup in jail." Tierney's edict stipulated that in the future all information releases about federal prisoners in the county jail would be routed through his office instead of the warden's.

"There hasn't been any censoring of news in the Cook County jail during the last ten years," one columnist complained. "Ever since Warden Jack Johnson has been in charge. Apparently Sam is getting special treatment—news-wise that is."

As it later developed, Sam's special treatment was considerably more personal. When first admitted to the county jail, Giancana was lodged in a basement maximum security cell in the old Death Row section. Here he was reportedly kept under constant observation and was not allowed to mingle with other prisoners. But almost immediately Marshal Tierney and Warden Johnson began squabbling over their prized possession. A month later Tierney ordered Giancana transferred to the federal prisoner cell block which housed sixty other inmates.

"That move gave Giancana a lot more freedom in the jail," Johnson complained. "In his new cell in the federal prisoners' block, Giancana is a troublemaker. Some prisoners cater to him because of his notoriety as a gang kingpin. Others try to pick fights with him. Either way, he is a problem for the jail administration and he wasn't a problem when he was down in maximum security."

Sheriff Richard B. Ogilvie, Johnson's superior, did not even want Giancana in the jail. "I'd like to get him out of the jail," he said. "He's causing trouble for Johnson and the guards. If he gets any privileged status out there, I'll hold everyone responsible, including the warden."

The inevitable scandal broke in late August when news leaked out that the U.S. Attorney's office and the Illinois Crime Investigation Commission were checking reports that Giancana was living it up in confinement with steaks smothered in mushrooms, whisky, and dollar

15

cigars being smuggled in by jail guards. Other privileges included laundry service, after-curfew television and an elaborate courier system that enabled him to flash secret messages to Syndicate lieutenants.

According to the warden, the entire jail staff volunteered to take polygraph tests to clear themselves. The first "liebox" casualties were two jail guards, Frank Barvitz and John Maraldo, who were accused of providing Giancana with laundry service in violation of the rule that required inmates to personally launder their underwear in cell washbasins.

Meanwhile, FBI agents arrested Anthony Rocco Silvestri, a Cook County probation officer, on charges of transporting stolen money orders. A known associate of James "Cowboy" Mirro* and other lower echelon hoodlums, Silvestri was the official liaison man between the probation office and the jail. Responsible for interviewing all prisoners slated for probation, Silvestri spent most of his time at the jail. When the Illinois Crime Investigating Commission identified Silvestri as one of Giancana's couriers, Johnson scoffed at the report. "Guys like Giancana don't take a draw [chance] by giving important messages to a warden, a guard, or a probation officer," he said. "Even if a jail official was on their payroll for ten grand, guys like Giancana wouldn't talk to him. They're too smart."

The third polygraph casualty was Sergeant Frank A. Rinella, an admitted close friend of Sam DeStefano, a convicted rapist and bank robber and a former Youngblood terrorist who now headed an Outfit juice ring. During the test, Rinella admitted to having dined at DeStefano's home on several occasions. Moreover, his wife had nursed the hoodlum back to health following an abdominal operation.

Rinella's appointment as a guard in 1963 had come about when Republican County Chairman Timothy P. Sheehan had written a letter to Sheriff Ogilvie stating that Rinella's political sponsor was John Wall, Republican committeeman of Mayor Daley's Eleventh Ward.

The test indicated that Rinella had received bribes for performing special services for both Giancana and DeStefano, who had occupied Giancana's former isolation cell earlier in the year. Rinella admitted he provided Giancana with dollar cigars, special meals and late evening snacks, but denied having had anything to do with smuggling in whisky or smuggling out messages.

* See Appendix.

16

Sheriff Ogilvie felt betrayed. "We fingerprinted every guard to be sure that none of them has criminal records," he said. "Now we're going to be certain that no guard is associating with gangsters. The Mob isn't going to have any servants in my jail."

A spokesman for the Federal Bureau of Prisons thought differently: "Conditions in the Cook County Jail are such that government witnesses seldom are lodged there in the federal tier. We found that if government witnesses were lodged in the jail, somehow they were talked out of testifying for the government. To avoid having government cases hurt by shenanigans in the Cook County Jail, most federal witnesses are kept in other jails in the Chicago area."

Eventually, the scandal suffered a typical Chicago death—asphyxiation under tons of newsprint. In late September, after a "thorough investigation" of his own jail personnel, Warden Johnson happily concluded that "none are connected with favors to Giancana or any other inmate." He was likewise "absolutely certain there is no evidence that illicit cigars, whisky or steaks smothered in mushrooms have been given to Giancana." The courier system was "highly improbable," and after-curfew television "ridiculous." In fact, the only favored treatment given Giancana was special handling of his laundry by a jail guard fired later with two other guards "suspected of favoritism." And that was the end of it. Earlier threats of a federal grand jury investigation of the jail never materialized. It was also pretty much the end of the federal grand jury investigation of the Syndicate.

3

Back in pre-Lindbergh-law days, kidnaping was a gangster specialty. During the Twenties, a colorful mobster with the unlikely name of Llewelyn Morris (Murray) Humphreys became one of the most proficient exponents of this lucrative racket. Known to his admiring public as "The Camel" and to his criminal associates as "Curly," Humphreys was perhaps the only kidnaper in history to have paid income tax on ransom money without being charged with the crime. The kidnapee was Robert G. Fitchie, president of the Milk Wagon Drivers Union, who refused to cooperate when Humphreys told him, "We're going to take over this joint."

After Humphreys departed, Fitchie and Steve Sumner, the union's eighty-three-year-old secretary, armed themselves and barricaded their offices. Among other assets, the union's $750,000 treasury was at stake. However, they did not stay behind the barricades long enough. On the evening of December 21, 1931, Fitchie was kidnaped in his own garage. Sumner paid $50,000 ransom and Fitchie was released. Later Fitchie refused to identify his abductors. "What the hell difference does it make?" he said. "I can't prove it and I wouldn't if I could. I'd get murdered." But Sumner was too old to be intimidated. He told IRS agents that Humphreys was the one who had collected the ransom.

A few days later, Humphreys invested $54,000 of his own money in new equipment for the Meadowmoor Dairy, a company he had muscled his way into. By then, of course, Humphreys controlled a variety of businesses and unions.

One of the major prizes in the 1920s was the cleaning and dyeing industry, which for most of the decade was involved in intra-industry warfare between operators who wanted to keep prices up and those who wanted to cut them down. Violence broke out when operators began hiring goons to intimidate rivals. Before long the goons were warring against each other, using dry cleaning plants as their battleground. The hoodlum generals were Al Weinshank of the Bugs Moran forces and Murray Humphreys of the Capone army.

Capone's services were first enlisted by Morris Becker, owner of a large dry cleaning chain of stores and plants in Chicago and suburban Cook County. "Our shops had been bombed, the union had bled us for three thousand dollars to call off a strike," Becker explained. "The police, the state's attorney, and the United States Attorney would, or could, do nothing. So we called in a man who could protect us—Al Capone. He did it well."

Humphreys was invited by Becker to attend a meeting of the six biggest wholesalers in his faction. He was to be introduced as an "arbiter" in labor disputes and as a "persuader" in discouraging price cutting. To demonstrate his persuasive personality, Humphreys brought "Machine Gun" Jack McGurn to the meeting. His fee of $10,000 for one year was considered most reasonable by his naive employers. In gangster arithmetic, it was merely a nominal down payment. Instead of leaving when the year was up, he cut himself in for a piece of the action, asking as high as fifty percent from one establishment. When the Michigan Cleaners withdrew from the agreement, hoodlums broke into the plant and ruined $20,000 worth of clothing with acid—just like in the movies.

While the operators argued about prices, the hoodlums fought over territories, with Weinshank running his operation from a big North

18

Side dry cleaning plant, and Humphreys from an equally large cleaning establishment on the South Side. Before it was over, more than twenty businesses were bombed, fourteen were subjected to acid attacks, five persons were murdered, and numerous others were severely crippled in brutal assaults. Usually a beating was enough to convince an operator of the sincerity of a hoodlum's intention to steal his business. To resist beyond a reasonable point was considered unrealistic. Benjamin Rosenberg was one of the few who disagreed with this viewpoint. In fact, Rosenberg continued to oppose Humphreys' intentions even after two goons, Philip Mangano and Louis Clementi, threw acid in four of Rosenberg's trucks and then nearly beat him to death. Instead of capitulating, Rosenberg testified against his assailants before a grand jury which returned indictments. But a few weeks before the trial Rosenberg was murdered and the case was dismissed.

Weinshank made an abrupt but glorious exit in 1929 as one of the seven celebrated corpses in the St. Valentine's Day Massacre. With Weinshank out of the way and Moran on the defensive, Humphreys saw his opportunity to move into the unions. Some of the competitors who were eliminated included Big Tim Murphy, a labor racketeer who was gunned down on his front lawn; John D. Clay, financial secretary of the cleaning drivers union, who was killed in his home by two assassins firing through a window; and Clay's successor, Patrick Berrell, and his bodyguard, Willie Marks, who were trailed to Shawano, Wisconsin, and mowed down by machine gun fire.

At the time of his death in 1965, Humphreys still controlled Local 46, Laundry, Cleaning and Dye House Workers International Union through nominee Gus "Windshields" Zapas, business agent and close friend of James R. Hoffa. Besides sporting a lengthy criminal record (more than forty arrests in Chicago), Zapas was indirectly linked to the kidnap-murder of Robert Greenlease by the McCellan Committee which charged that he had plotted to peddle Greenlease ransom money "for a few cents on the dollar."

Local 46 was expelled from the AFL–CIO in 1957 on charges of corruption and became affiliated with the International Brotherhood of Teamsters (IBT), also expelled on similar charges at the same time. Zapas' associates include Tom Firotta, William Skalley and Ernest Infelice,* all notorious narcotics dealers; Leonard Gianola, Joseph Aiuppa* and Felix Alderisio, Syndicate bosses; and Joe

* See Appendix.

19

Costello, owner of the Ace Cab Company in St. Louis, who was a suspect in the Greenlease kidnaping.

In Humphreys' hands, kidnaping was a convincing angle in the *modus operandi* of the Mob's extortion rackets. It had worked beautifully during prohibition. At one time or another, just about every successful bootlegger in Chicago was kidnaped. A "brainy" hood like Humphreys found it a lot easier to muscle into an operation than to create it from the ground up. Ransom was often only an incidental—compensation for the free ride and lodging. For example, bootlegger Maurice Gordon paid Humphreys only $5,000 in ransom for his freedom, but threw in a half-interest in his business.

At other times, murder proved to be a more direct route to the control of a union than kidnaping. In March 1932, Humphreys and Charlie Fischetti were arrested and questioned in the murder of Dennis H. Zeigler, secretary of Local 569 of the Hoisting and Portable Engineers Union. They both denied any knowledge of the murder and were released.

On May 6, 1933, the *Herald-Examiner* disclosed that the government was preparing income tax cases against fourteen racketeers, including Humphreys, who was described as: "Public Enemy No. 1, heir to Scarface Al Capone's power, the brains of the so-called Syndicate and the directing agent behind the muscle men and killers who have dominated numerous unions and so-called trade associations."

The indictment—rendered on June 27, 1933—charged that Humphreys had defrauded the government of $26,108.04 in 1930, 1931 and 1932. Humphreys fled to Mexico.

Meanwhile, the Cook County Grand Jury returned indictments against twenty-four hoodlums, with Humphreys and Capone heading the list, on charges of conspiring to control the cleaning, dyeing and laundry industries and the carbonated beverage and linen supply industries through kidnaping, strikes, bombings, slayings and acid throwing. Testimony was offered to show that Humphreys and Capone had conspired to gain control of these industries and had forced them to pay tribute to the Syndicate. The seventeen defendants present at the trial were acquitted, and the cases against Humphreys (who was in Mexico), Capone (who was in the Atlanta penitentiary) and other absentees were stricken off with leave to reinstate.

After sixteen months in Mexico, Humphreys returned to Chicago to plead guilty on the income tax indictment. He got eighteen months and a fine of $5,000. Before departing for Leavenworth, Humphreys told reporters: "While I'm down there, I intend to study English and maybe a little geometry." (His only other sentence was in 1918 when he served six months on a charge of burglary, reduced to petty larceny.)

In 1939, the aging Steve Sumner finally got his chance to testify about the Fitchie ransom (local authorities had failed to prosecute on the kidnaping charge) before the U.S. Board of Tax Appeals. The government's contention that Humphreys should have included the $50,000 as income was upheld by the Circuit Court of Appeals. Years later, Humphreys offered the government $15,000 to settle the tax lien, which by then (with interest and penalties) had grown to $74,617.77. Whether the offer was accepted is not known—the last public mention of the case was in 1942 when the Supreme Court refused to review the decision of the appeals court.

The next man to visit income tax grief on Humphreys suffered a fate worse than death before paying the ultimate gangland penalty. The curious twist to this story is that the victim was not a naive bystander. By the age of fifty-nine, Irving Vine had spent the best years of his life hustling on the fringe of the Syndicate. At one time or another, he had performed chores for Syndicate kingpins like Edward Vogel,* Ralph Pierce* and Gus Alex. In fact, until Humphreys married Vine's ex-wife, Betty Jeanne Neibert, a former tavern dice girl, Vine had no apparent need for a blueprint on Syndicate ethics. After that he either lost heart or gained courage. At any rate, he volunteered to testify against Humphreys in an income tax case.

In the course of a routine net-worth investigation, IRS agents had discovered that Humphreys' cash investment of more than $100,000 in his palatial Key Biscayne home did not correspond with earned income as reported in his tax returns. Humphreys' explanation that Betty Jeanne had contributed at least $50,000 (saved during her marriage to Vine) toward the purchase and decoration of their home was refuted by Vine, who claimed Betty Jeanne had never earned more than $75 a week as a dice girl in the six years she was his wife.

In subsequent months, Vine ignored all underworld warnings. Even Humphreys' threats failed to deter him. Then, the morning of May 6, 1963, Rosie Mitchell, a chambermaid at the Del Prado Hotel in Hyde Park, noticed that the door to room 507 was ajar. After a discreet knock, she stepped into the room, took one look, and stepped right out again, screaming. Homicide detectives found Irving Vine lying on the floor, dressed only in blood-smeared shorts, his mouth

* See Appendix.

21

and nose sealed with surgical tape, his legs also bound with tape, a shirt twisted loosely around his neck, and a pillow covering his head. Three of his ribs were broken, his face was scratched and his knees bruised, but the real damage was to the lower part of his body where savage tortures had been inflicted with an icepick during a period of several hours. Death was due to suffocation "by person or persons unknown." Police stated they would like to question Humphreys, Betty Jeanne, Gus Alex, Edward Vogel, Nathan "Butch" Ladon, Bernard "Pipi" Posner and Ralph Pierce, the hidden owner of the Del Prado Hotel. Betty Jeanne remained in Florida; Humphreys vacated his Chicago apartment and successfully avoided arrest by becoming a nomad for a few weeks.

4

From the era of Al Capone to the present, labor racketeering has been a multiedged sword in the hands of ruthless gangsters. The Syndicate's infiltration of unions was the first step in its invasion of legitimate business. It was basically an extension of the protection racket. A typical example was the take-over of the building-trades unions at the turn of the century. The primary objective was not the unions but the wealthy contractors who faced costly penalty charges unless work was completed on schedule. By threatening strikes and other operational tieups, the gangsters extorted tremendous penalties of their own. In time, of course, hoodlums like Louis "Lepke" Buchalter in New York City's garment district and Humphreys in Chicago recognized the potential in unionism itself.

The underworld view of unionism was succinctly expressed by Dan Sullivan, Operating Director of the Miami Crime Commission, when he testified before the McClellan Committee in 1958. Sullivan had asked one hoodlum why he had moved from other enterprises into the union welfare field, and the answer was: "Well, first of all, when you have a checkoff system, you have a foolproof system of collections. It doesn't cost you money to operate. Secondly, if you run into one of these insurance companies or welfare outfits, you don't pay any money out and you take it all in. And thirdly, you have no inspection on the local, county, state or federal level. So your funds are not audited."

Recent federal legislation inspired by the findings of the McClellan Committee has provided safeguards against certain flagrant abuses,

22

but in the beginning it was wide open. All it took to steal a union and its treasury was muscle. By terrorizing one or two officials, gangsters often inherited the entire membership. And once armed with the membership, they inherited an entire industry.

A case in point is the story of the Chicago Restaurant Association and the Syndicate-manipulated unions which have dominated it since the mid-1930s. Formed in 1914 to defeat legitimate unionization, the association was destined to become the victim of its own greed.

The Syndicate launched its offensive early in 1935. For a rare insight into its muscling tactics, there is no better text than the testimony given by George B. McLane in 1940 before the Cook County Grand Jury and before a master in chancery in receivership proceedings involving Local 278 of the Chicago Bartenders and Beverage Dispensers Union.

McLane testified that his troubles began in the spring of 1935 with a telephone request from Danny Stanton, a union organizer for Frank Nitti. Stanton wanted $500 to finance his trip to the Kentucky Derby. When McLane refused, Stanton replied, "You son of a bitch. We'll get the money and take the union over."

A few weeks later, McLane was summoned to the LaSalle Hotel for a brief meeting with Nitti, who came right to the point: "The only way to overcome this [Stanton's request] is to put one of our men in as an officer." "But it's impossible," McLane argued. Nitti boasted, "We have taken over other unions," pointing out that he had made his man, George Browne, president of the International Alliance of Theatrical Stage Employees and Motion Picture Operators. Nitti told McLane that he had made Mike Carrozzo czar of the Chicago Street Cleaning Union and George B. Scalise president of the Building Service Employees International Union. Nitti allowed McLane a few days to think over the proposition.

When McLane accepted another invitation, this time at the old Capri Restaurant on North Clark Street, Nitti lived up to his reputation. Seated at his table were "Little New York" Campagna, Paul "The Waiter" Ricca, Joseph Fusco,* Jake Guzik and Fred Evans, who substituted for Humphreys while the latter studied English and geometry at Leavenworth P.

Nitti opened the conversation by informing McLane he would have to put his man in as an officer of the Union. McLane explained that it was impossible without the approval of the executive board.

"Give us the names of anyone who opposes and we will take care of them," Nitti replied with his usual candor. "We want no more playing around. If you don't do what we say, you will get shot in the head. How would your wife look in black?"

After mulling that prospect over for a few days, McLane was again summoned to the Capri Restaurant for another conference. "Why haven't you put our man in as an officer?" Nitti demanded. "What are you stalling for? The slugging of your pickets and intimidation of your business agents will stop if you put our man to work. I will give you a man without a police record. The places that our syndicate owns will join the union. There will be no pickets and no bother." McLane nervously explained that the proposition had been turned down by the executive board. "What are their names?" Nitti asked. "We will take care of that. Now this is your last chance. This is the only way we will stand for anything. Either put in our man or wind up in an alley."

And so by terrorizing one man, the Syndicate gained control of another union.

Nitti's man, Louis Romano, was elected president of Local 278 in July 1935. Romano, it should be noted, was not as clean as Nitti had promised. Actually, he was known in police circles as a psychopathic killer. And not all of his murders were in the line of duty. For example, during a barroom brawl in 1922, Romano had shot three men, one fatally. All three indictments, one for murder and two for assault with intent to murder, were subsequently stricken off. Ten years later, in the heat of a traffic argument, Romano shot and killed one Albert Lucenti. Witnesses refused to testify against Romano and the case was dropped.*

McLane's testimony before the grand jury in 1940 precipitated a small crisis when a four-count indictment was returned against Nitti, Humphreys, Ricca, Campagna, Evans, Romano, Thomas Panton and James Crowley, secretary-treasurer of the union. They were charged

* Not all the sons of Syndicate hoodlums attend fancy Eastern colleges as legend goes. That Albert Louis Romano was created in the image of his father, Louis, was evident from an early age. When just a young punk, he too became involved in a barroom brawl with three patrons. But instead of whipping out a gun and doing them in on the spot, he waited until they left and followed them to their car. Then he opened fire, wounding one and missing the others. Albert's career, which included arrests for rape, burglary, armed robbery, assaults of every description, extortion and narcotics peddling, was considerably shorter than his father's. In 1964 a Negro narcotics operator shot him through the heart and unceremoniously dumped him among the trash cans in the rear of a parking lot.

with conspiracy to loot the treasury of Local 278 by threatening to murder, maim or wound McLane and by coercing and threatening other members of the union.

McLane's courage, fortified by five years of brooding, faltered in the face of the inevitable "shot in the head." When the case was called for trial, he invoked the Fifth Amendment. The prosecution failed, but the union was thrown into receivership. A few months later, the receivership was dissolved and elections were held in the courtroom of Judge Robert Jerome Dunne. Ex-defendant James Crowley was elected president. "The Nitti mob is still in control," said State's Attorney Investigator Dan Gilbert, "but I'm glad to see McLane defeated." Crowley's first job as president was to rehire all officials fired during the receivership because of alleged Syndicate taint. The year before his election, Crowley had gone about the city with a goon squad, breaking windows, slugging proprietors and throwing stench bombs. Arrested and charged with smashing windows, he was acquitted in a bench trial.

His performance as president was apparently satisfactory until 1947, at which time gunmen drove up alongside his fancy Cadillac and opened fire. Crowley's wife was hit with twenty-five shotgun slugs and instantly killed. Crowley escaped with recoverable injuries and a new outlook; he continued as president of the local for another ten years.

Within a month from the time Romano assumed control of Local 278, Nitti moved to extend the Syndicate's power. On August 13, 1935, an application to charter a similar union to operate in suburban Cook County was filed with the international union in Cincinnati. It was granted the same day. The charter for Local 450, Bartenders, Waiters, Waitresses and Miscellaneous Workers Union was granted to Joseph Aiuppa, a Mafia lieutenant who bossed vice in Cicero, and who also supplied machine guns to the Dillinger-Karpis-Barker mobs. His representative in Local 450 was Claude Maddox, alias John Manning (nee John Edward "Screwy" Moore), once the operator of the infamous Circus Cafe, headquarters for a mob bearing its name and headed by "Tough Tony" Capezio. Its most illustrious alumnus was Tony Accardo.

Aiuppa, Maddox and Robert J. Ansoni (alias Robert Taylor) were the owners of Taylor and Company, a firm that manufactured gambling casino equipment, including marked cards and loaded dice.

Maddox's domination of Local 450 lasted until his death in 1958. His replacement was Anthony Spano, who at this writing still heads the union for Aiuppa, who in turn controls it for Giancana.

Along with Locals 278 and 450, the Syndicate also controlled Local 593, the dominant affiliate of the Hotel and Restaurant Employees and Bartenders International Union within the city of Chicago. The front bosses were James Blakely and John Lardino. Blakely was a vice-president of the international and secretary-treasurer of the local, and Lardino was administration director of the local and the real controlling force in the union. Having earned his Syndicate stripes as an executioner under "Machine Gun" McGurn, Lardino was Humphreys' nominee. Blakely was a close friend of Danny Stanton, a renegade gangster who was slain in 1943 for ignoring an edict to surrender control of the Checkroom Attendants Union.

Daniel Lardino, a brother of John, was boss of Local 658, Drugstore, Fountain and Luncheonette Employees Union. An investigation by the Chicago Crime Commission in 1951 revealed that Daniel Lardino was extorting monthly payments from druggists as insurance against acts of violence and strikes. A few years later, Local 658 was merged with Local 593, of which Daniel Lardino became a business agent.

Thus, when the Syndicate decided to move against the Chicago Restaurant Association in the late 1930s, these locals became the principal control points. Violence erupted in 1939. Goon squads smashed windows, slugged owners and patrons with baseball bats, slashed tires, dumped sugar in gasoline tanks, tossed stinkbombs, set fires and planted black-powder and dynamite bombs, and when everything else failed, resorted to murder.

To restore peace, the Chicago Restaurant Association retained the services of Abraham Teitelbaum as its labor relations counsel at $125,000 a year. A former attorney for Capone, Teitelbaum has often stated, "Alphonse Capone was one of the most honorable men I ever met." As his labor relations expert, Teitelbaum hired Louis Romano. The hoodlum strategy had now come full circle: The Syndicate controlled the unions, and its attorney handled the association's "labor relations." In effect, the money flowed in from both ends at once.

A compromise was reached—owners paid initiation fees and dues for a limited number of employees, who were not consulted and rarely knew they had become members of a union. The arrangement usually continued for years. Dues were collected on members who had changed jobs, left the state or country or even died. It made no difference to either party in the deal. The important thing was that the terrorism had stopped.

It was an ideal shakedown racket. There was little bookkeeping involved; only names and dues were important, not animated members agitating for union benefits, welfare, meetings, elections or any other kind of irritating legitimate union practices. It was strictly a paper organization. Meanwhile, the association members were pushing Syndicate beer, liquor, meats and produce, and were utilizing its myriad services: laundry, dry cleaning, garbage disposal, vending machines, jukeboxes, and buying its fixtures and appliances.

The association members contributed to a "voluntary fund"— aside from its regular membership dues—for use when labor troubles arose, which happened with unerring regularity. Attorney Teitelbaum somehow always managed to arrange "settlements" at a cost that kept the voluntary fund flowing from the restaurateurs to the gangsters. Millions flowed through this fund. It was a classic "sweetheart" arrangement, for the restaurateurs were still coming out ahead by paying below-scale wages, the lowest in most instances in the country. There was something in it for everybody but the workers.

The grift was endless. For example, one investigation disclosed that the Cleary Transport Company was remitting 25 percent of its gross billing obtained from the Palmer House to one of the hotel's porters, who was a member of Local 593 and the bagman for Blakely and Edward "Red" Donovan, secretary-treasurer of Teamsters Local 755, Film and Exhibitors Truck Drivers Union.

In 1953 Teitelbaum fell into disfavor with Tony Accardo. He lost his magical arbitration touch immediately after Paul "Needlenose" Labriola and James Weinberg threatened to push him out of his office window. These two hoodlums had organized the Cook County Licensed Beverage Dealers Association, which was specifically formed to shake down owners of liquor establishments. The president of the association was Joseph Nicoletti, a tavern operator and associate of Accardo, who perjured himself at Accardo's 1960 income tax trial and was sentenced to federal prison. In 1954 Labriola and Weinberg were garroted and their bodies stuffed in a car trunk.

Teitelbaum's replacement was Anthony V. Champagne, a legal batboy for Giancana. Before his appointment to the $125,000-a-year post, Champagne's *reported* annual income was $9,000. As his assistant labor relations expert, he hired Sam English, brother of

Charles English,* Syndicate overlord of the Twenty-ninth Ward and a business partner of Giancana.

Within a year, Champagne incurred the wrath of Accardo and was ordered murdered forthwith. Giancana interceded on his behalf and Champagne was allowed to resign with his life and limbs still intact. His replacement, Ralph J. Gutgsell, also lasted one year. He was succeeded by Thomas E. Keane, alderman and committeeman of the Thirty-first Ward, and presently city council floor leader for Mayor Daley. As a member of the state legislature in the Thirties, Keane had represented the Restaurant Association at Springfield.

During their appearance before the McClellan Committee in 1958, both Teitelbaum and Champagne invoked the Fifth Amendment. Louis Romano gave one of the most arrogant exhibitions before the senate committee. When Chief Counsel Robert F. Kennedy asked about the various murders he had been accused of, Romano snarled, "Why don't you go and dig up all the dead ones out in the graveyard and ask me if I shot them, you Chinaman?" (The Oriental aspersion, which baffled the committee members, is Chicagoese for bagman.) Later, Romano explained how he was able to retire in Florida on a reported income of less than $600 a year. "Well, one reason is I buy very little food . . . I catch a lot of fish for food. And I can eat it six times a week. If you want any good hints how to cut the high cost of living, there is a good one."

"There wasn't much else during the Chicago restaurant hearings that was calculated to draw smiles," Senator McClellan later observed in his book, *Crime Without Punishment.* "Those sessions were among the clearest examples in all the hearings of how the crime syndicate has infiltrated into legitimate business enterprises. The restaurant industry didn't do very much to bring glory upon itself, either; the investigations brought nothing but abuse on the one hand or equivocation on the other from the very people who should have been happiest to see these conditions exposed and ended. . . . Whenever the committee's staff launched an investigation . . . their [gangsters'] normal criminal activities usually came to an abrupt halt. . . . That wasn't what happened in Chicago, however, in the spring of 1958, when committee investigators were digging into the unsavory record of shakedowns in the city's restaurant industry. Instead, the crooks fought back in their own vicious fashion."

Testimony before the committee disclosed that forty restaurants

* See Appendix.

28

had been destroyed by arson in the eighteen months preceding its hearings in July 1958. Before the Syndicate's invasion of the industry, there had been about one or two cases a year. A total of 39 unsolved murders were connected with the criminals under investigation.

Another bombing and arson epidemic flared up in 1963. By the end of 1965, the score totaled 124.

"What is there about the Chicago area that makes bombing a safer occupation than window washing?" one reporter asked. "Why so many in Chicago and so few elsewhere?"

"It is a vicious, sneering, but eloquent demonstration of the failure of Chicago, Cook County, and state law-enforcement agencies to mount anything more than a verbal defense against the latest assaults by the crime syndicate," the *Daily News* charged in 1964. "It has gone on too long; the risk to the citizenry of Chicago is too great; the civic embarrassment of a community trying to live down a miserable, gang-ridden image has passed the point of toleration." A few months later, the *American* was proclaiming a national emergency.

Although the Syndicate maintained its four-figure batting average against the cops, at least one error added a little suspense to the game. Shortly after three A.M. on January 18, 1963, as patrolman Richard Martin was cruising by Dimitri's restaurant in Countryside, a black Ford came barreling out of the restaurant's deserted parking lot and shot through a stoplight. Martin curbed the Ford within a block and began questioning the driver. A moment later the area was rocked by a loud explosion. Dismissing the motorists, Martin drove back to Dimitri's to find it in flames. Hours later, after the fire had gutted the building and investigators had found positive evidence of arson, Martin recalled the name of the motorist.

That afternoon Lawrence Rossano was arrested and identified by Martin. Besides being an ex-convict, Rossano had once managed the Turf Lounge, a Cicero strip joint owned by Joseph Aiuppa, the friendly charterer of Local 450. For the first time, police had discovered a link between a syndicate-controlled union and the bombing of a restaurant. The press applauded patrolman Martin. For a while the event seemed a millennium. And in terms of convicting a Syndicate torchman, it certainly was. Of course, there was no precedent on which to base such optimism.

Through changes of venue and continuances, Rossano managed to delay his trial for an entire year. Then, in less than two hours, he walked out a free man. Judge Alexander J. Napoli, presiding without a jury, ruled that the evidence was insufficient. Rossano did not even have to testify. It was a disappointing verdict, but one that kept the record clean.

Besides being a major source of revenue for the Syndicate, labor racketeering is an integral part of machine politics. The control of this tremendous pool of manpower inevitably carries with it the clout of patronage, which in Chicago is the original fountain of political perpetuity.

William A. Lee, president of the Chicago Federation of Labor and Industrial Union Council, was Mayor Daley's first civil service chief. The fact that the wage scale of local government workers is above union rates, sort of a sweetheart contract in reverse, is another indication of the political muscle of labor bosses. The power of numbers is even more meaningful when coupled with the power of ruthless terrorism. Thus, it becomes a combination impossible to top—or topple.

Even the prestige of Lee's lofty status has failed to insulate him from the facts of political life in Daley's Cloutville. For the past seventeen years, William Lee has been guarded by a two-man police detail. His moment of terror began on a cold November night when three hoodlums approached him on a dark street and said, "We want in." Lee, who was then president of Local 734 of the Bakery Wagon Drivers Union, shook his head. "We want in or something might happen," they warned. "Nothing doing," Lee said and quickly walked away. And that, reportedly, was the end of it. That is, except for the two bodyguards peering over their shoulders for seventeen years. Through the years, there have been some who have questioned Lee's survival tactics, explaining that bodyguards in Chicago have been known to bleed as profusely as anybody else. If there was a secret to Lee's subsequent success, John A. Kilpatrick could have used a clue.

As the International President of the United Industrial Workers of America, Kilpatrick was deeply concerned about the machinations of Angelo Inciso, president of the union's Chicago Local 286 and also chairman of the board of the American Continental Insurance Company, which carried the welfare insurance of the union's four thousand members. A known associate of Tony Accardo, Inciso had a criminal record dating back to 1930, with convictions for auto theft, illegal transportation of liquor and grand larceny.

30

Shortly after his release from prison in 1938, Inciso emerged as a labor leader, and like most hoodlum unionists, was soon involved in wholesale violence. After he was shot in the right knee in 1953, he had two police bodyguards at his side for several years. What these two minions of the law were doing while Inciso was cracking skulls with baseball bats or consorting with Accardo *et al.* remains a mystery.

Following his appearance in 1955 before a U.S. Senate subcommittee investigating union health and welfare funds, Inciso was indicted by a federal grand jury on charges of illegally collecting $420,267 in insurance payments from twenty-two companies employing members of his local, and for squandering union funds on fancy gifts and European travel for hoodlum *amici*—in a moment of amorous extravagance, Inciso had even purchased a $65,000 home in Encino, California, for his paramour.

Four years after his indictment, on June 23, 1960, Inciso was convicted and sentenced to serve ten years in federal prison and fined $22,000. Meanwhile, Kilpatrick had filed a civil action against Inciso to recover misappropriated union assets, a move that did little to improve Inciso's frame of mind, since he already blamed Kilpatrick for his present predicament.

On the morning of April 28, 1961, while Kilpatrick and Gregory Grana, vice-president of the International, were standing in a courtroom corridor awaiting their turn to testify in the civil suit, Inciso approached them and pointed a finger at Kilpatrick: "I'm going to kill you," he said. "I'm not going to do it personally, but I'll have it done." Kilpatrick reported that threat, plus a score of others that came over the telephone, but was not granted the standard protective escort.

The threat was realized on October 20, 1961. That morning Kilpatrick's body was found slumped in the front seat of his car, a single bullet hole behind his left ear. Two sticks of dynamite, found wired to the brake pedal and connected to the ignition system, had failed to explode because they were water-soaked, presumably as a result of a recent rainfall.

Attorney General Robert F. Kennedy remembered Kilpatrick as a witness who had cooperated with the McClellan Committee while he had been its chief counsel. After explaining the circumstances to J. Edgar Hoover, Kennedy issued an emphatic order: "Find out who's behind this killing, and get him." Kennedy's edict marked the first time the FBI was ordered to investigate a gangland slaying in Chicago. Fifty special agents were assigned to the case. Within a week an estimated two thousand persons had been interviewed, including Inciso, who was free on bond pending appeal of his conviction, and his chief organizer, Ralph Polk, who was then awaiting trial on charges of having assaulted a nonstriking employee with a baseball bat.

The break came from an unexpected source. A month after the murder, William Triplett was arrested in Detroit for a liquor store robbery. At the time of his arrest, Triplett vaguely hinted that he knew something about a Chicago murder. Upon checking his background, the FBI learned that he was a nephew of Dana Horton Nash, an ex-convict on parole from Jackson (Michigan) state prison for passing bogus checks. Nash had relatives in Chicago and had once been the co-owner of a Detroit restaurant with Ralph Polk.

Confronted with this information, Triplett confessed. He began his confession, a twenty-page document, by saying he was with Nash in Detroit on October 16 when Nash made a telephone call to Chicago.

"During the telephone conversation, Nash turned to me and stated that some others had 'muffed' on the job in Chicago. After he finished the call, Nash approached me and asked if I'd like to make two hundred fifty dollars. I asked him on what and he stated to me that Ralph Polk had a [beating] job for him to do on a man that had done his boss an injustice. . . . Nash said the payment for the job would be five hundred, of which I was to receive one half." After arriving in Chicago on October 19, Nash and Triplett made a couple of "dry runs" by Kilpatrick's residence. The next morning "when I got out of bed, I found in my suitcase a .32 caliber pistol. I asked Nash what the weapon was doing in my suitcase and he told me . . . it was to be used only to keep the victim in line until the beating could be administered."

The following morning Nash selected an alley and instructed Triplett to "put the gun on Kilpatrick and drive him in his car to the alley." But when he delivered Kilpatrick as ordered, Nash took the gun from him and promptly shot Kilpatrick in the back of the head. Later, when a news report mentioned the two sticks of dynamite, Nash became furious at Polk. "That's going to cost him two thousand instead of five hundred," he told Triplett. Back in Detroit, Nash warned him to keep his "mouth shut because there are some pretty big people in this." Triplett never received the money he was promised.

On October 9, 1962, almost a year to the day of the murder,

32

Triplett and Nash were convicted in Superior Court in Chicago. Nash was sentenced to serve a minimum of ninety-nine years in the Illinois State Penitentiary; Triplett received a sentence of fourteen years.

Although it was the first gangland slaying conviction since 1934 when Sam Bruno was convicted as an accessory in the murder of Joseph Adduci and sentenced to fourteen years, it was at best a partial victory. No action was taken against Inciso or Polk, proving once again the effectiveness of the insulation between the order and the deed.

The union changed its name to Local 44, Amalgamated Industrial Union, but continued under the domination of the Syndicate. The leads supplied by Kilpatrick in 1961 resulted in a seventy-one-count indictment in 1964 against five officials of the local on charges of embezzling $46,000 in union funds. Four entered guilty pleas: Angelo Inciso (five counts) was given one year, the sentence to run concurrently with his previous ten-year term; Ralph Polk (sixteen counts) was given three years; Benjamin Tarsitano (thirty-two counts), a business agent and chief contract negotiator, received two years, and John Barkowski (twelve counts), a strike organizer who has since been promoted to secretary-treasurer, was sentenced to one year.

"I don't feel those two men [Barkowski and Tarsitano] took anything for their personal gain," said Elmer H. Karnuth, the newly elected president of the local. "If the law says they can hold jobs in the union, I'll welcome them with open arms. The membership will back them up, too."

With the first conviction of Inciso, Tarsitano had become the new hoodlum liaison of the local and consequently the new boss. One of Tarsitano's associates was Charles G. Lucenti, an official of Kingsbury Iron and Metal Company (this firm was actually owned by Titus Haffa, a Chicago industrialist whose holdings included the Checker Taxi and Yellow Cab companies), who was considered a mystery man by police until it was discovered that he was mainly a bagman for Joey Glimco, a labor racketeer not exactly unknown to Haffa, or Hoffa for that matter.

From the day Tommy Maloy was gunned down in a wild automobile chase on Lake Shore Drive in 1935, Local 110 of the Motion Picture Operators Union has been under the domination of the Syndicate. This is not to say that Maloy's leadership was founded on

33

brotherly love. By any definition, Maloy was a tough customer; he merely lacked the proper credentials. As a young man, he chauffeured for Mossy Enright, boss of the building-trades unions. On occasion Maloy drove the "Gray Ghost," a long sedan crammed with well-equipped sluggers and killers, which Mossy dispatched whenever he had an important message to deliver. For a while there was a busy exchange of messages, the final one being delivered to Mossy in 1920 by rival gangsters.

After that Maloy became a projectionist in a small movie house, where he ran a crap game under the stage. Maloy established himself that same year when two gun-toting organizers informed him that he had better join a new union they were forming, or else. Maloy, who had done a little more than just drive the Gray Ghost, literally knocked the two gunmen senseless, pitching them and their guns headlong down a flight of stairs. This made Maloy business agent of Local 110. Other exploits soon gave him complete control of the union.

Quick to learn the ropes, Maloy began clipping theater owners on threats of strikes. One grateful owner presented Maloy with a $4,000 toilet. Discordant voices were silenced with bullets. His two top gunmen were Ralph J. O'Hara, who was to become a kingpin in the Syndicate's wire service, and Joey Montana, who had cut down two policemen at the age of sixteen and could still walk the streets armed like a bandolero. The slightest opposition was punished. Operator Jacob D. Kaufman backed a rival candidate and was murdered by a sport in white pants. Fred F. Oser, another rebel, was enticed into Maloy's office and shot in the head by O'Hara (he pleaded self-defense and the judge instructed the jury to acquit him because nobody had actually witnessed the shooting).

On January 25, 1935, Maloy was indicted on income tax evasion charges for failing to report $350,000 for the years 1929–1932. A week later, a couple of Nitti's boys poked a machine gun into his limousine and saved the government the expense of a trial.

George Browne, International President of I.A.T.S.E., took a tip from Nitti and appointed Nick Circella (alias Nick Dean) to succeed Maloy. (Browne and his partner, Willie Bioff, were later convicted for extorting millions from Hollywood studios. It was on their testimony that seven of Chicago's top gangsters—including Ricca and Campagna—were convicted in 1943 in a New York City federal court. Nitti escaped by committing suicide. Ironically, the extortion

34

plot had its inception in the early Thirties when Hollywood was busily producing its greatest Chicago crime epics with Robinson, Cagney, *et al*. Simultaneously, the movie moguls were paying the real Chicago gangsters for the privilege of operating their studios and theaters sans labor strife.)

Paul Ricca has been the Syndicate boss of this local for thirty years. His present liaison, Clarence A. Jalas, collects $21,000 annually as business agent plus $6,000 for expenses, while the president of the local receives only $2,500 and no expenses.

According to Assistant U.S. Attorney David P. Schippers, head of the Justice Department's organized crime unit in Chicago in 1965, Local 110 is a kind of "hiring hall" for relatives of elite mobsters. "When they're not doing anything else, that is, out on jobs for the Mob, there's work for them through the union as a movie projectionist," he says. "It's easy and it pays well." Most of them, however, have never seen a projector. They hire other union members to substitute at a much lower rate of pay and pocket the difference. Their membership cards establish them as respectable members of the working class. It is also a good income front. Included in the union's membership are Accardo's son, Anthony J., and his brother John; Humphreys' brother, Jack Wright; Aiuppa's brother, Sam; the late Frank Nitti's nephew, Frank Dolendi; the late Charles "Cherry Nose" Gioe's brother, Anthony Gior; Paul Ricca's brother-in-law, Pat A. Gigante, and at least a dozen more.

Herman Posner, a seventy-two-year-old projectionist, attempted to lead a rebel movement in 1960. A few days before he was to turn over to federal investigators a black leather briefcase allegedly containing evidence of shakedowns and kickbacks, Posner was knifed to death near his home; the killers fled with the briefcase. Posner's murder was the seventh in the bloody history of the union.

Five years later, on April 23, 1965, Clarence Jalas was indicted by a federal grand jury on twenty-five counts of violating the Taft-Hartley Act: twenty counts of receiving illegal gifts of money, stock certificates and services from the Essanay Electric Manufacturing Company, a film company headed by Jalas' sister, Mrs. Alma Long (also indicted); four counts of embezzlement of union funds, and one of conspiracy. The government charged that Essanay used nonunion employees to run films at McCormick Place, Chicago's mammoth convention center (destroyed by fire in 1967), and was the almost "exclusive supplier" of projectionists to conventions and other private

35

affairs. The firm also enjoyed a monopoly of the renting of movie projectors for such occasions, and was reportedly moving into the newly opened field of in-flight movies on major airlines.

5

The Syndicate is well represented in the plush executive suites of union bosses who control the rank-and-file in industries which run the gamut from minor to major—candymakers to hod carriers, street sweepers to electrical workers, tortilla bakers to machinery erectors, orchestra truck drivers to funeral directors.

But of all the corrupt labor czars who have pounded their "muscled" imprint into the congested face of Chicago, the biggest "Little Caesar" of recent years has been a five-foot-four bleak-eyed Sicilian who most likely was picked by Central Casting after muttering: "Listen, you mugs, I'm taking over, see. The first guy that rats gets a bellyful of slugs in the head. Understand?"

In the world of Joseph "Joey" Glimco, these precious clichés are still amazingly effective. Nobody on the receiving end ever thinks they are funny. Testifying before the McClellan Committee in 1959, one witness quoted a Glimco gem: "If anybody double-crosses me, I'll get 'em if they go to the other side of the world." The threat certainly indicated impressive connections.

Glimco's early mentor was William "Witt" Hanley, a Teamster leader of a handful of unions. He was known as "Boss" of the Fulton Street Market. Besides controlling the Produce and Florist Drivers, the Poultry Handlers, the Poultry Drivers, and the Fish Handlers unions, Hanley also headed the Taxicab Drivers, Local 777 (IBT), a union with six thousand members.

On the death of Hanley in 1944, Glimco quickly took over: "I'm the new boss, see. From now on, you guys take orders from me, see. The first guy that tries something wise gets a bellyful of slugs in the head. Understand?" Everybody understood. "Glimco is the Mob," one police official observed. "When he opens his mouth, it's the Syndicate talking."

Ten years later, federal investigators estimated Glimco's gross annual revenue from unions and business interests at about $840,-000, with most of it filtering back to his Syndicate backers. There was enough left, however, to keep him in silk underwear, Cadillacs and mistresses.

That kind of yearly boodle requires more than colorful dialogue. It

36

takes perseverance and plenty of larceny. Nothing escaped the watch-ful eye of the Boss. For example, there was the item of chicken feathers. All proceeds from the sale of feathers to mattress and bedding manufacturers were turned over to Glimco as a "kickback." In a period of eight years, it amounted to $24,069.

The Taxicab Union yielded $16,000 a month with no public accounting. Yet Glimco had a lot of other angles working for him. According to payroll vouchers, Dominic Abata, president of Local 777, was supposed to get a salary of $125 a week. Actually, he received $71, the balance bouncing back to Glimco. Five other union officials enjoyed a similar arrangement. This raised Glimco's weekly stipend of $125 to $608. But that was not all of it. The officials also kicked back their $100-a-month expense allowance. And to add the final indignity, the officials were required to pay income tax on the full amount of their salaries. In Abata's case, it meant that he paid income tax on $6,500 a year while actually receiving only $3,692. Asked to explain why he had allowed himself to be subjected to such an injustice, Abata told the McClellan Committee: "Well, that is the way it was set up, and that is the way I went along with it. I batted absolutely zero against him [Glimco]." In the latter part of 1951, Abata left the union "for my own safety."

Among a variety of strange practices, none intrigued the McClellan Committee more than the union's arrangement with the Yellow Cab and Checker Taxi companies. In a period of twenty years, Local 777 had rebated $327,491.46 in union dues to the two companies to defray administrative cost of collections, which meant that union members were actually paying back part of their salaries to their employers.

Another unique situation uncovered by the McClellan Committee was the health and welfare plan carried by the Occidental Life Insurance Company and their Chicago agent, the Dearborn Insurance Agency. It was the only program of its kind underwritten by Occi-dental without a board of trustees—Glimco was the sole trustee of the fund. In the case of just three locals controlled by Glimco, Occidental paid over $515,000 in excessive and overwrite commis-sions to the Dearborn agency. The McClellan Committee concluded that there was evidence of "collusive arrangements" between in-surance officials and labor leaders, and that the excessive commis-sions were part of the payoff.

On the other hand, Glimco did his zealous best to protect Occi-dental, which had authorized him to pass on the validity of claims and to write checks on the company in payment thereof. Handling this detail for Glimco was his paramour, Laverne Murray, who was also the cobeneficiary of a $44,000 home purchased through union funds. Miss Murray was not easily moved by the ailments of union members. In fact, most claims were flatly denied without explanation. Stubborn claimants were fired on the spot and stripped of their union membership. One cab driver who insisted on going to the top to collect a $60 claim later quoted Glimco as stating: "You are going to get a hole in your head if you don't get out of here and stay away from here and behave yourself. You are not going to get it." The cab companies, which contributed to the health and welfare fund, showed no interest in what happened once they fulfilled their obligations under the contract. They even paid insurance premiums on part-time employees who were not eligible for benefits. However, when called upon to substantiate alleged payments of more than a million dollars in insurance and welfare benefits paid by Glimco, the Dearborn agency informed Senator McClellan that the necessary documents and records had vanished mysteriously soon after committee investigators indicated an interest in them.

Still, it was not easy to ante up $840,000 a year to impress hard taskmasters like Accardo, Ricca, Guzik, Campagna, Capezio, Alex, Giancana, Pinelli, LaPorte, DeGeorge and Humphreys. They were always expecting improvement.

The mayhem squad on the Fulton Street Market was handled by Dominic Senese, a brother-in-law of Accardo, and John Smith, business agents and officers of Local 703, Produce Drivers Union (IBT). Senese and Victor Comforte, a hoodlum associate of Glimco, were found to own a two-thirds interest in the Broadway Sheet Metal Works, Inc., which held government subcontracts to construct Nike sites in the Chicago area. Senese and Comforte, along with Frank V. Pantaleo and Frank Senese (a brother of Dominic), were also partners in the Vernon Farm Products Company, a wholesale egg business in the Market, which made Senese a businessman as well as a union official. In 1954, federal indictments charged Glimco with operating a shakedown racket and reign of terror in the Fulton Street egg market. Through various legal maneuvers, the case was delayed until 1957—and Glimco was freed when many of the witnesses changed their testimony. The legal defense cost Local 777 about $140,000, which was considerably less than the $600,000 Teamster boss Hoffa drew to fight criminal prosecutions in Nashville, Chattanooga and Chicago.

38

Pantaleo, a partner of Charles "Cherry Nose" Gioe in a construction business, was hired by Glimco in 1952 to build an additional office into the union hall of Local 777 "to provide more space for additional records regarding hospitalization only." Pantaleo was paid $85,325 for this work, which was estimated by an expert hired by the McClellan Committee to have cost no more than $35,803, allowing for a generous margin of profit. The differential was used to build a house in Oak Park which in 1953 was transferred from Pantaleo, the builder, at a price of $44,000, to a trust agreement. The beneficiaries were Laverne Murray and Glimco. The next year when Gioe was found stuffed in a car trunk, Glimco denied any connection with the slaying but refused to submit to a polygraph test.

Local 777's mayhem squad was handled by George Marcie, secretary-treasurer and chief henchman, and Oscar Kofkin, vice-president, whose criminal record included such items as murder and assault with a deadly weapon, but no conviction. Marcie also dabbled in business, with interests in such enterprises as Don Marcie, Inc., a cosmetic company, and Best Sanitation and Deodorizing Company, both of which occupied space in the building owned by Local 777. Besides deodorizing the toilets at the Checker Taxi and Yellow Cab companies, Best Sanitation was mighty popular with many companies employing union labor as well as a large number of individual local unions. One of its customers, the Orchid Flower Shop, owned by the wives of Capezio and Campagna, sold Local 777 $12,000 worth of flowers in a little over seven years. Best Sanitation's most persuasive salesman was Joseph Glimco, Jr.

There was little doubt in police circles that Senese, Comforte, *et al.* were business fronts for Glimco, who in turn was fronting for a dozen top hoods. For example, Glimco's associate in the Industrial Garment Service, Inc., a large chain of laundries, was Fred Evans, a devoted underling of Humphreys. With the aid of union "muscle," the company had cut heavily into the business of supplying coveralls and towels to service stations and garages. In 1959 when Evans was backed up against a brick wall and executed in firing squad style, Glimco denied any association with him. At the time of his death, Evans was also involved in five other companies: Infant Diaper Service; Linen of the Week, Inc.; Western Laundry Service; Crib Diaper Service, and Dust and Tex Cleaning Company. A slip of paper found in a drawer of his desk indicated various financial notations including "Total resources $11,000,000." Three safety deposit boxes yielded tangible assets valued at about $500,000. Among his out-of-state holdings were two luxury hotels in Los Angeles. Another Humphreys-Glimco business enterprise came to light in 1964 when government investigators revealed that Glimco's son, Joseph Jr., and Humphreys' brother, Jack Wright, were on the payroll of Paolo Salce, Inc., a paving firm that received city contracts totaling $4 million. Victor P. Salce, president of the firm, was a close associate of Glimco.

After its investigation of the coin machine industry in 1960, the McClellan Committee named Glimco as a major figure in a $200,000-a-year extortion racket against Chicago operators which was "enforced by coercion, violence and murder." Glimco's hidden interests in this field included the Mercury Record Corporation, Automatic Phonograph Distributing Company, AMI Music Company and Automatic Music Instrument Company.

(An investigation disclosed in 1966 that Joseph "Gags" Gagliano,* a syndicate loan shark, was a director of Commercial Phonograph Survey, which collected monthly tithes of ninety cents from each of the 6,975 jukeboxes owned by 492 distributors. Vincent Angeleri, a syndicate front in Recorded Music Service association, charged twenty-five cents per machine. Both men were associates of Glimco and Fred "Jukebox" Smith, a strong-arm tactician for Chuck English and Eddie Vogel.)

Glimco ran into trouble for the first time in 1961 when Dominic Abata came out of retirement to lead a rebel movement in an election supervised by the National Labor Relations Board. Although James Hoffa stood staunchly behind Glimco, the movement resulted in a rank-and-file defection from the Teamster local to Abata's new Democratic Union Organizing Committee, Local 777, Seafarers International Union (AFL–CIO).

"Well," said Hoffa, "since they want to join the Seafarers, let's see if the goddamn cabs will float." Four taxicabs were dumped into the Chicago River and two others were burned.

Although Glimco lost out in the election to disaffiliate the Teamsters and ceased to be the bargaining agent for six thousand Yellow Cab and Checker Taxi companies employees, he solicited a dollar a month from cabbies to keep the local alive; by 1965 three thousand were still contributing to the fund. Almost immediately Glimco organizers began moving on a number of industries to boost the depleted membership. Dock workers, bus drivers, laborers and even candlemakers were inducted into the local.

* See Appendix.

40

One of Glimco's boldest moves came in 1964 when he successfully invaded the Chicago waterfront. In November 1963, a contract was signed between Local 777 and Midwest Triumph Distributors and Mid-State Jaguar Ltd., franchised dealers of Triumph and Jaguar automobiles for seven midwestern states. Then, in April 1964, the Calumet Harbor Service Company, a newly incorporated subsidiary of the Midwest firm, leased seven and a half acres inside the port confines and rented space on the pier. Glimco's contract was to unload and drive the imported cars from the dock to their destination, a move not exactly sanctioned by Local 19, International Longshoremen's Association. The latter promptly called for a boycott of the importers in a move to oust Glimco from the post.

Since few things in Chicago are ever what they appear to be, it is necessary at this point to delineate the machinations in the woodwork. According to the U.S. Attorney's office, Hal Opper and Don Ross, president and vice-president respectively of the Midwest and Mid-State firms, were actually business fronts of Humphreys and Glimco. In two previous automobile agencies, Opper had withheld state sales tax amounting to $211,000, and was a defendant in a suit filed by Illinois Attorney General William G. Clark, who charged that Opper had dissolved the agencies "on paper" and started another in the same location and with the same owners as a ruse to avoid payment. Ross, whose real name was Donald Rosenberg, was the brother-in-law of Frank "One Ear" Fratto,* a Syndicate terrorist on the North Side, and Rudolph Fratto, known as the "garbage king" of the Rush Street saloon strip. Also associated with Midwest was Attorney Donald Mitchell, who incorporated the Mayfair Acceptance Corporation, headed by Larry Rosenberg, son-in-law of Meyer Ditlove, who had fronted for the Syndicate in a multimillion-dollar horsemeat scandal during the Stevenson administration. Larry Rosenberg, along with Leo Rugendorf, his partner in a number of Syndicate ventures, was a well-known associate of Felix Alderisio and Jack Cerone.*

Wonders never cease in Chicago, so it was not particularly surprising when Midwest appealed to the National Labor Relations Board to protect its contract with Glimco. The previous month, Glimco had been named by the Chicago police before the McClellan Committee as one of the city's top nineteen Syndicate leaders. However, the NLRB, after holding hearings (the Glimco forces were represented by the august law firm of Jake Arvey), ruled in favor of Local 777,

* See Appendix.

giving Climco official labor jurisdiction on the waterfront, which is under the administrative supervision of the Park District (Arvey is a board member) as well as the Port of Chicago.

Both surprised and angry, Harrison Tyler, president of Local 19, called for a U.S. Senate inquiry into the labor board's handling of the case. "The order," said Tyler, "was so strange and it ignored so much of the testimony given in hearings that we think there may have been some conniving in the board. Putting Glimco on the docks is moving the crime syndicate into the Port of Chicago. The battle of Local 19 to keep Glimco off the docks is a fight against crime even if these gangsters are protected by the government agency [the NLRB]."

"These arrangements now establish the Syndicate as an employer, as a stevedoring firm hiring labor, and as a labor union in competition with legitimate unions in the Great Lakes ports," one federal agent told this writer. "Thousands of vehicles from foreign countries are entering American ports. These vehicles could easily become, if they are not already, carriers for such things as narcotics, gems, gold or other contraband. Right now there are ten custom inspectors for the entire Port of Chicago, which includes Navy Pier and Calumet Harbor. These men are spread so thin that it is problematical of the extent, if any, of the inspection these automobile shipments receive. The potential in terms of contraband and further growth of the Syndicate can't be overestimated."

The NLRB order was issued on February 18, 1965, two months after a federal grand jury had returned a seventeen-count indictment against Glimco et al., for violating the Taft-Hartley law, the very same law the labor board later interpreted in Glimco's favor. Named in the indictment with Glimco were Don Ross and Frank Pesch, an officer of the Best Sanitation and Supply Company, also housed in Local 777's headquarters. Fifteen counts charged that Glimco had received gifts from Ross and Pesch ranging from an XK-E Jaguar roadster to a turkey. Two other counts concerned Glimco's receipt of television sets from Ben Stein, head of the National Service Company, who had been indicted a year earlier on ten counts of making illegal payments to union officials, including Glimco, Edward "Red" Donovan and Ralph Stark of the Building Service Employees Union (AFL–CIO).

A flashy associate of top hoodlums, Stein was known as "King of the Janitors" at McCormick Place. One of his rackets was to pay workers recruited from skid row $1 an hour while the firm collected $2.65 an hour—the union rate. Edward Lee, general manager at

McCormick Place, explained that he met Stein through Erwin "Red" Weiner, general superintendent of the Park District. At the time, Lee was having trouble with sloppy workers. "They used to splash acid on the walls," he said. "When Mr. Stein took over, all that stopped. It was amazing."

Even more amazing was how Mr. Stein continued under Lee's good graces even after the *Daily News* exposed his skid row racket. Stein merely changed the name of his firm to Midwest Maintenance Company—from 1961 to 1964, Stein's firm received $1.2 million from McCormick Place. Among his clientele were some of the city's largest hotels. An ex-convict (he served a year in 1938 for setting up his business partner to be robbed) with vast business interests, Stein has admitted that he paid $50,000 in "sales" commissions to Louis Arger (deceased in 1965), a cousin and henchman of Gus Alex, who operated a string of Loop strip and peep-show dives. (Convicted of labor racketeering on May 23, 1966, Stein was sentenced to eighteen months in federal prison.)

The Glimco case was more expeditiously resolved by Federal Judge Michael L. Igoe, who one morning quietly dismissed the indictment. The first time the government learned of the dismissal was when the ruling reached the court clerk. Igoe did not specify any reason for his ruling. However, when pressed by newsmen, he suggested that the "charges were imperfectly framed. All they [the government] have to do is get another indictment. My only reason for dismissing the indictment was because the defendants were imperfectly charged. The merits of the case were not at issue, and they were not passed upon." The eighty-year-old Igoe was in semiretirement at the time. Still, he had an interest in Glimco going back twenty-two years. In 1932 Glimco's first petition for citizenship was denied for lack of good moral character: he testified he had been arrested five times while his record showed eighteen arrests. He was again denied in 1939 when examiners discovered four more arrests on his record. It remained for Judge Igoe to grant Glimco citizenship in 1943. (When Glimco was reindicted in June 1966, the statute of limitations had run out on thirteen of the seventeen counts.)

In his thirty years as a labor terrorist and extortionist, Glimco has held one elective office—president of Local 777. Yet for most of those three decades he has been the moving force behind at least fifteen Syndicate-dominated unions, exercising muscle through the collective strength of drivers, salesmen and workers in such diverse industries as coal, produce, laundry-dyeing-cleaning, steel and metal

43

and alloy fabrication, scrap iron, food processing, canning, coffee vending, excavating-grading-asphalt, florist, ambulance-embalming, beer-liquor-soft drink, carbonic gas, fair-film-radio-television orchestra, cigar-tobacco-cigarette, vending machine, garage-service station and frozen food.

The underworld's stranglehold was so intricately executed that even the McClellan Committee, which devoted three years to its exhaustive study and compiled twenty thousand pages of testimony, could not untangle it. The legislation that followed was at best a partial answer. "Well intentioned though it may have been, it is far from adequate," Senator McClellan wrote in 1962. "Even without the advantage of the passage of time needed to judge the law's effectiveness, it can be said that it is not strong enough to do the job that must be done."

6

Lawrence Wakefield was a penurious old man who lived in a house with barred windows and slept behind a locked steel door. He had four watchdogs and one common-law wife. That he was a busy man was obvious to his neighbors; his movements were as precisely planned as an Illinois Central timetable. But what he did for a living was a well-kept secret.

Mrs. Rose Kennedy, Wakefield's "wife," was every bit as frugal as her mate. She certainly proved it the night he had a heart attack. Instead of summoning a private ambulance, she called the fire department. One of the officers with the inhalator squad noticed a large stack of coin wrappers and a bag of money on a table and notified the authorities.

The next day, moments after Wakefield died, detectives secured a warrant and searched the premises. They found nothing too exciting until they peered behind the steel door of Wakefield's bedroom. "There was money everywhere but on the ceiling," said one officer. It took thirty-two money bags and pillow cases to transport the loot to the Kensington police station on Chicago's South Side. (Shortly before the police arrived at the Wakefield home, the maid had pleaded for an advance of twenty dollars on her salary because of illness in her family. "I'm sorry," said Mrs. Kennedy, "there isn't a penny in the house.")

The police worked in shifts for twenty hours to count the money with IRS agents hovering overhead. It amounted to $763,233.30 in cash, $15,825 in government bonds, and about $30,000 deposited in various banks for a grand tally of $809,058.30. Also recovered from the Wakefield home was the physical evidence that explained the hoard—two policy wheels, eleven policy presses, two check-writing machines, five revolvers and two shotguns.

It was a sad night for the IRS agents. Income tax forms found during the raid indicated that Wakefield had been making systematic payments of over $3,000 a month to the federal government for his own income tax and withholding tax for six employees. The most they could clip the estate for was $102,000. Cook County appropriated $60,000 as contraband because it was wrapped in policy slips. Eventually, the probate court awarded $431,385 of the hoard to Rose Kennedy; the balance was held in escrow pending settlement of any claims against the estate.

Meanwhile, Wakefield's customers did not desert him in death. Eleven hundred jammed Metropolitan Community Church for the services. Mrs. Kennedy, in a black dress and mink coat, was escorted by two women in white nurses' uniforms. Interrupted by laughter when he praised Wakefield for his "skills of frugality and administration," the Rev. Paul E. Turner forged ahead with his eulogy. "He could have been chairman of the board of a large institution if the doors were open to him," Turner concluded. "Well," explained one mourner, "I just wanted to see the man who took all of my quarters."

Back in the Kensington station, Police Captain Edward Egan was expounding on the financial rewards of gambling. As policy operators went, Wakefield had been "just a small-timer." The Syndicate, Egan observed, had thought of "muscling in on his operation two years ago, but decided not to bother because it was too small to worry about."

By comparison, the profits reaped from one notorious policy wheel, the Erie-Buffalo, grossed $21 million from 1948 through 1950, according to U.S. Tax Court findings. State's attorney auditors estimated that while the Jones boys were languishing in a twelve-room hacienda in Mexico City, their policy wheel, the Maine-Idaho-Ohio, under the astute management of Theodore Roe, netted them $4,556,766 between July 1, 1949, and June 30, 1950. And this was just one out of thirty to forty big wheels in daily operation on the South and West Sides, each employing from a hundred to a thousand people.

Gambling has always been big business in Chicago. Through the years there has been little public opposition. Al Capone's answer to bootlegging—"All I ever did was supply a demand that was pretty popular"—applies equally to gambling. Because bookmaking is now conducted almost exclusively by telephone instead of the open horse-room of the past, the prevailing fiction is that gambling is on the decline. Even reform groups have lowered their voices.

However, no one denies that gambling could not exist without official sanction. After two decades as head of the Chicago Crime Commission, Virgil W. Peterson noted in his book, *Barbarians in Our Midst,* that the "whole law enforcement structure was geared to provide a healthy climate for a flourishing gambling industry." Peterson linked ward committeemen, judges and policemen in a conspiracy to deceive the public: "Many of the arrests in gambling cases were the products of 'phony' raids. It was all a big game to fool the public and protect the gamblers. The testimony of police officers in court usually made it easy for the judge to dismiss the cases on the ground that the evidence was illegally obtained and therefore inadmissible in court. The courts also applied the most technical rules of evidence in gambling cases, sometimes appearing to lean over backwards to discharge the violator."

A recent four-year study of the problem on a national scale by the Massachusetts Crime Commission concluded that the "price of protection has reached the stage where illegal gambling is *police business instead of bookie business* [italics added]."

Crime experts believe that 90 percent of all gambling could be eliminated overnight by determined law enforcement. The same holds true for most other forms of organized racketeering. Bona fide arrests, as opposed to phony circuses staged for appearances, are still made by honest policemen who have resisted the lure of instant money. But if they persist, many of them find themselves pounding a beat in outlying districts.

That there are more straight cops than judges and prosecutors in Chicago is borne out by the statistics of arrests as opposed to convictions. For example, of the 11,158 arrests for gambling in 1963, there were only 173 convictions. Exactly 13 persons viewed the inside of a jail cell. Of the 160 others who were fined, the fines were suspended in 123 cases. So the answer actually comes down to rather basic arithmetic: 13 jailed and 37 fined out of an army of 11,158 violators.

"And that's the best record we ever compiled," the late Deputy Police Superintendent Joseph Morris confided. "We have to work within the framework of our laws, which makes it virtually impossible to get a conviction. Even if we have a warrant [on a raid], it's difficult. I suppose the courts are only reflecting the attitude of the public."

The federal government has fared no better in Chicago. Federal judges are also local boys who made good. Still, FBI and IRS agents are often out on the street making elaborate coordinated raids that bag a half-dozen betting joints at a clip for some of the fattest headlines in town. For example, three days before Christmas 1964, sixty IRS agents, assisted by some forty Chicago policemen, swept down in simultaneous raids on nine Near North and Near West Side gambling establishments. The raid was the result of seven months of intense investigation in which agents actually infiltrated the gambling operation.

Twelve men were arrested and charged with failing to purchase $50 federal gambling stamps. (Federal law requires gamblers to buy either a $50 wagering [betting] stamp or a $250 gaming [for pinball and slot machines] tax stamp; they must also register with the local federal tax collector and pay a 10 percent tax on the gross amount wagered.)

U.S. Attorney Edward V. Hanrahan was pleased with the results of the coordinated raid. "Raids such as these have a disastrous effect on organized gambling," he said. "They keep handbook and wire-room operators on the move. The men in control of the operation lose customers. Phone service must be established in new locations. Such raids hit crime syndicate chieftains where it hurts—in the pocketbook." But Hanrahan was less enthusiastic about the ultimate results expected in federal court. "I hope the charges against these men will be treated with more seriousness by the courts than in the past. *We have had a few mild fines and no jail or prison sentences.* It is ridiculous. Such light treatment makes it scarcely worth the effort to bring these cases into court, although each raid and arrest costs the crime syndicate money. A few decent convictions will be better than any praise for the police agencies who work long and hard to bring law violators to court."

A multibillion-dollar-a-year extravaganza, gambling in Chicago makes Las Vegas look like a Saturday night crap game in the rear of Schultz's delicatessen. For example, even something as innocuous as punchboards and lottery jars was costing the public "half a billion dollars" a year, the Illinois Crime Commission discovered in its 1966 investigation of Empire Press, a Chicago firm which produced 1.5 million punchboards and 2.5 million lottery jars yearly. The punchboards, which sold for $2 each, took in about $300 from cus-

47

tomers—the company supplied "key charts" so operators could punch out the big winners before putting them on display. Empire was owned by Abraham H. Zimmerman, an ex-convict and associate of Syndicate hoodlums.

Variety in gambling is infinite—from football parlay cards to roulette wheels in plush gambling casinos, from nickel policy slips to multithousand-dollar horse and sports bets, from pinballs to cock fights. Most all of it is Syndicate controlled and politically insulated.

Few Chicagoans cannot find the action, whatever their pleasure. Judges and politicians of note, along with celebrated gangsters and newspaper columnists, prefer the basement poker parlor at Fritzel's restaurant, operated by Joey Jacobson, former owner of the Chez Paree with the late Mike Fritzel. *Sun-Times* Columnist Irv Kupcinet touts Fritzel's as the "Midwest equivalent of New York's Toots Shor's." An authentic Chicago saloonkeeper, Mike Fritzel operated the Frolics, a notorious dive frequented by gangsters and flappers during prohibition. Fritzel's basement really jumps at midday when judges repair from the bench for a little relaxation with cronies of the political and sporting world. One interesting facet about Fritzel's basement is that it has never been raided. Even newsmen have shunned making mention of it. In fact, it appears to be one of the most widely known and best kept secrets in Chicago.

Roulette wheels are found only in swanky casinos, but cards and dice are the staple diet of many neighborhood restaurants and taverns. These games are operated by the Syndicate and most of the time rigged to fleece the suckers in record time.

The way it works is quite simple. Mrs. Claire Stelmaszek knows the story well. She and her husband, Raymond, owned a small tavern on the South Side called Kola's Klub. One evening in March 1965 two men entered the tavern and promptly knocked the bartender up against a wall. The gist of the conversation was that they wanted a "piece" of the business and intended to install a rigged dice game in the back room "to take" the steel mill and railroad workers who patronized the place. The bartender mumbled something about not being the owner and the thugs reluctantly released their grip on the front of his shirt, promising they would be back. They returned later that night and repeated their proposition to the Stelmaszeks. The crap game would be held twice a month, on the tenth and twenty-fifth, pay days for steel and railroad workers. Card games and a "few horse bets" would be in continuous operation. And to show they were good guys, they offered the Stelmaszeks a third of the action, later changed to a fourth.

Mrs. Stelmaszek flatly rejected their proposal and the threats began. For the next three weeks, hoodlums came to the tavern at all hours to reemphasize their request. Mrs. Stelmaszek was followed night and day by a man in a black convertible. Finally, on April 26, shortly before closing time, nine burly musclemen silently entered and seated themselves at the bar. This was to be the last time words would be used, they warned. After they had left, Mrs. Stelmaszek notified the police and was advised to accede to the demands. Police installed tape recording equipment in the back room and a detective became the Kola Klub's new bartender. With the trap well set and baited, police waited to spring it.

Within a week, the Mob's electronic experts were at work in the back room. An old pool table was converted into an electronically controlled crap table. Magnets were placed under the top of the table and holes were drilled through the floor to connect the intricate wiring complex to the basement power source. Additional electronic gear was installed to allow the croupier to control the roll of the dice (loaded with powdered magnesium) with a remote unit that was actuated whenever he moved his body a certain way. A crap shooter never had a chance. The dice always came up seven at the most inopportune time. The electronic force was so great that the dice actually jumped a foot off the table (coming down seven) and the house lights dimmed whenever the device was used.

The game on May 10 lasted only eleven minutes before twenty-two cops came smashing through the door. Four hoodlums, eleven customers and Mrs. Stelmaszek were arrested. Her role in the deception was not disclosed until she had testified before the grand jury. "I told those hoodlums the first time," said Mrs. Stelmaszek, "that I wouldn't go their route. They thought I was a pushover. Maybe they know now."

"For Mrs. Claire Stelmaszek, 34-year-old mother of four, we feel admiration bordering on awe," said the *American*. "In helping police round up a gang of swindlers and musclemen, Mrs. Stelmaszek went far above and beyond the call of duty. . . . Her courageous service has earned her the heartfelt thanks of the whole community."

Police Superintendent Wilson presented Mrs. Stelmaszek with a citizen's award of appreciation. "Your acts, your courage, and your determination to see the job through with police is highly commendable. I wish we had more citizens like you." As she received the award, Mrs. Stelmaszek was guarded by two policemen, and armed guards were staked out at her home and tavern. Mayor Daley presented her with the city's official Medal of Merit. "You have given our people an outstanding demonstration of good citizenship and bravery," said the mayor.

Mrs. Stelmaszek received twenty fan letters. Not all were complimentary. One said: "Congratulations on being a stool pigeon and getting Mayor Daley's stool pigeon award of the year."

The fact that a free American citizen would dare protect her property rights is cause for celebration in Chicago!

7

Go with me to a notary, seal me there your single bond.
And, in a merry sport, if you repay me not on such a day,
in such a place, such sum or sums as are expressed in the
condition, let the forfeit be nominated for an equal pound
of flesh, to be cut off and taken in what part of your body
pleaseth me.

—SHAKESPEARE, THE MERCHANT OF VENICE

Shylock's method of collecting a loan is old hat in Chicago. Many cornered Bassanios would gladly settle for a pound of their quivering flesh when the juicemen put the squeeze on them.

Frederick P. Ackerman was a successful attorney until the juicemen got to him. Today he is under a Syndicate death mandate for having testified before the Illinois Crime Investigating Commission during its probe of the juice loan racket in January 1966.

There was standing room only in the hearing chamber when Ackerman made his appearance. Ten detectives and United States marshals, armed with revolvers and machine guns, formed a semicircle at his back, facing the spectators, as he unfolded his nightmarish story:

"I first got into the juice about five years ago when I needed $1,000. I had been to the race track. I got a loan for 5 percent a week." (The rate is usually 20 percent a week or 1,040 percent a year and the principal must be paid in one lump sum.) "I paid $50 a week for about a year and a half. I had some contact with a couple of fellows who were in the service of Chuck English.* I got behind in my payments and met some of these people in a basement at Wells and Madison. When you are doing business with these people, you never want to meet them in basements because they brainwash and torture you. They sit you down at a round table in that basement and intimidate you. They may torture you, squeeze you—that's what it is—they squeeze you until there's no juice left. It destroys a man. This racket is a squeeze. I think this is where the word juice came from because they drain everything out of you."

Ackerman conceded at the outset that he was far from "unsullied or untarnished." He had cashed forged checks, handled stolen bonds, embezzled from clients, made fake applications for bank loans, abandoned his wife and seven children, resigned from the bar after he was convicted of forgery, lost a $200,000-a-year law practice, owed more than $400,000 in income taxes, consorted with thieves and Syndicate hoodlums and compulsively gambled away his future.

"When you operate with these people, the money flows one way— into their pockets. If you don't pay them, you're dishonorable. If they don't pay you, you're a sucker. They change the rules [interest rates and due dates] to their own convenience." When he fell behind on payments on his first loan, William "Potatoes" Daddano, an associate of English, told him: "If you don't pay the thousand, I'm not going to shout; I'm not going to holler. I'm going to hit you in the head." ("Hit" in the underworld means only one thing—murder.) Ackerman later borrowed from Sam DeStefano and continued to gamble. He sold his home, his car, a diamond wristwatch, and cashed bad checks amounting to $27,500 to pay the juice. "The fear of the juice victim of criminal prosecution is far less than his fear of the juicemen." DeStefano warned him to be prompt with his payments because part of the juice went to Accardo and Ricca.

On one occasion, Rocco Infelice and Americo DePietto* offered him $50,000 to act as the courier for 10 kilograms of heroin from Beirut, Lebanon, to New York City. "I had some conscience, if you understand. Anyway, if I made a few trips then they would say: 'Meet us on the river front some night when the moon is down.' They would pay you off with a couple of peas [bullets] in the head." In Ackerman's opinion, DeStefano financed a large portion of the narcotics traffic. He frequently saw Thomas Durso, a policeman and narcotics peddler (convicted of murder in 1965), at DeStefano's

* See Appendix.

51

home. DeStefano was also involved in the 1961 torture-murder of William "Action" Jackson, a three-hundred-pound juice collector and terrorist. "DeStefano and I were talking in a breezeway at his home," said Ackerman. "He was laughing and talking about the Jackson murder. He offered to show me pictures of the mutilated body, but I didn't want to look."

Shortly before he was murdered, Jackson had told Ackerman: "Dyno [DeStefano] is crazy. He even killed his own brother, so you know how far he will go." But Ackerman did not need anyone to tell him that DeStefano was a mad-hatter. "DeStefano is not normal mentally, physically or spiritually and he knows it." One time outside the courtroom of the chief justice of the criminal court, DeStefano shoved Ackerman into a telephone booth, pressed an icepick to his stomach, and took $1,000 from him in payment on a defaulted juice loan. And there were always threats: "I'll put you in a sewer. I'll pull your eyeballs out. I'll put icepicks in you."

Ackerman told the story of Peter Cappelletti, a bail bondsman, who incurred the wrath of DeStefano by making juice loans on his own. Cappelletti fled to Milwaukee, but it was not far enough. "DeStefano went up there with two carloads of men. They took along a shovel because DeStefano wanted to kill Cappy and bury him on the roadside. They brought Cappy back to Chicago to a pizza place owned by DeStefano's brother, Mario, in Cicero. They stripped him naked and chained him to a radiator. They tortured and beat Cappy and urinated on him in the presence of his [Cappelletti's] wife. Then they unchained him and threw him at the feet of his wife, and DeStefano said, 'I'm giving back his life to you.' Bob [Attorney Robert J.] McDonnell told me he was present and that DeStefano said his life wouldn't be spared if he did what Cappy had. DeStefano is a mental deviate. He must attempt to destroy people to bring them to his level. He must degrade and debase them, even kill them so that he can rise and be a supreme person. That's his type of personality."

McDonnell, Ackerman said, still owed $80,000 in juice loans, many of them to DeStefano, even though he had paid $150,000 to $200,000 in usurious interest [juice] rates.

An attorney for DeStefano on numerous occasions, McDonnell was the typical juice victim. He once borrowed $12,000 from Daddano to pay DeStefano. "Instead of going to DeStefano, [he] went to the airport and got a plane for Las Vegas. Bob lost the twelve grand at a crap table in thirty minutes. He had to borrow money to return to Chicago because he had bought only a one-way ticket."

Ackerman recalled that DeStefano once bought a wrist watch for McDonnell as a birthday gift, instructing the jeweler to take it off the jeweler's juice bill. "Have it engraved 'From Sam to Bob'," DeStefano told McDonnell, "so when they find you in a trunk they'll know I was your friend."

McDonnell, Ackerman said, was once forced to carry the bodies of two murder victims from DeStefano's basement. In time he became so desperate that he formulated a plot to kill DeStefano. Assisted by five other juice victims, "they decided they'd darken their faces and that McDonnell would furnish hand grenades. All of them had access to service jackets [military uniforms] and they were going to get M-Is [army rifles] and the hand grenades, and roll one into Sam's breezeway. Unfortunately, they changed their minds."

Ackerman accused Sergeant John Chaconas, a sheriff's policeman later convicted of perjury in a $250,000 drug burglary investigation, of having sold to Cicero gangsters information about gambling joints known to authorities. Nick Kokonas, a bail bondsman, served as the intermediary between Chaconas and Joey Aiuppa, who paid $500 a month for the intelligence reports the Chicago Crime Commission turned over to the sheriff's office. When Kokonas defaulted on a juice loan, Ron Polo, a collector, threatened "to put icepicks in his eyes." Kokonas appealed to another old friend in the sheriff's office, Sergeant William Witsman, who was also indicted for perjury in the drug burglary case. Ackerman was present when Witsman told Kokonas that he would "go out and shake up those greaseballs because you are my friend."

"He went out and rattled a few cages in Melrose Park and Cicero, and woke up the animals. Maybe it saved Kikonas, but his mother, who is a good woman, borrowed $1,500 and had it delivered to the juicemen." Kokonas had borrowed $10,000 from Fiore "Fifi" Buccieri and had paid $8,000 in juice and still owed $16,000 on the loan, including interest and penalties. "Different men would take the money from me," Kokonas later testified, "and I knew none of them." Kokonas said that Ackerman had warned him that Cowboy Mirro, a Buccieri lieutenant, was advising other borrowers not to ride in cars with Kokonas because he was going to get "hit."

(Attorney Robert J. McDonnell, Ernest Infelice, James Mirro, Frank Santucci and Americo DePietto were brought to trial in federal court in May 1966 on conspiracy charges to pass forged money orders that were stolen from a supermarket across state lines. Ackerman, the government's star witness, said that Santucci stole the

money orders, and a few days later Infelice, DePietto and Mirro gave
them to Ackerman to forge and pass. He and McDonnell arranged
for a convicted forger, John O'Connor of Kansas City, to pass the
orders in Missouri. The scheme backfired when an associate of
O'Connor was seized by the FBI and O'Connor went into hiding. "It
looks bad," Mirro told Ackerman. "He is the only guy who can put
us in the pen. There's only one thing to do. We've got to bury him
[O'Connor] in McGurn's private cemetery." One day while riding in
northern Indiana, Mirro had pointed out a spot on some farmland
and said that it was the late "Machine Gun" Jack's private burying
ground. Through Ackerman's testimony, all five men were convicted
and sentenced to five years in prison.)

When it came time for DeStefano to face the interrogators, he
strode majestically into the hearing room, his overcoat draped over
his shoulders, an ivory cigarette holder thrust upward in Rooseveltian
fashion, and a smirk on his face. "This hearing is a three-ring circus,"
he announced. Then he carefully crossed his legs and spit on the
floor, rolling his eyes at the spectators.

Asked if he had murdered his brother, he giggled.

"On September 26, 1955, were you . . . contacted to remove
your brother [Michael—a drug addict] from a Cicero gambling
casino where he was causing a disturbance? . . . Did you go there
and remove him? . . . Did you put your brother Michael into his
auto and shoot him four times with your pistol?"

"Did you say *four* times? Did you say shoot or stab?" he asked,
grinning, a hand cupped behind his ear.

"Did you take Michael's body to your brother Mario's home in
Cicero? . . . Did you there remove all of his clothing and wash
down his naked body? . . . Did you also wash his clothing? . . .
Did you also clean the trunk of his automobile? . . . Did you then
put Michael's wet clothing back on his dead body? . . . Did you
then put Michael's body back in the trunk of his car? . . . Did you
then drive Michael's automobile to the sidewalk of 1507 Flournoy
Street in Chicago? . . . Did you the following afternoon call a Chicago newspaper without identifying yourself and tell them where the
car was parked? . . . Did you also make an anonymous phone call
to the Chicago police and tell them the same information?"

Throughout the questioning, DeStefano managed to elicit nervous
laughter from the audience. He pretended lapses of memory, feigned

54

ignorance of various terms ("Do you mean electric *juice?*"), and dramatically paused to sip water from a little plastic cup, or to spit into a cardboard carton supplied by an anxious janitor.

Hidden behind a blue drape and speaking through a microphone that distorted her voice into a gargle-like sound, one housewife told of the beatings and threats received when her husband fell behind in his payments to Donald and Joseph Grieco, juice bankers for the Buccieri brothers. Although her husband had borrowed only $400 in 1963 and had since made payments of from $20 to $40 a week (his weekly salary was $78), the original amount of the loan was still outstanding. All of the payments, nearly $1,000, had gone for interest—juice. When her husband became ill and fell behind in his payments, the Grieco brothers paid her a visit.

"They said that since I was a good-looking woman I could probably help and make a little money on the side to pay for the loan. By that I knew they meant becoming a prostitute. They told me that no matter how, why or where, the money has got to be paid. They said, 'Your husband works nights and if you want him to come home again some night, that money has got to get in. If you ever want to see him again, get that money in. Then one night I answered our doorbell at two in the morning, and when I opened the door my battered and beaten husband passed out in my arms. When my husband became ill, I personally made payments at the Vic Damone Pizza joint at 2015 North Larrabee. . . . I received a telephone call last week to 'keep my mouth shut' and they warned: 'You have a child who goes to school close by. I suggest you don't ever let that child alone.' "

Four months after her appearance before the crime commission, "Mrs. Smith" was identified as Mrs. Dorothy Franchina after her husband Anthony "committed suicide." Despite the security precautions of the blue drape and microphone distortion, the juicemen had identified the Franchinas. But whatever had happened in the interval between the date of the hearing and the night of her husband's suicide was left blank by Mrs. Franchina. "If they ask me about juice, I'll have a lapse of memory," she told police. "The juice people are no people to fool with. They have no feelings. My life is in jeopardy. My boys' lives are in danger." Police theorized that threats from the juicemen had broken Franchina's health—he suffered from epilepsy and weighed about a hundred pounds—and were the immediate cause of his suicide. "My husband was in bed," Mrs. Franchina testified at the inquest. "He asked me if I loved him. I told him, 'Yes.' Then I went into the kitchen. When I returned to the bedroom he was lying there holding a pistol to his chest. Then it went off." The verdict was "suicide while under a despondent frame of mind." Franchina had been employed by the *Sun-Times.*

Other victims testified behind the blue drape about the Vic Damone Pizza Corporation operated by Frank Buccieri* and the Grieco brothers. A "Mr. Boyd" told how Donald Grieco got him out of bed in the middle of the night. "He takes me out in his car. There's a girl out there. They ride me around the block and he pulls out a gun and I'm looking down the barrel. He tells me: 'I don't care how you get the money, but you get it and don't try to leave town.' " One night Mr. Boyd was escorted to the pizza factory: "When they brought me in they started saying things like: 'Look, here comes the lemon. He looks nervous. Why not put him in the cooler and cool him off.' Then they point out this big guy they call 'The Beast' and they tell me he breaks bones pretty good."

Singer Vic Damone (nee Vito Farinola) was president and the Grieco brothers and Frank Buccieri were directors of the Vic Damone Pizza Corporation at 2015 Larrabee Street. Also at the same address was Nickey's Frozen Pizza, a firm which sold to retail outlets in twenty-six states and chain stores in the Chicago area. The Damone corporation used letterheads decorated with the singer's photograph. "I'm a guy who trusts people," Damone told newsmen on January 12, 1966. "I guess it doesn't pay off sometimes. I lost a big contract for a television show when this first came out. Now it will probably cost me another television show that's coming up."

Damone went on to explain the circumstances that had led to his business association with the keepers of The Beast. It began in 1963 during a game of golf. "I can't remember the name of the club," Damone said. "Anyway, I played golf with this guy [Joseph Grieco] after someone introduced us and he told me he was having trouble with his pizza company. The second time we played he made the offer. I thought it would be a swell idea and I told him my mother had a recipe for pizza sauce we could use. I don't remember if I signed anything. I visited the place. It was clean. They made pizzas. That's all I knew. What am I going to do? I never knew anything. I never got a dime out of them [the deal was for 50 percent of the net]. In fact, I sent them a letter six months before this all came

* See Appendix.

56

out. I told them I never got any money. Never got anything. I told them I wanted out. I never heard anything until the headlines came out." Damone smiled when asked if he had made any inquiries about Grieco before entering into the business arrangement. "All I knew about him was that he drove a Cadillac, his pizza company was in financial trouble, and he played golf."

Besides exposing the juice racket in bold headlines, the Illinois Crime Investigating Commission's purported purpose for the probe was to recommend new legislation in a state where the so-called legitimate consumer credit practices were the most corrupt in the nation. The legal ceiling on interest charged by small-loan companies is 3 percent a month (or 36 percent a year), but the real gouge comes in hidden costs such as service charges and penalties. Illinois has no legal limit to the interest rate a seller can charge on installment sales of automobiles and retail goods. It is not unusual for the buyer to pay double and triple the true value of the purchase. And if he defaults, the seller can repossess and still collect the full inflated price with a court order.

"Every spring credit reform bills are introduced with a flourish," said one legislator. "Then no one hears of them again until they die in the Senate. It's a very old tradition." Speaking of the 1965 legislature, Senator Alan J. Dixon, Democratic sponsor of a credit reform bill, said: "We were beat before we started. I had a devil of a time even getting a hearing so we could put people on record. It was opposed by business, loan companies, banks—the kind of people who influence Republican thinking." "It was Joe Meek [lobbyist for the Illinois Retail Merchants Association]," said another senator, "who gave it the kiss of death." "It does no good to call everybody a loan shark," Joe Meek answered. "You have to compromise—to walk a few steps if you can't walk a mile. Credit reform won't come at first blush."

If after a century the legislature had not yet learned to walk more than a few steps, what could the crime commission do about the victims of juicemen? As one reporter asked, "How do you protect guys who get loaded in bars, or busted in a crap game, then go to pizza joints to borrow money from strangers?"

But not all the victims of juicemen were pathetic wretches. Many substantial citizens had fallen into their clutch. (A member of the crime commission, a noted attorney, resigned when it was disclosed that his son was a juice victim.) Captain William J. Duffy, director of the Chicago police intelligence division, testified that businessmen with better-than-average risk ratings secured loans as large as a million dollars from Syndicate lieutenants, and that the lieutenants often lent that much to "business factors," trusted middlemen who distributed the money to better risks. In detailing the operation, Duffy said lieutenants received their working capital from respective Syndicate bosses at weekly interest rates of one to two percent. The lieutenants parceled it out to "soldiers" at an additional interest rate of one-and-a-half to three percent a week. The soldiers worked the street, lending it to gamblers, alcoholics, victims of extortion, thieves in need of a bankroll to finance a heist, and the whole spectrum of poverty where desperate souls always reach out hungrily for "easy money." Juice was the squeeze. Like the proverbial stone, the victims suddenly found money oozing out of their pores. They found money where it never existed before. They embezzled, committed burglaries and robberies, put their wives and daughters into prostitution, peddled narcotics, betrayed friends. And there was no protection. Even the cop on the beat could be a juice collector, and the ward politician was often up to his fat cigar in the rackets.

Two enterprising hoods, Joseph "Joe Gags" Gagliano* and William "Wee Willie" Messino,* had an arrangement with a West Side politician who owned a chain of employment agencies. Rejected job applicants were handed these two gentlemen's business card.

Wee Willie had started out as a handyman at Accardo's River Forest mansion, but he was not destined to be a small-timer. He had as much greed and sadism as the next hood. And like all lower echelon helpmates, he aspired to bigger things.

So in June 1964, when Sandor Caravello, head of Bee-Gee Builders, hooked a live one, Wee Willie was ready. It began when the Chiagouris brothers (Jack, George and Albert) became interested in a real estate deal promoted by Caravello. Since financing was needed, Caravello introduced the brothers to Wee Willie and George Bravos, a West Side bookmaker and loan shark (a popular mating of occupations). After some friendly conversation, they handed the brothers $50,000 in hundred and thousand dollar bills. In return, the brothers signed promissory notes agreeing to repay $70,000 over nine months. The 40 percent interest rate did not appear too indecent under the circumstances. A few weeks later, Caravello informed the brothers

* See Appendix.

58

that more financing was needed to consummate the deal. This time they borrowed $100,000 from their angels. When the smoke cleared, the brothers unhappily realized that they were stuck for $10,000 a month interest on the second loan and $1,500 a week on the first, for a grand total of about $16,000 a month interest on a loan of $150,000—considerably more than 40 percent.

When the brothers missed a payment in September, they were vigorously threatened and assessed a $2,000 penalty. When the missed another payment a few months later, they were summoned to the Flying Carpet Motor Inn in Rosemont for a conference. Wee Willie was visibly upset. "These guys belong to me," he said to Bravos. "Give me permission to shoot them through their heads." The brothers, who by then had paid $82,000 on the debt, were told that they still owed the full amount of the principal.

Eight months later, in May 1965, the brothers again defaulted on a payment. At this point they had paid $165,000 in interest and still owed $124,000. There were a number of loud telephone calls from Wee Willie, and then one night Jack and George Chiagouris were kidnaped from the dining room of an Elmwood Park restaurant by Wee Willie, Bravos and Joseph Lombardi, their version of The Beast. They were choked with their own neckties, kicked and beaten senseless before being dragged from the premises in the presence of a roomful of nervous diners.

Their first stop was the apartment of Alice Erwin, where the brothers were questioned and physically abused. Later they were taken to the basement of Wee Willie's $80,000 home in Elmwood Park for the grand finale. Ribs were cracked, teeth knocked out, heads badly bent. They were held captive for fifteen hours until they agreed to comply to certain unpleasant stipulations. The following day, as per instructions, they visited the Service Savings and Loan Association in Summit, where they were greeted by its director, Sam Mercurio, who assisted them in signing away titles to $200,000 worth of property they held in southern suburbs for construction sites. It was after this disillusioning experience that the brothers decided to unburden their souls to Charles Siragusa, head of the Illinois Crime Investigating Commission. Messino, Bravos and Lombardi were convicted of conspiracy—intimidation—assault—kidnaping, and Mercurio of conspiracy.

Juice is second only to gambling in illicit revenue in Chicago. And it is a lot easier and a great deal less expensive to operate than gambling. There is no complicated system of handicapping, bet recordation, relay systems, wire services and other inconveniences which are basic to the successful function of gambling. All that juice requires is cash in one hand and a baseball bat or an icepick in the other. An indication of its prominence in Outfit circles these days is the protocol which calls for approval in advance by respective loan sharks whenever one of their borrowers is about to be defaulted with a couple of "peas" in the head.

8

Murder remains the Outfit's most persuasive weapon. In the old bootlegging era, quantity rather than quality was the keynote. By knocking off seven of Bugs Moran's henchmen at one clip in a North Clark Street garage on St. Valentine's Day in 1929, Al Capone achieved immortality. Chicago newspapers still note the anniversary of the event.

Although it never gained the prominence of that North Clark Street garage, Death Corner (at Oak and Cleveland), in the heart of the alcohol-cooking belt, still managed to account for forty-two corpses in eighteen months. To accommodate prospective widows, the Mafia (then known as the Black Hand) thoughtfully tacked notices with the names of the intended victims on a nearby "death tree."

But with the sharp decline in quantity in recent years, the quality has improved. The standard shot-in-the-back-of-the-head method is often preceded by colorful deviations. Typical of the new technique was the 1961 torture-murder of William "Action" Jackson, a three-hundred-pound juice collector suspected of being a stool pigeon.

The circumstances surrounding Jackson's death remained a mystery until a year later when a squad of assassins journeyed to Hollywood, Florida, bent on another mission of death. The prospective "hit" was to be Frank "Frankie the X" Esposito, union boss of five thousand city and county workers and a top political clouter who had sponsored a host of Syndicate gamblers and hoodlums for city patronage jobs. Apprised of the Chicago gunmen's departure for Florida, federal agents managed to "bug" their rented Miami residence and subsequently recorded some lively dialogue. Included in the cast of characters were John "Jackie the Lackey" Cerone, James "Turk" Torello,* Dave Yaras,* Fiore "Fifi" Buccieri, Vincent "The Saint" Inserro, James "Cowboy" Mirro, Felix "Milwaukee Phil"

* See Appendix.

60

Alderisio and Louis "Lou the Tailor" Rosanova, a sandwich-fetching, minor-league hood with one federal rap for theft from an interstate shipment and routine local pickups for questioning.

In the evenings, after a hard day's work of "casing" Esposito, the Boys would gather in the living room to drink and talk shop. The subject of Jackson's murder was first brought up by Buccieri during a discussion of techniques. Apparently Jackson's doom was sealed when Buccieri received word that the "big fat slob" was a "stool pigeon for the 'G'." Jackson had been observed conferring with two FBI agents at the corner of Laramie and Jackson Streets on the West Side. Shortly afterward, Buccieri and Torello brought Jackson to the "Plant," a place described as having a large meat hook on the wall. There they were joined by Cerone, Yaras and others not mentioned by name. They shot him "just once in the knee," stripped him naked, tied his hands and feet, and hung him on the hook for "a little bit of fun." Buccieri's interpretation of fun included a cattle prod (a large battery-powered stick) which he placed against Jackson's penis. "You should have heard the prick scream," he recalled. While Buccieri was amusing himself with the electric stick, others were playing around with such toys of torture as icepicks, baseball bats and even a blowtorch. "Then," said Buccieri, "I shoved the fucking stick up his ass and he shit all over the fucking joint. Boy, did he stink."

Buccieri's nostalgic account convulsed his audience into fits of hysterical laughter. A moment later, Torello became serious: "I still don't understand why he didn't admit he was a pigeon." Buccieri ignored the remark. "I'm only sorry the big slob died so soon," he said. Since Jackson had lasted two days impaled on that hook, the comment was good for another round of laughs. "Believe me," said Buccieri, "I'll never forget how the big slob looked hanging on that hook in the cubby hole." Credit for the cattle prod was claimed by Cerone, who said he got the idea from "some coppers who used the same thing on hoods."

The conversation then shifted to the time Cerone had attempted to kill Big Jim Martin, a West Side policy operator. Cerone said he fired several shotgun blasts at Martin but only wounded him because the ammunition was "old stuff." Yaras interrupted to observe that whenever he used a shotgun to kill anybody he always made sure that the "Double O" buckshot was new stuff. Cerone said that Accardo had given him the ammunition. After shooting Martin, Cerone said he returned to the scene of the crime and mingled with the crowd.

Engaging a bystander in conversation, he remarked, "It's a shame the way these niggers are always killing each other." (More laughter.) After the shooting, Cerone said he met with Accardo and reported that he had killed Martin, only to learn the next day that he was still alive.

Nobody laughed this time. Then it was Yaras' turn to tell a tale of murder concerning the time that he and Inserro "got a guy in the bushes and bowled him over" (killed him), ending his yarn with the moral that one should always take advantage of bushes "if any are around."

After a while it was Cerone's turn again. (The plot line was similar to *The Decameron*'s.) He recalled an old homicide buddy called Johnny Whales (phonetic), who "bowled over" people in the old days. Whales was a "Polack" but was "a real nice guy" with "plenty of guts." On one occasion, Whales was so anxious to "hit a guy" that he jumped out of their car while it was still moving and chased the guy "a full block" before he caught up with him and "bowled the guy over." He jumped back into the car, laughing. Later, however, Whales "went off his rocker or something" and just disappeared from sight. Whales, it developed, was afraid of the "Dagoes" and thought he was going to get hit himself. "You see, Dave," Cerone said, addressing his remark to the only non-Italian in the group, "he didn't understand that we [the Mafia] got Jews and Polacks also. I told him this, but he was still afraid. He just seemed to go off his rocker. I told Accardo and he asked me if I wanted the guy hit. I told him I liked Johnny too much to see him killed. But we didn't have anything to do with him after that."

Throughout their stay in Florida, Cerone frequently reminded the others that "Moe" (Giancana) had awarded *him* the contract, and that Moe wanted the job finished before he arrived in Florida for a vacation. Various murder plots were hatched, but none pleased Cerone quite so much as the one he dreamed up himself. It was simple and gory. They would approach Esposito (who knew each of them personally) when he was alone. They would invite him into their car and force him to lie on the floor. They would then take him to a boat, where they would shoot him, cut his body into small pieces, and feed them to the sharks.

Meanwhile, Esposito and his Hollywood neighbor and close friend, John D'Arco, a Chicago politician, were enjoying the Florida sun, unaware of the carload of hoodlums circling their homes and dogging their steps. Buccieri thought it was a shame they could not include

D'Arco in a package deal, and this prompted Cerone to remind the others that he had the knife they would use to dissect the body. At regular intervals, Cerone would caution the others about not being seen in Florida by Ross Prio* and Chuck English.

In trying to entice their prey within abduction range, they once used a woman as a decoy. But something always went wrong. It seemed that each time they were about to close in a car would suddenly intrude upon their privacy, scattering them to the four winds. What they did not realize, of course, was that FBI agents were the cause of those annoying intrusions. Later, when they began to suspect that something was up, they abandoned the project and returned to Chicago. Briefed by the FBI on the situation, Esposito returned to Chicago and apparently managed to have the contract rescinded. The *why* and *how* of the episode remains a mystery. Esposito refused to talk. "We're not concerned about his silence and I don't think it bothers the FBI, either," the state's attorney's chief investigator observed. "The important thing is that he's still alive to keep his mouth shut."

(A note for golf fans: Cerone and Rosanova teamed with George Keyes, club professional at Riverwoods Country Club, and "Lefty" Strummer [whoever he may be], and won the 1966 Illinois Professional Golf Association pro-am tournament, an event widely reported in local sports pages. With the closing of the Tam O'Shanter Country Club in 1965, the Outfit moved en masse to Riverwoods up in Deerfield. Not only were the gangsters welcomed with open arms, but Rosanova was elected president of the club, which has two excellent courses, several swimming pools and most of the comforts one usually expects for dues of $1100 a year. The exclusive membership is limited to 250 members. "As far as I know, this is the first PGA-sponsored golf tournament in which victory is shared by the Cosa Nostra," Mike Royko noted in his *Daily News* column. "Most other professional sports try to discourage their members from getting close to Cerone and his friends. In baseball or football, it would cause a scandal. But, then, golf is not like most other sports. It is a gentleman's game." Riverwoods was the scene of the Chicago and suburban police's annual golf outing in 1966.)

Testifying before the McClellan Committee, Police Superintendent O. W. Wilson spelled out the problem: "Much of what we know [about organized crime] confirms common impressions: that certain

* See Appendix.

key racketeers have amassed great wealth, that they make income tax returns in which tremendous incomes are reported from undisclosed sources; that they continually associate with others of their kind who have no known legitimate sources of income or wealth; that when called before Senate and House investigating committees they invariably plead the Fifth Amendment; that they are continually the subjects of comments in the public press and on the radio and television where they are labeled as gambling czars and vice-lords, and that they never deny such accusations or bring suits for libel or slander against news media for making such accusations. We know who they are and where they live. We are well informed about their comings and goings and we make all of this information available to Federal law enforcement agencies. We strongly believe that they control vast gambling and other vice operations, that they divide up and secure monopolies of various territories and drive out all competition, and that they are responsible for gangland killings to further these ends. We have not been able, however, to prove any of these beliefs." Still, it was quite a concession, considering Wilson's predecessor remained convinced up to his replacement in 1960 that there was no such thing as a crime syndicate. Wilson continued: "The most nefarious action of those engaged in organized crime is their resort to murder in order to maintain discipline within their organization. Since 1919 there have been 976 gangland-type slayings in the Chicagoland area. [Of these] only two have been cleared by arrest and conviction of the killers."

Senator McClellan's shocked reaction was expressed later in the hearing: "That struck me as one of the most frightening developments of information that I have heard regarding crime."

This frightening "bowling over" record is not just happenstance. Some of the top hoodlums are members of "hit" squads as illustrated in the Esposito episode. This should lay to rest the fiction that out-of-town punks carry out *important* gangland contracts. When the chips are down, lieutenants and bosses gleefully roll up their sleeves to indulge in their favorite sport.

There are more than a score of top-rated exterminators who work strictly on contracts for the board of directors. Alphabetically, they include Felix Alderisio (touted as lord high executioner), Fiore Buccieri, Marshall Caifano, Frank "Skippy" Cerone,* "Jackie the Lackey" Cerone, Eco Coli,* William Daddano, Americo DePietto,

---

* See Appendix.

64

Sam DeStefano, Joseph DiVarco, Albert Frabotta, Joseph Gagliano, Ernest Infelice, Vincent Inserro, Sam Lisciandrello, William Messino, James Mirro, Charles Nicoletti, Rocco Potenza, Rocco Pranno,* Rocco Salvatore,* James Torello and Dave Yaras.

(Many sharpshooters practice their art at the Santa Fe Saddle and Gun Club in Hinsdale. Listed as a nonprofit organization, its president is Joseph Scaramuzzo, owner of Scaramuzzo & Sons, a West Side gun shop. Back in the old days, Scaramuzzo's father, Louis, was identified by police as a "Capone gang armorer"—one raid on his gun shop produced sixty-four guns with their serial numbers defaced and a supply of bomb material. Early in 1967, Joseph Scaramuzzo sponsored a bash at Chicago's exclusive Edgewater Beach Hotel in honor of Fiore Buccieri. Attended by two hundred of the Syndicate's top brass, it was called by police, who checked license plates outside, the "Little Apalachin dinner." The conclusion was that "Buccieri is definitely moving up.")

There are many other assassins, of course, but the above named work directly on contracts issued by the board of directors. Each is either a top lieutenant or operates one or more lucrative rackets in territories protected by Syndicate edict. Alex and Yaras, the only non-mafiosi in the group, are highly placed associates of top Mafia bosses, having earned their positions with the blood, sweat and tears of a long list of victims and their heirs.

Not all gangland slayings, however, are "contract" murders approved by the Syndicate's board of directors. Police believe that as many as 50 percent of the "hits" involve fringe characters requiring only a single "thumbs-down" vote from a district boss or juice banker. For example, robbers who recklessly knock over a Syndicate gambling spot are swiftly executed on orders from the gambling overlord of the area. The same applies for bosses of other rackets and districts.

A not-so-typical example of the latter type of gangland execution was the case of Anthony "Lover" Moschiano, a heroin addict murdered by Thomas N. Durso, a Chicago policeman and Syndicate narcotics dealer. In describing the murder to federal narcotics agents, Leonard "Torpe" Fiorenzo (also a heroin addict) told how he and Moschiano were brought to the policeman's $40,000 Westchester home on the afternoon of January 21, 1964, by Durso and Michael Gargano, a Syndicate terrorist. Ordered to take off their shoes before

* See Appendix.

65

entering the house, they sat in the living room while Durso questioned Moschiano about reports that he was a "stoolie for the feds." After a few minutes, Durso went into another room to make a telephone call. When he returned fifteen minutes later, they were told to put on their shoes.

"We got up," Fiorenzo said, "and we walked into the garage. When I got into the garage I noticed the trunk of the Pontiac was open and spread with newspapers. There was no spare tire. Durso ordered Lover and I into the back seat where we remained for approximately sixty seconds. I saw him turn to Gargano and whisper something, but I didn't hear what it was. Then Durso ordered Lover out of the car. He told Lover to put his hands behind his back and Lover said, 'Don't handcuff me; don't put me in the trunk.' Durso handcuffed Lover and Gargano then began shoving rags into Lover's mouth. After that Durso tied a gag around his mouth. They forced him into the trunk and when I turned around to see what was happening I saw Durso stick a knife into Lover's throat. I saw this through the crack created by the trunk opening and by looking through the rear window. I saw him jerk the knife back and forth and heard the blood gurgling from Lover's neck. Gargano handed Durso some rags and I saw that both Durso's hands were covered with blood."

"Durso told Gargano, 'Get Torpe out of the car. I want him to see this.' I got out of the car and Durso told me to come there. 'I want you to look at this, Torpe. This is what happens to stool pigeons and people that fuck me.' I looked into the trunk and saw Lover laying there with blood all over his tee shirt. Durso then told me, 'I'm going to give you the break of your life. I'm going to let you go now because I think you can stand up and when this thing is over in a couple of days, we're going to make some big money.' Durso looked at Gargano and told Gargano they were going to wait until dark to get rid of the body. I saw Durso wipe the knife on Lover's sleeve and throw the knife into the trunk. Durso removed Lover's gloves from his jacket pocket and handed them to Gargano. He also removed a quantity of money and a billfold and handed these to Gargano."

"Durso asked me if I wanted to stay until dark. To this I said, 'Yes, whatever you want.' Gargano then told Durso: 'I don't think it's a good idea to have him wait. I think you ought to let him go back to the neighborhood and be seen. He hasn't been gone that long.' Durso told me to take the Cadillac and to take it to the neighborhood and park it at the County Hospital. He said to take a cab to Jimmy Green's [tavern] and to stay there until either himself or Gargano showed up that night. He said, 'If anybody says anything about you picking up Lover don't deny it. You picked him up and dropped him off a block away.' He said, 'I don't know if it will be myself or Mike, but whoever it is, don't talk to us. I'll have a drink and I'll leave first. After that you can leave, go where you want to, but make sure you go to Green's and stay there until one of us shows.' I got in the Cadillac and backed out in the street and then Gargano came running out and told me to move over. He said, 'It's better that you take the El. You can take that to Western Avenue and walk to Jimmy Green's from there.' Before Gargano and I drove off, Durso told me he wanted to see me every day around noon by Jimmy Green's tavern. He told me if you see me don't try to talk to me, just let me see you, and in a couple of days, when this all blows over, I'm going to make some money. Again Durso told me, 'The only reason you're getting a break is because I think you can stand up.' "

"Gargano then drove me to the El station at Desplaines Avenue and the Congress Expressway. I caught the El, went back to the neighborhood, stayed awhile and then went to Eleventh and State Street [Police Headquarters] to find officer [Bernard] Brown. I didn't find Brown so I went back to the neighborhood and stayed at Jimmy Green's until eight-thirty or nine o'clock at night. The following morning I contacted Detective Brown and told him what had happened."

In April, the nude decomposed body of Moschiano was fished out of the Des Plaines River in River Grove, and murder indictments were returned against Durso and Gargano. The trial was staged six months later. Meanwhile, it was found that three other Chicago policemen had been members of Durso's West Side narcotics ring, but authorities refused to disclose their identity.

Moschiano's problems had begun about three weeks before his murder, following his arrest by federal narcotics agents who confiscated four ounces of uncut heroin belonging to Durso which Moschiano had mistakenly tried to peddle to an agent. To escape imprisonment, Moschiano turned informant.

In an attempt to explain the disappearance of the $4,000 worth of heroin, Moschiano telephoned Durso and told him that thieves had stolen it from his room. Accompanied by Gargano and Fiorenzo, Durso broke into Moschiano's room to search for the missing drugs. Unable to find the drugs or Moschiano, the three men drove to the rooming house of Lupe Riviera, a drug addict friend of Moschiano.

During the murder trial, a seventy-two-year-old widow testified about what happened when Durso arrived at her rooming house. Prefacing her testimony with, "I'm not afraid to testify—I am old enough to die," Mrs. Nancy Bourne said that she admitted the three men after Durso told her they were policemen. But when they began searching Miss Riviera's room, "hurling clothing and papers on the bed," Mrs. Bourne asked to see their credentials. "Here's my credentials," Durso replied, striking her in the face with his .38 caliber revolver. Mrs. Bourne fell to the floor and Durso placed the gun to her head. "Any more lip from you and I'll blow your fucking head off," he snarled. "He used dirty, filthy talk all the time. He said he would break me in two or break my back. He told me, 'Get up, you dirty little bitch.' I told him I couldn't get up, and he finally helped me to my feet."

Durso then telephoned Moschiano's home and told his brother, "You get Tony out in the open where we can get at him." Moschiano appeared at the rooming house a few minutes later, and Durso handcuffed him to Fiorenzo. Fiorenzo testified that Durso released them later with the threat that this is "your last chance," either produce the heroin or the money within two weeks. The ultimatum was delivered on the eighth of January and Moschiano was murdered on the twenty-first, one day ahead of schedule, when Durso learned that he was a police informant.

Durso and Gargano were convicted of first-degree murder and sentenced to 100 to 150 years in prison. (Gargano's attorney was Robert J. McDonnell.)

"It's the first crime-syndicate murder conviction in Chicago in my memory," Captain Duffy told newsmen.

(Narcotics is so important in Syndicate economics that Mafia traffickers require approval from the board of directors. They in turn rule their organizations with iron-fisted discipline. The narcotics overlord—Giancana's first assistant—is Sam Battaglia, the so-called heir-apparent, which again demonstrates the importance placed on this lucrative racket. Licensed lieutenants under Battaglia include Felix Alderisio, Rocco DeGrazia,* Sam Cesario, Charles Nicoletti, Joseph Gagliano, Sam DeStefano, Leonard Gianola, Vincent Inserro, Frank Teutonico, Joseph LaBarbera,* Joseph Cordovano, Charles and Joseph DiCaro, Frank Caruso, John DeBiase and Americo

* See Appendix.

DePietto, who was convicted with eleven underlings in federal court in 1964 of conspiracy to operate a $10 million-a-year narcotics ring, and sentenced to twenty years in prison.)

9

Quite often the most bizarre element of a gangland slaying is the hoodlum victim himself. The penalty for transgression is clear. Yet, year in and year out, hoods violate sacred trusts that primarily concern money, rackets or territories, the traditional cause for the celebrated "bump off." Or they default on gambling or juice debts, they embezzle racket funds, they talk too much or they fail to carry out important assignments.

A typical example was Mandel "Manny" Skar, who on September 11, 1965, became statistic 990 on the gangland murder roster.

"Manny Skar was murdered over the weekend," said a *Daily News* editorial. "Speak no evil of the dead. But if you speak of Manny Skar at all, you speak of a cheap, blustering, boasting, vicious hoodlum who lived and died by violence. Without in any way condoning murder, one can say about Manny Skar that he asked for it."

Indicted for income tax evasion shortly before his death, the underworld rumor was that Skar was "interested in a deal with the feds" and was ready to "blow the whistle" on his gang associates.

The murder investigation turned up a long list of suspects and motives, but nothing concrete enough to take into court. Among the prime suspects were Rocco De Stefano* (no relation to mad-hatter Sam), a Capone-era hoodlum and the man behind Skar's financial ventures; Dominic Senese and Victor Comforte, who earlier had pursued Skar to Palm Springs and Beverly Hills in an unsuccessful attempt to collect a $35,000 debt; Rocco Salvatore, chauffeur and horsetrainer for Sam Battaglia; Joseph "The Clown" Lombardi, a juice collector and terrorist for Gagliano and Messino; Felix Alderisio, Rocco DeGrazia, Sam Battaglia and Fiore Buccieri, all of whom were believed to have argued with Skar in Rush Street clubs the month preceding his murder.

One theory was that Skar had collided head-on with mob collectors when he ventured into the Rush Street nightclub belt. It was rumored that he had bought into one and possibly two Near North Side joints

* See Appendix.

in the last year, and then had refused to pay the Syndicate's monthly tax imposed on tavern owners. This tax is in addition to the increased price of doing business with hoodlum-backed firms supplying food, liquor and other restaurant and bar needs.

After weeks of investigation, John Glas, a North Side homicide lieutenant, concluded that "Any one of a thousand men could have killed him." However, Glas was fairly certain it was not the Syndicate. "I don't know that I would call Manny that important a person."

Who, then, was Manny Skar, the "nothing" who died at forty-two owing the government $2,246,988? What was he besides a five-foot-five loudmouth in a silk suit and pointed alligator slippers?

In underworld terminology, Manny Skar was a beard (front). Once, for a brief moment, he was one of the star players in the Syndicate's smash production of *How to Succeed in Business While Failing.* His name was up in lights on Mannheim Road (the West Side's glitter-gulch version of Rush Street) where he officiated as mein loud host at the "fanta-bulous" *Manny Skar's Sahara,* a $10.8 million hostelry described by one press agent as a "little bit of Broadway, a little bit of Hollywood, and a whole lot of Miami Beach and Las Vegas."

Opening night, June 6, 1962, found Manny resplendent in a metallic red tuxedo, jumping about and yelling at the top of his lungs as he greeted television and movie personalities, along with celebrated criminal personalities, in the splendor of his deeply carpeted and stone-walled lobby.

Meanwhile, the fans outside had to give way to a company of cops made up of platoons from the state police, sheriff's posse, state's attorney's office, Chicago police's intelligence unit, and agents from the FBI, IRS and Federal Narcotics Bureau. They lined both sides of the driveway as they feverishly jotted down license numbers and tried to identify celebrities.

Their crude behavior offended Skar. "What's the matter with you guys?" he cried. "Don't you believe in rehabilitation? I made some mistakes, and now I'm trying to make good. If society is not willing to give a man another chance, it should take a man out and shoot him."

Skar's words were punctuated with jabbing arm movements that called attention to the fascinating tableau. Anyone but a dumb suspi-

70

cious cop would have known instantly of the owner's rehabilitation. There was the scarlet decor of the Club Gigi where Bobby Darin was knocking three hundred celebrities dead. Two hundred other celebrities dined at the Sultan's Table in the luxuriating atmosphere of gold carpeting, gold nylon chairs and gold foil-covered walls, listening to the romantic strains of strolling violinists. And for forty celeb-celebrities there was the exquisite Gourmet Room, with Chateaubriand served on 14-karat gold plates and wine in crystal goblets at a mere $35 per. There was even a Celebrity Lounge catered by "Sahara Starlets" in jeweled gold lamé harem costumes of minimum dimensions. At poolside, between gourmet treats and Bobby Darin, celebrities could cool off with highballs served by shapely bikini-clad nymphs.

Among the celeb-celebrities were three celebrated Roccos: De-Grazia, De Stefano and Pranno (Roccos have been popular on the nightclub circuit a long while); Marshall Caifano, Gus Alex, Felix Alderisio and others with lower register ratings. Giancana was conspicuous by his absence.

Skar spent most of the evening screaming that he was "absolutely" and "categorically" the sole owner of the joint. "I put in every dime of my own and borrowed from every source I can think of. There's a lot of borrowed money in here, but I own all the stock, every share of it." Asked if he knew Giancana, Manny replied: "I never even met the man. I'm willing to take a lie test on that, too." (A year later, Skar was observed at Lake Tahoe visiting Chalet 50 during Giancana's much publicized tryst at Sinatra's Cal-Neva Lodge.)

However, there was some evil gossip, phrased as "disquieting reports" in the *American,* that some of the "newly built motels and clubs" along Mannheim Road "are a new-found haven for investment of crime syndicate profits earned in gambling and prostitution." Nothing could have been further from the truth. The Syndicate had invested its muscle, not its money. Syndicate money is for Swiss banks, the New York Stock Market, and national and international corporations with impeccable financial ratings—not Chicago joints. That is always with somebody else's money.

There is little known about Skar's early life except that he had a habit of talking like Joey Glimco. For example, when he was caught behind a tavern Christmas morning, 1943, in the process of loading fifty cases of whisky on a truck, Manny told the arresting officers, "I can fix this rap." He was only twenty years old at the time, but he was right. Found guilty of burglary, he was placed on one year's

71

probation. Arrested by the FBI in 1952 for using the mails to defraud, Manny shrugged: "I can fix this rap." Brought to trial before Federal Judge Walter J. LaBuy, Manny explained how he had lost $40,000 betting on horses in Chicago and $10,000 shooting dice in Miami. "Everybody I know is a high roller," said Manny, trying to clarify his problem for the court. As a consequence, his two clothing stores, one in Aberdeen, South Dakota, and one in Chicago, had been forced into bankruptcy. Manny was convicted and sentenced to two years in prison and fined $2,000. Then Judge LaBuy suspended the sentence and imposed probation for three years conditioned on his paying $16,000 to more than a hundred creditors as restitution.

For the next three years Manny was silent. Then on June 1, 1955, the State of Illinois issued a charter of incorporation for the Jefferson Garden Builders Inc., with Mandel Skar as president, treasurer and director, and Frank De Stefano as director and as an incorporator. A brother of Rocco, Frank, and another brother, Vito, had operated (as fronts for Rocco) the Tarr Tobacco Distributing Company until the firm's license was revoked in the 1952 state cigarette tax stamp scandal—investigators estimated the racket had netted the Syndicate $13 million. Frank and Vito were indicted twice on cigarette tax stamp violations. The first indictment was for counterfeiting tax stamps and conspiracy. Both were acquitted. The second indictment came after state police seized a hijacked and unstamped cargo of cigarettes in a garage owned by the brothers. The first trial ended in a hung jury. A second trial was ordered, but the disposition remains one of those mysteries so common in Chicago.

Also in 1955, Skar and Frank De Stefano incorporated the Southwest Community Builders Inc. While Jefferson Garden was building sixty homes at Ogden Avenue and County Line Road in Cook County, Southwest Community had a project of three hundred homes in Cicero. Both projects were financed by C. Oran Mensik's three savings and loan institutions (City Savings Association, First Guarantee, and Chicago Guarantee) with total assets listed at nearly $50 million—none insured by the Federal Savings and Loan Insurance Corporation (FSLIC). Mensik bankrolled Skar and De Stefano to the tune of $1,693,750. Evil times fell upon Mensik almost immediately. In 1956, his close friend State Auditor Orville Hodge was convicted for embezzling $2.5 million of the taxpayers' money and sentenced to prison (he served six and a half years).

Early in 1957, Hodge's replacement, Elbert S. Smith, seized Mensik's three S&Ls, which he claimed were short more than $2 million of capital to offset claims. Smith charged "unsafe and unsound" practices (including a "questionable $200,000 loan to Hodge"), "excessive loans to favored firms, illegal investments and inadequate reserves." A ban was placed on savings withdrawals. But even after Smith had taken over the financial institutions, they continued to contribute to Skar's building fund for a total of $158,-000 in a period of two months. Asked to explain this strange procedure, Smith said that State Senator Roland V. Libonati, who had accompanied Skar to the bank, had urged him to make the loans promptly. (Once a personal friend of Al Capone, Libonati was the leader of the Capone Bloc, known as the West Side Bloc, in the state legislature. He was later elected to Congress.)

First Guarantee and Chicago Guarantee went into receivership, while City Savings was declared solvent by Judge Cornelius J. Harrington and returned to Mensik. A trade journal, *Savings and Loan,* labeled the day of Harrington's decision as Black Tuesday. "The court's action was interpreted by some as meaning that the state supervisory powers were practically invisible," the magazine concluded. It was an invitation "for some fast money boys" to set up operations without much danger.

The prediction was unhappily accurate for thousands of investors. Within a few years, open fraud and mismanagement cases in S&Ls involved assets totaling $175 million in the Chicago area alone. (In January 1965, Mensik was convicted of mail fraud and sentenced to five years in prison by a federal court in Richmond, Virginia. He was charged with conspiring to set up a phony insurance firm to claim that thirteen savings and loan associations he and two associates controlled in Maryland were "insured." City Savings was liquidated in 1965 at substantial loss to investors.)

Rocco De Stefano's name appeared with Skar's for the first time in 1957 when it was disclosed that they were partners in the R. and M. Construction Company, which worked as a subcontractor for Southwest Community Builders Inc. According to the State Auditor's office, the prices charged to Southwest by R.&M. "were about 50 percent too high."

By this time Manny Skar had come a long way from that 1943 Christmas morning whisky job. His two housing developments had received loans totaling $4 million. One day when a process server tried to slap a lien on a Skar-De Stefano interest, Manny upbraided him: "Don't you know whose money this is?" When the process server admitted his ignorance, Manny wised him up: "Sam Battaglia and the Outfit."

On June 5, 1959, Skar stepped into the major leagues. On that date the Sahara Motel Corporation was formed with Rocco as president, Frank as treasurer and Manny as secretary. The corporation built a 61-unit (later expanded to 150-unit) motel at 4501 South Cicero near Midway Airport. Called the Sahara (South), it was a less pretentious edition of the yet unborn Manny Skar's Sahara (North).

Equipped with a $150,000 yacht and a skipper's cap, the diminutive beard began entertaining Henry J. Moravec, owner of Marshall Savings and Loan Association in Riverside (a bank which went from $3 million in assets in 1952 to $100 million in 1960), in the grand manner of a Rush Street con man. Pictures were taken of the gamboling sportsmen on the yacht at Miami Beach and in nightclubs there. When the touch came, Moravec advanced $1.7 million on the Sahara (South). Skar boasted loudly to his friends, laughing as he cited a credit report to the effect that his credit was worthless.

When most of the air traffic was switched from Midway to O'Hare Field in the early Sixties, just about when construction was completed at the Sahara (South), the entrepreneurs incorporated the Sahara Inn North, Inc., to build a 267-unit motel only two miles from O'Hare at 3939 Mannheim Road in Schiller Park. Records on file at the Secretary of State's office show Rocco as president and treasurer, Frank as secretary, and Rocco, Frank and Vito as directors. Skar's name did not appear on the records. But on the company's letterhead he was listed as "chairman of the board."

Skar was again dispatched to negotiate with Moravec. When the bank's attorneys pointed out that Skar's credit was worthless, Skar argued that the new motel would be a gold mine. Three years later, Moravec attempted to explain his rationale for having advanced $6.6 million on Skar's verbal phantasmagoria. "We sent some of our people familiar with motels out to appraise it and to get routine credit information on Mr. Skar and Mr. De Stefano," Moravec said. "Mr. Skar had some conviction or suspended sentence 15 years ago [sic] or something. De Stefano was called before the Kefauver committee and took the Fifth Amendment. Prior to this they had been in partnership and had built substantial housing. All we asked is has this individual been rehabilitated and does he have a sound venture? It is not our duty or job to sit in moral judgment on an individual."

In gangster arithmetic, the real profit in such a venture is in the sleight-of-hand manipulations involved in the construction itself which is bankrolled by fat multimillion-dollar loans. The projected cost is always overstated to the point where only a vivid imagination, induced by generous consideration, can miraculously bring it back

74

into focus. In the case of Moravec, investigation disclosed that a six-figure "commission" was the inducer. (Moravec, his son, and five others were indicted on charges of misappropriations of $2.7 million —the case is pending at this writing.)

Later, federal investigators were to charge that Skar had diverted from $2 million to $3 million from the construction fund to his own private bank account, and from there to the long pockets of the Syndicate. The siphoning process was not overly intricate. First, of course, the Syndicate was quite well-represented in the construction and supply business. These companies submitted inflated bills which Skar further inflated before passing them on to his yachting buddy at Marshall Savings. Additional devices included fraudulent liens, kickbacks from non-Syndicate contractors and, as it later developed, disappearance of over a million dollars' worth of construction materials from Edmier Inc., a company which supplied materials for both Saharas to the cement contractor, Frank V. Pantaleo, the builder who provided Glimco with that additional space for hospitalization records.

(In 1966, contractor Pantaleo was slightly embarrassed when curbs and gutters he installed on a city contract began to crack, calling attention to the fact that the curbs were six inches shallower than called for in the specifications. Some four hundred home owners had to ante up $165,000 for the project.)

It was the exposure of the Edmier theft and the subsequent grand jury investigation that set Skar on the road to ruin. At 1:30 A.M., November 25, 1962, some six months after the grand opening of Manny's Mannheim Road Taj Mahal, two arsonists crept up behind watchman Frank Lapiane as he sat in the Edmier office. A hard object was pressed into his back, and when his hands automatically shot up over his head, he was bound, gagged, blindfolded and dragged outside and left in the yard. Two hours later, when Lapiane freed himself, he discovered that an unusual ritual had taken place in his absence. Records and papers had been dumped from filing cabinets and soaked with gasoline. But two roadside emergency flares had failed to ignite the pile because the arsonists had heaped wet leaves taken from a pickup truck on top of the intended bonfire.

An investigation of the fire led to the disclosure of the loss of $1 million worth of materials over a three-year period. Larry Edmier, president of the firm, could only scratch his head. "Even banks lose pencils," he said. However, the loss was quickly traced to two dispatchers, Theodore Kaczminski and Michael Russo, who had been with the company six years prior to their dismissal the previous month. Both men, police learned, were hopelessly in debt to gamblers and juicemen. Beginning in 1958, Kaczminski had dropped $40,000 to Syndicate gamblers. His juice payments to Alderisio, Rugendorf, Messino, Sam DeStefano, Fiore Buccieri and George Bravos ranged from $300 to $500 a week. When the scandal broke, Skar was in Florida on his yacht, Kaczminski was vacationing in Las Vegas and Russo was registered as a permanent guest at the Sahara (North), where he was known as a big tipper.

From the moment the grand jury investigating the Edmier theft was convened to the time Marshall Savings foreclosed on both Saharas in April 1963, a period of some four months, Skar did not pay a single bill except for issuing a slew of rubber checks. Shrewd enough to realize that the deception was over, Skar and his associates milked both motels for every penny not nailed down inside the decorative paneling. Even the telephone company was bilked out of $20,000.

Manny's performance before the grand jury was also standard in gang circles. Asked to bring in complete books and records, Skar sadly explained they had mysteriously disappeared while in transit by air from Florida to Chicago. Sentenced to six months in jail for contempt, he mumbled, "I can fix this rap." A few months later he was vindicated by the Illinois Supreme Court.

Although the mortgages totaled nearly $8 million, Marshall Savings paid Skar $60,000 to surrender his interests in both corporations. Some of the bills left outstanding by Skar included $80,000 to 140 unsecured creditors; $18,314 to the federal government on unpaid withholding and corporate income taxes; $51,584 in delinquent excise and unemployment taxes; $600,000 to the Albert Pick Company for equipment and furnishings; $6,900 in liquor sales taxes; $104,866 in mortgage payments; $3,000 in deposits from prospective guests; one month's wages for 150 employees, plus thousands more for liquor, food and utilities.

One of the most fascinating items for investigators interested in discovering the true ownership of the Sahara was the unraveling of the secret land trust at the Exchange National Bank. It listed ten separate beneficiaries, beginning with Rocco De Stefano and ending with Skar, the fall guy. Curious as to its actual market value, the *Daily News* hired an appraiser, who concluded that $2.5 million would be "a lot of money" for Manny's fabulous $10.8 million oasis.

Moravec sold his controlling interest in Marshall Savings to Louis

J. Verive and Anthony Navarolli, west surburban contractors, for $1.2 million. At the time of the sale, approximately 40 percent ($47 million) of the institution's loans were delinquent. Watered loans totaled millions. As it later developed, Verive and Navarolli were partners in a land deal with Rocco Salvatore, financed by a $1.5 million loan from their new institution.

In January 1965, the state seized the association; in April a receiver was appointed and the bank was subsequently liquidated.

A pure Chicagoese item (*American*—January 14, 1966) in Maggie Daly's column aptly sums up the Chicago psyche: "We talked to Mrs. Manny Skar at noon yesterday. She was wearing a cloth coat (she always had magnificent furs but all are gone now). She said, 'I've been crying a lot today. . . .' She looked beautiful as she always does. Her loyal friends are still around and her former elegant society friends, some of whom pretend not to know her anymore, . . . she finds she doesn't need."

And so ends the soggy saga of Manny Skar, the "cheap, blustering, boasting, vicious hoodlum" with the "elegant society friends."

10

In recent years, bankruptcy has become a major source of income for the underworld. New York hoodlums call it "bust-out"; in Chicago it is known as a "scam." The difference in the two operations is only in terminology.

The acknowledged "king of scams" is Felix "Milwaukee Phil" Alderisio, the Outfit's former lord high executioner. In 1962, Alderisio and Charles Nicoletti were arrested while crouching on the floor of an automobile later described by police as a souped-up "hit-car." Under the dashboard police found three switches. Two of the switches controlled the tail lights and license light. The third switch activated an electric motor which opened a hidden compartment in the backrest of the front seat. This compartment was fitted with brackets to hold shotguns, rifles and pistols. There was also room for a submachine gun. Alderisio and Nicoletti, who were dressed in black pants and black leather jackets, explained they were merely resting while waiting for an unidentified person; naturally, they had never seen that car before. A check of the registration led police to a vacant lot.

Alderisio works so many scams that his fronts have fronts who have fronts. Basically, a scam is the controlled bankruptcy of a legitimate business with solid credit references. The Syndicate has various ways of gaining a foothold into such businesses. One popular method is extortion. Sometimes this can be accomplished simply with a show of muscle, particularly if the businessman is from the old neighborhood and has a nodding acquaintance with the hoods through protection payoffs. Then there is the "love-nest" frame, complete with photographs and tape recordings. And, of course, there is always the gambling or juice debtor. He is the most vulnerable of all victims because he has provided them with the most devastating motive imaginable—money, *their money*.

Once the hoodlum's front is in control of the business, the firm's credit rating is used to make heavy purchases from wholesalers and to secure bank loans. The merchandise is then disposed of as quickly as possible. It can be transferred to legitimate businesses owned by Syndicate members or sold in wholesale lots to cheap discount houses at two-thirds the wholesale price. In sixty or ninety days, when creditors start clamoring for their money, the business goes into bankruptcy. There are no assets available and the books are either nonexistent or so inadequate as to be worthless for an audit.

When there is only limited success in acquiring merchandise from creditors on original orders, the hoodlum switches to what he calls a "rehash," which is a refinement of the scam. In this case, a small portion of the original order is paid for according to credit terms, and a subsequent and much larger order is placed. This order is then disposed of as scam. At times a hoodlum will even use his own money to buy into a firm with a particularly fine credit rating. At other times, he will start a new firm and carefully plant phony credit references.

A few of Alderisio's principal fronts include Leroy Silverstein (aka—also known as—Leroy Sterling and Lee Schmidt), George J. Harris, Morton Schulman, Alan Robert Rosenberg (aka Alan Rich), Edward W. Winel (aka James Davis), Harriet Meister (aka Rene Crawford), Leo Rugendorf, Lawrence "Larry" Rosenberg, Irwin "Pinky" Davis, Al Solomon, Lou Brown, Benjamin Feldman, Arthur Charles Tarantino, and Burton S. and Robert A. Wolcoff (fronts of Pinky Davis). Others include Pat Manno, Jr., son of Pat Manno (aka Pat Manning), a South Side policy operator; Mathew "Ace" Carbone, nephew of Ralph "Bottles" Capone, brother of the late Scarface Al; Robert "Bob" Berk, Larry Freedman, Morton Don Hartman and Joseph Pignatello.

78

A scam can be big or small, simple or complex. Sometimes a small one will be complex and a big one rather simple. But whatever the situation, it is always fast and thorough, as travel agency owner George Hoyt sadly discovered in June 1965.

George Hoyt met Alan Robert Rosenberg one spring morning, and two months later his company, Corydon Travel, Inc., was a creditor's nightmare. "Rosenberg seemed to know the travel business," Hoyt later recalled, "and everything seemed fair and aboveboard. He agreed to sign a 'hold harmless' contract relieving me of responsibility for his operations once he took over. He paid me $15,000 in cash and promised another $45,000. He asked me to wait until he had obtained his own bond, required by the airlines because of the ticket stock, and he took over the corporate note, about $45,000. About the first of June I went away on a trip to Morocco, with his assurances that he would notify the Air Lines Traffic committee of the change of ownership, get his bond straightened out, and finish up the transfer of my stock, in toto, to him."

When Hoyt returned twenty days later, he discovered that Rosenberg "had done none of these things he promised." Then "our company checks started bouncing and Rosenberg disappeared." On June 22, agents of the domestic airlines appeared at Corydon and removed all remaining ticket material. They informed Hoyt that he "still was the owner of record and that Corydon owed the airlines almost $100,000." The foreign airlines claimed "at least $50,000." And there was even worse news the next day when the operators of a commercial factoring agency informed Hoyt that they had paid Rosenberg $236,000 for accounts receivable represented by various types of travel tickets given to customers on credit. They then displayed a stack of checks valued at $35,000 which had been returned marked "insufficient funds." The factoring agents said that Rosenberg had "paid right on the dot" the first eleven days in June, and as a consequence they had introduced him at the National Boulevard Bank and had guaranteed Corydon's checks at that institution. Rosenberg had then taken that guarantee to a number of currency exchanges throughout the city and had cashed Corydon's checks "made out to real people who had, however, no claim to the money." With this device, Rosenberg managed to drain $165,000 from the bank in ten days. The last item was $28,000 from customer deposits and prepayments for travel.

In a period of twenty days, Rosenberg parlayed a $15,000 investment into nearly $500,000. These are the kind of odds the Syndicate appreciates. Consequently, Rosenberg has been kept busy. At the time he was "scamming" Corydon, he was under two federal indictments in New York City, one in Bettendorf, Iowa, and another in Paducah, Kentucky. Los Angeles had a fugitive warrant out charging grand theft, and Chicago had indicted him for theft by deception. Meanwhile, federal authorities in Chicago were busily investigating four other Rosenberg scams. The "take" from all these financial shenanigans ran into the millions.*

In one of the federal indictments in New York, Rosenberg's codefendants were Arthur Nasser, former Internal Revenue Service attorney, and James Pigano (aka Pagano and Agano), a member of the Mafia "family" of Vito Genovese in New York City. The indictment alleged that the three men gained control of S. L. Suth Company, a small Chicago jewelry store with an excellent credit rating, which they incorporated under Illinois law as the S. L. Suth Jewelry Company, Inc., with Rosenberg, Nasser and Pigano representing themselves as agents of the firm. They opened two accounts with minimum deposits in a suburban bank to establish an atmosphere of financial responsibility. Then they purchased jewelry valued at a quarter-million dollars from thirty New York City diamond importers and jewelers in a period of three weeks. Included in the credit purchases were a 125.5-carat star sapphire and a "cat's eye" precious stone of 24.47 carats, valued at $20,000. Shortly thereafter the company went into bankruptcy—not a single stone was recovered by creditors.

The diversity of businesses used in scams is illustrated by the names of just a few recent operations: National Lumber Company, Hilton Carpet Company, Combined Industries, Inc., Fiesta Warehouse Center, Chicago Discount Center, Harvey's Furniture Company, Reddi-Sales Company, Hansen Paper and Storage Company, Market Introduction Corporation, Riley Management Corporation, Chicago High School for Home Study, Newport Construction Company, Sterling-Harris Ford Agency, Central Casualty Insurance Company and Mount Prospect Country Club.

According to one federal report: "We have found a veritable spider web of interconnecting personalities in these bankruptcies, the web seeming to have at its center the person of "Milwaukee Phil"

* On March 16, 1967, Alan Rosenberg became Chicago's 1,003d gangland victim. Shortly before his murder, police said he was beaten by hoodlums in a dispute over money he owed Alderisio.

Alderisio. Unfortunately, witnesses usually refuse to testify against these characters out of fear for their own safety."*

One of the most brazen scams was the Sterling-Harris Ford Agency of 2626 North Cicero Avenue, incorporated by Leroy Silverstein and George J. Harris in 1960. On the weekend of March 4 and 5, 1961, the owners withdrew and concealed all of the corporation's available cash (about $30,000) and transferred $25,000 payable to the corporation to a bank account under their control. That weekend three hundred automobiles vanished from the agency's lot and showroom.

A platoon of car hikers directed by Leo Rugendorf drove a hundred of the automobiles to a lot in Park City, near Waukegan, where they were auctioned off. Silverstein and Harris sold ninety-nine for cash at big discounts—some patrons came in taxis and drove away in new Thunderbirds, boasting of their bargains to friends who in turn rushed to the agency to take advantage of the first real automobile sale in history. The remaining cars were driven north beyond Waukegan to an unknown destination. Meanwhile, Alderisio had crossed over into Wisconsin to attempt to sell fifty cars for $50,000 to car dealer Edward Bembenster, who rejected the offer when Alderisio was unable to furnish certificates of origin. This promptly led to vigorous threats and to Bembenster being placed under police protection.

Weeks later, titles for twenty-eight of the cars were cleared through the Secretary of State's office in violation of an order of the Federal District Court in Chicago. Most of the titleholders were friends or associates of Syndicate hoodlums, and included: Leo Rugendorf; Charles Nicoletti; Milan Dragin; Mrs. Florence Battaglia; Mrs. Carmen Buccieri; Mrs. Albert Frabotta; Leonard Franzone and Frank Bruscato, manager and owner respectively of the Talk of Town, a Near North Side nightspot; Dominic Galiano, a hijacker-pander-bagman slain in 1966; Michael "Nick" Nitti, a partner with Accardo's son, Ross, in the Plan-It Travel Bureau; Dolly Pontone, a guest at the wedding party of Accardo's daughter at the Villa Venice on April 27, 1961; Joachin Silvan, an indicted jewel thief, and Joseph Pignatello, who turned up in Las Vegas with a new Thunderbird for delivery to a well-known singer and entertainer.

Associates Discount Company, which had originally financed all the cars for Sterling-Harris, was left with $600,000 of worthless

* The testimony of Joseph Polito led to the convictions of four Alderisio associates for the $50,000 scam of Vogue Credit Jewelers. On March 7, 1967, Polito was killed by four shotgun blasts as he walked from his home.

paper. Both Silverstein and Harris, who invoked the Fifth Amendment at bankruptcy proceedings, later returned to the automobile business. The records of the agency were eventually located in the basement of the Apex Waste Company, owned by Lawrence "Larry" Rosenberg, a business partner of Rugendorf. Five years later, four of the principals were convicted on charges of fraud: Silverstein and Harris were sentenced to ten years in federal prison, and Rugendorf and Rosenberg to five years.

Being grade school dropouts has not discouraged hoodlums from the merits of higher education. Take, for example, the case of the Chicago High School for Home Study, a correspondence institution fronted by Bruce Helwig of Kenosha, Wisconsin. The school shared offices with the Mayfair Acceptance Company, another Alderisio enterprise fronted by Larry Rosenberg. Mayfair's responsibility was to make sure that students paid for their education. Although not accredited by any educational body, CHSHS nevertheless maintained firm standards when it came to matriculation fees: one year, $195; two years, $275; three years, $335, and the works for $395. Students were advised they could pay in installments of $10 a month, but CHSHS sold the contracts to Mayfair. Raymond Hilliard, Cook County Welfare Director, charged that the school was selling courses to illiterate welfare recipients, who were then hounded by strongarm collectors.

CHSHS went into bankruptcy on September 18, 1964, owing its creditors $44,600, mostly for textbooks. Its assets were turned over to S. Harvey Klein, a receiver and trustee in bankruptcy court. On September 25, Mrs. Irene J. Lurie and Miss Evelyn V. Siegel bought the assets of CHSHS for $12,500, which included mailing lists, 20,000 textbooks and examinations, ten typewriters, four adding machines, five filing cabinets, one grapho-type machine, and one addressograph. The name was changed to General High School for Home Study, but everything else remained the same: the address, brochures, diplomas, stationery, and the matchbook and public-transportation advertising. GHSHS, like good old CHSHS, was referred to simply as "High School for Home Study."

A check of records revealed that Evelyn V. Siegel was the sister-in-law of the late Fred Evans, Syndicate financier executed firing-squad style in 1959. Among the papers in Evans' pockets, police had found a penciled notation, "E. V. Siegel," which had mystified them for years. Mrs. Irene J. Lurie was the wife of Harold Lurie, president of the Gaylur Mercantile Corporation, a firm which salvaged disaster merchandise for insurance companies. An ex-convict, Lurie had served five years (1955–1960) for obtaining by fraud war surplus goods valued at $531,231.

Police were pretty certain that Alderisio had not turned his back on scholastic pursuits. In 1966 they received proof positive when Lurie and the Gaylur Mercantile Corporation became involved in a grand jury investigation concerning a million-dollar fire which had destroyed the Fullerton Metals Company. Although Lurie had told the insurance company that nothing could be salvaged, police charged that 118,000 pounds of steel was recovered from the demolished building and trucked to a warehouse rented by Alderisio, who allegedly sold the metal to steel brokers for $200,000. When Lurie balked at producing his records for the grand jury, he was sentenced to six months in jail for contempt. (His appeal is pending at this writing.)

Many fronts have more than one Syndicate mentor. Rugendorf, for example, has fronted for a whole battery of hoods. In the 3250 Wentworth Building, his associates included Battaglia, Alderisio, Caifano and Frabotta, plus Irving Weiner, a business front allied with Rugendorf. Other Rugendorf-Weiner enterprises operated for the four above-named hoodlums included P&S By-Products Company, Twin Distributing Company and Twin Food Products Company.

Rugendorf and Morris Lasky operated the C&B Meat Company for DiVarco and James Allegretti,* who twice in court identified himself as a meat magnate. When the Illinois Crime Investigating Commission began focusing on the company's sales tactics during its 1964 probe of restaurant bombings (five restaurants shifted to C&B after such acts of terrorism), Allegretti and DiVarco stepped out of C&B. Adverse publicity later folded the company. Meanwhile, Lasky appeared on the payroll of the Simon Meat and Provision Company on the Near North Side. Within six months, the sales volume of Simon doubled, leaping to an annual gross of $2.7 million. A state audit revealed that 70 former C&B customers had switched to Simon, including Valentino's restaurant, long known as Allegretti's base of operation. (For years, police had watched the strange ritual of Rush Street operators—estimated as high as forty—bringing their cash

* See Appendix.

83

register tapes to Allegretti or Lawrence "Larry the Hood" Buona-guidi* at Valentino's after closing hours each night.) Lasky's salary and commissions amounted to $41,600 the first year. Besides catering to some of the finest restaurants in Chicago, the Simon firm was also very popular with hotels, including the Palmer House, Sheraton Chicago, Blackstone, Sherman, Congress, Allerton, Webster, Atlantic and many others.

11

No one would more readily agree that "there's no business like show business" than the good old all-American gangster. The criminal fraternity always has been shoulder-holster deep in nightclubs, saloons and restaurants. The late-late show with the pinstriped, slick-haired, bleak-eyed torpedo in the sound-proofed back office is pure Americana—past, present and interminable future. Rocco and Tony and Nick and Sam and Joe and Vito are still at the old booze-stand, be it the poshiest joint in town or the lowest dive in skid row. But, for obvious reasons, 99 percent of the time there is a different name on the liquor license and records of ownership.

Since Chicago issues nearly nine thousand liquor licenses every six months (as many as New York City), the game of pinning the right hoodlum tag on the proper beard is not an easy one. However, regardless of the true ownership of an establishment, a fair percentage of the guest's tab is certain to trickle into the long pockets of somebody big.

A recent federal report states: "The criminal element is in complete control of many establishments serving liquor to patrons and all of the cabarets featuring strip tease entertainment in the [six] main Chicago night life areas. The effect of this condition has been threefold. First, it is providing a tremendous source of illegal income to the Syndicate. Second, the position of the honest businessman who is left in the tavern business has become so jeopardized that he is often presented with the dilemma of going out of business or following the whims of the Syndicate in the running of his business. Third, the lack of public awareness and the apathy lend credence to Syndicate claims of being immune from law enforcement."

The six main nightclub belts are the South State Street-Wabash

* See Appendix.

Avenue section, Cicero, North Clark Street, Rush Street, Wells Street in Old Town and Mannheim Road.

That the Outfit dominates the nocturnal entertainment of Chicagoans is a fact that has been sporadically deplored since the first liquor license was issued. As recently as December 1965, Howard Cartwright, chairman of the Illinois Liquor Control Commission, was promising to conduct an extensive inquiry into the books and records of retail liquor business establishments suspected of mob ownership. "We expect a bitter struggle," he said, "but the law will be enforced to drive the gangsters out of the liquor business."

The *Daily News,* which ran a series of Mob exposés in 1964, was delighted when it discovered a non-Outfit sponsored nightclub: "There are no saints in the nightclub business, no matter how often the band plays 'When the Saints Go Marching In.' But Bill and Ruth Reinhardt, owners of Jazz Ltd. at 164 E. Grand, qualify as near-saints by night-life standards. While many other nightclubs and jazz spas have fallen prey to hoodlum control, Jazz Ltd. has stayed clean. . . . Not that the crime syndicate hasn't tried to syncopate at Jazz Ltd. But the Reinhardts have been remarkably anti-footsie. They have barred the way to known mobsters, dames, cigaret vending machines, juke boxes, and a well-known but 'kinky' brand of whiskey. The contrast with many dives here is total. . . . The Reinhardts sounded their anti-hoodlum note two weeks after they opened Jazz Ltd. in June, 1947. Its address then was 11 E. Grand, in the depths of the syndicate-infested E. Chicago Av. police district. . . . They ran the show themselves. Unlike many other liquor licensees here, they are not mere stand-ins for the hoodlum big shots who secretly control the action. . . . [Once a district police captain] sent a message to the effect that 'you can operate a place too cleanly.' The Reinhardts interpreted this as a crude bid to let them operate after-hours, in return for contributing on their part. They ignored him—'but I [Mrs. Reinhardt] was more afraid of him than the hoodlums.' "

One of the latest announcements from the Chicago police was in March 1966: "Fresh efforts to expose gangsters' secret ownership" of some twenty Rush Street cabarets were imminent. The probe was also to focus on musclemen and collectors who "taxed" independent owners at an average of $500 a month for the privilege of operating in their territory, and forced them to purchase all supplies and services from their firms at inflated prices.

Whether it be a tavern, a cocktail lounge in a first-rate hotel, a restaurant, a skin emporium or a nightclub, the Syndicate has a variety of wares, supplies and services to offer the industry. These include beer, liquor, meat, produce, milk, bread, grease rendering and garbage collections, laundry, dry cleaning, steam cleaning of the tap beer coils (required thrice weekly by law), linens, uniforms, glassware, glass-washing machines, detergents, plumbing, car parking, jukeboxes, vending machines (from cigarettes to contraceptives), fuel oil and coal, interior decorations (drapes, carpeting, etc.), furniture, fixtures and insurance.

Since the Syndicate controls related unions such as bartenders, cooks and waitresses, and the Teamster locals who deliver supplies and haul off garbage, they can apply the kind of muscle an owner must recognize if he wishes to remain in business. Political connections also give the hoodlums influence over city licenses and permits.

Fifteen years ago, A. J. Liebling explored this monopoly in a *New Yorker* article: "Syndicate administration of the saloon-with-entertainment business is equally smooth, a man on a theatrical publication told me. 'In the twenties, two or three different outfits might try to muscle in on the same place,' he said. 'If the fellow didn't pay off, they went in for rough stuff, and even if he did, they might get rough with each other. Now just one man arrives and says he is from City Hall, and he is a partner, drawing down a hundred and a half a week, or two hundred—whatever the club looks good for. It's a part of the nut, like the rent. After all, if everybody has to pay, nobody has an unfair advantage.' . . . 'But is the fellow who declares himself in really from City Hall or from the Syndicate?' I asked. 'Well, he's known as a Syndicate fellow, but the police enforce what he says,' the man said. 'I don't know what the split is.' 'Maybe the Syndicate is just a front for the city government,' I suggested, 'instead of its being the other way around.' And maybe, I have thought since, the city government is just a front for Colonel McCormick and for the railroads that don't want to be moved off the streets and for the landlords who don't care to lose the swollen rents from their hovels and for all the nice, earnest people who constantly form committees but really don't want anything changed if it costs money. If no Syndicate existed, it would be necessary to invent one, to blame it for the way things are."

Liebling discovered, as writers always do in Chicago, that Chicagoans take secret pride in their knowledge that the Syndicate has most of the lucrative businesses in town locked up, including, said

Liebling, "any hotel a visitor happens to be stopping at. 'Did you know that was a Syndicate place?' is a staple of small talk. The answer is 'Sure. Who doesn't know that?' The out-of-towner's accompanying mental reservation is 'Who does?', but he should not voice it if he wishes to be popular."

The "who does" question has perplexed everybody from Senate Committees to inquiring reporters. Since hoodlums have been remarkably adapt at camouflaging their operations, rules of thumb have been developed through the years to help pinpoint their various spheres of influence. One unerring clue is the big spontaneous success, particularly if located on Syndicate turf as in the case of the Playboy Club at 116 East Walton Street, in the heart of the Rush Street glitter gulch belt.

Investigators from the McClellan Committee expressed curiosity about the Playboy Club in 1963 when they learned that some of the Club's most prominent playboys were Giancana, Alderisio, DiVarco, Gus Zapas, Chuck English, Allegretti, Prio, Vogel, Fusco, Alex and the Buccieri brothers, among other notable purveyors of Syndicate wares. The Boys were also observed squiring the Club's "unapproachable" Bunnies after hours, a privilege reserved exclusively for holders of Number One Keys, usually awarded only to Playboy executives, members of the press, radio and television, and other clouters whose payola includes a free tab.

Eddie "Big Head" Vogel, the Outfit's slot and coin machine czar, was enamored of Bunny Mother Peg Strak, who later became private secretary to Tony Roma, operations manager of Playboy Clubs International, Inc.

Roma's success story is one that has inspired many lively discussions in the "who does" fraternity. Born in Chicago on December 9, 1923, as Tony LoPresti, and deserted by his father three years later, Roma spent the early years of his life in foundling homes in Philadelphia and Brooklyn. At the age of ten he was reunited with his mother in Brooklyn, and attended public schools until the age of sixteen, when he quit while still in the seventh grade. For the next three years, he shined shoes, peddled, worked on the docks and spent three months in Gimbel's restaurant. Then he served four years in the Navy. His career from 1946 until his employment by Playboy in January 1961 is what personnel directors classify as checkered: two years as a dress operator with the Harry Koldin Dress Company in New York; three years at odd jobs; one year with Lennie's Wagon

Wheel, a night club in Bridgeport, Connecticut; one year with Star Attraction, a theatrical booking company in New York; six months with Chez Zizzi on New York's East 54th Street; one year with the Midwood Restaurant in Brooklyn; three months with Mama Lina's Villa Nova in Miami; six months with the Fountainbleu Restaurant in New York; one year with Rocky Graziano, promoting the former middleweight champion's book, *Somebody Up There Likes Me;* one season with the Cotton Club in Miami; one year with the Chauffeurs Club, a nonprofit drinking club in Miami; one summer with the Green Acres Country Club in Northbrook, Illinois; one month with the Yorkshire Room, a restaurant in Chicago's Park Lane Hotel and two years with the Idlewild Country Club in Flossmoor, Illinois.

In Flossmoor, Roma's nomadic existence took a dramatic turn toward stability when he met Josephine Costello, daughter of Frank Costello, a partner with his brother Joseph in the Chicago Heights Distributing Company (beer and liquor wholesalers), a firm started by their father, the late Charles Costello, a Capone-mob bootlegger. Joseph Costello was also a co-owner of the Regal Vending Company with Frank LaPorte, Tony Franze (a brother-in-law of LaPorte) and Ralph Emery, son of the late Big Jim Emery (née Vincenzo Ammeratto), the Mafia boss of Chicago Heights and southern Cook County. In 1953, police seized thirteen of Regal's cigarette vending machines in Calumet City on charges that the cigarettes bore counterfeit tax stamps. Joseph Costello was a character witness for Tony Accardo at his 1960 income tax evasion trial, testifying that he had known the gang chieftain for more than twenty years.

Soon after Tony and Josephine married, Tony got the most important job in his diversified career. In January 1961, he became general manager of the Chicago Playboy Club, and three and a half months later was promoted to operations manager of Playboy Clubs International, Inc., an organization which grossed $19 million in 1965. Roma's title and salary made him the chief salaried executive officer in the firm. The only executives above him in the chain of command were Hugh Hefner, president and a director, and Arnold Morton and Victor Lownes, both vice-presidents and directors.

As operations boss, Roma's authority extended to the location and designs of new clubs, including licenses and permits, the hiring and firing of personnel, the selection of purveyors, and the general supervision of policies and operations once a club was established, including the receipt of daily reports on food and drink sales and personnel matters. In the past five years, Roma has officiated at the preopening and opening ceremonies of fifteen Playboy Clubs in the United States, Jamaica and London.

One of Roma's first acts as general manager of the Chicago Playboy Club was to award the garbage collection to Willie "Potatoes" Daddano's West Suburban Scavenger Service. But he did not exactly set a precedent in Syndicate-Playboy relationships. Attendant Service Corporation, a Prio-DiVarco enterprise, was already parking playboy cars, checking playboy hats and handing playboy towels in the restrooms. Other playboys were drinking Fusco beer and liquors, eating Allegretti meat and smoking Vogel cigarets. In other words, there was little chance of confusing the Playboy Club with Jazz Ltd.

A master union contract was signed in 1964 between Playboy Clubs and the Hotel and Restaurant Employees and Bartenders International Union, but it provided that local contracts were required at each club. None, however, were negotiated in Chicago. Illinois Director of Labor John Cullerton was quoted in 1966 to the effect that the Bunny pay system was "legal, but probably the single situation of its kind in the state." Previous to his appointment to the state post, Cullerton was the president of the Syndicate-controlled Local 593 and head of the joint board.

While harmony reigned in Chicago, where scantily clad Bunnies frugged with playboys and performed the Bunny dip as they served drinks on low tables, chaos was the keynote in New York City where Hefner planned to open his fifth club on December 8, 1962. (Besides Chicago, there were clubs in Miami, New Orleans and St. Louis.) The fact that the Gaslight Club, a Gay Nineties type of key club, had experienced considerable difficulty with the State Liquor Authority (SLA) did not unduly affect Hefner's optimism. By December 6, Hefner's investment was reported at $3.5 million. Still, there was not a bottle of liquor in the place. Then in a dramatic climax, a liquor license was granted a few hours before the club was to open.

"I would not deny," Hefner said later, "that pressures were brought to bear on us. I am certain they were on anyone getting a license in New York during the last several years. It is a shame that the biggest city in the country should have this sort of problem." Then he added: "We did not attempt to accomplish anything of an extra-legal nature."

However, the club was denied a cabaret license by City License Commissioner Bernard J. O'Connell. "It would appear clear that the applicant's main appeal to its prospective customers is the lure of its scantily clad waitresses," O'Connell ruled. "The impression is created by the club's publicity releases, truly or falsely, that they are available to twist with club members at private parties."

Not entirely convinced by Hefner's plea that nothing of an "extra-legal nature" had taken place, Manhattan District Attorney Frank Hogan continued with his investigation of the State Liquor Authority.

A few days after the club's opening, Hefner, Morton, Lownes and Robert Preuss, secretary-treasurer of all Playboy enterprises, paid a visit to the offices of District Attorney Hogan to complain of a $150,000 "blackmail" scheme involving L. Judson Morhouse, then New York Republican State Chairman and a close adviser to Governor Nelson A. Rockefeller; Martin C. Epstein, then chairman of SLA and Ralph Berger, a self-styled Chicago public relations man.

According to the four Playboy officials, who testified under immunity from prosecution before a grand jury, Berger had first made overtures to them in May 1960 following the announcement of the plans for the New York Club. Berger allegedly approached Arnold Morton with the information that he personally knew Epstein and would "put in a good word for you on your license."

(Berger, back in March 1935, was indicted with Capone gangster James Weinberg and others in connection with an attempt to dispose of $237,000 worth of bonds stolen from a mail truck. Seventeen years later, a gambling raid on Berger's office bagged Paul "Needle Nose" Labriola and attorney Abraham Teitelbaum. As noted earlier, Weinberg and Labriola ended up side by side in a car trunk in 1954. During the Second World War, Berger was a Syndicate front in the Latin Quarter, a nightclub on Chicago's West Randolph Street. OPA officials later charged that Berger had bilked customers out of $330,-750 in violations of price ceilings. Berger settled for $3,289. At the time of his arrest in 1963, Berger operated Lee Berco Inc., a real estate and public relations firm.)

During his trial in New York, Berger kept a closed stiff upper lip while all about him his former "alleged" allies acted like fugitives from the Tower of Babel. He was charged with conspiracy to pay a $50,000 bribe to SLA Chairman Epstein for the Playboy Club license. The asserted conspiracy took place between July 1960 and December 7, 1962, when SLA finally issued the Playboy license. Not indicted at that time, but very much a part of the trial, was L. Judson Morhouse and the $100,000 bribe he allegedly solicited.

Assistant District Attorney Jeremiah McKenna described Berger as a "conduit" and "go-between" for Playboy Club officials and Epstein. Under cross-examination by defense counsel Joseph E. Brill, Arnold Morton admitted that his group was under pressure from creditors and from 63,000 persons who had paid $25 each for keys in the proposed New York Playboy Club. But he denied any intention of bribing either Epstein or Morhouse to do anything illegal. Brill suggested that the Playboy officials were so "desperate" to get a license that they were willing to resort to bribery.

Morton denied the allegation. "I felt I was being blackmailed," he said. "I didn't think I was bribing a public official."

Morton said that Berger first took them to meet Epstein who set the price for a license at $50,000. Later, Berger arranged for Morton to meet someone "big in the state who thinks he can help you." But the $50,000 deal with Epstein "was still on." "You are going to have to make your own deal with Morhouse," Berger allegedly told Morton. Morhouse asked for a retainer of $100,000, an option to buy $100,000 worth of Playboy stock and a concession to run a string of gift shops in Playboy Clubs. Subsequently, Epstein settled for $25,000 and Morhouse received $18,000. Berger was convicted and sentenced to a year in prison. Epstein, a seventy-three-year-old invalid, was never brought to trial for reasons of health. Morhouse was convicted in 1966. In his testimony, Berger did make one curious statement: He said he was promised $5,000 for making contact with Epstein. When the money was not forthcoming, Berger contacted Marshall Korshak "who called someone in the bunny organization, and the money was delivered."

During the grand jury investigation of Morhouse in 1965, Berger continued to remain silent, even when granted immunity by the court. "It's obvious from his refusal to testify that he's protecting other persons," said the prosecutor, who refused to comment on whether the persons shielded were in Chicago or New York. Berger was sentenced to thirty days for contempt. In first sentencing Berger to a year in prison, the court had said: "The evidence was established clearly that you are a broker in corruption or a wheeler-dealer in corruption, as this case proved conclusively." And the court was absolutely correct. But is not a broker or a "conduit" merely an instrument for the convenience of others? (In December 1965, the Playboy Club was granted a cabaret license by the outgoing Wagner administration.)

Back in Chicago, Maggie Daly included the observation in

her column in September 1965 that: "IT ALL ADDS UP. . . . In spite of the fact that a columnist said that business was way down in the night clubs during conventions here, Playboy club's take for one week was $75,000 . . . $50,000 more than the same week last year."

It also adds up that every dollar gained by Playboy is a dollar lost by another club in the most tightly gangster-controlled entertainment condominium.

BOOK TWO
THE CLOUT MACHINE

The partnership between politics and crime begins with the seizure of a city such as Chicago, by bosses who have risen to power in their party on the backs of the boys in the bad lands of a town that has been the dumping ground for criminals of all classes from all over the country. Behind the blazing automatics of the beer runners and through a maze of murder, bombings, blackmailing, bribery of public officials, jury and witnesses, robbery of the mail, and race riots, runs a red thread of the partnership between politics and crime back beyond the labor wars since the days of the old red light district.

—ANONYMOUS CHICAGO JUDGE, IN A
RADIO ADDRESS ON FEBRUARY 19, 1926

Everywhere we went the committee found a certain amount of political immorality, but in Chicago the rawness of this sort of thing was particularly shocking. . . . There was no doubt in the minds of any of us, after the sort of testimony we heard in Chicago, that organized crime and political corruption go hand in hand, and that in fact there could be no big-time organized crime without a firm and profitable alliance between those who run the rackets and those in political control.

—ESTES KEFAUVER, *Crime in America,* 1951

1

Prostitution was a lucrative occupation long before man invented the currency system. In Chicago it has always been an integral part of its economy as well as its reputation. Within a decade of its founding in 1837, Chicago was the "wickedest city in America."

In those days, the red-light district was an area north of the river called the Sands. Cheap lodging houses, rattletrap bordellos, noisy saloons and crooked gambling dens stretched for blocks on land nobody owned. After the great fire of 1871, the center of the tenderloin shifted to Clark and Van Buren. Known as Little Cheyenne, the area could boast of 119 brothels employing a thousand prostitutes. There were plush houses and panel houses (where a hand reached through to clean out a customer's pockets), goosing slums, circuses, cribs, dance halls and opium dens. When streetcar tracks were laid on Clark Street at the turn of the century, political pressure forced the madams to relocate around Twenty-second and Dearborn, which became known as the South Side levee. By now the prostitute population had grown to five thousand, and the number of separate acts of prostitution committed each year was curiously estimated by one vice commission at 27,375,000. The commission reported that children sold gum or candy or newspapers late at night under the red lights, and 300 white children and 1,500 Negro children lived in the heart of the levee under "the worse forms of bestiality."

Inmates were allowed to ply their trade even when in the last stages of venereal disease. Except for a few "elegant" madams like the Everleigh sisters, "men were the gainers, women the victims." But the biggest "gainers" of all, said the report, were the hoodlum proprietors. "With this group stand ostensibly respectable citizens, both men and women, openly renting property for exorbitant sums."

The Everleigh Club, the creation of Minna and Ada Lester, was the most elaborately furnished house on the levee. The legend of its grandeur continues to grow. It is said the girls wore only evening gowns and discoursed politely on Oscar Wilde or Longfellow according to the intellectual whims or abilities of the patrons. There was a music room, a library, an art gallery, a grand ballroom, a dining room and a buffet lunch for those on the run. There were twelve soundproof parlors where private parties might retire to enjoy a little circus

95

or journey around the world. The names of the parlors were Gold, Moorish, Silver, Copper, Red, Rose, Green, Blue, Oriental, Chinese, Egyptian and Japanese. Every room had a $650 gold spittoon to accommodate wealthy consumptives, and the Chinese room provided a large brass bowl and a supply of firecrackers for gay patriots. All the beds were brass and inlaid with marble and fitted with specially built mattresses and springs.

Three orchestras played without interruption from sunset to dawn, and a large staff of cooks and maids worked around the clock. The gentleman was not obliged to bed down with the young lady. He could have dinner, play a brisk game of casino, browse in the library, admire the fine paintings, play the $15,000 gold piano or just sip champagne and chat. If he did go to bed, the staff would press his clothes and shine his shoes. He paid as he left and his check was always good, coming back discreetly endorsed "Utopia Novelty Company."

Although the Syndicate currently pulls in some $200 million annually, prostitution today is more on a cash-and-carry basis. The day of the posh whorehouse is gone. The action now centers around the B-girl (often a stripper) whose specialty consists of masturbation and oral copulation in a dark booth, and the call girl who almost invariably is in league with the electronically equipped extortionist. There are no statistics on the blackmail take, but police estimate it at far more than prostitution itself. Recent raids in Chicago have uncovered vice rings that worked in collusion with employees (sometimes officials) of exclusive private clubs, restaurants, country clubs and first-class hotels throughout the United States. B- and C-girls work Syndicate circuits that take them to New York, Miami, Houston, Dallas, Phoenix, Las Vegas, Denver and as far west as Seattle. VIP swingers are card-indexed in vice rings across the nation. In a raid on one North Side call-girl operation, police found sixteen address books containing the names of ten thousand patrons and hundreds of prostitutes and madams from several cities.

Frank "Shirley" Tournabene bossed a vice ring that mailed credit cards to six thousand patrons from coast to coast. The cards bore the signature "Shirley," his gangland cognomen, and a message: "When in Chicago, come and see me." Tournabene is listed in police files as an enforcer for Joey Glimco. Federal agents recently raided a chain of six North Side bars involved in a sex-blackmail ring where the

96

victims were drugged, robbed and shaken down for five-figure payoffs by extortionists posing as Chicago policemen. The boss was Dominic Galiano, murdered gangland-style March 11, 1966. The Chicago police conducted 3,747 vice raids in 1964, with arrests totaling 6,049. Of these, 731 were convicted, but the overwhelming majority paid only nominal fines. Women's Court Magistrate Ben Edelstein estimated the prostitute population at 10,000 in 1965.

The chain of command on the levee started at the top with committeeman Michael "Hinky Dink" Kenna and alderman Bathhouse John Coughlin, bosses of the First Ward, the wealthiest plot of real estate (it contains the Loop) in the Midwest. Their bagman was Ike Bloom, a ward heeler and proprietor of a busy dance hall. Ike's autographed picture was prominently displayed on the wall behind the Captain's desk in the Twenty-second Street Station. The next in command was Big Jim Colosimo, an Italian pimp and restaurateur, who started out as a street cleaner. When he married a madam with a pair of dollar houses, Hinky Dink made him a precinct captain in charge of getting out the Italian vote. An aggressive thug, Colosimo was to become Chicago's overlord of crime in a relatively short time. Today he is revered as the patron saint of the Capone syndicate.

"Mr. Big" was an Irishman named Michael Cassius McDonald, a Clark Gable "divil-may-care" type, who ran the operation from a plush gambling den. Mike was king of Chicago gamblers and saloon keepers. He was also the political king, founder (1873) of "Mike McDonald's Democrats," a party and philosophy which have survived to this day. Mike's favorite mayoralty candidate was Carter H. Harrison, a real estate speculator from Kentucky, a Yale man and a lawyer. "Our Carter," as the mayor was fondly known, served four terms, retired for a few years, and then returned only to be assassinated by a disgruntled patronage seeker. McDonald's next favorite candidate was the son, Carter Jr., who also served four terms at Mike's option. Many years later, when he had grown old and full of civic virtue, Harrison Jr. gained perspective. "A rare conglomeration of city fathers ruled Chicago in the nineties," he wrote. Chicagoans "permitted the control of public affairs to be the exclusive appanage of a low-browed, dull-witted, base-minded gang of plug-uglies, with no outstanding characteristics beyond an unquenchable lust for money." And there was more, he went on to explain. Each ward was largely under the domination of a single man or of a small group, and

97

with few exceptions these men were gamblers or saloon keepers. Yet their word "as far as the choice of delegates was concerned, was supreme."

Bathhouse John aptly summed up the situation in 1903 after the fourth term election of Harrison Jr. Surprised at his reelection, the mayor wondered "just why the people had chosen me again?" "Mister Maar," The Bath bellowed, "you won because of the well-known honesty which has caricatured your every administration." In those days, the mayor referred to The Dink and The Bath as my "Two Rocks of Gibraltar."

The day before Mike McDonald died (from a "nervous break-down" suffered when his young bride shot and killed her sixteen-year-old lover), August 8, 1907, the *Daily News* reminisced: "Mike McDonald is dying. When the city had a scant half million [people] this man ruled it from his saloon and gambling house by virtue of his political power. During many succeeding years he had a controlling influence in the public affairs of this community. . . . Bad government was accepted as a matter of course. Vice sat in the seats of power and patronized virtue with a large and kindly tolerance, asking only that it remain sufficiently humble and not too obtrusive. Gambling was a leading industry. Clark Street was thronged night and day with men going in and out of the wide open gambling resorts. The wretched conditions then prevailing were excused on the theory that vice 'made the town lively.' Gambling was necessary, it was said, to attract strangers. As for the 'king of gamblers' he was a 'good fellow.' He 'always stood by his friends.' Boodle aldermen lorded it in the city council. Boodle county commissioners stole everything they could lay their hands on . . . contracts for public works that had thievery written between the lines were let and carried out to the large profit of the conspirators. Elections were controlled by the sweet and simple methods of chasing away voters and stuffing ballot boxes."

But times had changed. The *Daily News* continued: "Compared to the present, McDonald's days seemed almost like those of a 'mystical period.' " It was hoped that good morals and good government would prevail henceforth under the vigorous leadership of the present Republican administration, prodded along by the courageous voice of the Fourth Estate.

Of course, nothing had changed. In fact, the city was in the midst of a bomb war as gamblers scrambled for power. Five days after McDonald's death, James O'Leary's gambling resort on South Halsted Street was bombed. A few days later, the home of gambling czar Mont Tennes was bombed for the second time. Then, in quick succession, several more bombs exploded across town, one at the distributing office of Tennes' racing wire service, another at the home of Cook County Sheriff James Pease and still another at the Western Cash Register Company store, a front for another Tennes gambling enterprise. The total inaction on the part of the police made it plain that law enforcement had capitulated to the underworld.

Harrison was elected for another term in 1911, again receiving the backing of the vice and gambling interest. Harrison himself attributed his victory "beyond a shadow of a doubt" to the foreign element support and the flophouse votes of the First and Eighteenth Wards. Said Harrison: "On election day, as previously on primary day, my old-time friends of the First Ward, Hinky Dink and Bathhouse John, came through with flying colors."

Following the election, the number of gambling houses in the Loop doubled. Bookie drops ran into the thousands and gaming tables could be found on every block. And all of it was under the protective services of Tennes. There was a set fee for everything. Operators of crap games paid 60 percent of their net profit; horse race, poolroom and faro establishments 50 percent, and roulette wheels 40 percent. Tennes' General News Bureau (wire service) was rapidly becoming nationwide. Another wire service, the Payne News Agency, tried to oppose Tennes in his expansion outside of Illinois. With the aid of dynamite and arson, Tennes eliminated all opposition in twenty cities and drove Payne out of business. By 1914, Tennes was the most powerful horse-race gambler in the country.

A civil service inquiry into police practices was the most unnerving event of Harrison's fifth term. Every known method of bribery and intimidation was employed to thwart the investigation. A slush fund was raised to bribe the prosecutor and witnesses, and when that failed, the homes of the witnesses were bombed. Even the prosecutor received a warning on September 23, 1911. But despite violence and publicity, the gambling joints continued to operate openly. The only tangible results of the inquiry was the eventual discharge of a few policemen.

The inquiry was followed three years later by a grand jury investigation of the First Ward organization. This probe disclosed that precinct captains and other ward heelers held jobs as bailiffs and clerks in the courts; served as guards in the city jail; held high offices in the sheriff's department, the county jail, the House of Correction, the county treasurer's office, the state's attorney's office, and had

99

generally infiltrated every sensitive organ of the law enforcement body. Minna Everleigh testified she paid over $100,000 to the organization for protection. Violence and murder in brothels was hushed up by the officials. A $3,000 donation to the Kenna-Coughlin fund had helped defeat a bill introduced in the legislature forbidding the sale of liquor in disorderly houses—a most peculiar bill considering brothels were illegal.

As Harrison's fifth term came to a close, the press announced that finally Chicago was growing up and stood at that very moment on the threshold of a new golden age of reform. Chicagoans then went to the polls and elected a new mayor—William Hale "Big Bill" Thompson.

2

After three generations of social and political corruption, Chicago was about to reap its well-sowed harvest. All that was needed was a little fertilizer called the Volstead Act. But Big Jim Colosimo, the harbinger of it all, was dead on the eve of the decade, the victim of an assassin's bullets. Johnny Torrio buried his boss in the grand manner that was to become the mode for the underworld. The honorary pallbearers included Mike Merlo, head of the Unione Sicilione, three judges, an assistant state's attorney, Congressmen John W. Rainey and Thomas Gallagher, State Representative Michael L. Igoe (a machine politician who today is a Federal judge in Chicago) and several aldermen including Hinky Dink Kenna, Dorsey Crowe, John Powers, James P. Bowler and John Toman. Bathhouse John Coughlin and State Senator John Griffin were among the active pallbearers. Mike Fritzel, a friend of Terrible Terry Druggan and in later years the owner of the Chez Paree and Fritzel's restaurant, was among the honored guests.

A specialist in extortion and mayhem along the East River waterfront in New York City, Torrio had first come to Chicago in 1910 as a bodyguard for Colosimo. Now with his boss laid away, Torrio decided that he too needed a bodyguard, and he summoned a young ruthless thug from Brooklyn by the alias of Al Brown (nee Alphonse Capone—newspapers of this period only refer to an Al Brown).

In those days, Torrio's headquarters was in a building at 2222 South Wabash Avenue called the Four Deuces. It was a four-story building dedicated to drinking, gambling and fornicating. The first floor housed a saloon and Torrio's office; the second and third floors

100

were devoted to gambling, and the fourth floor was a whorehouse. Naturally, it was a busy place, frequented by the aristocracy of the underworld of crime as well as the overworld of politics and business.

An even dozen unsolved murders were committed in the Four Deuces, but compared to what was happening off the premises, it was probably the safest place in town. In the short twelve years (1920–1931) that Al Brown was in town, there was a total of 629 unsolved gang slayings within the city limits, not counting the more than 5,000 homicides not classified as gang killings. Policemen and politicians were shot or bombed as readily as hoodlums.

But, as always, the name of the game was *quid pro quo*. Aside from paying for protection, the gangs' operations provided the aldermen and committeemen with thousands of patronage jobs such as bartenders, waitresses, bookies, alcohol cookers (Torrio and Capone paid thousands of Italian and Sicilian families in West Side tenements to cook alcohol for them), bookkeepers, clerks, runners, bouncers, bellhops and any other position open to voters. Then, of course, they provided the gunmen and thugs to supervise the polls on election day. It became a vicious circle: the politician needed the gangster and the gangster needed the policemen and the policemen needed the politician whose city patronage included the police force. The Chief of Police did not hire his own personnel. It was provided by the central committee of the party in power.

Thompson's Chief of Police, Charles C. Fitzmorris, publicly admitted that a large percentage of his officers were actively engaged in the illicit liquor business. Although State's Attorney Robert E. Crowe criticized the mayor for the condition of the city police, he personally had very little faith in his own small police contingent of forty officers headed by his Chief Investigator, Ben Newmark, who had been forced on him by the same political bosses. Privately, the state's attorney referred to Newmark and his crew as "Ali Baba and the forty thieves." A racketeer in his own right, Newmark was the victim of a typical gang killing in 1928.

By the mid-Twenties, beer vans rumbled through Chicago streets night and day in long convoys, and high-powered black limousines swept in deftly disconnected caravans to Canada and New York and Florida and New Orleans. The deluge of money was breathtaking. The Internal Revenue Service estimated the *weekly* net for Torrio and Capone as $100,000, which was split down the middle between the two bosses.

Then Torrio's luck went bad. Not only was he swept up in a raid on one of his breweries, but he was convicted and sentenced to a year in jail.

A few months later, the legendary black sedan pulled up alongside Torrio's car and four gunmen opened fire with sawed-off shotguns. The chauffeur and a dog beside him on the front seat were killed instantly. Torrio stared incredulously at the two bullet holes in his derby. Two days later, as he and his wife were tiptoeing from their car on a street directly behind their home, intending to sneak through to their own backyard, a big black sedan roared down the street and cut loose with two machine guns. Fifty slugs—"poisoned in garlic"—riddled the buildings and trees about them; three of the shots found their mark.

After a month in the hospital "wavering between life and death," Johnny Torrio called it quits. Desperate for a way out, he recalled the one-year sentence he was appealing and withdrew his bail and appeal. He was promptly lodged in the Waukegan Jail, where six of his thugs—in addition to the jail force—guarded him around the clock. Torrio suddenly decided it was time to visit his family back in the old country. In a grand gesture, he surrendered the entire Syndicate to Capone for his assistance in getting him safely out of the country. Years later he was to return to New York City and become one of the leaders in the international Mafia.

While the gangster melodrama occupied center stage, a round little actor in the wings "crept slyly into power, and in silence, but with swiftness coiled the city as a boa-constrictor can enwrap and crush even a tiger. . . ."

"In Chicago," wrote Edgar Lee Masters, "Samuel Insull ruled with the hand of a despot the domain of gas and electricity; he had the elevated lines in his grip which by this time (1931) ran northwest and west as well as south, to Milwaukee and across Illinois. The busses and the surface lines were his and much of the central heating. He could throw Chicago into darkness and cold by the wave of his hand. The banks were dominated by him, their presidents and officers were his liegemen, his clerical staff. He could call them to him or send them from him; he could remove them from power by a scowl, by the flush of his apoplectic wrath."

Born in 1860 in a London house on a street with a workhouse name, Samuel Insull migrated to Chicago in 1892 and in two decades

102

built a $2 billion utilities empire out of tissue paper. By the time he arrived in Chicago, he had advanced from confidential secretary to Thomas Edison, then general business manager of the Edison enterprises, to vice-president of the General Electric Company—a consolidation of the Edison and Thompson-Houston interests.

In quick succession, his company began swallowing up smaller electrical concerns, moving through a sea of utilities like a starving shark, until finally there was nothing left to consume. He formed the Commonwealth Edison Company in 1907, Middle West Utilities in 1912, and a few years later the Peoples Gas Light & Coke Company. Still not surfeited, he reached out through Illinois, Indiana, Kentucky and Ohio. On the eve of the 1929 stock market crash, Samuel Insull operated factories supplying gas, light, ice and heat in five thousand communities to 1,718,000 customers (a population of at least ten million); he employed thirty-two thousand men and had six hundred thousand security holders for his corporations; he manned 324 steam plants, 196 hydro-electric generating stations, 328 ice plants, 44,500 miles of transmission wires and 10,600 miles of gas mains.

In the words of Masters, Insull "was a connoisseur of nothing but city grants which could be capitalized in the swelling of his fortune." He built his paper colossus on the hot coals of corruption. Corrupt politicians and predatory law firms kept it precariously fireproof for forty years in a continuing conspiracy that provided low taxes and favorable legislation, plus safe judges, reasonable mayors, pliable aldermen, patronage officeholders and anybody else who could serve Insull's undivided interest.

However, wholesale corruption, as Capone, Inc. discovered, is expensive. One basic difference between Insull and Capone was in the *modus operandi* of the payoff. Capone paid off with tainted cash in a small black bag. Insull reciprocated with generous investment opportunities that permitted the "investors" to purchase large blocks of stock at prices far below the market value, with a down payment of 5 to 6 percent of the purchase price and balance due only after resale. Seven pools, aggregating $185,683,900, were formed specifically for the enrichment of the top political elite. The total down payment was $11,424,334 and the profit was a cool $3,161,683.50—all seemingly legitimate and quite respectable. Some of the buyers included Pat Nash, Democratic boss and a political descendant of Mike McDonald, and Tony (Anton J.) Cermak, chairman of the powerful Cook County Board and a leading mayoralty contender for a decade, each with $100,000; politicians Michael L. Igoe and E. J. Schnackenberg, both presently federal judges in Chicago, $50,000 and $25,000 respectively.

Between August 1, 1928, and September 10, 1930, Insull and his associates unloaded on the public securities valued at $650 million. Those were the critical years when the hot coals silently consumed the innards of the paper colossus. When it finally caught fire in 1932, the losses to investors and speculators were estimated at $2 billion.

One London newspaper epitomized the Insull collapse as "the downfall of a financial dynasty which rose from the gutter and fell back into it." Insull died in Paris in 1938, leaving $1,000 in cash and $14 million in debts—an impressive swindler right to his near-octogenarian grave.

3

During the mid-Twenties, when the Insull and Capone dynasties were at their zenith, junkmen Mike and Moe Rosenberg were the royal chamberlains of backroom politics. Their power as Democratic bosses over the entire West Side was so vast that it transcended party lines.

Mike was the committeeman of the Twenty-fourth and a trustee of the sanitary district, the most graft-infested unit of municipal government in the annals of corruption. Moe, an ex-convict, succeeded his brother as committeeman when Mike died in 1928. Jacob M. (Jake) Arvey, a protégé of the Rosenbergs, became the ward's alderman in 1923 at the age of twenty-eight.

Years later, after the Insull debacle, when Moe was trying to avert indictment by the federal government for evading income tax payments, he went to Washington and confessed his part in the wholesale purchase of political henchmen for the Insull utilities, and revealed that although Insull did not personally use a small black bag, he nevertheless availed himself of more direct means of compensation.

The secret testimony rendered under oath on December 27, 1933, was not made public until March 12, 1934, two months after his death. ("Politicians and officeholders drew a sigh of relief," the *Evening American* observed. "They thought Moe's secrets went to the grave with him.") The following is a partial transcript of Moe's confession:

Q. What happened when you went into the business with Mike?

A. When Mike and I got together he told me all about the business, told me he had the utility business, which was a very profitable business, with a lot of expense attached to it that I don't want to carry on the books. He says, "I take care of the political end. I take care of all the candidates and the general organizations, and it is charged to the business." He says, "Of course, I take it from time to time as I need it for different elections, and you will have to take my word for it."

Q. Did he say just how he took it out of the business?

A. He would sell some merchandise, take that check and cash it, and use it for campaign purposes, election funds, what he calls XX. . . .

Q. What happened after Mike passed away?

A. Right after Mike passed away I went up and saw Mr. Insull about keeping the business, and Mr. Insull said he did not see any reason why I could not keep it if I carried on as Mike did in all the years. . . . Keeping a friendly attitude between the different aldermen and politicians for the companies.

Q. What was the condition of the Democratic party in 1928?

A. After George Brennan died [1928] there was not much left to the Democratic party and we got together and reorganized the Democratic party, Cermak and myself. And when we reorganized it and took the party over there was a deficit of about $200,000 in bills payable.

Moe testified that he presented his own price and bids for the Insull utility junk and no questions were asked. His bids were nominal and his profits astronomical. He estimated his personal fortune at a million dollars in 1929, and his income at about $640,000 a year. Moe financed the party's reorganization with utility junk money, spending $500,000 in 1929 and 1930. Cermak had been influential with the utility companies from the time he was an alderman (first term 1909), and had helped originally to obtain the junk business from the utility companies for the Rosenberg Iron & Metal Company. In one election Moe gave $95,000 to Cermak; $92,000 to elect favorable aldermen; $8,000 to Joseph McDonough, chairman of the council's traction committee; $2,500 each to scores of legislators, and $12,000 to Jake Arvey, chairman of the council's finance committee and attorney for the utilities. Arvey was also attorney for Moe's junk yard and his Cook County Trust Company. When a Citizen's Traction Committee was formed to work out a favorable unified traction settlement, the legislation was drafted by Insull-owned officials, approved by the city council and sent to the legislature. Sidney S. Gorham, later president of the Chicago Bar Association, was sent to Springfield at $50 an hour, and Allan T. Gilbert at $30 an hour (total of $28,449), at the city's expense, to lobby the bills through. They passed 111 to 10. The companies' properties were valued at only $260 million by the act. The council passed a franchise and the mayor signed it.

Q. Now then, what was your idea? How would you profit by the passage of the traction ordinance and the construction of the subway?

A. Well, if they had built the subway, they had to tear out all the old cables in the ground and if that happened, and I think it would have happened if the depression hadn't come along, I would have had enough to do for a couple of years hauling every day of the week all of the cables of the Edison Company, Telegraph Company and the lines of the Peoples' Gas Company.

Q. You mean by that, that the construction of this underground railroad right of way would require the reallocation of all the utilities?

A. Yes, sir, separate gallery for Edison and Telephone Company and everything else. . . . .I thought I could make a million dollars or more out of the junk alone if they ever built the subway.

Scattered in the testimony was a remark that he had spent $25,000 in the 1929 judicial election. Asked if he had any need for the judges, Moe replied: "The chances are we would some time. I was building up Cermak at the same time. . . . We were not only looking to those judicial elections to have Cermak become leader, but then we were looking to put Cermak in the Mayor's chair, which we did."

Moe neglected to elaborate on the usefulness of "kept" judges. For example, he did not mention the 272 receiverships awarded to his Cook County Trust Company by twelve judges, and that his personal attorney, Jake Arvey, had been appointed a master in chancery. (When the *Tribune* refused to back Thompson in 1931, the mayor charged in a signed statement that the *Tribune* law firm [Kirkland, Fleming, Green & Masters, founded by Colonel Robert R. McCormick and presently known as Kirkland, Ellis, Hodson, Chaffety &

106

Masters] appeared with Arvey's law firm as attorneys of record in a trust company incorporated by Moe Rosenberg and Anton Cermak for the sole purpose of going into the receivership business on a mammoth scale.) The fantastic earnings of receivers in six years in Chicago totally eclipsed the illicit profits of gangsters. One congressional committee investigating real estate foreclosures for a six-year period reported in 1936 that "there appears in the State courts serving Chicago and its adjacent territory approximately 100,000 foreclosure cases filed since January 1930, representing approximately $2,000,000,000 in face value. About 40,000 cases, representing $800,000,000, have been disposed of." Lawyers, masters in chancery, receivers and trustees, all Phi Beta Kappa graduates of the System, were allowed at least $100 million in fees during this period.

4

One bright afternoon (June 9, 1930), Alfred "Jake" Lingle, a veteran *Tribune* reporter, strolled into a subway entrance to catch a train to Washington Park racetrack. Two men walked beside him. Just at the foot of the stairs in the kiosk one of the two men stepped back and bought a newspaper. He put it under his right arm, ran quickly back to Lingle, and with his left hand placed a snub-nosed revolver just over Lingle's collar, sending a bullet upward through his head. Lingle, cigar still in his mouth, fell dead. The slayer, described as blond and hatless, dropped the gun beside the body and darted up the stairs and across Michigan Avenue, escaping into anonymity forever.

The newspapers were outraged. Large black headlines, front-page editorials, messages of condolence from newspaper executives throughout the country, filled the pages of the Chicago press for days. Fifty-five thousand dollars was offered for information leading to the apprehension and conviction of the slayer.

The funeral procession was one of the most spectacular in the city's history, surpassing even Colosimo's. Nothing was left undone, except to omit the black horse troop.

But after the funeral, indignation was swiftly replaced by curiosity and suspicion. Why had Jake been killed? That is, why had he been the target of a carefully planned gangland execution? How could a $65-a-week reporter afford to live in a suite at the Stevens Hotel? Where did he get his money—the fourteen $100 bills found in his pockets at the time of his murder; the $60,000 he had spent the first six months of that year; the $100,000 stock market account held jointly with Police Commissioner William F. Russell; the $180,000 in Simmons Bed he had lost in the stock market crash; the vast loans received from gamblers and politicians, including $2,500 from the president of the Civil Service Commission and $5,000 from Corporation Counsel Samuel H. Ettelson? And then there was the diamond-studded belt buckle given to him by Capone—the gang chief's favorite token to very special friends. And, finally, how much truth was there in the persistent rumor that in underworld parlance Lingle was the city's unofficial Chief of Police?

In time, reform Police Commissioner Russell was given a furlough "so that he cannot hamper this investigation." Later, his resignation was demanded and accepted. Deputy Commissioner John Stege resigned under pressure.

Lingle, it developed, had two very close and dear friends—Police Commissioner Russell and Crime Commissioner Capone.

"Jake's like a son to me," Russell had often remarked. Their friendship, which went back twenty years to the days when Russell had pounded a beat, was a fairly common phenomenon among police and crime reporters. What was uncommon was the series of events which placed this friendship on a mutually beneficial monetary basis.

One of the first noteworthy events took place on April 10, 1928, when Negro lawyer Octavius Granady decided to run for committeeman in the "Bloody" Twentieth, a South Side black-belt ward ruled by political boss Morris Eller, a Thompson incumbent. After the polls closed that day, assassins hunted down Granady and murdered him in the street. This vicious crime, piled on top of hundreds of others, was the final straw.

Reform became the order of the day. At the forefront of the crusade rode Colonel McCormick astride the "World's Greatest Newspaper" and applauded in the winner's circle by the "World's Richest Reporter." A grand jury was immediately impaneled for the usual perfunctory investigation. To no one's amazement, it discovered a thriving multimillion dollar policy racket on the South Side.

"The [grand jury] report paints a picture of conditions no community pretending to be self-governed and civilized can afford to tolerate," said the *Tribune*. "It demonstrates with proven facts that there is a vicious alliance between corrupt politics and crime. That alliance is a disgrace to the intelligence and conscience of our citizenship, as well as an unsleeping enemy of competent government and

108

even of public security. It poisons the public service. It robs the public funds. It demoralizes the administration of justice. It shames the city before the eyes of the world."

And then to prove its own grand and noble intentions, the *Tribune* reprinted a New York *World* editorial laudatory to itself:

> The Chicago *Tribune* deserves congratulations for its victory in the lawsuit to compel Mayor Thompson to restore $2,245,000 to the city. It may well record its achievement by full page advertisements in other papers.
>
> Judge Friend states in his decision that Thompson and his allies needed great sums for political purposes. To obtain them they made a plan by which nearly $3,000,000 was paid to five experts for appraising public improvements. The experts turned back the greater part of their receipts into Thompson's political treasury. . . .
> The Chicago *Tribune* has done the state and city a service which has sometimes seemed ill-appreciated by the voters. In Illinois there is a cynicism which distrusts motives and—with some justice—pronounces one Republican crowd about as bad as the other. But the *Tribune* vindicates its unselfishness and public spirit by announcing that, although the costs of its prosecution are recoverable, it will seek no recompense.

But as always there was a "recompense." The *Tribune* had the mayor over the proverbial pork barrel. A deal satisfactory to both sides was negotiated through the good offices of Corporation Counsel Ettelson (Thompson was recuperating in the north woods). It was basically a simple *quid pro quo* arrangement: The mayor would appoint William F. Russell commissioner of police and the *Tribune* would see to it that the $2,450,000 judgment was stayed. The mayor was more than happy to reciprocate. The deal was consummated to everyone's satisfaction—especially Jake Lingle.

As to Russell's qualifications as a policeman and his philosophy on law enforcement, there could be little confusion on anybody's part. In March 1928 (barely four months before his appointment), Russell, then deputy commissioner, was quoted in the *Daily News* on the policy situation in the black belt. "Mayor Thompson was elected on the 'open town' platform," said Russell. "I assume the people knew what they wanted when they voted for him. . . . I haven't had any

109

orders from downtown to interfere in the policy racket and until I do get such orders you can bet I'm going to keep my hands off."

Two days after Colonel McCormick made the deal with the mayor, the *Tribune* portrayed Russell as a thoughtful, conscientious man engaged in a difficult mental audit of the grave responsibilities presented by the proffered office and not quite certain which way to jump.

From that date on, up to the time of Lingle's murder, the *Tribune* kept its poisoned anti-Thompson arrows in its quiver. And even fewer were directed at Alphonse Capone, who in 1928 had "settled" a pending strike of the newspaper's chauffeurs and drivers union. The meeting between the Colonel and the gangster was later made public in a signed statement by Daniel A. Serritella, a political protégé of Capone. "I attended this meeting," Serritella wrote, "at which Capone agreed to use his influence to stop the strike, which prevented the same. Max Annenberg [*Tribune*'s circulation manager] then brought in Robert McCormick . . . and introduced [him] to Capone. McCormick thanked Capone for calling off the strike and said: 'You know, you are famous like Babe Ruth. We can't help printing things about you, but I will see that the *Tribune* gives you a square deal.' "

A front-page story by a Lingle hireling on April 21, 1930, jubilantly proclaimed, "Alphonse Capone had achieved considerable power and wealth through bootlegging, vice and gambling before his imprisonment [ten months] in Philadelphia for carrying a gun. Upon his return to Chicago a month ago he decided to embark on new conquests because the bootleg business wasn't what it used to be, inasmuch as Police Commissioner Russell has shut down all gambling. Vice rings also had been routed and couldn't be reorganized."

The reporter who wrote this story resided at the Lexington Hotel, Capone's Chicago fortress. (The gang occupied three floors, sixth, seventh and eighth; Scarface Al was ensconced on the sixth. Hallways and lobby were crowded with wary-eyed gunmen—Tony Accardo, then only a punk kid with a rod, spent long hot hours in a lobby closet, a submachine gun in his moist hands, ready to jump out at a moment's notice and riddle away.) The true facts of the crime situation, published in other newspapers at that time, were in complete contradiction to the *Tribune* story. The income from Chicago rackets was estimated at a fantastic $6 million a *week*.

Ted Link, noted St. Louis *Star* crime reporter, was one of the first outside newsmen to comment on the deplorable condition of the Chicago press following Lingle's assassination: "One of the most curious discoveries made in connection with the situation here as it relates to the activities of a certain class of newspaper men involved in 'rackets,' is the fact that a voice has been crying out charges of this nature for years without results. The Rev. Elmer Williams . . . [in his] little magazine, *Lightnin'* . . . told as far back as 1925 of 'Jake' Lingle's arrest [with two other *Tribune* reporters] with an automobile load of alcohol. It also printed in 1928 and 1929 stories about the activities of Lingle in protecting gambling places. Likewise it told of his being known as the 'unofficial chief of police,' and also of his connection with race-track publications."

Not only was the press silent when its members were caught dipping into the rackets, but in some cases its columns were open, if not to defend the criminal, at least to castigate anyone brazen enough to interfere. When Williams' home was bombed for the second time, the reactionary *Tribune* curiously solicited the biased opinion of Democratic Boss Brennan to the effect that the publisher of *Lightnin'* had actually bombed his own home. Replied Williams: "If I bombed my own home, then Brennan [who had lost a leg in a mining accident in his youth] bit off his own leg."

Before the climax precipitated by the violent demise of Lingle, the peculiar mouthings of the *Tribune* were mostly regarded as symptomatic of the Colonel's gargantuan ego and mulish attitude. But afterward it became clear that the *Tribune's* daily vitriolics against certain reformers, labor leaders and public officials were not always sans ulterior motive. It became a standing joke in the underworld that the "Big Fellow" on the 24th floor of the *Tribune* tower did not know what the "little fellows" on the 4th floor (editorial offices) were doing at any given time of day or night. The *Tribune's* city editor was Robert M. Lee, and his assistant was W. D. "Don" Maxwell, who today is the paper's editor in chief.

The Chicago *Herald-Examiner* did not mince words: "The work of these newspaper reporters is directed by the city editor. A good city editor knows pretty well just what his men are doing for the paper— and on the outside. It is understood that Robert M. Lee . . . had for about nine years been a close friend of Jake Lingle. The grand jury might call Mr. Lee and inquire what he knows and what his records show of the activities of Lingle in the months before he was murdered. But the 'board of strategy,' the *Tribune* lawyer [the

Colonel had his own attorney appointed a special prosecutor to conduct the grand jury investigation], the State's Attorney, the police and all the rest of officialdom have never called a witness that might be expected to know anything about: Who killed Jake Lingle and why?"

As the unofficial chief of police, Lingle had been in a position to "hand over the town" to Capone. But long before that came to pass, Lingle liked the gang chief and frequently said so. They attended the prize fights and horse races together and took several vacation trips to Florida and Cuba. When Capone was imprisoned for two days in connection with the murder of assistant State's Attorney William H. McSwiggin in 1926, he refused to eat any food except that brought to him by Lingle personally. But after Jake connected in 1928, the money and power, not to mention the underworld prestige, went to his head. He began peddling protection wholesale, and more often than not (except with Capone) it was a low-grade product at a high price.

Following the St. Valentine's Day massacre, the order to "get Capone" issued by the Moran-Aiello gang (also disgruntled customers of Jake's inferior merchandise) became virtually nationwide. New York Mafia chieftain Lucky Luciano called a meeting at Atlantic City to effect a truce between the gang leaders, and when it failed, Capone arranged to have himself picked up in Philadelphia for carrying a concealed weapon. Taking a page out of Torrio's strategy book, he pleaded guilty and shook (served) a year in prison, safe and untroubled, while back home in Chicago, Lingle and Russell dutifully minded the store. The raids on Moran-Aiello interests steadily increased in scope until the entire operation was on the verge of collapse. Alky cookers defected to the protected ranks of Capone enterprises, and a number of top aides, including Frank Foster, Ted Newberry and Harry Marks, turned renegade. A barrage of machine gun bullets accounted for eighteen dead gangsters in February 1930, and in the group was Julius Rosenheim, a crime informant employed by the *Daily News*.

Released from prison in March, Capone found Chicago still too hot for his health and left immediately for Florida where he bought himself a $375,000 fortress on Palm Island. It is interesting to note that Capone was never in Chicago when a major killing attributed to his outfit occurred. And he was in Florida when notified of Lingle's

112

murder. Eleven of his competitors had met violent death in the preceding ten days.

Although the Lingle murder was never officially solved, there were some significant developments. The .38 caliber snub-nosed Colt which killed Lingle was traced to Frank Foster and Ted Newberry, two Moran defectors who had joined the Capone organization. The revolver, a type popular with well-dressed hoodlums (small enough to fit in a specially tailored waist pocket), was one of six similar guns sold to Foster and Newberry by Peter von Frantzius, an underworld gunsmith and armorer, who for years supplied gangsters with the tools of their trade, including the two machine guns used in the St. Valentine's Day massacre.

"Newberry took three and Foster the other three," von Frantzius told police. "Later Newberry came back and asked me to file off the number of one of the guns very carefully, deeper than I usually do. I filed it very deep, so it could never be traced. Newberry called for the gun and was satisfied."

The filed-off numbers were resurrected by Colonel Calvin Goddard, head of the Northwestern University crime detection laboratory. Police searched about for Foster and Newberry and began to question the undying friendship that had supposedly existed between Lingle and Capone. Big-spender Capone, it seemed, had resented the reporter's habit of visiting his (Capone's) tailor and charging four and five suits at a time to the gangster's account. Then there was the matter of Lingle's faulty advice on the dog tracks. It had cost the gang chief about a million dollars. The first year Russell was commissioner the protection had been a hundred percent pure. But later Russell and State's Attorney Swanson started squabbling in the pages of the newspapers, and Swanson's investigators began raiding the tracks. For a time they were kept open by repeated court injunctions issued by Judge Harry Fisher, but finally even Capone's judge had to bow to the superior judgment of the Supreme Court which ruled dog racing illegal in Illinois. When this happened, Capone and Lingle reportedly quarreled, with Capone saying: "Well, the racket is through, and as far as I'm concerned, so are you."

The best indicator of the Capone-Lingle disenchantment occurred the day Capone was released from prison. Lingle arrived in Philadelphia a few days early, ready for the big "inside story" of Capone's release. Capone, however, had been plotting with prison officials to keep secret the time, location and means of his departure. More concerned with his own safety than in Lingle's journalistic responsibilities, Capone left the world's richest reporter waiting, suitcase in hand, for hours in front of the penitentiary. It was said that Lingle bitterly resented that episode.

The two primary suspects, Foster and Newberry, were arrested, briefly questioned, and released. Ted Newberry was picked up by New Jersey police while on his way to the Sharkey-Schmeling fight in New York. When he and his six gangster companions were searched, the smallest bankroll found on any of them was $8,500. Newberry had $17,000. They were released in time for the fight.

The last major suspect was Jack Zuta, a tough, fast talking hood who bossed North Side vice for the Moran-Aiello mob. He was interrogated briefly by police and released. One month later, Zuta's luck ran out in a dance pavilion near Delafield, Wisconsin. Five men, one carrying a machine gun, stepped into the ballroom and headed for the gaily whirling Zuta, who immediately fell to the floor, the color draining from his usually florid face. They calmly picked him up and carried him bodily to a chair before an electric player piano. Not a word was spoken. Rigid and glassy-eyed, Zuta was just falling from the chair when the machine gunner sprayed a row of bullets across the piano with a crash of glass and a tinkle of music. Twenty-eight of the slugs found their mark.

Garrulous in life, Zuta was no less silent in death. A prodigious scribbler, his detailed records belied his usual "Aw, forget it" when grateful grafters thanked him for "little favors." Ledgers recovered from three banks retained under aliases revealed that no fewer than fifty officeholders had received substantial payments to protect his $400,000-weekly vice operation.

Among Zuta's documented beneficiaries were Joseph W. Schulman, a municipal court judge; Emanuel Eller, a criminal court judge and son of Morris Eller, political boss of the "Bloody" Twentieth Ward; Diamond Joe Esposito, murdered political boss of the even bloodier Nineteenth Ward and Republican aide of U.S. Senator Charles S. Deneen (former governor of Illinois); George Van Lent and Harry W. Starr, Republican state senators; William O. Freeman, Chief of Police of Evanston—then "the world's wealthiest suburb"; Louis I. Fisher, former assistant state's attorney, counsel for hoodlum-owned dog tracks and brother of Harry Fisher, circuit court judge who kept Capone dog tracks open with a series of injunctions; Charles E. Graydon, sheriff of Cook County who issued Zuta a signed

114

card which read: "To all members of the department: The bearer, J. Zuta, is extended the courtesies of all departments"; Richard J. Williams, police sergeant and aide to Frank J. Loesch, a special prosecutor who had attempted to indict political thieves involved with gangsters; the East Chicago Avenue police precinct, which received a $3,500 weekly payment; William R. Skidmore, a saloonkeeper-gambler and junk-yard operator, who was to become the foremost political fixer and underworld bagman during the Kelly-Nash regime; the Regular Republican Club of Cook County and the William Hale Thompson Republican Club—Big Bill was caught once visiting Zuta at his home in Middlesboro, Kentucky—to the tune of $50,000; and one small donation of $1,500 to a poor patrolman to pay for his promotion to sergeant.

Not to be neglected was one Arthur X. Elrod, the subject of earlier publicity in a variety of high jinks. An *American* story on December 30, 1929, said in part: "While George 'Bugs' Moran waited warily in the lobby of the building at 127 North Dearborn Street today, detectives opened the vault in the Acme Products Company on the fifth floor, where four alleged gangsters were seized and plans for a nation-wide punchboard syndicate uncovered. The vault contained four quarts of Scotch whiskey, more than 200 cancelled checks signed with the name Arthur X. Elrod, who was formerly connected [assistant office manager] with the Corporation Counsel Samuel A. Ettelson's office, and punchboards and numerous premiums."

Aside from being treasurer of the Acme Sales Company, Arthur X. Elrod held a variety of lucrative positions. He was a gambler, a saloonkeeper, a business front for North Side hoodlums, a bail bondsman for the Moran-Aiello gang, and a private secretary for Jack Zuta. Simultaneously, Elrod was a bailiff in the criminal court, a realtor, an insurance broker, and to quote Jake Arvey, the "best precinct captain in the Twenty-fourth Ward." Such a native talent could not go unrewarded for long in Chicagoland. In subsequent years, Elrod was to prosper financially and politically as Arvey's designated heir.

5

As the great Depression settled over Chicago, the crime rate soared. After years as the victim of vicious plunderers, the city finally sank to its knees. With its credit cut off, there were no funds to pay the salaries of policemen, firemen and school teachers. Desperate and

115

defiant, the citizens refused to pay taxes. Wrote one observer: "Citizens already paying heavy taxes to racketeers, who can deliver what they promise, are refusing to pay taxes to a city government which cannot."

Anton J. Cermak was elected mayor in 1931. The four architects of his victory were Moe Rosenberg, Jake Arvey, Al Capone and Patrick A. "Pat" Nash, committeeman of the Twenty-eighth Ward in the heart of the West Side Irish ghetto and Brennan's successor to the Irish leadership of Mike McDonald's Democrats. Nash was also a "fat cat" sewer contractor and grafter whose income was among the city's ten highest. Nash Brothers did more sewer contracting for the city than any other firm. In a three year period, 1926–1928, Nash and his nephews, the Dowdle Brothers, received contracts from the Sanitary District alone totaling $13 million. An income tax investigation in 1930 forced Nash to ante up another $177,000 to the government. That same year the Dowdle Brothers were indicted for income tax evasion amounting to $203,654.07, but the cases were delayed for six years and finally nol-prossed by the new United States Attorney, Michael L. Igoe.

The money and patronage controlled by these four bosses, combined with Cermak's own political fortunes, created the most invincible political machine in modern times. Cermak, a ward politician, had been at the public trough for thirty years. He had been a member of the Illinois General Assembly, where his record was distinguished largely by his conflict-of-interest work as secretary of the United Societies, a large and formidable lobby of saloonkeepers, brewers and distillers.

That the brewers got value in kind was attested to by one contemporary historian who wrote: "As leader of an organization which assumed the misleading name of United Societies, Cermak aroused and organized the underworld to enforce its demand for a wide-open town. For a quarter of a century, any politician, whatever his party, who dared to support any measure that would curb the license of those anti-social hordes, was immediately confronted by Cermak, snarling and waving the club of the underworld vote."

Where the Thompson machine had been a *quid pro quo* grab bag of political spoils and diffused power structure, the Cermak machine was a pyramidal structure of tempered discipline, molded around a dictatorial committeeman in each ward at the base and moving vertically up through the organizational structure to the pinnacle of power, Cermak. His patronage, the foundation of Illinois politics,

116

was the largest ever controlled by a mayor. Then with the election of Henry Horner to the governorship in 1932, Cermak became the boss not only of Chicago and Cook County but of the state of Illinois as well. In the wards, the strength flowed from lucrative gangster-operated rackets which supplied both money and jobs. The West Side (particularly Hinky Dink's First Ward loop and wards bossed by Nash, Arvey and Rosenberg) became popularly known as the Capone Bloc.

After Capone was sentenced to 11 years in federal prison in October, 1931, Cermak began looking for an underworld boss who would be subservient to the Democratic machine.

James P. Allman was appointed police commissioner with the understanding that law enforcement policies regarding gambling and vice would be dictated by the individual ward leaders. Ted Newberry, Capone's North Side boss following the demise of the Moran-Aiello-Zuta gang, became Cermak's favorite candidate for the underworld post.

A prime suspect in the Lingle case and a prime suspect in a variety of heinous crimes during his violent career, Newberry was unquestionably the most popular among the gangster fraternity. And he was apparently quite popular with judges, too, for he was never convicted even of a misdemeanor. Often he was a tenuous suspect. For example, when labor racketeer George "Red" Barker, a Capone mob lieutenant, was cut down by eighteen machine gun slugs on June 17. 1932, federal investigators checked Newberry's various bank accounts with an eye to income tax violations and came up with some coincidental withdrawals and deposits. Again Ted made headlines as a prime suspect.

According to a newspaper account: "A check of machine gun sales showed that the gun [left at the scene of the crime] had been purchased over the counter of the Von Lengerke & Antoine sporting goods company . . . by the Haber Screw Machine Products company . . . headed by Titus Haffa, former alderman and ex-convict. . . . The [federal] investigators found the Newberry banking affairs intertwined with those of Henry Finklestein, known to the north side gang circles and said to be a follower of Haffa. Newberry, investigation showed, had drawn $300 from the bank the day before the purchase of the gun . . . $3,000 on the day of the purchase . . . and another $300 on the next day." Records showed no further

117

withdrawals for two weeks. (Finklestein, who was listed by the Chicago Crime Commission as one of eighteen public enemies, was once fined $500 for operating distilleries for Titus Haffa, and was a prime suspect in the slaying of Zuta. A bootlegger and gang leader, Haffa later diversified his interests into more legitimate fields. Today, as a multimillionaire industrialist, he is a "respected" Chicagoan of considerable clout.)

Frank "The Enforcer" Nitti, a cousin of Capone and heir apparent to his crime empire, was not overjoyed at the prospect of being replaced by Newberry. Nitti's espionage system was in every way as efficient as Cermak's, who was not adverse to using surreptitious means such as wire taps, mail drops, surveillance and stool pigeons to ferret out information concerning the weaknesses and foibles of administrative and political friends, taking great pains to learn the identities of his enemies.

In his book *The Twenty Incredible Years,* William H. Stuart wrote: "Mayor Cermak was a master of detail. He dealt closer with the mysterious, menacing line of the underworld than any mayor in Chicago's history. This phase was something the bankers, big business, were not concerned in. . . . The high hats did not want to know about it, beyond seeing that they got their share of deposits from that business as well as from legitimate business. . . . It was apparent that Cermak had no conscientious aversion to the business of gambling and beer running. . . . He was mayor now, but that made no difference to Cermak."

Cermak maintained the *status quo* in the underworld until the 1932 national elections were over. Then he began the dangerous redistribution of territories controlled by the Capone mob. Three months later he was dead. Cut down by bullets in Florida, he suffered (according to the press) a "martyr's death" when he was "accidentally" shot by Giuseppe Zangara, a "crazed fanatic" who had "tried to assassinate" Roosevelt.

Prior to this bizarre development, Sergeant Harry Lang, a member of Cermak's hoodlum squad, had placed several bullets into the back and chest of Frank Nitti during a raid on the mob's Loop headquarters. But Nitti had survived.

Months after Cermak and Newberry (his bullet-riddled body was found in a ditch on January 7, 1933, less than three weeks after the attempt on Nitti's life) were buried, Sergeant Lang was charged with "assault with intent to murder" Frank Nitti and brought to trial. Chris Callahan, a detective who had accompanied the raiders, testi-

118

fied that "As we entered the suite, we looked into a small office and saw Nitti and three others. In another room there were two more men. We took the men out one by one and searched them. I searched Nitti. Nitti was taken into another room. He appeared to be chewing something. I told him to spit it up. When I found he had no revolver I put mine back in my pocket. I was holding him by the wrists behind his back. Lang came up and said, 'What is your name?' He then shot him three or four times. I jumped away. Nitti staggered toward the other room and Lang shot him again."

Lang's partner, Sergeant Harry Miller, testified that Cermak had given them the address "where you will find Nitti, 'Little New York,' and several others," and had "ordered" the raid for Monday because "that was payoff day for them." Asked if the mayor had feared for his life, Miller said Cermak believed that Louis "Little New York" Campagna was the man Nitti had imported to kill him. Miller's testimony before the grand jury to the effect that Newberry had paid Lang to murder Nitti was not introduced in the trial.

When the jury brought in a verdict of guilty of "assault with a deadly weapon," Lang threatened to "blow the lid off Chicago politics and wreck the Democratic party" if he served one day in jail. The next day Judge Thomas Lynch granted him a new trial. Lang never served a day of confinement. The new trial never took place.

The swift gang retaliation against Newberry is said to have terrified Cermak. He moved from the Congress Hotel to a penthouse bungalow with a private elevator at the top of the Morrison Hotel, and increased his bodyguard force from two to five. Guards were placed at the homes of his daughters.

Cermak's trip to Florida to see Roosevelt was prompted by his uneasiness over federal patronage. There was also the problem of mending political fences. During the national convention in 1932, Cermak had backed Al Smith, refusing to release the fifty-eight-vote Illinois delegation through three ballots. On the fourth ballot, Texas and California broke the log jam and Roosevelt was nominated. The politically astute Cermak was left at the rail while the wheelhorses rejoiced in the winner's circle. Although Roosevelt subsequently polled almost a million votes (330,000 majority) in Cook County, Cermak had yet to make his peace with the President-elect.

On the evening of February 15, 1933, Mayor Cermak, seated in the front row on the gaudy bandstand in Miami's Bayfront Park,

119

anxiously awaited the arrival of the President-elect. Ten thousand people filled every seat and aisle of the amphitheater. After an eleven-day fishing trip off the Florida coast aboard Vincent Astor's yacht *Nourmahal,* Roosevelt looked tanned and in good spirits as his motorcade swung into the amphitheater and came to a stop some fifty feet in front of Cermak. The crowd cheered and Roosevelt smiled and waved gaily from his open touring car. When the cheering subsided, he raised himself up and sat on top of the rear seat of the car and delivered a pleasant, short, informal speech. Then, still smiling, he slid down into the seat again.

Followed by other dignitaries, Cermak was the first one to reach and shake hands with FDR. They chatted a moment before Cermak stepped away and moved toward the rear of the car. Then it happened. Five rapid shots, which sounded like firecrackers to Roosevelt, rang out in less than fifteen seconds. Cermak, and four others near him, were simultaneously cut down.

Zangara's asserted motivation for the crime was that he suffered from severe chronic stomach pains and that he blamed capitalists for his physical discomfort. "Back in Italy," he said, "the capitalists get to be boss to my father, and my father send me to work, and I have no school, and I have trouble with my stomach. And that way, I make my idea to kill the President—kill any President, any king." (An autopsy report stated that he was a "healthy, well-nourished individual." It found nothing organically wrong with his "stomach.")

During long hours of interrogation, Zangara repeatedly admitted he had no personal grievance against Roosevelt. Curiously enough, he admired him. And for all his so-called resentment against capitalists, he was neither a Communist, a Socialist, a Fascist nor an Anarchist. He was, in fact, a registered Republican. He had thought, he said, of assassinating President Hoover, but it was cold in Washington that time of year, and since Roosevelt was in Florida, it was more convenient that way.

Zangara had lived in Florida two years and his principal occupation (except for a brief stint as a tourist guide) was betting on horses and dogs. He traveled to Los Angeles and as far south as Panama during this period, and spent some time in Palm Beach and Key West. The Rev. Elmer Williams wrote that Zangara had been employed in a Syndicate "cutting plant" in Florida "convenient to a canal where the whisky was run in from the islands." Williams then theorized that Zangara got into trouble with his bosses and was ordered to kill Cermak. It was either that or be tortured and murdered himself. He allegedly chose the lesser of two evils.

120

The full report of the two psychiatrists who examined him ran less than a hundred words: "The examination of this individual reveals a perverse character wilfully wrong, remorseless and expressing contempt for the opinions of others. While his intelligence is not necessarily inferior, his distorted judgment and temperament is incapable of adjustment to the average social standards. He is inherently suspicious and anti-social. Such ill-balanced erratic types are classified as a Psychopathic personality. From this class are recruited the criminals and cranks whose pet schemes and morbid emotions run in conflict with the established order of society."

The murder weapon, a .32 caliber revolver, was purchased in a downtown Miami pawnshop for eight dollars. Although not classified as an expert marksman, Zangara served five years in the Italian infantry, and recalled that he had once bagged a rabbit on the run with a pistol.

Yet on the night of the assassination, he could not even hit an automobile standing still. Instead, he hit a group of five people some eight to ten feet away—and only Cermak was shot fatally. His failure to hit Roosevelt has been attributed to the alert and heroic responses of fearless spectators who assertedly grabbed his arm and pushed it upward just as he started to fire. Although he did not publicly dispute any of these claims, privately Zangara told his attorneys that his arm was nót seized until after he had fired all shots, and a policeman who helpèd overpower him agreed.

Cermak was convinced that he was Zangara's target. He told a reporter friend, John Dienhart, that he had been threatened before leaving Chicago because of his intention to break up the syndicate's control—this phraseology created the image of a crime-fighting reform mayor. He told Dienhart he had bought a bulletproof vest, but had not worn it on that day even though he had had a premonition of such an occurrence. When his Chicago secretary, Clara Beasley, first arrived at the hospital, the dying mayor greeted her with, "So you arrived all right. I thought maybe they'd shot up the office in Chicago too."

Cermak died on March 6 and Zangara's murder trial took place on March 9. It lasted all of one day. The next morning he was sentenced to death. No appeals were taken. Ten days later, at nine-fifteen on the morning of March 20, 1933, he walked unassisted into the death chamber. "I go by myself," he told the guards. "I no scared of electric chair." And to prove it, he sat down with a defiant smile, saying, "See, I no scared of electric chair." When the guards placed a black cowl over his head, he said in a muffled voice, "Good-by, adios

121

to all the world." Moments later, as final preparations were being completed, he impatiently shouted, "Go ahead. Push the button." And they did.

6

As for Nitti (whether or not he had engineered the murder of Cermak was inconsequential as long as highly placed politicians believed that he had) the next ten years, until his suicide in 1943, were the best. He reigned as the undisputed boss of a unified underworld which enjoyed a decade of great prosperity and immunity from arrest—local and federal. Those were the years of consolidation and integration; the years when the criminal foundation that supports the Outfit today was laid deep in the fertile soil of Chicago corruption. For the first time, the Italians became the absolute rulers of organized crime; and for the first time, the Mafia welcomed talented hoodlums from other ethnic groups into its inner circles. Murray "The Camel" Humphreys, Eddie "Bighead" Vogel, Lester "Killer Kane" Kruse,* Lenny Patrick, Gus Liebe, Dave Yaras, Joseph Corngold, Gus "Shotgun" Alex, Joseph "Big Joe" Arnold,* and William Block, all tough mobsters—many of them contract killers—have survived to this day within the orbit of the Italian Outfit. Jake "Greasy Thumb" Guzik, regarded as the brains behind Al Capone, was listed among the top three crime bosses before his death in 1956.

By 1933 the integrated Italian organization had ruthlessly destroyed all gang opposition except for the defiant Touhy mob headed by Roger Touhy, a Northwest suburban bootlegger who had switched his *modus operandi* to labor unionism (a Nitti monopoly) as Repeal dawned over the horizon. No amount of "persuasion" could convince Touhy of the merits of capitulation. Then, in typical Chicago fashion, fortuitous coincidences solved the problem. Enters center stage one John "Jake the Barber" Factor, a notorious international confidence man and stock swindler. It just happened that Factor, an intimate friend of Capone, Nitti, Rosenberg, Arvey, Kelly and Nash, was then a fugitive from British justice in a $7 million stock swindle and was about to be extradited back to England to serve prison sentences amounting to twenty-four years. But Jake the Barber vanished mysteriously, the alleged victim of a kidnapping scheme engineered by none other than the recalcitrant Touhy.

Since it followed in the wake of the revulsion created by the

* See Appendix.

122

Lindbergh abduction, public sympathy was quickly aroused in favor of Factor and against Touhy. The newspapers had a field day. Reporters waited for hourly bulletins from command headquarters (Factor's expensive fortieth-floor suite) at the Morrison Hotel. The *American* kept its readers informed as to facts and theories: "And despite Roger Touhy's indignant statement that he never had stooped to kidnapping—a statement made to a Chicago *American* reporter in a personal interview—there was a mounting conviction that the Northwest mobster and his cohorts were in some way mixed up in the Factor case. . . . Alderman Jacob M. Arvey, friend of Factor, was in and out of the headquarters at the hotel, obviously arranging some plan for the release of the prisoner. . . . One intimation was that Factor may be released on his own recognizance—'on parole,' as it were, to pay his kidnappers his ransom afterward. Factor, it was pointed out, has the *reputation of never having broken his word* [italics used—a rather clever touch when compared to the earlier disclaimer of Touhy's veracity]."

As it developed, Factor was released by his captors, unshaven, unharmed and unextraditable; Touhy was arrested, tried, convicted and sentenced to ninety-nine years in prison. He served twenty-five years before a federal court fully exonerated him, the ruling reading in part: "The court finds that John Factor was not kidnapped for ransom, or otherwise, on the night of June 30th or July 1st, 1933, though he was taken as a result of his own connivance. . . . The court finds that Roger Touhy did not kidnap John Factor and, in fact, had no part in the alleged kidnapping of John Factor." Legal vindication, but unfortunately not mob absolution. On December 16, 1959, twenty-three days after his release from Stateville, Touhy was cut down by five shotgun blasts as he arrived at his sister's Chicago home. At that precise moment, Jack Factor, by then a wealthy Beverly Hills and Las Vegas financier and self-proclaimed philanthropist, was in Chicago, enjoying a steak dinner at the Singapore, a syndicate-controlled Rush Street joint.

(On July 25, 1960, seven months after the shotgun slaying of Roger Touhy, Factor sold Murray Humphreys—questioned as a suspect in the Touhy slaying—400 shares of First National Life Insurance Company of America stock at $20 each for a total of $8,000. At the same time, Factor was paying $125 a share to other holders of the same stock in a bid to gain control of the company. Eight months later, Humphreys sold back the stock at $125 a share, reaping a long-term capital gains profit of $42,000. Suspicious IRS agents were not so sure it was a long-term capital gain. Questioned under oath in Los Angeles, Factor explained that when his son, Jerome, was kidnapped for ransom in 1933, a few weeks before his own alleged kidnaping, he contacted Humphreys to arrange for the safe return of his son—it was suspected that the Capone mob had engineered the abduction. His son was returned and now, 27 years later, Factor had suffered a pang of conscience. He felt he owed Humphreys something for his help.)

By late 1940, gloom had settled over the scandal-ridden Democratic machine. The ten-year cycle of opulence and skullduggery seemed about complete. By a process of political erosion, Mayor Edward Kelly (Cermak's successor) had become the titular head of the party. Jake Arvey resigned from the city council in time to join the Illinois National Guard as senior judge advocate, and was succeeded in the Twenty-fourth Ward by Arthur X. Elrod, described in the press as "The No. 1 Arvey henchman."

Chicago business and rackets boomed during the war years. War plants operated to capacity, wages were high and unemployment almost nonexistent. Gambling and prostitution provided the serviceman with entertainment around-the-clock. The Loop and near North Side were riddled with gambling and assignation joints, many of them operated by precinct captains and other deserving politicians.

Mayor Kelly was reelected for another four-year term with typical machinelike precision. A few months later, on October 6, 1943, his political sponsor, Patrick A. Nash, who had been in ill health, died. Kelly automatically assumed chairmanship of the Cook County Democratic Central Committee and the stewardship of the forty-thousand-odd patronage jobs that was the muscle behind the title. For the first time in Chicago history, a mayor had become the absolute ruler of his Party organization.

Gambling along West Roosevelt Road in the Twenty-fourth Ward continued to flourish under the intermediary control of Elrod, who according to a government report was "running the ward in a high-handed manner and is the protector of the mob in the locality and reported to receive $700 monthly from Louis 'Little New York' Campagna, the Syndicate's gambling boss on the West Side."

In the days of Moe Rosenberg, the aristocrat of gambling on the West Side had been Julius "Lovin' Putty" Annixter. After Rosenberg's death, Annixter was replaced by Ben Zuckerman, an intimate

124

friend of Arvey, who was affectionately known as "Zucky" in high political circles. Once well-connected with the power bloc (political and criminal), Zucky's connections were permanently severed on January 14, 1944. One of his associates, Ben Glazer, a convicted rapist, died of a heart attack when he heard the news. A few months later, two other associates, Dago Lawrence Mangano and Michael Pantillo, were cut down in a hail of shotgun slugs. Louis "Danny" Dann (aka Dan Reusch) fled to California. Still not satisfied, the Syndicate eliminated eight more West Siders in quick succession.

With everybody dead, wounded or missing in action, Willie Tarsch, the last member of Zuckerman's group, continued to operate as if nothing had happened. A secret government report reveals that Tarsch's fate was sealed at a meeting in the Chez Paree between Elrod and members of the Syndicate. After listening to various complaints, Elrod allegedly raised his hand and said, "Take care of it in your own way." A few days later Tarsch was gunned down in the rear of a building on West Roosevelt Road.

In the national election of 1944, the Twenty-fourth Ward again produced the largest number of votes in any single ward in the United States, rolling up 29,533 votes for Roosevelt as opposed to 2,204 for Dewey. Elrod was personally congratulated by Roosevelt.

Meanwhile, his connections had become national as evidenced from a list of telephone calls obtained by New York officials. Among the calls made from Frank Costello's Sands Point, New York summer home on May 27, 1945, was one to ROckwell 4177, which at that time was the telephone number of Arthur X. Elrod, 1333 South Independence Boulevard, Chicago. Costello was then publicly acclaimed as the prime minister of the national crime syndicate. (At the 1932 Democratic National Convention in Chicago, Costello had shared a room at the Drake Hotel with Jimmy Hines, head of the Tammany machine, while Lucky Luciano doubled up with Albert Marinelli, a Tammany district leader.)

When Arvey returned from the war in 1945, Elrod gracefully stepped aside to let his old boss resume his Twenty-fourth Ward committeeman post. A year later, when the slatemakers met to nominate the mayoralty candidate, Arvey was ready for Kelly. Said the *Tribune:* "Kelly soon arrived looking cheerful. Arvey, beaming, took him into the committee room, waving reporters in at the same time. Kelly was loudly applauded, and Al J. Horan, head of the slating group, remarked, 'That's from the heart.' Arvey in rapid sentences said to the mayor that he could have the organization bid if he

125

wanted, but that because of Kelly's reluctance to run they had picked [Martin H.] Kennelly [a political amateur and wealthy warehouseman]. . . . The mayor's face registered amazement. . . . The mayor said the news was a surprise at this time, while reporters on the scene declare there were tears in the eyes of hardbitten ward chiefs."

Kennelly was elected by the usual solid majority. For those who had looked to the new mayor with hope of reform, it soon became apparent that they had been duped once again. Kennelly had no intention of disrupting the *status quo*. Former Kelly department heads were retained, including Police Commissioner John C. Prendergast. To Kennelly, the Capone mob was a myth. When queried about the steps he was taking to combat the Syndicate, he replied, "I don't know about any syndicate. Isn't that man Capone supposed to be dead?" (Al Capone died of paresis, a disease of the brain caused by syphilis, in his Palm Island fortress and his body was brought back to Chicago on February 4, 1947, for burial in Mount Olivet Cemetery. Another link between the Syndicate and the Machine came to light when it was learned that a mortgage amounting to $35,000 on Capone's palatial Florida home was held in the name of Frank E. Harmon, committeeman of the Twenty-fifth Ward, a personal friend of Arvey and a political protégé of Kelly.)

The only difference between the new administration and the previous one was in the repository of patronage and clout. With Kennelly the Machine had shifted into reverse all the way back to the days when mayors were merely figureheads for the boys in the smoke-filled backroom.

Apprehensive of the swelling Dewey tide in the coming 1948 elections, Arvey decided to embark upon the role of national kingmaker by initiating a draft-Eisenhower movement. In travels across the country, he argued with other Party bosses that the Democrats were not obliged to nominate Truman at the Philadelphia convention. Then he spoke of an "open" convention. Mayor Hague of New Jersey, Mayor O'Dwyer of New York and James Roosevelt joined forces with Arvey. They bitterly held on to this hope until Eisenhower irrevocably withdrew his name in Philadelphia.

Convinced that Illinois could not win with Truman, Arvey had earlier urged the State Central Committee to endorse Adlai E. Stevenson for senator and Paul H. Douglas for governor. The com-

126

mittee approved the two candidates, but reversed their roles in the belief that they would get nothing from Douglas, a University of Chicago economist and a former alderman. Stevenson, while not directly promising anything, offered hope, both as an unknown quantity and as a novice—his experience had been as a diplomat, a delegate to the United Nations and assistant to the Secretaries of State and Navy. Although Truman finished only about 30,000 votes ahead of Dewey in Illinois, the two machine candidates scored smashing victories: Douglas won by 407,000 and Stevenson by 572,000, the largest plurality ever polled by a statewide candidate.

7

As chief investigator for three state's attorneys from 1932 to 1950, Captain Dan "Tubbo" Gilbert was an elder statesman in the field of political corruption. To the underworld, he was the most important cop in the county; to the press, he was the richest cop in the country; to the Rev. Elmer Williams, he was the most corrupt cop in the world, and to Jake Arvey, he was the ideal candidate for sheriff of Cook County.

According to newspaper files, the first time Gilbert got into the news as a policeman his name was misspelled. On November 9, 1920, the *Tribune* published an article captioned "Whiskey Running" in which Police Chief John J. Garrity stated that "I have learned that certain captains assigned detectives and policemen to guard whiskey shipments. My investigators have obtained affidavits from policemen and others involving whole police stations in the whiskey traffic." Assistant United States District Attorney John J. Kelly was quoted in the same story to the effect that the "Chicago Police Department is honeycombed with booze graft. Within the last week we have been forced to issue warrants for a dozen policemen. There is a police taint in every illicit whiskey deal that has so far come under our attention. Chief Garrity says he has given all the evidence in his power. This is false. Chief Garrity has double-crossed me and from this moment I am through with him." Federal warrants on a charge of attempting bribery to violate prohibition laws were issued against five policemen, including Daniel "Guilbert" (another officer was Harry Miller, of Cermak hoodlum-squad fame). Later newspapers tell of indictments against the other detectives but there is no mention of "Guilbert." Gilbert's ascendancy in the police department was jet-propelled. In nine years, he went from rookie to captain.

In the middle Twenties he met Thomas J. Courtney, then sergeant-at-arms for the city council, plus three other public payrolls. They became close friends, played golf together and while so pleasurably engaged, Tubbo expounded his ideas of crime fighting and Courtney listened. On December 5, 1932, Courtney became state's attorney and promptly appointed Gilbert as his chief investigator. So began the twelve-year Courtney-Gilbert reign of power on the "West Side"— location of the Criminal Courts building.

Gilbert was indicted by a federal grand jury in 1938 for participating in a racket to maintain a high price for milk in Chicago, which was set by the big distributors. He was charged with using "unlawful threats, intimidation and acts of violence" against the drivers of milk wagons of independent distributors, and with preventing "the delivery of daily supplies of meat, bread, bakery goods, vegetables and other foods to places of business served by independent distributors" who refused to maintain trust prices for milk. The indictment was later quashed.

Gilbert and Courtney allegedly worked closely with the Syndicate as hoodlums infiltrated unions. "Few labor crimes have been solved in Chicago because of the close association between labor gangsters and law enforcing agencies," said Frank J. Loesch, president of the Chicago Crime Commission, in a 1940 radio address. "A real state's attorney could either jail, electrocute or drive these labor goons from our gates. A fearless, courageous and honest state's attorney could accomplish that feat and the war on crime would be over. This has been done in other large cities. Why hasn't it been done here? Why? Because of the close and corrupt association between labor and gangsters and law enforcing agencies."

For several days in October 1941, the *Tribune* published a series of articles on protected gambling in Cook County. The newspaper was in possession of some secret accounting sheets which Jake "Greasy Thumb" Guzik had carelessly left in a cold oven when he moved out of a flat at 20 E. Cedar Street. The *Tribune* printed photostatic copies of these balance sheets. They indicated that the Syndicate had received gross income from certain slot machines and gambling houses in suburban Cook County of $322,966 in July 1941; that the gang paid out the sum of $26,280 to various persons and officials for protection. Under the heading, "July 1941—Kick Outs," there followed a column of names, nicknames and names of villages and towns. Opposite these names were amounts of money ranging from $50 to $5,500. Heading the list, which consisted of some forty-odd names and nicknames, were that of LAIRD (Chief of Cook County Highway Police) with the figure of $400; "SKID" (Billy Skidmore) with $2,500, and TUB with $4,000. The identity of "Tub" was never publicly established. Gilbert, however, insisted that his friends did not call him "Tub," although they sometimes called him "Tubbo." The records were turned over to Courtney, and that was the end of it.

During his thirty-three years on the force, Tubbo was a busy man. His sphere of influence was impressive. He worked as a labor organizer for the Syndicate in a score of unions; he kept an eye on gambling and handbook joints (informants for the Chicago Crime Commission saw him in so many places they could not keep track of the names and dates—one of his favorite hangouts was the Gym Smoke Shop, a combination handbook and poker parlor, where he played cards many an afternoon). He was a wheelhorse in the Democratic party—when Courtney was elevated to the bench in 1944, he raised $30,000 from among the hoodlum element for the campaign of William J. Touhy. He operated his own handbook at 166 W. Washington Street with Oscar Cutter, a top commission boss for the Syndicate; in March 1949, he occupied a suite of rooms in the Sherman Hotel with Izzy Levine and Rocky Vallo, two Syndicate gamblers; he visited the Criminal Courts building almost daily, where he wandered in and out of courtrooms and chambers, conferred with runners, fixers (they work directly for judges) and bondsmen, spending considerable time in Felony Branch, where tens of thousands of felonies are reduced to misdemeanors each year. He was interested in vending machines, jukeboxes, slot machines and a variety of vices, including prostitution. In his spare time, he speculated on the grain market. His third boss, State's Attorney John S. Boyle, once described Gilbert as "probably the most efficient . . . and one of the hardest-working police officers I have ever known."

The first ominous rumble of trouble came from the Democratic *Sun-Times* in a series of front-page editorials advising the voters to defeat Gilbert: "All right, Capt. Gilbert. Let's look at the record. . . . The proof that hoodlums can get away with murder in this town is not entirely a matter of statistics. How about Ernest D. Potts, a precinct captain, killed just last March 30? He was your personal friend. You attended a political meeting with him the night he was rubbed out. He was ambushed gang style in the vestibule of his home.

He was mixed up with gambling all his life. You said you knew him for 40 years but couldn't find his killers. . . . We could go on and cite 186 more UNSOLVED gang killings. Each is evidence racketeering flourishes in Cook County."

Replied Arvey: "All they can do is smear, smear and smear some more. But voters know men. We will ask them to compare Governor Stevenson, Mayor Kennelly, State's Attorney Boyle, and Senators Lucas and Douglas with their Republican predecessors."

The kiss of death was delivered by a soft-voiced Tennessean. Senator Estes Kefauver came to town three weeks before the 1950 November elections to preside over the first hearings held in Chicago of the Senate Crime Investigating Committee.

In typical Chicago fashion, a few days before the committee convened, two important witnesses (former police captain William Drury and attorney Marvin Bas) were silenced by gang bullets. Drury's first mistake went back four years, to the murder investigation of James Ragen, owner of Continental Press, a wire service in competition with the Syndicate's Trans-American. At that time, Drury brought in Jake Guzik for questioning. Police Commissioner Prendergast shook his head and said: *"They* won't like it." Dared by Drury to take a polygraph test, Guzik lost his temper and shouted: "If I took a test, twenty of Chicago's biggest men would jump out of windows." But instead of big men jumping out of windows, Drury was thrown off the force. State's Attorney Touhy and Chief Investigator Gilbert fervently endorsed the charge of depriving Jake Guzik of his civil rights all the way to the state's supreme court before the dismissal became final. On the other hand, Touhy and Gilbert were less successful in prosecuting Guzik's associates (Lenny Patrick, Dave Yaras and William Block) who were identified by four witnesses as Ragen's murderers and indicted by the grand jury. Then, in quick order, one witness was murdered, two recanted and the other fled in panic. The indictment was dropped.

Of the hundreds of anonymous letters received by law enforcement agencies in the wake of the Drury murder, the following to Kefauver is worthy of attention: "Jake Guzik and Charles Fischetti ordered Bill Drury killed. Guzik sent word to his North Side triggermen Dominick Nuccio* and two other Dominicks [Brancata* and Di-Bella*—known as the Three Doms], and Nuccio supplied three shotguns and .45 caliber pistol for job. After killing, killers returned

* See Appendix.

130

to Nuccio's saloon and hid guns. Everyone knows the Doms' last names. Now go and get them lined up for electric chair. They have good, crooked lawyers known as BB boys [George Bieber and Mike Brodkin, Syndicate specialists]."

One of the first witnesses to testify before the senate committee was Gilbert's new boss, State's Attorney John S. Boyle, elected in 1948, who was soon confronted with his past. Under prompting by the committee's counsel, Boyle admitted that he once was attorney of record for Trans-American, but denied having any knowledge that it was gangster-owned—it had been written up in the press countless times. "They [Accardo, Guzik, Fischetti, *et al.*] never let me know about it if [they were behind it]," he said. As to the type of people that purchased Trans-American's wire service, Boyle answered: "Pretty high-class-looking people." (Boyle is currently Chief Judge of the Criminal Court.)

Commissioner Prendergast's performance before the committee was a tour de force in sheer ignorance. A random sampling of the quiz follows:

Q. Do you know of any evidence or have you an opinion as to whether the Capone group of gangsters or their successors are still operating in any fashion in Chicago?

A. I have no personal knowledge. I have nothing in my reports to indicate that they are.

Q. Do you have any information at all, Commissioner, about the Mafia?

A. No. Years ago, of course, I knew a little about the Unione Siciliano. Was that it? . . .

Q. Was there such a thing as a Mafia or a Unione Siciliano operating?

A. They always referred to it as that. But of course they were all sealed. In fact, one day we had a murder over there, a boy was walking down Oak Street with his father at 12 o'clock noon, and they shot the father down. The boy didn't see anything, the son. I said to him, "That is your father. Please give us something on it." He said nothing. He was walking down the street with his father.

. . .

Q. Do you have any files at all on it?

A. We had a squad here known as the Black Hand. I

131

suppose most of those fellows are dead now. . . . It was my thought I would love to clean up a Black Hand case, but I was never successful. I think I cleared up every other case on the books, but not a Black Hand case. I came close to it several times. . . .

Q. Suppose a ward policeman was accepting graft to protect some gambling in his ward, would this detective bureau automatically and systematically check what was going on in that ward from time to time?

A. No. I have a special squad working out of my office consisting of three men. They do my work for me.

Q. Don't you think that you might have difficulty discovering a situation in a particular ward unless you did have somebody who made a general check over the city instead of just being concentrated in one particular ward?

A. If I had the manpower [seven thousand—ten thousand today], I would love it. . . . What I should have in my department is 10 men, trained investigators. That is what I should have, not policemen. . . .

But the star of the show was Tubbo Gilbert, who testified at a closed executive session of the committee on October 17, 1950:

Q. You said you had arrested a number of gangsters. I have seen it stated around here that you have been in this office 18 years and you never had arrested any of these big-time hoodlums.

A. In the kidnapping of different men we have arrested the Touhy mob, a notorious group up in the northwest part of the county. Bankhart, in Alcatraz at the present time, Basil Bankhart—

Q. What did you arrest him for?

A. Kidnapping of Jake Factor.

Q. Who else?

A. A fellow named Kator.

Q. What for?

A. For kidnaping.

Q. All in the same group?

A. Yes, Roger Touhy. A fellow named Gus Schafer.

Q. Specifically, it is said around here that you never arrested Capone or Fischetti or Guzik. . . . You have no hesitation and no fear of arresting them?

132

A. No, I have not. In fact, I never saw Fischetti on the streets of Chicago I think but once in my life. I think he was coming out of a show with his wife. I don't know whether it was his wife. He came out with a girl. . . .

Q. Would you say this long list of unsolved murders and the situation which has prevailed over the last 20 years has been one which through lack of cooperation or lack of coordination of law enforcement has not been what it should be?

A. No. I will say this to you, Mr. Halley. I have never violated my oath of office. When these gangsters go out and kill they are as precise and detailed in their work as an architect. If an architect makes a mistake, that architect can correct the mistake. If a doctor or lawyer makes a mistake, you can dig in the archives and get some help. These men, when they go out to kill, they don't leave nothing. . . .

Q. From the point of view of public confidence . . . isn't it only natural that when people realize that a man in your position has amassed great wealth, and you have rather considerable assets, that they should lose confidence in you? . . .

A. The failure of human nature is that we are prone to believe evil about our fellow man, and especially about a peace officer.

Prompted by the fact that the Committee was in possession of his income-tax returns, Gilbert began a long, garbled recital of his triumphs in the stock and grain market. He estimated his net worth at $360,000. The Committee expressed doubt since he had reported dividends of $42,000 in 1949. Gilbert blandly explained that he was getting over 10 percent on his investment. Questioned about his gambling activities, he admitted that he was "a gambler at heart." He wagered on elections, prize fights, football, baseball, but not on horses. Asked if it was legal betting, he replied: "No, sir; it is not."

The election results on November 7, 1950, were catastrophic for the Arvey machine, not only in the county but in the city itself. Gilbert went down to ignominious defeat. His Republican opponent, John E. Babb, was elected by a majority of over 370,000 votes. (In no time at all, Babb demonstrated that he was every inch as aggressive a crime fighter as Tubbo—and not a millimeter more.)

The defeat was not Gilbert's alone. The Republicans captured several key county offices and won control of the pork-barreled Sanitary District. But the most crushing blow of all was the victory of downstater Everett M. Dirksen to the United States Senate. In typical Chicago style—the deposed Senate Majority Leader, Scott Lucas, angrily blamed Senator Kefauver for his defeat.

The day following the election, Gilbert retired from the police department and a short time later headed for Southern California. With due respect to other enterprising police captains, it must be acknowledged that although Kefauver did not conduct an investigation of the police department, Gilbert was not the only wealthy cop. Arthur Madden, Treasury agent in charge of the Chicago Intelligence Division, estimated that at least forty police captains were worth more than a million dollars each.

For a while, Arvey's career was in the balance. The defeat was characterized in the press as "the major blunder of his career as a political manager." A few months before the election, Bishop Bernard J. Shiel (a politically oriented prelate with more clout than most committeemen) had presented Arvey with the Catholic Youth Organization's Medal of Champions, with a citation which read in part: "Some of his enemies have termed him a political boss; we believe he is a political leader, a distinction with a considerable difference."

What saved Arvey from obscurity was the coincidental death of Ed Kelly on October 20, 1950. At the time of his death, Kelly was still Democratic national committeeman from Illinois. Arvey promptly assumed the title, and Joe Gill, a party elder, succeeded Arvey as chairman of the Cook County Democratic central committee, the seat of clout and patronage.

Eighteen months later, Arvey began beating the "Stevenson for President" drum in a last chance for national fame and fortune. But, of course, in the event of Stevenson's ascendency to the nation's highest office, Arvey would not personally covet any cabinet post or appointment to any other government job. "I have no further political ambitions," he said. "I would just like to practice law leisurely and not be enslaved by causes, parties or projects."

After he successfully put Stevenson over at the National Democratic Convention in 1952 (at the expense of his arch rival, Senator Kefauver), he became the nation's undisputed political general. In an emotional post-convention statement, Senator Douglas observed: "My respect for Jack Arvey has broadened and deepened. He un-

134

doubtedly surpasses anyone in American history for political wisdom, astuteness and knowledge."

Dwight D. Eisenhower—not exactly a stranger in Arvey's dreams of empires—burst the bubble. The defeat of Stevenson in 1952 and 1956 marked the end of Arvey's career in national politics. He settled down to the role of benevolent elder statesman, a role he has played with elaborate skill.

After treading a thin line for fifty years, Jake has proved his political agility. As one writer remarked: "He is smooth. They'll never catch Jake Arvey."

8

On April 5, 1955, Richard J. Daley became mayor of Chicago, the third successive Irish mayor from the Eleventh Ward. He carried twenty-nine of the city's fifty wards, and some 55 percent of the total vote. The Republicans controlled every state office, a number of county offices, the Sanitary District, twelve seats in the city council, and they had won a majority of contests in a county judicial election. Democrats, however, fairly danced in the streets. Across Chicagoland rang the triumphal cry of Alderman Paddy Bauler: "Chicago ain't ready for reform yet."

By 1965, the Daley machine controlled forty-five of the city's fifty wards, every county office except sheriff, and all but two state patronage offices. With one exception, the only Republicans on the Circuit Court bench had been elected on a coalition ticket approved by the mayor.

The "dwarfs" (in Kennelly's time, aldermen were known as dwarfs and he as "Snow White") of the city council (also known as the "Gray Wolves" for their rapacious appetites) had been somehow magically metamorphosed into a gaggle of "Snow Whites"—Daley's personal chowder-and-marching society.

On the anniversary of "Daley's Decade," thirty aldermen completely lost their heads in a marathon oratory contest that reached the heights of a *Te Deum laudamus*. Thomas E. Keane, Daley's floor leader and chairman of the powerful finance committee, introduced a resolution congratulating the mayor "for ten years of the best civic and political leadership in the United States." Keane opened the eulogistic jag with the observation that next to the President, the mayor was better known than any other American. "When you travel, and you speak of Chicago, people say, 'That is Mayor Daley's town.' "

"The city has a rendezvous with destiny," Claude Holman proclaimed, "you are the north star that leads us."

Leon Despress was reminded of St. Paul of Tarsus, who had once said, "I am a citizen of no mean city."

"I hate to speak of this and make a comparison," said Casimir Laskowski, trembling with excitement, "but once on this earth there walked a man named Jesus Christ."

Daley's victory edge in 1955 came largely from the West Side river wards, the citadel of the old Capone bloc—now known by the more genteel appellation of the West Side Bloc.

What this means in terms of underworld control in the political hierarchy is not a hazy supposition to Chicagoans who are daily briefed on the latest intramural antics of their favorite gangsters and politicians. The Syndicate's trail of influence in both political parties is a well-lighted path. Its domination of politicians in at least half of the wards is a virtual dictatorship over the voters in their domain. "The bloc's hold is so powerful," the *Daily News* concluded in 1963, "that people in its territory are afraid to vote against it—on the rare occasions when they are given a choice. . . . The ease with which the West Side blocsters get elected and re-elected to the Legislature is another indication of their strength. Six legislators linked to the bloc have served a total of 109 years in Springfield. Thanks to an unspoken deal between the two parties, they don't even worry about token opposition on election day." To Cook County Sheriff Richard B. Ogilvie, a Republican, the Bloc was "a festering sore within the body politics of this community."

But to Mayor Daley the Bloc is nonexistent—all politicians, that is Democrats and pseudo-Republicans, are fine, upstanding public servants, elected by the people who have the "right to select their leaders." At a time in history when other cities have been subjected to abrasive reforms, the results in Chicago remain dismally negative. The reasons for this opprobrious stalemate have their roots in the anachronistic power structure of ward politics vis-à-vis organized crime.

Of the wards presently under the aegis of the Syndicate, the First Ward remains one of the most representative in the system. Its formidable architects were Hinky Dink Kenna and Bathhouse John

136

Coughlin. No bigger than a flyweight—under five feet and a hundred pounds—Hinky Dink was the ward's committeeman for fifty years (1895 to 1944). And for thirty-six of those years, he was the despotic head of the ward organization as well as the protector of the most vicious gang of hoodlums ever spawned by a political machine.

Colosimo, Torrio and Capone were Kenna originals. Until Kenna took him under his protective wing, Colosimo was nothing but a cheap pimp. Torrio and Capone prospered through his good will. A trail blazer in wholesale political corruption, Kenna was the master plunderer of his time. He operated the First Ward like a fever-driven miner pursuing a rich vein of gold. The yield was blinding. Known as Lords of the Levee for their blanket protectorate over the red-light district, Kenna and Coughlin collected votes and tribute from every racket and vice operation in their bailiwick.

They were specialists in public utilities franchises and in the general legal needs of the Loop—the world's most confined center of business, commerce, finance and amusement. They provided licenses, zoning variances, permits and tax reductions with the blinding speed of a magician—and revoked them with equal alacrity. The whole train of city services moved at their command. Parking privileges, driveways, conduits, overhanging electric signs and other requests were rubber-stamped by the city council. Their patronage representatives occupied city, county, state and federal offices. Their henchmen infiltrated every inspection service department, the courts, the prosecutor's and corporation counsel's offices and the jail. They had their own policemen, prosecutors, judges, state legislators and always at least one United States congressman for speechifying on patriotic occasions.

Besides owning two saloons, Kenna ran a cigar stand at 311 South Clark Street where bookmakers laid out hundred dollar bills for nickel stogies. Coughlin was in the insurance business, which is still a top-drawer gambit for grafting politicians.

Some gamblers, bootleggers and male madams were precinct captains, and some precinct captains were gamblers, bootleggers and male madams. Whatever their origin, precinct captains had a slice of the rackets, especially bookmaking. At election time a percentage of the profits went toward the financing of campaigns in their respective precincts. Kenna took his cut in ballots. As long as they delivered the magic number of votes, they remained immune.

But since a downtown book was worth at least a couple of Texas oil wells, precinct captains fared less magnanimously with Capone

137

and his assignee, Jake "Greasy Thumb" Guzik, the Outfit's overlord in the First Ward until his death in 1956 when his protégé Gus "Shotgun" Alex succeeded him.

In 1932, Guzik established a regency to rule in the name of Kenna, who was then seventy-four and growing more feeble, mentally and physically, with each passing year. The regency used his signature for documents and his magic name to accelerate requests through city departments. When Bathhouse John died in 1938, Kenna was ordered against his wishes to assume the aldermanic post. Now eighty and almost totally senile, he was virtually carried to City Hall on inauguration night for the swearing in ceremony. When Guzik again suggested Kenna in 1943, Kelly balked. The embarrassment of having a doddering eight-five-year-old front presented to the council was too raw even for the free-wheeling mayor.

Back in his Blackstone hotel suite, The Dink was guarded by city policemen and Syndicate gunmen, including Hymie "Loud Mouth" Levin and Christian "Barney" Bertsche. He spent a good deal of his time counting the hundreds of coins he had hidden in the room for tips—he suspected his male nurses of stealing them. Finally, in 1946, at the age of eighty-eight, Michael Kenna died. He left $1,100,000 in cash to relatives who proved to be just as greedy as he was—they ignored his request for a $30,000 mausoleum for his wife and himself; instead, their graves are marked by $85 headstones.

9

As successor to Kenna's committeemanship, Guzik selected Fred M. Morelli, a millionaire who had started out in life as a doorman at the Rex Hotel, then a well-known seraglio of Duke Cooney, whoremaster of the First Ward. Morelli's rise within the Cooney organization had been impressive—from doorman to bagman to business manager to keeper of the combination to Cooney's large office safe. After Cooney's death, police conjectured that Morelli had "inherited" his sudden wealth from that safe. Morelli had also "inherited" the Century Music Company, a jukebox enterprise founded by Cooney.

Century Music and Eddie Vogel's Apex Cigarette Service (vending machines) were, so to speak, politically allied: policemen, state liquor inspectors and politicians enthusiastically endorsed the Morelli-Vogel interests. Morelli's Practical Supply Company did business with the Chicago public school. In the entertainment field, his specialties ranged from walkathons to marathons to roller derbies.

A year after Kenna's death, the First Ward was merged with the adjoining "Bloody Twentieth"—the two wards had been separated by the south branch of the Chicago river. A typical West Side ghetto ward, the Twentieth had gone from Irish to Jewish to Italian. It was the old rumbling turf of the notorious 42-Gang, whose most celebrated alumnus was Sam Giancana. It was also the site of "The Valley," noted for a century as the toughest neighborhood in Chicago. The Italian gangsters moved into the Twentieth in 1920. The next year thirteen persons were killed in election violence during a power play for control. It became the nucleus of the bipartisan Capone Bloc. In those days, Morris Eller, the Republican committeeman, was Capone's political nominee. Political foes and honest voters were put on notice that the Mob had no aversion to killing. The organization got so taut that no precinct was allowed to report more than four or five votes for the opposition.

The 1947 merger created an awkward surplus in the power structure. Anywhere else in the nation, it would have resulted in a frenzied political contest. Not in Chicago. It never even got as far as the "smoke-filled" room. The orders came direct from the landed gentry in River Forest—specifically, Accardo, Ricca, Humphreys and Guzik.

Peter Granata, the Twentieth's Republican committeeman, replaced Daniel A. Serritella; Morelli deferred to Twentieth Ward Democratic Committeeman Peter Fusco, who deferred to Frank Annunzio, then secretary-treasurer of the state CIO's Political Action Committee, a powerful arm of the Democratic party which had backed Stevenson's gubernatorial campaign. When it came time to file for alderman in November 1950, both incumbents were dropped in favor of State Representative John D'Arco, who ran unopposed.

To simplify the channels of communication between River Forest and the First Ward, Benjamin "Buddy" Jacobson was appointed executive secretary of the ward's Democratic organization. Jacobson's career dated back to the prohibition era: first as a slugger for Morris Eller, where he became a policeman assigned to the Twentieth's police district, and then as a bodyguard (while still a cop) to gangster Earl "Hymie" Weiss, a bootlegging rival of Capone. Jacobson nearly achieved gangdom immortality on October 11, 1926, when Capone machine gunners ventilated Weiss in front of Holy Name Cathedral on North State Street. Some fifty errant slugs were imbedded into the walls of the church (one of Chicago's most revered historical shrines—a must for tourists who have never before poked a finger in real gangster bullet holes). Weiss and a bootlegger associate were killed. His lawyer, chauffeur and his bodyguard—Jacobson— were painfully riddled but eventually recovered. Two years later Jacobson was convicted on a vote fraud indictment and fined $400. In 1936, he was indicted on charges of conspiring to fix a jury, but the case was nol-prossed. Along the way to his present auspicious status in Democratic circles, he picked up arrests for armed robbery, kidnaping and obstruction of justice.

While Jacobson was frantically cementing ties with Capone in the late Twenties, John D'Arco was peddling vegetables from a pushcart in the Maxwell Street market. Although Chicago police files list no arrest record for a John D'Arco or (Darco), an indictment (No. 61493) for armed robbery was returned in 1931 against a John Darco and a Sam Losurdo. Darco was acquitted and Losurdo was convicted and placed on probation. During the Kefauver hearings in 1950, an official of the Chicago Crime Commission stated that Alderman D'Arco and indicted robber Darco were one and the same.

D'Arco's initial political success was due to a quirk of nature: an irresistible likeness to Al Capone. The Syndicate's dream was to have a mayor who resembled big Alphonse.

D'Arco's grooming began in the state legislature. When he failed to distinguish himself as a second Justinian, they decided to make him an alderman in the hope that proximity to the mayor would prove inspirational. Three years later, he collected his courage and rose to make his first public statement, a three-paragraph tribute to a late friend which he read from a slip of paper. Nine years later, he again publicly cleared his throat, this time to protest against the proposed West Side campus of the University of Illinois which displaced a number of consistent voters.

The appointment of Frank Annunzio as acting committeeman in 1948 was praised by the press and interpreted as an omen of reform. The fact that a political novice had inherited the seat of clout in the city's most tightly hoodlum-controlled ward did not arouse suspicion. Annunzio's record was clean, they reasoned, so he had to be straight.

140

Besides, there was no evidence of criminal associations. No one questioned the fact that he was a director of the Italian Welfare Council—along with Syndicate attorneys Anthony V. Champagne and Joseph I. Bulger and labor racketeer Frank Esposito—because it was a charitable organization which operated a summer camp for Italian children at Pistakee Bay. (It was dissolved in 1954, three months after Champagne succeeded Annunzio as president, at a time when its resources were estimated at $400,000.)

Described in the press as a protégé of Jane Addams, the new committeeman was ticketed for a fast ride up the political elevator when Stevenson appointed him director of the Illinois Department of Labor in 1949. It took the governor three years to discover that Annunzio was also First Ward committeeman, a conflict of interest which had received considerable publicity in Chicago newspapers. Faced with the governor's ultimatum of resigning as labor director or as First Ward committeeman, he chose the state job—D'Arco succeeded to the committeemanship. Then, to make matters worse, it was further revealed a few months later that Annunzio was in partnership with D'Arco and Jacobson in Anco, Inc., a Loop insurance business.

"In Chicago," said the *Sun,* "politicians have long peddled insurance as well as influence. So the political insurance firm, Anco, Inc., formed by Frank Annunzio and two unsavory characters . . . represents no departure from precedent. . . . Until that association was exposed, Annunzio enjoyed an excellent reputation. . . . That he—director of the state department of labor—would go into the insurance business at all, with or without D'Arco and Jacobson, is even more difficult to comprehend."

Annunzio explained: "It was a legitimate business transaction. . . . I personally feel that I am being persecuted because of my nationality and nothing else. . . . Every politician and his grandmother were doing business in the First Ward."

To Stevenson's distress, Annunzio was not the only director in trouble early in 1952, the year the governor made his first presidential bid. Faulty state inspections were blamed for the death of 119 miners in a West Frankfort mine disaster; bribery in the Agriculture Department had permitted the Syndicate to operate a multimillion dollar horse meat racket, and bribery in the Revenue Department had resulted in the counterfeiting of cigarette tax stamps which had netted the Syndicate an estimated $13 million.

141

Although he admitted a ten-year friendship with Jacobson, Annunzio denied having any knowledge of his police record or criminal associations.

Along about then, the Syndicate thoughtfully provided D'Arco and Jacobson with a helpmate, an ex-convict named Pasqualino Marchone, who after serving a prison term for robbery in the 1930s changed his name to Pat Marcy. His brother Paul, also an ex-robber, became an administrative assistant on the Cook County Board of Zoning Appeals.

Considering the pressure placed on the Stevenson administration only a few months before the convention, it was inevitable that Annunzio would be sidelined. In the first week of March 1952, Annunzio tendered his resignation and received a "Dear Frank" reply from the governor.

His retirement lasted twelve years. In the interim, his image was refurbished with public service awards. For his work with the Catholic Youth Organization, he received the CYO Bishop Sheil Medal; he received an award from the Chicago Council on Religious and Racial Discrimination for his civil rights efforts, and the Italian government conferred upon him the Star of Solidarity for his work in fostering good relations between the United States and Italy.

In 1964, a new Frank Annunzio emerged as the Democratic candidate for Congress from the Seventh District, which includes Chicago's Loop and Near West Side. During the campaign, Annunzio said that he thought Americans of Italian ancestry had been unfairly linked with crime syndicate hoodlums: "I feel our image has been created unfairly." His political sponsor was Alderman Vito Marzullo, political boss of the Twenty-fifth Ward. (According to a federal report, Marzullo was allegedly an associate of Giancana, Humphreys, Alex and other Outfit moguls, and "holds a position in the organization similar to D'Arco.")

10

A leader of the notorious West Side Bloc during his twenty-two years in the legislature (six years as a Republican representative and sixteen years as a Democratic senator), Roland "Libby" Libonati polled 89 percent of the votes in his Congressional "boat" race in 1957 (Annunzio had to settle for 82 percent in 1964). A criminal lawyer with a record of two hundred murder trials ("never got a death penalty, thank God!") and a few judges, Libonati is the epitome of a machine politician—he not only represented the Syndicate but gave all appearances of being a Mafioso himself.

Asked in a newspaper interview in 1957 about his friendship with Al Capone, Libonati replied: "Mr. Capone showed me great respect as a person of Italian extraction who represented one of the pioneer families in Chicago, and naturally I . . . ah . . . returned . . . I returned. . . I treated him in accordance with . . . I treated him with like respect as I would treat any American. Let's put it this way: He treated me with great respect and admiration and I never did anything not to merit his respect. You know, politically that man was not a politician. If people treat me nice, I treat them nice." Libonati also believed that Tony Accardo and Paul Ricca were "charitable" and "patriotic" fellows.

Having been photographed at a Cubs baseball game with Capone and "Machine Gun" Jack McGurn in 1931, Libonati, who was hardly in a position to debate the issue, managed to dress it up for sentimental readers: "I was very proud when he [Capone] asked me at the ball game to speak to his son, and under the circumstances today I would still be proud to speak to any man's son."

A few months before his "proud" day at Wrigley Field, a police raid on his campaign headquarters had bagged twenty gangsters and politicians, including Paul Ricca, Ralph Pierce, Murray Humphreys, Frank Rio, August Demore, a brother of "Machine Gun" McGurn, Alderman Al Prignano, Saul Tannenbaum, a member of the city's attorney's office and Libonati. Speeding to the rescue with writs and bail bonds were Alderman William V. Pacelli, State Senator James B. Leonardo and City Sealer Serritella.

Elected to the legislature for his first term a few days later, Libonati's arrival in Springfield was greeted by a furious debate about impounding the ballots in his district—it remained a debate. In the next twenty-two years, Libonati, who had a flair for unintentional comedy (dubbed Mr. Malaprop), became a powerful member of the West Side Bloc—he opposed crime legislation proposed by the Chicago Crime Commission and backed bills beneficial to gangsters and gamblers. One piece of legislation paid off handsomely: In the closing days of the general assembly in 1949, Libonati and eight blocsters pushed through legislation authorizing harness racing at Sportsman's Park. It later developed that all nine legislators or their wives were stockholders, having acquired thousands of shares at the insider's price of ten cents each. In the first two years of racing, their investment realized a profit of 1,650 percent.

143

As Mr. Malaprop, Libonati won the hearts of a number of quote-loving newspapermen as well as readers. "He rattled the walls at Springfield with his free-wheeling attacks on the English language," one columnist recalled during the 1957 congressional campaign. Some of his more ludicrous quotes were repeated *ad nauseum:* "Nobody can speak asunder of the governor's reputation. . . . Not by any creeping of the imagination. . . . I am trying not to make any honest mistakes. . . . The moss is on the pumpkin. . . ." (A debate between Libonati and Daley would sound like an old Amos and Andy radio script. Some of Daley's more memorable malapropisms include: "Alcoholics Unanimous. . . . I resent the insinuendoes. . . . Once they get the atom harassed. . . . [President Johnson] is one of the truly great living Americans of our time. . . . That isn't even true enough to answer. . . . Chicago [will] become the aviation crosswords of the world. . . . For the enlightment and edification and hallucination of the aldermen from the 50th ward. . . . And so, together with the University of Chicago the city will march on to new platitudes of learning. . . . Walking pedestrians [and] tantrum bicycles. . . .")

Libonati, who received considerable notice in the Kefauver report as a "bosom pal" of Capone and a leader of the West Side Bloc, was presented with a gold-inscribed watch by Governor Stevenson in 1950 for his legislative work in behalf of the Civil Service Protective Association. (Chicago is most lavish with awards, as noted by *Daily News* Columnist Royko: "Politicians, businessmen, civic leaders, athletes, and anybody else with a clean suit gets a plaque or scroll in recognition of what they have done, or what they haven't done. Anyone who can't win at least one award during the year gets the shakes.")

As a prominent slumlord, Libonati has contributed a few awards of his own, mostly to courts for violations of the building code. Another noteworthy Libonati award included a bill he introduced to exempt the office of former State Auditor Orville E. Hodge from statutory limitation on spending during the first two months of a two-year budget period. This generous little proviso made it possible for Hodge to steal $2.5 million from the taxpayers and eventually earned him a stretch in prison.

When Libonati arrived in Washington in January 1958, he was met at the station by his top aide, Anthony P. Tisci, a Chicago attorney. But Tisci was not just another Chicago attorney trying to crash through a political back door. A young man of twenty-eight,

144

reasonably handsome in a silk suit, he had the good fortune in 1957 of falling in love with Bonita Lucille Giancana, the nineteen-year-old daughter of the man who dispatched Libonati to Washington. Following their wedding in 1959, the couple moved into Papa Momo's rambling Oak Park manse, where they resided until 1963. It was obvious even to the most casual political observer that son-in-law Tisci enjoyed a rather sharp edge over congressional boss Libonati.

Libonati had been in Washington less than a week before a vigorous behind-the-scene movement was launched to place him on the powerful Judiciary Committee, much to the consternation of a number of committee members who did not relish the idea of having him among their ranks. Of particular concern was the fact that—in view of his Chicago connections—his reelection would be assured session after session, with the possible results that within a certain number of years he might become chairman of the committee, or at least one of its most influential members. Libonati's sponsor was Congressman Thomas J. O'Brien of Chicago, a member of the committee, who enjoyed a "very fine reputation" in Washington, a condition not substantiated by his previous performance as Sheriff of Cook County—the county was so wide-open that the press referred to him as Sheriff "Blind Tom" O'Brien.

Libonati's movements in Washington were a matter of grave concern to the Justice Department as the following excerpts from a secret federal report indicate:

—On May 23, 1960, Murray "The Camel" Humphreys was observed by FBI agents arriving in Washington, D.C., by airplane. He went to the Woodner Hotel, 3636 Sixteenth Street, and when he left this hotel, he was carrying a package about 5″ × 3″ × 2″ wrapped in blue and white gift wrapping paper. Humphreys proceeded by taxicab to 224 C Street N.E. and entered the building. The Congressional Directory reflects that 224 C Street N.E. is the local address for Congressman Roland V. Libonati, 7th District, Chicago. Humphreys left this address about an hour later, at which time he was not observed to be carrying any package. He returned to the Woodner Hotel and went to a room registered to Murray H. Olf, reputed big-time gambler, and a Syndicate Washington lobbyist. Later that same evening Humphreys went to the lobby of the Hamilton Hotel, 14th and K Streets N.W. At 8:30 P.M. he made a telephone call on one of the house phones in the lobby

145

and at 8:35 P.M. he was joined by Congressman Thomas J. O'Brien, 6th District of Chicago, in a small room off the lobby. About twenty minutes later he left this room and on the morning of May 24, 1960, he returned to Chicago.

—Advised on about August 24, 1960, that Roland V. Libonati, Congressman, 7th District of Chicago, who is on the House Judiciary Committee, visited the United States Penitentiary at Terre Haute, Indiana. Informant said that the visit of Libonati was approved by the United States Bureau of Prisons in Washington, D.C. The informant said that the visit to Terre Haute by Libonati was in regard to an article that Libonati wrote for the Congressional Record which appeared in the Friday issue, September 2, 1960. After Libonati inspected the penitentiary he asked to visit with Paul De Lucia [alias Paul "The Waiter" Ricca] and Frank Keenan, both serving sentences from Chicago for income tax violation. Informant said that at all times during the visit a Bureau of Prisons employee was present and that when De Lucia and Libonati met there was a disgusting display of affection by Libonati as Libonati hugged and kissed De Lucia [an ancient Mafia ritual still practiced when a lesser mafioso greets an elder under unusual circumstances].

—Advised in the fall of 1960 that Murray Humphreys had made arrangements with Congressman Roland V. Libonati to visit Paul De Lucia in the United States Penitentiary at Terre Haute. Humphreys himself actually talked to De Lucia subsequent to Libonati's visit and obtained information that De Lucia was very happy about the Congressman's visit.

—Advised in November of 1960 that at that time Murray Humphreys was apparently in frequent communication and personal contact with Congressman Libonati. The purpose of these contacts was to expedite the early release of Paul De Lucia from the United States Penitentiary at Terre Haute. [De Lucia served twenty-seven months of a three-year sentence—released October 1, 1961.]

—Advised that Humphreys and his associates have become very concerned about the investigations of them by the FBI and they are interested in taking measures designed to hinder surveillances and other investigations of the FBI. Humphreys is very concerned that the leaders of organized crime in Chicago are not convicted by the

146

Federal Government and is concerned with taking necessary steps to prevent further successful prosecutions of organized criminals. In this regard Humphreys has been meeting with Congressman Libonati with the result that Libonati has been making contact with the Department of Immigration and Naturalization in order to have that department sanction a bill which provides that if an alien has a son who has served in the Armed Forces of the United States they are not subject to deportation.

—On February 17, 1961, Murray Humphreys was observed by FBI agents sitting in a corner of the lobby of the Hamilton Hotel in Washington, D.C. conversing with Congressman Thomas J. O'Brien. A short time thereafter Humphreys left the hotel and went to the residence of Roland V. Libonati, 224 C Street N.E.

—Advised in the fall of 1960 that Murray Humphreys was in contact with John T. "Sandy" O'Brien, International Vice President, International Brotherhood of Teamsters, and an official of the Teamsters Local in Chicago. Humphreys was interested in obtaining a large yearly contribution from the union for the small camp for underprivileged boys located north of Chicago [Colona, Wisconsin] which Congressman Roland V. Libonati has an interest in. Humphreys felt that the Teamsters should show their appreciation to Libonati by making much larger contributions to the camp in view of the help which Libonati had given to the Teamsters Union in some unknown manner concerning investigation by Congress of the monitors appointed in Federal Court over the Teamsters Union.

Philanthropy among underprivileged boys is not only good immediate politics but carries a longevity clause. There are middle-aged people in Chicago today who still remember Big Bill Thompson's annual school picnic with misty-eyed nostalgia. It is also not bad economics, particularly if on a big enough scale to interest a master-fixer like Humphreys. The camp, which occupied a portion of Libonati's 188-acre farm, was supported by newspapers, the Post Commanders Club and philanthropic organizations throughout the state—not to mention politically-minded unions. Libonati's Wisconsin neighbor was James DeGeorge, a high-ranking mafioso of the old school, who took Libonati's animals onto his own farm in the winter.

By 1963, Libonati had run out his string as indicated in another secret federal report: "Congressman Roland V. Libonati stepped down on orders from Sam Giancana. It came to a head in January, 1963, when Libonati made a public announcement of his resignation because of the poor health of his wife and his desire to resume his law practice in Chicago. Giancana had already selected Frank Annunzio to replace Libonati. Annunzio will follow dictate of Mob."

An earlier secret federal report on West Side politicians indicated the Syndicate's attitude: "Advised in February, 1962 that Sam Giancana has emphatically instructed his associates and lieutenants not to call 'these politicians' or meet them at their houses. They were advised to meet 'these politicians' some place away from their homes because if they [the Syndicate] lost these men they 'were dead.' Among the individuals indicated by Giancana were Frank Annunzio; Anthony Girolami, Twenty-eighth Ward Democratic committeeman; Vito Marzullo, Twenty-fifth Ward Democratic alderman and committeeman; Robert L. Massey, Thirty-sixth Ward Democratic committeeman, elected to Circuit Court in 1964; Bernard Neistein, Twenty-ninth Ward Democratic committeeman and state senator; Anthony De Tolve, state senator from First Ward district and nephew-in-law of Giancana; Peter C. Granata, First Ward Republican committeeman and state legislator; Elmer Conti, Mayor of Elmwood Park, Illinois."

Libonati's unexpected announcement prompted the usual rash of speculation in the press. Asked whether he was disturbed over reports of hoodlum influence in Libonati's retirement, Mayor Daley answered: "As I understand it, Congressman Libonati has expressed a desire to retire to the committeemen in his district. The man says he wants to retire. I think this speaks for itself. I served with him in the [state] Senate and I know that he has always tried to do a good job for the people of this state and country." Annunzio also received the Mayor's blessings: "He did a very fine job as state labor director. He is a great leader in the Italian-American community. He is a fine family man. I know his wife and family very well. I think he will do an outstanding job in the United States Congress."

The Mayor's comforting observations failed to answer the question uppermost in the minds of law enforcement officials: Why had Giancana snipped Libonati's string? One intriguing morsel of scuttlebutt suggested to this writer by a high administrative official was that Robert F. Kennedy, who at that time was unquestionably the most powerful Attorney General ever to grace that office, had issued an

148

ultimatum to City Hall: If Libonati returned to Congress, Kennedy would personally see to it that he went to jail. The Kennedy dictum was relayed to the First Ward organization and on to Giancana, who officially tossed Libonati the black ball.

Two significant developments, one prior and the other subsequent to the alleged Kennedy ultimatum, lend credence to this theory. The first development concerns Giancana's petition in the federal court, seeking an injunction against the FBI which he claimed was violating his civil rights by constant surveillance. Shortly after Giancana instituted the action, Libonati introduced a bill in Congress which would have made it a crime for federal agents to keep gangsters and criminals under surveillance. The bill provided for a penalty of ten years in prison and a fine of $5,000, or both.

Interviewed by John Madigan, a Chicago television newscaster, Libonati said: "Yes. I know Giancana. Of course, my bill would cover him. It would cover anyone whose constitutional rights were violated in surveillance or investigation. And, I'll tell you something, there's a lot of interest down here [Capitol Hill] in my bill."

While Congressman Libonati was trying to hobble the Attorney General's investigators, Administrative Assistant Tisci, a federally paid employee, was diligently laboring in behalf of his father-in-law's civil rights, including a maudlin quasilegal plea on a television news program.

Subsequent to the announcement of his retirement, Libonati sponsored a resolution calling on the House Judiciary Committee to investigate the alleged "persecution" of Teamsters Union boss James R. Hoffa by the Justice Department. The action was aimed at Robert F. Kennedy, who had resigned as Attorney General to run for the United States Senate from New York. Among Libonati's early supporters were Congressmen George Meader of Michigan, Basil L. Whitener of North Carolina and Michael Feighan of Ohio, who was resentful toward the Justice Department because it had failed to find legal grounds to bar actor Richard Burton from accompanying Elizabeth Taylor to the United States.

Chairman Emanuel Celler (D-N.Y.) refused to convene the full Judiciary Committee to take up the matter, charging that Libonati's resolution had been prepared by the Teamsters Union—a kit of documents distributed by teamsters representatives at the Democratic National Convention at Atlantic City included one which was the same as the Libonati resolution—and that Libonati and his co-sponsors were acting as a pipeline for Hoffa's bitter feud with Kennedy. The drive to kick off the congressional hearing to correspond with Kennedy's senatorial campaign was spearheaded by Sidney Zagri, a top Hoffa aide and lobbyist.

Even as a lame-duck congressman, Libonati was powerful enough to secure an eighteen to fourteen vote over the objection of Celler and the administration. Two weeks later, a new resolution by Ohio Congressman William M. McCulloch was approved by a twenty-one to thirteen vote. It called for an inquiry of the Justice Department without mentioning Hoffa. "This might be called the Hoffa resolution," Celler told the press. "Nobody asked for the investigation except those involved with the Teamsters Union." The McCulloch resolution was a compromise to win the approval of some of the Democratic majority. It called for a special ten-man subcommittee to investigate the Justice Department's activities "concerning individual rights and liberties as guaranteed by the Constitution and the laws of the United States regardless of the administration in power."

Libonati's parting blow at Kennedy was also a slap at Celler, who had previously tabled Libonati's bill to curtail the surveillance and investigative activities of the Justice Department. That the investigation was not eventually successful does not alter the ominous fact that a hoodlum-controlled lame-duck congressman was capable of outmaneuvering the chairman of one of the most powerful committees in Congress.

Frank Annunzio's Democratic nomination to succeed Libonati in the Seventh Congressional district (including the First, Twenty-fifth, Twenty-sixth and Twenty-seventh Wards, and parts of the Second and Eleventh Wards) was tantamount to election. The GOP candidate, a Ray Wolfram, turned out to be a mystery man with no address or telephone. "I'd sort of like to meet him," Annunzio told the press. "Maybe we could debate." But it was not the first time the Republican Party had trouble finding and keeping track of a candidate in the district. Two years earlier, the party had picked Wolfram to run for the state senate after a phantom candidate was uncovered. At that time, Wolfram was described as a 49-year-old bachelor manager of two apartment buildings.

Annunzio not only retained Tisci but boosted his salary from $13,000 to $19,000 a year. No one seemed particularly disturbed

150

with the *status quo* until May 1965, when the Justice Department haled Giancana before a federal grand jury investigating organized crime in Chicago. Subpoenaed along with the gangster was son-in-law Tisci, who invoked the Fifth Amendment on all three of his appearances before the grand jury.

When the Better Government Association asked the Chicago Bar Association to recommend his disbarment, Tisci resigned his federal administrative post because of a "heart ailment" on the "advice of his physician."

"I'm hoping for the day when the American people will mature to the point that the sins of the father are not heaped upon the children," Annunzio observed upon receipt of Tisci's resignation—he had earlier stated that he would not fire Tisci.

However, the sins of the father-in-law were not at issue, as the St. Louis police discovered seven weeks later when they were alerted to a high-level crime conclave scheduled in their city. Among the invited delegates were Nick Civella, a rackets boss in Kansas City, Missouri; Frank "Buster" Wortman, bank robber, terrorist, ex-convict and racketeer in East St. Louis, Illinois; Tony Accardo, and Joseph Aiuppa. Alerted nine days in advance to the impending conclave by federal authorities, St. Louis police intercepted communications dealing with politics, a labor union, Nevada gambling projects and building construction plans. Bagged in the police raid were Pat Marcy, secretary to D'Arco; Charles Nicosia, a worker in the Illinois Attorney General's office; Anthony Esposito of Melrose Park, and Anthony Tisci, the prodigal son-in-law.

11

The adventures of Alderman-Committeeman John D'Arco continued to interest federal investigators. A few excerpts from a secret government file follow:

—On July 21, 1959, John D'Arco was contacted in his office on the 23rd floor at 100 North La Salle Street by [two FBI agents]. D'Arco was questioned concerning the fact that when Sam Giancana returned from Mexico on June 15, 1959, it was learned that he was carrying a piece of paper containing the names of approximately fifteen of the major hoodlums in this city along with the names of John D'Arco and Buddy Jacobson. D'Arco claimed that

151

he had no idea as to the significance or meaning of this list of names. He refused to speculate concerning its significance. He admitted that he was acquainted with Sam Giancana, but claimed that this was for the reason that Giancana grew up in D'Arco's ward and that they have been friends from youth. Concerning the fact that the first name on the list appeared to refer to Gus Alex, D'Arco refused to comment as to whether he was acquainted with Alex on four occasions. When informed that the FBI would refrain from making inquiries concerning his connections with the hoodlums appearing on this list for a week or so until he had a chance to learn of the significance of this list and pass such information on to the FBI, D'Arco replied that the agents had a job to do and they should do it as they saw fit. When told that the FBI would prefer to do this job without causing D'Arco any embarrassment, D'Arco replied: "You guys can't embarrass me in this town. I'm a big man here and if my constituents are satisfied with the way I represent them, I don't have to worry about nobody else."

—Advised that Gus Alex and Frank Ferraro [deceased 1964] frequently meet with John D'Arco at Postl's Health Club located on one of the top floors at 188 West Randolph Street and the Normandy Inn located on the ground floor of the building at 100 North La Salle; the building also houses D'Arco's offices.

—Advised on October 3, 1961, that Gus Alex and Eddie Vogel occasionally have conferences at Postl's Health Club with Alderman John D'Arco, Buddy Jacobson and Pat Marcy.

—Advised that between thirty and forty handbooks operated in the loop area, and in order for a bookmaker to operate he first had to make proper connections either with Gus Alex or John D'Arco.

—Advised in May, 1961, that many of the strip joints located on South Wabash and South State Streets in the First Ward of the city of Chicago give twenty per cent of their profits to Chicago area hoodlums, and over and above this pay a sum between $2,000 and $3,000 per month to Pat Marcy, who in turn furnishes this money to John D'Arco.

—Advised that the Chicago politician closest to hoodlum Murray Humphreys, Gus Alex, Frank Ferraro, Eddie Vogel and others is Alderman John D'Arco. These hoodlums meet frequently in the office of Pat Marcy, secretary to D'Arco, and are in close and frequent contact with D'Arco. They utilize his services whenever they desire that favors be done for them by public officials and politicians. In this regard, advised that D'Arco is generally the intermediary they use to contact public officials and local judges. Advised also that D'Arco is the individual they use whenever they attempt to obtain favors through Mayor Richard J. Daley of Chicago. In this regard, advised that Mayor Daley, particularly since the police scandal of 1960, has rejected attempts by D'Arco to obtain favors for the hoodlums. D'Arco assumes a subservient attitude when in the company of the above-mentioned hoodlums and there is no doubt that he considers their orders to be mandates to him.

—Advised that many merchants in the First Ward . . . must make contributions to the Democratic Ward Picnic sponsored each year by D'Arco in order to obtain the usual city services . . . such as garbage removal, etc. In many instances merchants in the First Ward find that they must take insurance from D'Arco's insurance company, Anco, Inc., in order to obtain such services.

—Advised in the summer of 1961 that Alderman John D'Arco . . . acts as a collector of the "Outfit's" money from the strip and clip joints in the loop area when Gus Alex is out of town. Advised that Joseph J. Laino helps D'Arco collect this money. It is noted that Laino currently is an investigator for the Sanitary District and formerly worked in D'Arco's office as a secretary.

A career payroller, Laino was rousted by Los Angeles police officers in 1953 while sharing a room in the Beverly-Wilshire Hotel with John Capone,* brother of the Mob's patron saint. Also present in the room was movie tough-guy George Raft—the original Method actor who goes directly to the source for his characterizations. Laino explained that he was employed as an inspector for the Chicago Street Department, and that his duties involved the dispensing of political favors such as passing on contracts and getting buildings approved. He said he had held political jobs in Chicago for the past twenty years, but neglected to mention his previous job as an investigator for the Revenue Department and the fact that he had been fired for his part in the cigarette tax stamp scandal. For a while

* See Appendix.

153

he was Deputy Clerk in the Superior Court, then he went to work for Frank Chesrow, president of the Sanitary District.

D'Arco's political flotilla went sailing corruptly along until 1962 without making too many turbulent waves. By then a man of substance, politically and financially, the former pushcart peddler nearly torpedoed his good-ship lollipop with a handshake.

It happened the afternoon of November 29, 1962, while the alderman was enjoying a late lunch with his boss in a North Riverside restaurant. They had appropriated a small dining room and had installed a burly type to guard its entrance. Then in walked one of J. Edgar Hoover's minions, unannounced.

"Ho, ho, ho, it's Moe," cried the agent, grinning at a startled Giancana. "And good afternoon to you, John. How've you been?" The agent stuck out his right hand and D'Arco automatically grasped it in a firm handshake. However, the reptilian glare from the other side of the table made him jerk away his hand as if he had clutched a live coal. The agent strolled out, and moments later Giancana scurried from the restaurant, sans dining partner.

The next day, D'Arco shuffled into a city council meeting and complained to his old friend and colleague, Vito Marzullo, that he was ailing. "I think I better go to the hospital," he said. That evening he entered Mother Cabrini Memorial Hospital and the word went out that he had suffered a heart attack. A week later, the First Ward Regular Democratic organization announced that their beloved leader was too ill to run for a fourth term as alderman. From his hospital bed, D'Arco told a visitor that his doctors had advised him to give up politics: "They told me if I didn't, I'd wind up in a box."

His successor was to be none other than that busy-busy senator, Anthony J. DeTolve, who had been reelected to a third term in the State Senate five weeks earlier. DeTolve had succeeded D'Arco to the senate in 1951, and now he was ready to occupy his city council chair.

However, D'Arco's apparent downfall was due to more than an indiscreet handshake. For example, his City Hall influence had diminished considerably with the growing interest of Attorney General Kennedy in Chicago politics. Mayor Daley's increasing deafness to hoodlum-inspired requests was hurting the Syndicate in its most sensitive spot—the pocketbook. And for the first time in the history

154

of the Justice Department, J. Edgar Hoover was motivated to square off against organized crime—it took an Attorney General with a brother in the White House to plant the incentive. Suddenly, FBI agents were raiding bookmakers and gambling dens. Although nobody of any importance was arrested, the raids were a costly nuisance which generated a certain degree of heat in the underworld. D'Arco should have been powerful enough to stave off, at least to some extent, the federal crackdown on rackets in his ward. Public disclosures of his mob connections had tarnished his image and consequently reduced his effectiveness as a frontline spokesman.

While D'Arco's image had survived for twelve years, DeTolve's lasted eleven weeks—not because Giancana was his uncle by marriage, but because he refused to be interviewed by the press. *American* reporter Sam Blair dogged DeTolve's footsteps for a week in an effort to interview him. After leaving a dozen messages at DeTolve's law office and home, Blair finally received a telephone call from the candidate. "Let's get one thing straight," DeTolve told Blair. "I haven't been hiding. I'm just busy, all the time busy." When Blair suggested that all he wanted was a few minutes of his time for an interview, DeTolve replied: "Well, I can't be running around talking to reporters all the time. I'm busy, all the time busy." The senator did hint, however, that his program would include the advancement of cultural enterprises: "I go for all that cultural stuff." From then on newspapers referred to the senator as Anthony J. "Busy-Busy" DeTolve.

Meanwhile, the Republicans put up their token candidate. He was Thomas J. Curran, a former member of the West Side Bloc in the legislature, who embarked on a whirlwind schedule—he made one speech when a "bunch of women" asked him to address them "out there in that Hull House." Curran, who had voted to legalize bingo "for the benefit of the poor people," saw "zoning" as the big issue in the aldermanic campaign. "The way I see it," he said, "is that sometimes they make residential zones into business zones and sometimes they make business zones into residential zones and that has got to stop. It gets confusing." (Of course, he was right.)

Four weeks before the election, Sam Blair compiled the following box score for DeTolve: "Number of speeches—0; number of campaign posters displayed—0; number of meetings with ward workers— 0; number of campaign pamphlets distributed—0; number of radio and television appearances—0; number of interviews with the press

—0." Blair then toured the First Ward questioning twenty-five citizens about their voting plans. The censensus was: "What's a DeTolve?"

Interviewed by the *Tribune* on the reports that DeTolve's selection had been dictated by crime syndicate leaders, Mayor Daley insisted it was a matter for the voters to decide. Asked if following Blair's articles he had "second thoughts on DeTolve," Daley said: "The greatest democracy is when the people have the right to select their leaders. This is the right of the people. I repeat I talked to Mrs. D'Arco and she said that because of his health he would not run." Did the mayor understand that D'Arco would remain as the ward's Democratic committeeman? "Yes, I haven't heard otherwise. Is there anything wrong with DeTolve? Has he a record? He is a member of the Illinois Senate." Apprised by a reporter that DeTolve was a member of the notorious West Side Bloc and a relative and associate of hoodlums, the mayor angrily replied: "An implication. Is there any proof or evidence of this? Is relationship with anyone the basis for condemnation?" When a reporter suggested that such inferences could affect the Democratic party, of which Daley was county chairman, the mayor failed to make the connection. "I don't think that's true," he said. "Aren't there newspapermen who have evidences of bad characters? Here's a man who is a graduate of a law school. They didn't disqualify him from the Senate because of his relationship." (When the government placed a mail cover on Giancana's Oak Park residence during the Kefauver hearings, his mail was directed to DeTolve's address.) Would DeTolve remain on the staff of the city corporation counsel's office where he had been a patronage payroller for more than twelve years? "Yes," said Daley, "I assume that, like every other city employee, he's doing a great job." (Busy-Busy was busily "moonlighting" as a lawyer, a violation for which he had been briefly fired from that same office in 1951.)

The mayor's paternalism could not save DeTolve from Blair's humorous barbs—he literally laughed DeTolve out of the race. Even Uncle Momo was soon disenchanted with the buffoon antics of his piccolo-playing (noted for his solos at gay Springfield parties) nephew. Fifty-five hours before the polls were scheduled to open, two hundred precinct captains and workers gathered in a Loop hotel and listened in stunned silence as DeTolve announced he was withdrawing from the campaign to protect the party from further embarrassment. "In the city council, I would be a rookie anyway," DeTolve offered by way of explanation. "My loud voice is needed in the state

156

Senate, where the Democrats are in trouble. You are not going to vote for me. You are going to elect Mike FioRito as the alderman of the First Ward."

Accustomed to following orders, the ward organization quickly endorsed FioRito, a political unknown, as their eleventh-hour candidate. As the city metaphorically scratched its head, the *Daily News* concluded: "If we knew root and all of this, we'd know the answer to all the questions about the mysterious half-world of Chicago."

If the publicity-shy Syndicate was trying to "cool it," FioRito was a rather unfortunate choice. A resident of Wilmette, he claimed he had established a legal residence more than a year before at an uncle's home on the Northwest Side, which satisfied the requirement of a year's residence in the city, and had moved into the Conrad Hilton Hotel the previous month, which gave him the necessary thirty days in the ward.

Meanwhile, another last-minute candidate materialized, Mrs. Florence Scala, a "peppery" little housewife who was backed by Sheriff Ogilvie.

For the next two days and nights, the "magnanimous foot soldiers," as DeTolve called the precinct captains, marched through the ward, instructing in Italian, Greek, Chinese, Spanish, Yiddish—and English—how to write "Michael FioRito," or an acceptable facsimile. Election day (February 28, 1963) produced no surprises: FioRito won by a 9 to 1 margin.

Mrs. Scala later revealed in confidence to a high police official that following her election defeat D'Arco's brother-in-law, Joe "Pep" Briatta, told her: "You know, if anybody really had a chance they would wind up in a sewer. We knew you couldn't win and we let you have what you got."

Following the election, Sheriff Ogilvie called for a grand jury investigation of the new alderman's registration credentials. In a letter to State's Attorney Daniel P. Ward requesting the grand jury probe, Ogilvie bitterly charged: ". . . there is no more flagrant example of crime syndicate interference with the free election processes than exists in the First Ward, and this goes for both parties."

The inquiry centered on a strange affidavit filed with the Chicago Board of Election Commissioners on January 28 by an official of the Conrad Hilton Hotel. It purportedly listed fifty-nine "permanent residents" of the hotel. The state's attorney concluded that a typewriter in the offices of the election board had been used to add the names of FioRito and his wife to the affidavit. A week later, Ward closed the

157

investigation with a report that FioRito had registered in the First Ward through an "irregularity." However, he could not determine whether a crime had been committed in the registration procedure.

When FioRito was sworn in as alderman on April 17, Republican Alderman John J. Hoellen attempted to challenge FioRito's qualifications but was shouted down by the Democratic majority. His resolution was shunted to the rules committee in a parliamentary maneuver to kill it.

After a talk with Attorney General Kennedy, Daley acceded to the demands of Alderman Hoellen and issued an ultimatum to FioRito: Either swear that he met all legal qualifications for the office or resign. Leading Democrats, including D'Arco and Frank Chesrow, pleaded with the mayor to withdraw his ultimatum, but he did not budge. FioRito resigned.

Two months later Sam Blair found D'Arco in his office at 100 N. LaSalle with "Alderman" still painted on the door, performing practically the same duties he had when the title was official. First Ward matters needing council attention were handled by Vito Marzullo.

Donald Parrillo, a thirty-two-year-old banker, was selected to succeed to D'Arco's council chair. "There's no connection between me and the crime syndicate," Parrillo hastily told the press. "Life is too short. . . . My past and present are an open book." Besides, he came from a "wealthy family" and would neither solicit nor accept campaign contributions. And for those cynical reporters who might uncover a closed book, Parrillo offered the standard rejoinder: "Because I am of Italian birth, I have been subjected to persecution, insinuations, and innuendo."

A son of the late William Parrillo, former Twenty-fifth Ward Republican committeeman and West Side blocster, he first came to public notoriety in the early 1950s when it was disclosed that he was vice-president of the Meadowmoor Dairy, a hoodlum-controlled company that received the personal attention of such Syndicate moguls as Ross Prio, Murray Humphreys, Phil Katz and Samuel Lewis. The sales manager was Harry Hochstein.

From this pristine beginning, the young "reform" candidate entered the respectable world of business in 1957 by chartering two finance companies: Parr Loan and Parr Finance in Oak Park. There was no adverse publicity until 1961 when one of his employees was found murdered in gangland style. The victim was William "Action"

158

Jackson. Upon closer examination, police investigators discovered that Parrillo's partner in the Parr firms was Samuel Lewis, a Syndicate "juice" operator who had served an eighteen-month sentence in the old days for bootlegging. The enforcer of the Parr juice operation was Joseph Lombardi, who ordered customers to telephone him at the Parr office. A check of police files further disclosed that three other victims, all Parr delinquents, had preceded Jackson in gangland deaths.

Lewis, Parrillo explained, had been a close friend of the family. "I happen to be in the unfortunate position of knowing these guys," he said. "They were friends of my dad. I knew them from the old neighborhood."

Parrillo's next business ventures included two considerable purchases: the Safeway Insurance Company and the Scala National Bank of Chicago, with assets of about $15 million—the purchase price was $1,080,000. The money, he explained, had been left to his mother by his father. "The days of the finance companies are coming to an end," he said. "At least, their heyday is gone."

After his automatic election to the aldermanic post, Parrillo's affluence became a popular topic with gossip columnists. "All those big, rich Texans who have all those big, rich houses on the ski slopes of Vail, Colo., are gnashing their teeth because the latest, big rich house under construction there has something they don't have," wrote one columnist. "It's a huge swimming pool [forty feet long] in the glassed-in living room where the ceiling is 29 feet high. Furthermore, the house doesn't even belong to a Texan but to a Chicagoan—Don W. Parrillo, alderman of the 1st Ward. And Parrillo's diggings in the Outer Drive East [nine rooms, $600-a-month rent] aren't so bad, either."

"I give my alderman's salary away to various First Ward charities," he said. "I live on my business interests." And his affluence has not diminished his compassion: "I spend most of every day in my ward, talking to my people, and seeing they're taken care of. I frequently eat lunch in the homes of my people of my ward. My biggest accomplishment so far is getting them to realize I'm here to help them."

On May 25, 1965, Alderman Parrillo addressed students in a community-relations welcome meeting at the Chicago Circle Campus of the University of Illinois—the project D'Arco had failed to sabotage. "I am sponsored by the best Democratic organization in the city," he told the students. "We go to all the wakes, write wills for people, and help them manage estates. We do a thousand and one favors for them. No one can sit down and talk with them like we can. . . . I don't believe the University of Illinois can ever affect our First Ward as the University of Chicago has influenced the Fifth Ward. The people in this area would resent you college people." Faculty members who chose to live in the area, he conceded, might have more effect on politics than the transient students, but he doubted it since the apartment buildings for faculty members were being built north of Roosevelt road—just outside the First Ward.*

Meanwhile, First Ward politicians were being subpoenaed to testify before the federal grand jury investigating organized crime. The mayor was interviewed on December 18, 1965, concerning the possibility that D'Arco and Marcy might land in jail with cohort Giancana if they continued to refuse to testify. Asked if, as Chairman of the Democratic County Central Committee, he thought it would help the party if D'Arco and Marcy resigned, the mayor replied: "As long as I'm chairman of our party, I feel that the people in the respective areas have the right to select the men and women they want to represent them."

When Sam Giancana walked out of the County Jail a free man on May 31, 1966, the talk of taking the hoodlum before another federal grand jury for a repetition of the immunity tactics suddenly dissolved into a bitter controversy that nearly toppled U.S. Attorney Edward Hanrahan from his patronage pinnacle.

For weeks the press had speculated about the legal alternatives available to Hanrahan and the dire consequences awaiting Giancana in the event he persisted in his refusal to testify before a new federal grand jury. What followed was par for the Chicago optimism course.

William J. Campbell, the federal judge who had jailed Giancana for contempt, struck the first blow when he ordered Giancana freed. Addressing the jurors of the expiring grand jury, Campbell began by apologizing for having wasted their time: "At the time you presented a recalcitrant witness to me a year ago and I committed him for his continuing contumacious refusal to obey my lawful order, you and I were assured by the government that it would vigorously continue to pursue its stated investigation of organized crime before you and that my incarceration of that witness until he testified was a necessary part of such investigation which should lead to indictment of many of those engaged in this deplorable activity. . . . After his imprison-

* Parrillo's opponent in the 1967 election, Dallas O. Littrell, withdrew because "some of my workers received threats." Parrillo ran unopposed.

ment, many Department of Justice statements—at least one by the Attorney General personally—were made to the effect that the government had scored a major victory in the battle against organized crime by the imprisonment of this witness. The fact is that they have never prosecuted him for any crime nor asked you to indict him for any substantive offense."

Campbell then praised Hanrahan as an "able, conscientious and knowledgeable" prosecutor who was "under direct orders from the Attorney General" not to indict Giancana for "obstruction of justice or criminal contempt, or both." Hanrahan had earlier agreed to the freeing of Giancana "reluctantly but obediently, on the instructions of my superiors." Campbell said he considered the decision of the Justice Department to be "unwise" and "paradoxical" in view of the earlier announced intentions.

This collective attack on the Justice Department touched off immediate retaliation in Washington. "I've been around here a long time," a Justice official told the press. "I've never seen such an act of connivery and chicanery in my life." Hanrahan, he charged, had "obviously misled" Judge Campbell and the public by falsely reporting that the government had no substantive evidence against four First Ward politicians: John D'Arco, Benjamin Jacobson, Pat Marcy and Anthony Tisci. All four politicians, the official stated, were connected by the FBI with shakedowns, police payoffs and the crime syndicate's vice and gambling network in the First Ward: "All Hanrahan did was sit and reject all suggestions that he take action against the four witnesses. If Hanrahan had immunized the four politicians and begun a full-blown grand jury investigation of the information furnished by the FBI, a racketeering case might have been made against Giancana. The FBI furnished plenty of material and plenty of leads for such an investigation. But after Giancana went to jail, Hanrahan kept his plans for future prosecution secret from David Schippers and Sam Betar [prosecutors in the Department's organized crime unit in Chicago—they later resigned]. Hanrahan and his first assistant [Robert Collins] got together in closets to talk about the case. No one knew what they were up to as far as Giancana and the rest were concerned. As it turned out, Hanrahan did nothing. When Giancana's jail term ended, the only thing Hanrahan could do was move on him again for criminal contempt of court or obstruction of justice. Either course raised the issue of persecution because of Hanrahan's inaction when Giancana was in jail."

The week before Giancana's release from County Jail, Hanrahan

161

had been summoned to Washington. "The grand jury's term was nearly over and we found out that Hanrahan was up to shenanigans," the Justice official explained. "When he got down here, Hanrahan suggested a criminal contempt case or an obstruction of justice prosecution against Giancana. We ordered him not to proceed. If cases like that went up to the Supreme Court, the justices might wipe out the whole immunity law on the theory of persecution." During the entire period of Giancana's incarceration, Washington had prodded Hanrahan to move in on D'Arco, *et al*. At one point, Hanrahan had promised to deal with the politicians after getting another top case out of the way. On various other occasions, Hanrahan had informed Washington that he was exploring angles in addition to, or other than, D'Arco. Meanwhile, Washington was receiving "feedback" from Chicago politicians that Hanrahan was "politically ambitious" and would "never touch the First Ward—you wait and see."

"He [Hanrahan] told me he had absolutely no evidence against them [the politicians]," Judge Campbell told the press.

And when the press began agitating for Hanrahan's resignation, Mayor Daley was forced into the arena. "Hanrahan's reputation for integrity, intelligence and courage is unequaled," said the mayor as he promptly pleaded ignorance of the facts in the case, adding however that he was "confident that Mr. Hanrahan and Judge Campbell can take care of themselves. . . . There's no reason for Hanrahan to quit. He's a man who'll stand up for what he believes is right and say so."

Washington explained that Hanrahan had not been fired because U.S. attorneys were presidential appointees who held office for four-year terms.

As the controversy escalated into a full-scale furor, Justice Department officials got down to specifics. Hanrahan, they disclosed, had received detailed information from the FBI concerning two separate payoffs to Giancana from First Ward politicians. A payoff of $10,000 on December 14, 1964, was described as a regular payment on Giancana's take from First Ward rackets. This was followed in 1965 by a $20,000 payoff from D'Arco's insurance firm, noted as Giancana's cut of First Ward insurance deals. The $10,000 payoff had been delivered personally to Giancana by Jacobson in an Oak Park restaurant. The $20,000 payoff was made by Marcy in a suburban parking lot while Giancana's bodyguard, Dominic Blasi, stood sentry duty to guard against federal agents. Marcy was described in the FBI report as the courier who delivered Giancana's commands to poli-

162

ticians in City Hall. Although apprised of the two payoffs, Hanrahan had failed to apply immunity procedures after the politicians had invoked the Fifth Amendment.

"This office," said Hanrahan, "has been, is and will continue to be operated on the basis of being interested solely in the conduct—and not in other characteristics or affiliations—of persons investigated or indicted by us. The common goal of myself, all assistants in this office and of all Department of Justice officials has been, is and will continue to be the eradication of organized crime."

But Hanrahan was not the only one who had failed to act against the First Ward power bloc. The State's Attorney's office had also ignored the federal report. State's Attorney's aides said they had been waiting for Hanrahan to act before beginning their inquiry. Mayor Daley, equally reluctant to bruise reputations, deftly demonstrated the versatility of the political cliché at a press conference:

> "As chairman of the Democratic Cook County Central Committee, are you proud of the kind of leadership your party has in the First Ward?"
>
> "I am proud of the leadership I have exerted in this entire community."
>
> "What about the leadership in the First Ward Organization?"
>
> "The leadership in the First Ward is selected by the people of the ward."
>
> "But the Justice Department has said that Pat Marcy . . ."
>
> "The leadership of the First Ward is selected by the people."
>
> "But do you have an opinion on whether that leadership is good?"
>
> "Opinion on what? I know nothing about the facts."
>
> "But, Mr. Mayor, you are the leadership of the leadership of the First Ward. You run . . ."
>
> "I'm chairman of the party and I'm proud of the record I've made in the party, and proud of the record that I've made in this city."
>
> "Can't you do something, though, to get rid of the leadership in the First Ward?"
>
> "I've told you what the leadership is. The leadership is elected by the people."
>
> "Are you satisfied with D'Arco's record in the First Ward?"

"What is his record? Have you documented it? What's he guilty of?"

"He is accused of having refused to testify before a federal grand jury."

"Do you know that of your own knowledge?"

"Through newspaper accounts."

"Let's get on the record here. Let's get talking common sense. Let's get talking the kind of conversation that you would want talked about you. Let's have some evidence on these charges here, and I'll answer if any of you have any evidence of what we're talking about."

"But what about D'Arco's performance?"

"I know his record. I know that there's no law he violated, or he would be tried by either the state's attorney [Daniel Ward] or the district attorney [Hanrahan]."

At his own press conference, Hanrahan stood pat on his stand not to prosecute the four politicians. "I haven't seen anything in print that would warrant prosecution where we have not prosecuted."

"I've got several grand juries and they're ready to go to work," Judge Campbell told newsmen. "I wish the juries would be brought some work."

"Giancana, not too long ago, was quoted as saying he'd pay $1,000,000 to any lawyer who could get him out of jail," one columnist noted. "Now the gag is who gets the reward—lawyers in the Justice Department or Ed Hanrahan?"*

12

The Syndicate's influence is not an exclusive prerogative of the First Ward. A comparable analysis of the remaining forty-nine wards would reveal other Syndicate-political alliances, vote frauds, vice and corruption. A single tree does not make a forest, nor a single ward a political machine. Yet in Chicago it is far more than numerical strength. It is the ruthless muscle that breaks the strong, and the sugar that pacifies the weak. It is survival of the lower precursor animal over twentieth-century *Homo sapiens*. It is, in fact, the law of the jungle, debased and diffused in its *modus operandi,* but pure and simple in its basic motivation.

* While politicians squabbled in Chicago, Giancana traveled to Mexico and established "headquarters" in a castle near Cuernavaca. Meanwhile, police were convinced that although Accardo had ostensibly resumed active control of the Outfit, Giancana was still making the important decisions.

An exhaustive survey of the entire ward complex would prove repetitious. A few choice items can demonstrate the universal nature of the political beast.

Vito Marzullo, who, according to a secret federal report, "holds a position in the organization similar to that occupied by D'Arco," is the Democratic committeeman-alderman of the Twenty-fifth Ward. His political sponsor was State Senator James B. Leonardo, who in turn was sponsored by Al Capone. Back in 1929, while on an errand for Leonardo, 'Marzullo fell into the clutches of the law when he attempted to bribe a witness in a case against an alleged pickpocket. Marzullo told the police that Leonardo had dispatched him to the home of the witness with a hundred dollars to persuade him to drop the case. At the time Marzullo was thirty-two years old. A few months later, the bribery case against him was dismissed when both the prosecution witness and the prosecutor failed to appear in court on the day of the trial. Ten years later, Marzullo became a member of the Illinois House of Representatives where he gained prominence as a leader of the West Side Bloc. After fourteen years of dedicated service in Springfield, he was rewarded with a chair in the city council. Since then Marzullo has prospered in wealth and clout.

In 1965, he succeeded the late Paul M. Sheridan to the chairmanship of the Local Transportation committee, considered one of the top-ranking posts in the machine because of its vast patronage. (Sheridan, who was Democratic alderman and committeeman of the Sixteenth Ward, left an estate in excess of $400,000—not bad for a man who held no other job for twenty-two years.)

A professional undertaker, Marzullo sponsored John P. Kringas, a mortician in business with Marzullo's son, William, to a seat on the Zoning Board of Appeals. Kringas' brother, Gus, served prison terms for armed robbery, grand larceny and assault with a deadly weapon, and in recent years has been an associate of Syndicate hoodlums in Cicero where he was linked by police with the operation of a gambling casino. One of his more colorful associates was Frank Eulo, a Syndicate gambling supervisor in Cicero and part owner with Kringas of Gus' Steak House—steaks downstairs and gambling upstairs (poker, dice and horse book). Police observed William Marzullo in the company of Syndicate thugs Mike Spranze and Leonard "Needles" Gianola.

"His [Kringas'] standing as an expert on zoning," the *American*

165

observed, "may be judged by the fact that he joined Marzullo in the mortuary business in 1938, soon after he had received his training as an embalmer."

State Senator Bernard S. Neistein, Democratic committeeman of the Twenty-ninth Ward, is another accredited member of the West Side Bloc. Although listed in a secret federal report as one of the politicians controlled by Giancana, Neistein takes orders from Charles "Chuck" English, the Mob's overlord of the ward. Neistein's relationship with English was publicly revealed in 1964 when used county furniture, purchased at salvage by the senator, turned up in Phoenix, Arizona, on English's Rim Rock Ranch.

"I don't know anything about it," Neistein protested. "I'll check into it." (This is always a good answer in Chicago since chances are the story will be dead within twenty-four hours and no one will be around to check on the checker.)

J. Gail Strader, county salvage expert, reported that Neistein and "three tough-looking guys" had picked up the furniture. "Neistein said the tough-looking guys were his precinct captains," Strader reported. "Neistein told me he wanted the furniture for his ward headquarters. He said the ward organization would send us a check for $59.28."

To make sure that the "tough-looking guys" loaded up all the furniture (thirteen chairs and two benches) in a truck, Fat Sam, Chuck's 270-pound brother, went to the County Building to supervise. They crated the furniture to the 5th Jack Club, the English racket command post at 3340 West Jackson Boulevard, a few doors from Neistein's political headquarters at 3350 West Jackson.

A racetrack bookie, gambler, policy operator, extortionist, loan shark, terrorist and political fixer, Chuck English went national in the early 1950s when he invaded the jukebox business with Giancana, Glimco and Vogel. One partnership, Lormar Distributing Company, a phonograph record distributorship which muscled jukebox operators, netted Giancana $296,188 in five years according to tax records, Lormar not only sold records nationally, but counterfeited trademarks as well. George Hilger, the company's front, entered a plea of guilty in the counterfeiting case and was fined $200, later reduced to $50. Charges against English were dropped.

When the English brothers incorporated the Rim Rock Ranch in 1963, they had more on their minds than ranching. According to

Arizona authorities, the spread was incorporated as a multimillion dollar enterprise to deal in real estate, contracting, construction, public works and loans, and as a base of operation for the invasion of the jukebox industry. Located in the mountains about ninety miles north of Phoenix, the spread was previously operated as a dude ranch. The purchase price was $331,400—$186,400 for the buildings and $145,-000 for the 265 acres of land. Except for a small airstrip about a mile away, it is accessible only by winding dirt and gravel roads. In the winter, it is a pleasant hideaway for Chicago hoodlums and politicians, a place where they can fraternize and discuss business in private—an ideal setting for Apalachin-type meetings.

The English local gambling and jukebox operations extend from Chicago into Will and Kane Counties. Their political influence transcends physical boundaries—hoodlums of their stature are allowed room to maneuver as long as the play does not violate the vested interests of a peer or superior. Politicians are always fair game. The hunt consists of isolating a particular weakness and then gratifying it.

Until George Vydra met Jane Darwyn in 1959, life had been rather dull. He was a husband (widowed in 1963), a Berwyn alderman and the owner of the Vydra Produce Company. Then the Hitchcock-type ride began. Jane was young, pretty and ambitious. She wanted to be a sexy chanteuse like the slinky dames on the late late show who nightly won the hearts of cold-eyed hardcases like Alan Ladd and Humphrey Bogart. The first item on Vydra's agenda was to find a suitable spot to exhibit her latent talents.

It was a blow for Vydra to discover that a Berwyn alderman did not swing much clout on the nightclub circuit. The only alternative was to open his own place, but since Miss Darwyn was a chanteuse and not a go-go singer, he decided on a classy supper club—the Continental West—in Cicero. But even here he needed a connection. The next logical alternative was to take in one of the "boys" as a partner. Vydra invited Fat Sam English. With Fat Sam at his elbow, Vydra not only opened the club but managed to operate for more than a month without a liquor license. Miss Darwyn sang her heart out every night, but the typical Cicero clientele is not celebrated for its appreciation of music. Fat Sam knew about such things, of course, and had provided against the contingency. The next thing Vydra knew, the Sheriff was raiding the joint and he was out of business. It must be noted in passing that the closing of a Cicero club is a rather unusual situation, especially when the landlords are Sam and Mario

167

DeStefano—they conducted a juice operation in another part of the building.

Growing somewhat desperate, Vydra decided to skip the preliminaries of a nightclub success. With the help of Fat Sam and Chuck, Vydra formed his own recording corporation. Now it is an undisputed fact that a record-selling deal such as negotiated by Vydra is 99 percent foolproof. Imagine a record being distributed to thousands of jukeboxes all over Cook County. A certain percentage of drunks are bound to get confused and punch the wrong selection button. "My records just didn't sell," Miss Darwyn later told police. "The public wants rock 'n' roll. I'm a chanteuse. But Sam English did his best for me."

But what about Vydra? He had called her on Christmas Eve, 1964. "He wished me a Merry Christmas," she said. "But he sounded depressed. He'd been that way for a long time."

On Christmas morning, Frank Vydra found his son, George, lying face down in the cab of his pick-up truck parked in the garage behind his home. The coroner's verdict was death due to carbon monoxide fumes and acute alcoholism. A four-page suicide note was found beside the body. The note contained a number of interesting observations. It said Vydra had been living as man and wife with a young woman for the last five years, and that "she took me for $50,000. . . . The FBI have my story about walking the tightrope."

Miss Darwyn was puzzled. "Where is the fifty thousand?" she asked. "I certainly haven't got it."

Although listed by Berwyn police as "an apparent suicide," there remained a few intriguing questions. When Frank Vydra discovered his son's body that morning, he also discovered the truck's ignition key turned off, the engine cold, gasoline in the fuel tank, a door to the vehicle open, and not a whiff of carbon monoxide fumes anywhere. The suicide note puzzled handwriting experts.

"There are those who believe Ald. George Vydra died because his true identity was discovered," wrote one columnist, "and he actually was an informant for the FBI. If this is true, it will never be revealed." Amen.

"He was the boss of the teeming 24th Ward, on Chicago's West Side. He was the ward's first Negro alderman. He wore $200 suits, and his friends called him 'Duke.' He held real estate valued at more than $100,000. He had just leased a shiny new political headquarters, with autographed photos of people like John F. Kennedy on the wall. That was how it was with Benjamin F. Lewis, 53. Everything was going his way. Last week he was reelected as alderman by a pretty decisive margin—12,189 to 888. It almost seemed as though Ben Lewis had not an enemy in the world. But he did." (*Time,* March 8, 1963.)

A notation in a secret federal report revealed the name of the real boss of the Twenty-fourth Ward: "Advised in 1961 that Ben Lewis . . . is Lenny Patrick's* boy and that he does not do anything without Patrick's O.K. Anyone who operates a book in the 24th Ward is required to give Patrick 50 percent of the proceeds from all operations and the person operating the book must make all payoffs to the police from his own fifty percent. Advised that Patrick could not be stopped in his gambling and other illicit activities since he was backed politically by Jake Arvey, Sidney Deutsch [former Finance Committee Chairman of the Cook County Board of Commissioners—deceased 1961], and Arthur X. Elrod [deceased 1959]. Advised that Patrick grew up in Arvey's ward and that Arvey would often call upon him for strong arm tactics in connection with stuffing ballot boxes."

Patrick's first serious encounter with the law was in 1932 at the age of nineteen, when he was arrested for the gang-type murder of one Herman Gleck. The grand jury returned a no-bill. A year later, at the height of the Dillinger bank-robbing spree, Patrick deserted the sanctuary of the Twenty-fourth Ward and ventured to Culver, Indiana, for a bank job of his own. The results were catastrophic: ten years in the Indiana State prison, of which he served nearly seven. Upon his release in March 1940, he flew to the bosom of his native ward, where politicians appreciated him. For these many years, Patrick has been the overlord of all Syndicate rackets and vice in the ward.

Today the Patrick muscle keeps the ward, which is 99 percent Negro, in line with the Syndicate's wishes. Alderman Lewis called it "a socio-economic garbage heap . . . there are 75,000 people squeezed into my ward, more than Joliet or Waukegan, and almost as many as Springfield. We have the highest percentage of high-school dropouts and the highest percentage of people on relief. We have the highest rate of unemployment, the highest rate of juvenile delinquency and a very high rate of apathy and disillusionment."

* See Appendix.

On the evening of February 27, 1963, Alderman Lewis was rewarded Chicago-style, joining a long list of Syndicate-backed political predecessors. The next morning a janitor discovered him lying face down on the new carpet of his political headquarters, wrists bound in handcuffs, arms stretched above his head, a dead cigarette in his fingers and three bullet holes in the back of his skull.

Superintendent O. W. Wilson vowed "to apprehend and bring before the bar of justice the culprit who committed this dastardly crime. I'm surprised that a killing of this sort would be effected against him."

Mayor Daley, who brushed aside questions on reports that Lewis might have been involved in a clash over policy in his ward, termed Lewis "a superior alderman," and offered a $10,000 reward for the capture of the murderer—the money was as safe as a cut from a cold deck. An investigation of Lewis' background resulted in several fruitless allegations: He was pocketing and spending insurance premiums received from customers of his insurance agency; he showered women with gifts and was heavily in debt; he was involved with Fillmore district policemen in the shakedown of jitney taxicabs—ancient hacks without a proper city license, whose operators were making payoffs of $20 to $40 a month; and he was linked to the multimillion dollar policy racket. Within a week, however, Lewis was just another statistic—the 977th unsolved rubout since 1919.

"Every time that iron ball bats down one of those slum buildings on the South Side," Lewis had happily observed shortly before his assassination, "twenty Negro families move west. Every time that ball strikes, my position as West Side Negro leader becomes stronger."

But as events dramatically proved, Lewis' optimism was short-lived. The undisputed boss of the South Side was Congressman William L. Dawson, Democratic committeeman of the Second Ward, who also controlled the Third, Fourth, Sixth and Twentieth as well. Unquestionably the most powerful Negro political leader in the country, Dawson was chairman of the House Committee on Government Operations, vice-chairman of the Democratic National Committee and a powerhouse in the Cook County Democratic Central Committee. In 1964, at the age of seventy-eight, he was elected to his twelfth term in Congress.

During his interminable career, Dawson has vividly demonstrated

170

that a political machine based on policy is unbeatable. Policy runners and writers are the most active kind of precinct workers. They visit homes and shops in their precincts two and three times a day, and most are glib persuaders who can also supply muscle if and when needed. Consequently, the gambling syndicate's Negro infantry has been a potent factor in South Side politics.

In the days before Anton J. Cermak was elected mayor, Chicago Negroes voted Republican as a matter of course. Following his election, Cermak transferred Police Captain John Stege to the South Wabash station, in the heart of the Negro community, with orders to "raise all the hell you can with the policy gang." Stege complied by arresting two hundred a day and packing them so tightly into cells none could sit down. The more Negro politicians protested, the better Cermak liked it. "Fine work," he would tell Stege. "Keep it up. Act tough with them." Finally, the Negro leaders capitulated. "What do you want us to do before you take that wild man out of our territory?" they asked. "Become Democrats," Cermak replied.

Other factors contributed to the total conversion—the Roosevelt administration with its alphabet-soup relief programs, federal jobs for Negro faithfuls, repeal of prohibition (Mayor Kelly controlled saloon licenses), state patronage from Governor Horner's Democratic administration.

When Dawson, the Republican, ran for Congress in 1938, he was defeated. In 1939, still as a Republican, he was defeated in the aldermanic election. But in 1940, *Democrat* Dawson went to Washington, where *he* has tenaciously remained these many years. His victory in 1964 was 142,688 to 25,719 against a civil rights candidate who labeled Dawson a machine politician with two basic interests—personal power and wealth. "The politicians laugh at us when we go to the polls time after time and vote against our own best interests," said the Rev. Arthur M. Brazier, founder of The Woodlawn Organization (TWO), which called the city's first school boycott ("the issue was getting soap and toilet paper for Carnegie School, and it worked"), and the first rent strike. In explaining Dawson's power, Brazier suggested that it was based on fear: "His precinct captains can threaten to turn people out of the housing projects, or cut them off welfare."

"I didn't make one speech in this campaign," said Dawson. "Why make a speech when the people out here know me so well? The people know what I can do." A few months later, "the people" were picketing his office, charging inaction on civil rights. The same people also paraded a few times around Mayor Daley's block.

Negroes on the South Side have no illusions about the Syndicate's tie-up with politics. Since the turn of the century, gambling, prostitution, booze and narcotics have reaped untold billions in lawless profits to the Caucasian gangsters who dominate their social as well as political life. Negroes, whether gangsters or political leaders, are merely lieutenants to the white usurpers. Dawson's link to the Capone mob reaches back into history. As a lawyer, he specialized in defending Negro gamblers and other lawbreakers in his district. Accused before a Congressional Committee in 1948 of having defended "the racketeers out there in Chicago—the policy racket, in the district he represents—to the tune of millions of dollars every year," Dawson offered: "I would defend any man."

In 1954, a federal investigation of the South Side policy racket resulted in indictments against—and guilty pleas from—the Manno brothers (Nick, Sam, Fred, Thomas) and Sam Pardy, all hirelings of Jake "Greasy Thumb" Guzik and Tony Accardo. One of the names most often heard during the probe was that of Congressman Dawson. During the investigation, it was later discovered, several calls from telephones used by Guzik and Accardo for personal business, and tended by Phil Katz and Harry Hochstein, were made to Dawson's unlisted Washington number. Three hundred long distance calls were made from these telephones during this period of a few months, including calls to Tony Pinelli in Sierra Madre, California; to George T. Wilson in Phoenix, Arizona, attorney for Guzik's son, Charles Girard, who was sentenced to 98 years in prison for repeated homosexual attacks on children; to Harry "The Muscle" Russell, Accardo's front man in Florida gambling, and to Frank "Buster" Wortman, Syndicate representative in southern Illinois.

On December 15, 1960, the *American* published the following news item: "President Elect Kennedy offered the job of postmaster general to Rep. William Dawson, Chicago Negro Congressman, but Dawson turned it down. Kennedy announced the offer and the refusal in a surprise statement today on the doorstep of his Georgetown home near Washington. . . . Kennedy added: 'I regret that he will not be with us in the administration.' "

"There would be special irony in appointing Dawson Postmaster General," the *Daily News* observed. "A few years ago Dawson's own secretary was convicted and served time for selling nine civil service jobs in the Chicago post office for $3,508 in bribes. Otto Kerner, then

172

U.S. district attorney, prosecuted the case, but he said he had no evidence connecting Dawson with this corruption."

Some politicians are crooks and some crooks are politicians. Through the years, the Twenty-seventh Ward has produced its share of both varieties. For example, in the late 1920s and early 1930s, James Adduci's name was followed in the press by such colorful appellations as "hoodlum . . . gangster . . . notorious member of the murderous Capone gang . . . vice monger . . . West Side gambler . . . racketeer." He was arrested eighteen times between 1920 and 1934—the year he was first elected to the state legislature. However, his election to that august chamber did not free him from suspicion whenever violence erupted on the West Side.

When his Democratic opponent from the Second District, Representative John Bolton, was slain gang fashion in 1936, the police suspected Adduci and called him in for questioning. On another occasion when he was picked up following the bombing of a theater, police charged him with carrying a concealed weapon. His attorney, a rather ingenious shyster, gained his release on the technicality that the gun Adduci carried was not concealed—it was in his hand. A few months before the 1934 election, Adduci was picked up by police in the company of Willie Bioff. Police charged they were trying to muscle into the poultry handlers' union.

Adduci's closert friend in those days was Dago Lawrence Mangano, one of Capone's most important West Side gamblers. Testifying before the Kefauver committee in 1951, Adduci described his friendship with Mangano: "On the primary and election, Lawrence used to give me a little finances to help me finance my precinct when I was a precinct captain." "Do you generally accept political help from gamblers and bookmakers?" Kefauver asked. "In my precinct I would accept a little finances from any kind of a business."

Adduci's closest friend in those days was Dago Lawrence Man-Mancin, who was seeking a third term in the legislature. Not long after Adduci announced his candidacy, two gunmen marched Mancin down Harrison Street with a gun at his back. They gave him a choice, withdraw or end up in a box. He first refused but later changed his mind when threats were made to kidnap his daughter. Adduci reigned unopposed until 1942, the year William John Granata filed for the Republican nomination to the Second District seat. Then sluggings, bombings and shootings became the order of the day. Adduci's brother, Joe, traded blows with Granata, after warning him to

173

"Watch yourself, you're getting too big for your pants." Adduci defeated Granata in the primary and then faced Scott Vitell, an independent, in the general election. This time it was Adduci's nephew, Joe Mondo, who did the slugging, and it was with a baseball bat against Vitell's head. Vitell became the first candidate in history to campaign in a Brinks armored truck. He lost, naturally, and a few months later Joe Mondo also lost—gangland style.

Granata again challenged Adduci in 1944, but this time Governor Dwight H. Green personally importuned Granata to desist "for the sake of harmony." Although he reluctantly complied, Granata was bitter over what he characterized as "the lack of moral fiber in a governor who not only would not fight the influence in the party of such a man as Adduci, but would not even permit other members of the party to do so, though they were ready, willing, and hopeful of success."

Granata was not politically naive. As Republican committeeman of the Twenty-seventh Ward, he was accustomed to violence. Two predecessors had displeased the Syndicate. William Garrison, elected in 1930, suddenly departed for the hills of Tennessee in 1935, telling friends he had been chased out by the "Mob." He sent his resignation in by mail. His successor, Mike Galvin, head of a teamster union not affiliated with the International Brotherhood, lasted two years before a shotgun squad executed him on Madison Street.

Granata's third attempt to unseat Adduci proved fatal. Shortly after midnight (October 8, 1948) an assassin virtually decapitated him moments after his chauffeur had dropped him off in front of his skyscraper home at 188 W. Randolph Street.

"John Granata's current political relationships were somewhat ambiguous," the *Daily News* observed three days after his death. "His brother, Representative Peter Granata,* has recently had no difficulty in getting along with Adduci and was regarded as his close ally in the legislature. In the last session, they both helped to kill the Crime Commission bills to improve law enforcement."

Granta's murder remains unsolved. His chauffeur, Amoth C. "Al" Cope, an ex-convict, who had driven Granata on the night of the murder, managed to avoid the unemployment line. Within a few weeks, he was chauffeuring for Adduci.

For many years, Adduci and Peter Granata ruled the West Side Bloc in the Legislature. When State Representative Clem Graver was kidnaped in front of his home in 1953 by three "hoodlum types,"

* In 1967, Giancana and Miss McGuire were observed in Mexico driving about in a white Oldsmobile licensed to Peter Granata.

174

police learned that Graver had had a falling out with Bloc leaders. Graver, who was politically sponsored by his brother-in-law, Harry Hochstein, a top Syndicate hood, was also Republican committeeman of the old Twenty-first Ward, now part of the First and Twenty-fifth Wards. No ransom was ever claimed and Graver was never seen again.

The Democratic leaders of the Twenty-seventh are Committeeman John J. Touhy and Alderman Harry L. Sain, who have been in office for more than forty years. Their insurance company (Touhy & Sain) writes some 90 percent of all the policies issued on the dives and clip joints on West Madison, Chicago's authentic Skid Row. Touhy's son, John P., was Speaker of the House during the 1965 session of the Illinois General Assembly. He has been in the legislature seventeen years, and is one of the two men—the other is George W. Dunne— presently being groomed by Daley as possible successors. The elder Touhy is a county commissioner and a party potentate of considerable clout.

The Twenty-eighth Ward, once the political roost of Pat Nash, lies directly north and northwest of the Twenty-seventh Ward. For a number of years, Nash's protégé, George D. Kells, officiated as Democratic alderman and committeeman. One of his most trusted lieutenants was Big Jim Martin, the West Side policy king, a man who could corral votes as readily as policy slips. For reasons never fully explained, Kells ran afoul of the Syndicate in 1950 and was handed the usual ultimatum. While Kells debated the alternatives, Big Jim Martin was offered the opportunity to switch allegiance, but he also vacillated. On November 15, 1950, Tony Accardo assigned the "contract" to Jackie Cerone, who "fired several shotgun blasts at Martin but only wounded him because the ammunition was 'old stuff.'" Few examples would more graphically illustrate the connection between the executive level of the Syndicate and ward politics.

The moment Big Jim was able to perambulate, he hot-footed it to California. Kells unceremoniously bowed out of politics and left for an extended motor trip to Florida, explaining that Mrs. Kells was in ill health.

Mrs. Kells' ill health, said the *Tribune,* ". . . arises principally from telephone calls from agents of the Capone mob, telling her that her husband would be killed if he did run. . . . Martin has been run out of town, the home of the alderman's secretary has been bombed.

. . . Alderman Kells is one of the Mayor's leaders in the council. He was until recently state chairman of the Democratic party. He is Kennelly's man, and Kennelly can't protect him from the hoodlums. . . . The Chicago police are Kennelly's police. . . . Maybe the gangsters own too many of the captains. If that is the situation it is time the people of Chicago found out who is really running the town, the Mayor or the gangsters."

The Syndicate's replacement was Patrick Petrone, a cousin of Robert "Happy" Petrone, boss of the Twenty-sixth Ward and a close friend of Tony Accardo. Petrone, a night-school law student, served his apprenticeship in the law office of Roland V. Libonati. By rubbing the Syndicate's magic lamp, he became alderman, running unopposed, and Democratic committeeman in one fell swoop. The most interesting notation in his police file refers to his attempt in 1954 to order Lieutenant Joseph Morris and a squad of curious policemen from the wake of Sam Giancana's wife at the Rago Brothers' funeral home.

The latest Democratic committeeman, Anthony C. Girolami, was mentioned in the secret federal report as one of the politicians Giancana had instructed his associates to meet "some place away from their homes because if they lost these men they 'were dead.' "

The Republican Committeeman, Joseph Porcaro, worked closely with Petrone, thus keeping all politics safely in the hands of the West Side Bloc. In 1963, Porcaro tried to branch out into suburbia but was stopped by Joe Woods, the Better Government Association's (BGA) chief investigator.*

"Porcaro decided he was going to move to the Park Ridge area and take over as committeeman out there," Woods told this writer. "The reason being that in the Twenty-eighth you may have only about three hundred Republicans voting in the primaries, where out in the suburbs you may get forty thousand. Naturally, this would give him more clout at the slate-making convention where a committeeman can vote the total number of votes cast in the previous primary in his ward or township. The BGA's idea was to stop him, and we were successful in planting an informer inside his organization. Every time they held a meeting, it would be splashed in the newspapers. This embarrassed Porcaro. In addition, we went out and asked people who were normally Democratic to vote for Tom Cunningham, Porcaro's opponent. As I remember, he was defeated about 5 to 1. He is now back in the Twenty-eighth. We feel we stopped the Syndicate from taking over in Park Ridge; at least, we slowed them down some.
* Elected sheriff of Cook County in 1966.

176

From what I've been able to discover, Porcaro had been caught by judges out at Twenty-sixth and California [Criminal Court building] practically in the act of buying off various people. Also down in Springfield, he was even charged with it in the legislature once. Now I'm told he's never really done anything wrong except sell insurance. A few years ago he sponsored one of Accardo's daughters for a job in the Sanitary District."

Porcaro's brother, Frank, who is more popularly known as "Porky," was sentenced to a one-to-five-year prison term in 1966 for theft of state funds and bigamy—his difficulties arose from the larceny end of it. Prior to his incarceration, he was chief investigator in the secretary of state's driver's license division. Porky and his staff set up shop in a soundproofed basement office in Chicago, with an unlisted phone number which was changed every week. His top sleuth was Charles C. Crispino, a $500-a-month payroller who lived in a $50,000 home and owned a half-dozen businesses.

Porky first made headlines when he launched a campaign against thirsty teen-agers with "phony" driver's licenses. Out of 280 arrests, 21 stood up. Other branches of the department were kept busy wheedling waivers from indignant parents.

Suddenly, the headlines were on Porky. There was the little item of his twelve arrests and five convictions. Then there was the matter of his two wives. And finally, Porky was exposed as a thief. In a period of five months, he had padded his mileage expense account by $3,745. Until this intelligence hit the front pages, Porky had enjoyed a close relationship with his superiors. As he later explained to Undersheriff Edmund J. Kucharski (and a hidden tape recorder), at least one of his superiors had trusted him implicitly.

"Mr. Z got this girl in trouble," Porky told Kucharski. "She worked in the secretary of state's office. He called me in Chicago and says, 'Frank, can you get a room in Chicago?' I says, 'Why?' He says, 'I got a doctor who's going to take care of this girl.' So . . . I went over there and paid for it. Then he says, can I get $650. . . . He says, 'Put it on the expense account.' He says, 'I'll work it out for you.' He used to OK my vouchers. . . . I was giving him money all along. . . . All of a sudden the Internal Revenue . . . wants $1,300 for this $3,700 I was supposed to take. So I tells Mr. Z and I says I ain't got thirteen cents. He says, 'Call me in a week.' I called and called and never got him. . . . But I'm going to get him."

Even if Porky failed "to get him," he did manage to get a few superiors before three grand juries on far more serious charges. In his

177

tape-recorded conversations with Kucharski, Porky charged that the state had been defrauded out of millions of dollars by cartage firms, many of them owned by the Syndicate. By paying bribes to state officials, the trucking companies were allowed to cheat on their license tax which ranges from $10.50 for a small panel truck to nearly $2,000 for a huge semitrailer. The secretary of state's office had fewer than 150 men to check on a half-million trucks registered in Illinois.

"I gave them all the information on the trucking thing. . . . I gave it to Mr. X and Mr. Z . . . and they never followed up. I wouldn't give it to Mr. Y cause he was the one who was planning [collecting] on this stuff. . . . Listen, I have too much on these guys. . . . You see, the Outfit has got a bunch of trucks and they operate with them. Say Mr. Y gets a complaint, but they don't follow it through, and he'll tell them what to do. I mean tell his friends [hoodlums] what to do and that's it. Hell, you should go down there some days to his office and you would think it was the Apalachin meeting there."

Among the hoodlums identified by Porcaro were Tony Accardo, Chuck English, John Lardino, Joey Glimco and Willie "Potatoes" Daddano. "I used to holler. I used to tell them, for Christ sake, how can you take care of state business with all of those hoodlums hanging around?"

The meeting with Kucharski was arranged by Crispino in September 1966 when he learned that the undersheriff was investigating trucking violations in Cook County. "You haven't scratched the surface yet on this trucking thing," Crispino told him. "We can tell you stuff that will blow this wide open." Crispino then brought up Porky's name. "Porcaro is about ready," he said. "He's about ready to blow his top. Frankie expected to get probation, but a big politician double-crossed him."

Secretary of State Paul Powell, a downstate politician whose career at times appears to be one long uninterrupted scandal, was properly shocked by the disclosures: Porky was a "cheat and liar. . . . I didn't even know the man until 1963." To Nicholas Ferri, Porky's immediate superior, he was a "monster. . . . The man is sick." Another superior, Charles C. Smith, lashed out at Kucharski for "scoundrelly acts," calling him a "political charlatan" who used the "Hitlerian technique of the big lie in a callous effort to obtain political publicity and votes [Kucharski was elected State Revenue Director in 1966] at the expense of other persons' lives, reputations and happiness." Smith, a political press agent and troubleshooter who usually has more clout than his clients, resigned his $21,600-a-year job as top aide to Powell (whose own salary was $20,000) after the *Daily News* uncovered evidence that he too was padding his expense account.

Shortly before midnight, November 22, 1966, Charles C. Crispino became Chicago's 1,000th gangland murder victim. Six .45 caliber bullets ended his life as he walked from his car to his home with a case of gin in his arms. Back in Stateville prison, Porky was so upset by the news that doctors had to administer oxygen. "I don't know nothin' about nothin'," he told investigators. "I don't want to leave here. I won't be taken out for more questioning. I want to serve my full time."

Directly north of the Twenty-eighth Ward is the Thirty-first Ward, the most autocratic of the fifty banana republics. The ruler is Thomas E. Keane, Democratic alderman and committeeman, who ascended to power following the death of his father, Thomas P. Keane, in 1945. Keane is the city council's acknowledged master of political artifice. His clout derives not from the position of his ward, which is small and impoverished, but from a long string of connections and wealth beyond the wildest dreams of most politicians. The *Daily News* once estimated his fortune at more than $10 million, tracing its source to "profitable real estate deals, a lucrative law practice—and a substantial inheritance from his father."

As chairman of the council's Finance Committee, Keane has vast investigative powers over city contracts—a privilege he exercises in reverse: (up to this writing) he has not permitted a single major City Council investigation of any charge of contractual irregularities by city contractors. As the mayor's floor leader, he is the "de facto" chairman of the council's committee on committees and rules, which determines council rules and the composition of its committees. He selects the chairmen and vice chairmen. However, his primary source of power is a negative one—the caliber of the Chicago City Council. As the *Daily News* phrased it: "Keane shines in the vacuum."

The patriarch, Thomas P., left a tannery job in 1914 to become committeeman of the Fifteenth Ward (changed to Thirty-fourth Ward in 1921 and to Thirty-first Ward in 1931). He was elected to the Legislature in 1918, and five years later Mayor Dever appointed him City Collector, a position which considerably broadened the leverage of his clout at a period in Chicago history when money flowed like booze. Capone's vice and booze designee on the Northwest Side, with headquarters in the Thirty-first Ward, was Marty Guilfoyle, who was not a stranger to Thomas P. In those days, Thomas P.'s brother-in-law, Nick Waterloo, operated a busy saloon at California and Chicago Avenues. Early in 1925 Waterloo became involved in a dispute over beer territories, and Thomas P.'s home was bombed, which immediately settled that dispute. Two items in *Lightnin'* in 1925 are of particular interest: "Who gets the dough that is being collected by Marty Guilfoyle, the killer of Pete Dentlemen? Marty is collecting from gamblers, saloons and other law-breaking establishments. He has a gambling house at 163 N. Cicero Avenue. Perhaps his position is that of a 'City Collector.' . . . Tom Keane is a friend of Lieutenant Al Winger, touted by Chief Collins as a great policeman, indicted by the Federal Grand Jury in the Morton-Gove beer scandal. Keane was active too in moving captains who would not let beer go."

Like his father before him, Thomas Earl Keane began his political career in the Legislature, serving as a state senator from 1935 to 1945. During this period, he became associated with the West Side Bloc, often voting along with its members. A vociferous advocate of the status quo, Keane has been an anxious guardian of the Democratic machine. He helped defeat a new Chicago charter which would have brought the archaic city government up to date with the rest of the nation by reducing the number of aldermen from fifty to fifteen. A payroll scandal inquiry in 1953 disclosed that Keane commanded more high-paying patronage jobs for his political minions than any other alderman. (One Keane-sponsored payroller, a court bailiff, was fired in 1953 following his arrest on charges of operating a pool hall, complete with handbook and gambling tables. Ten years later, this same payroller was again fired from the same job for operating the same gambling establishment.)

Evidence of the Syndicate's proprietary interest in the internal affairs of the ward was emphasized with a burst of shotgun fire on the evening of February 6, 1952. The victim, Charles Gross, had been repeatedly warned not to run for the post of Republican committeeman. Gross not only ignored the threats, but initiated a "reform" campaign against the influence of Syndicate gangsters in politics.

During its investigation of the murder, the homicide detail expressed considerable interest in Sam Mesi,* a brother of James Mesi,

* See Appendix.

180

who had opposed Gross for the committeeman post. As an illustration of the complexity of the ties between politicians and hoodlums, Sam Mesi was arrested back in 1934 as a suspect in the gang murder of Joseph Adduci (a kinsman of James Adduci)—he was shot while seated in a barber chair by two killers who lifted hot towels from his face to identify him before emptying their guns into his head. Seven months later, Sebastian Sapienza, a witness to the Adduci murder, was similarly disposed of by two killers after he identified Mesi as one of Adduci's executioners. In 1954 Mesi was a suspect in the gang slaying of Paul "Needlenose" Labriola (stepson of Dago Lawrence Mangano) and James Weinberg. A year later, the government attempted to collect $45,555 in taxes from Mesi's $800,000 a year bookmaking operation. The case resulted in a decision that a bookmaker may not deduct for income tax purposes the "wages he pays his employes." The next time Mesi received publicity was four years later when the *Tribune* revealed that he was on the sanitation department's payroll at $472 a month for "supervising" three garbage trucks. His job, he said, was to "see that truck drivers and laborers do their work." His sponsor was Mathew W. Bieszczat, Democratic committeeman of the Twenty-sixth Ward, chief bailiff of the Municipal Court, and secretary of the Democratic county organization. Bieszczat said he sponsored Mesi because "he helped pile up a Democratic majority" in the Twenty-sixth Ward during the 1959 city election. "I met Phil Mesi [brother of Sam] at the World Series," Bieszczat explained. "Phil Mesi was in a box with Frank ["Frankie the X"] Esposito, the union boss. I was sitting in the same box with Matt Danaher [Daley's top adviser], from the mayor's office. Esposito turned around and introduced Phil Mesi to me and Danaher." Bieszczat said he knew Sam Mesi "had a reputation as a gambler" but he was interested in "rehabilitating" him. "If I didn't give him a job, where could a man like Mesi go to work?" (Mesi lived like a gangland prince in River Forest.) Informed that Mesi had served a year in jail for robbery, Bieszczat dropped the rehabilitation story: "I wouldn't have sponsored him if I had known he was wrong." According to a secret federal report, the boss of Bieszczat's Twenty-sixth Ward was James Adduci: "Advised in October, 1961, that James Adduci, State Representative, had offered Sam Giancana the placement of anyone he chose as representative or committeeman in the Twenty-sixth Ward." However, Bieszczat's political sponsor was Thomas E. Keane, whose Thirty-first Ward borders the Twenty-sixth. On December 8, 1965, the *Tribune* announced that Keane was backing Bieszczat as the Democratic choice for sheriff of Cook

County. "Bieszczat . . . has often been criticized for hiring gamblers and former convicts for city payrolls," said the *Tribune*. "He became secretary of the county organization, with Keane's help, in 1953 when Daley first became party county chairman."

The strange complications in the above paragraph are typical of the Chicago condition. A politician is killed in Keane's ward, the suspected murderer is sponsored to a city job by Keane's political protégé (Bieszczat) in a neighboring ward where the Syndicate boss is James Adduci, a kinsman of the slain Joseph Adduci and an erstwhile friend of the late Dago Lawrence Mangano, step-father of the slain Paul "Needlenose" Labriola. Politics does indeed make strange bed-fellows.

In the immediate excitement following Gross' murder, Keane was assigned a police bodyguard, identified in a news story as Thomas Durso. This was the same Durso who was linked to the narcotics branch of the Syndicate in 1964, and convicted for the brutal knife slaying of police informer Anthony "Lover" Moschiano.

Bounded on the east by Lake Michigan and on the south and west by the Chicago River, the Forty-second Ward, known as the Near North Side, is the sweetest political plum in Chicago next to the First Ward. Once the booze domain of Dion O'Banion and Bugs Moran, it is now dominated by gangsters who take a cut—one way or another—from most of the area's more than four hundred establishments with retail liquor licenses. The Syndicate's overlord is Ross Prio, and his lieutenants include some of the top brass of the Outfit. (A reversed blueprint of the ward's boundary lines resembles a machine gun.)

Better known by conventioners for its "swinging" Rush Street joints and "reeling" North Clark Street dives, and by discriminating tourists for its Michigan Avenue shops, the ward once housed such colorful districts as Little Hell, Little Italy, Smoky Hollow, Bughouse Square, Goose Island, The Sands, Streeterville and Death Corner. Within its borders today are some of the city's finest hotels and high-rise apartment houses, Lake Shore Drive, The Gold Coast, Tribune Tower, Wrigley Building, Marina City, Northwestern University's downtown campus, hospitals, expensive restaurants, cathedrals, and modern office buildings. And then there are teeming rat-infested slums and flop houses, and perhaps the world's most unique unmelting pot—one-third Negroes and the rest Italians, Irish, Germans,

Puerto Ricans, Japanese, Mexicans, Filipinos and hillbillies from Kentucky, Tennessee and other points south. How do they get along with each other? "Each group has a sufficient number of taverns on Clark Street," replied one politician. "Woe unto him who strays."

Although historically Democratic, the ward's political complexion was abruptly changed in 1924 by Dion O'Banion a few days before he was ambushed by Capone assassins. On election day that year, O'Banion's gang swept through the ward in black limousines, kidnaping Democratic workers, frightening others away, protecting ghosts who busily voted under many names, ordering judges and clerks to tally vote counts as directed. The police, under Democratic Mayor Dever, did not interfere with the disorderly process of democracy, and the ward went 2 to 1 Republican—but it was only a temporary condition. The Forty-second has been a stronghold of the Democratic machine, notorious for its violence and vote frauds on election days.

"Chicago's 42nd ward is ruled by a king," the *Daily News* proclaimed in 1934. "A politician wears the diadem in that domain. His name is William J. ["Botchie"] Connors." Besides being king, Connors was Democratic ward committeeman, state senator and chief deputy bailiff of the Municipal court.

Since a political king is not as self-perpetuating as a royal one, Connors was particularly astute in selecting the members of his privy council. The prime minister was George Kries (nee Creff), an ex-bootlegger and a former manager of the C.&O. Restaurant, 509 North Clark Street, a hangout for the Bugs Moran gang and the scene of three killings in two years. Eddie Sturch, chancellor of the exchequer, was also the King's bodyguard. A former convict and gunman, Sturch served six years of a ten-years-to-life sentence for armed robbery. Walt Rogers, keeper of the privy seal, specialized in brothels. He was also the King's "Man Friday," and was once arraigned on charges of murder and assault with intent to kill. The King's brother, John, the noted Duke of Keno, was the gambling baron of the domain and the owner of the C.&O. Restaurant—his password was, "Don't say nothing."

King Botchie, who proclaimed in one campaign that he was "pardonably proud of the record I have made," was himself indicted in 1929 on charges of conspiracy in connection with the $5 million Sanitary District swindle. His Majesty refused to testify on the grounds of self-incrimination and was subsequently cleared of all charges. In 1930, the federal district attorney invited the King to explain why he had made false statements in connection with a

183

$15,000 surety bond he had filed in behalf of State Representative Lawrence C. O'Brien, later sentenced to prison for income tax frauds. An investigation revealed that the property the King had pledged as surety had been scheduled on two other bonds, both forfeited in state courts. In fact, several notorious gunmen, thugs and burglars had achieved fugitive status on the strength of the King's magic bond— although it was ordered forfeited countless times, it remained in the King's possession. Needless to say, his insurance and bonding agency was a wild success.

Charges that the ward reeked of vice and gambling never upset the King. Only "blue-nosed bastards" managed to penetrate the royal blubber of the three-hundred-pound King. He once snarled at a Chicago Crime Commission investigator, "Why you bunch of blue-nosed bastards, coming down to Springfield and trying to get some undesirable legislation passed." Included in the gratuitous purple tirade was Mayor Kennelly, who had had the audacity to close up the gambling dens of people who wanted them open, with the resulting effect of seriously depleting the King's weekly ransom. As far as His Highness was concerned, Kennelly had committed political hari-kari and would never again be elected to any office.

Until his death in 1961, the King was considered "Old Reliable" at downtown Democratic headquarters. Never once had he wavered in a political battle. He was a favorite of Boss Brennan in the Twenties; of Bosses Nash, Kelly and Arvey in the Thirties and Forties, and of Boss Daley in the Fifties.

His boyhood pal, Dorsey R. Crowe, was the ward's alderman from 1919 until his own death in 1962. Damon and Pythias were never closer. They shared ambition, wealth and ideology. In 1953, Crowe succeeded in blocking a Council resolution of regret over the death of Police Captain John T. Warren—while in charge of the East Chicago station, the captain had closed several of the area's worse honky-tonks. Until his last illness, Crowe was president pro tem of the Council, presiding in the absence of the mayor; and for a number of years Connors, a vigorous advocate of the West Side Bloc, was Democratic whip of the state Senate.

Of the original members of the King's privy council, Eddie Sturch proved to have the most stamina. Known variously as the "dictator of North Clark Street" and the "Napoleon of the Forty-second Ward," Sturch packed two pistols to impress upon the King's subjects the nature of his mission. Occasionally, he would dash into a night spot and pummel a complete stranger senseless as a form of exercise. He

184

also enjoyed smashing up tavern furniture, especially if the owner forgot his weekly ransom. On these occasions, he would stroll into a tavern brandishing his two shooting irons and declare, "I'm going to smash up the joint." A moment later, he was heaving chairs and tables at patrons lined up against the bar. Once a New York salesman actually laughed at Sturch, and the next thing he knew bullets were whizzing about his head. The two detectives who rescued the salesman by arresting Sturch found themselves back in uniform, pounding a beat in Outer Mongolia. Afterward, the personnel of the East Chicago police station had no trouble in distinguishing the powers of a king from a mere commissioner.

The Republican committeeman, Paul C. Ross (nee Rosario P. Ceffalio), was sponsored by Peter Granata. In 1942, one year before he was elected committeeman, Ross married Ursula Granata (sister of William and Peter Granata), and former secretary and fiancé of Edward J. O'Hare, a Capone underling and president of Sportsman's Park racetrack, whose career was ended rather abruptly in 1939 by buckshots. Ross, who has been accused of vote frauds on numerous occasions, denied in 1963 that Victor "The Gaff" Musso, a Syndicate policy operator, was one of his precinct captains, even though Musso's name was listed on a chart in the ward's Republican headquarters. "The Gaff comes into my headquarters occasionally," Ross protested, "because there are a lot of fellows there he grew up with. But a precinct captain he isn't. I might have put The Gaff's name in to have all the precincts covered, but he's never been a captain in the sense that he canvassed the precinct or really plugged it. I may have used the guy to get the count in the Fourteenth precinct." The Gaff can often be found in the Subway Poolroom, 1136 North Clark Street, identified in federal court testimony as headquarters for Near North Side vice and gaming bosses. Ross was also included in the secret federal report: "Advised that Murray Humphreys through his contacts with Alderman John D'Arco has been put in touch with Paul C. Ross. . . . D'Arco has been using Ross as an informant for obtaining information concerning the strategy of the Republican Party leaders for the past several years."

George Dunne, a county commissioner and chairman of the county board's finance committee, succeeded to Connors' committeemanship. A close personal friend of Daley, Dunne has yet to indicate any irresistible impulse toward reforming the empire he inherited. His Near North Insurance Company, Inc., 14 East Chestnut, is a business with a capital gains future.

185

Today the Near North Side is the Syndicate's most fertile breeding ground. Its investment in hotels, apartment houses, restaurants, nightclubs and taverns runs into the millions—all of it made possible through "protected" gambling, prostitution and extortion.

Chicago loves good old beer-guzzling, globe-trotting Mathias "Paddy" Bauler, that jovial, earthy, raucous, jolly, witty, roly-poly, lusty, cherubic, tough old warhorse with the twinkling eyes, infectious grin and heart of gold. These adjectives, and many more, have been used a thousand times over to soften the image of the one authentic Chicago masterpiece—a saloonkeeper-alderman with the morals of a spider and the mouth of a broken parrot.

In 1965, the City Council unanimously passed a resolution designating January 27 as Mathias Bauler Day to celebrate the rotund alderman's seventy-fifth birthday. It was Bauler who uttered one of the city's most famous cracks: "Chicago ain't ready for reform yet."

The resolution praised Bauler for his long success in "representing dramatically the most variegated constituency in all of Chicago consisting of the high born and the low born, the rich and the poor, the artist and the businessman, the native born and the foreign born, the white and the nonwhite, and the old and the new. Although Alderman Bauler is a confirmed world traveler, no one exceeds him in the depth and breadth of his knowledge of Chicago life. He is the avowed and effective enemy of hypocrisy, cant, sham, humbug, bunk, pomposity and false pretense."

"I had a great time and I represent a great ward," Paddy told his council colleagues. "Every election comes up, and they put some egghead against me. When the election is over, yours truly would come back to this City Council. I'm glad the Almighty has let me live seventy-five years, but that ain't enough. I'll settle for ten more years. . . . One thing I like to do is have a good time."

Some of Paddy's knee-slapping witticisms include: "Hey, shut up you bums and siddown or you're gonna get threw out!" To a group of sober guests standing against a wall, he once bellowed: "Siddown, you slobs. You look like a federal grand jury." To reporters: "You newspaper guys, don't you take anybody's hat and coat when you leave. I don't want to get sued." On reformers: "Them new guys in black suits and white shirts and narrow ties, them Ivy League types, them goo-goos, they think the whole thing is on the square." On his wealth: "Listen, I'm still opening 1927 money." ("It is not unusual for Paddy to fly to San Francisco or New York for dinner and return the same night," wrote Jay McMullen in the *Daily News,* "to Paris or Hong Kong for a weekend. Sometimes, if he shows up at O'Hare Airport and his flight to, say, Phoenix is delayed inordinately, he will catch the first plane out, no matter where it's bound for; he once flew to Zurich just to get another half dozen pairs of his favorite underwear.") On his formula for success: "I never get out of my class." On philosophy: "What's it all mean? Nuttin'. All you get out of it, all you get out of life, is a few laughs."

Known as the Clown Prince of the City Council, Paddy used to entertain Mayor Cermak by rolling on the floor in wrestling matches with himself. However, like his pal King Botchie, he too was the king of his domain. When a policeman tried to gain admittance after hours to Paddy's saloon a few days before Christmas of 1933, the king lost his royal patience. "Johnny, why have I got this coming to me for?" he roared plaintively. "I never done nothing to you." And then proceeded to do something: He shot the policeman, who in turn shot a bystander. Not long afterward, Mayor Kelly, an avowed admirer of Paddy, brought the house down when he described the alderman as "a real straight shooter."

Lying directly north of the Forty-second Ward, Paddy's Forty-third enjoys the same profitable alliance with the Syndicate as its southern neighbor. An investigation of police graft in Paddy's bailiwick by the Big Nine in 1953 publicly revealed his ties with the vice, graft and gambling in his ward. Paddy retaliated by delivering a blistering attack against the goo-goos from the floor of the Council, but never submitted to questioning under oath.

On one occasion, Ross Prio saved Bauler from a million-dollar suit by *persuading* the plaintiff to drop the case. "Humphreys," the federal report noted, "has been friendly with Bauler for a considerable period of time."

When another anniversary rolled around, Paddy deserted his legion of admirers. "You guys ain't gonna kill me with parties," he bellowed, as he hastily departed for Miami and the simple pleasures of his fifteen-room mausoleum, once the property of the late Rocco Fischetti, aping cousin of Al Capone.

Then, in 1966, Paddy bowed out of the aldermanic "race." The candidate he sponsored (against Daley's wishes), Frank Cale, also soon bowed out when it was disclosed that he had a police record and was a known associate of Syndicate hoodlums. Of course, others run with records far worse than Cale's, but their connections are far better.

13

"One of the open-sewer scandals of Illinois is that the Chicago crime syndicate usually gets what it wants from the Legislature," the *Daily News* observed in 1964. "The Hoodlum Establishment has the notorious West Side Bloc of legislators going for it—and that's not all. When it comes to blocking bills the hoods don't want, legislators can be counted on from East Side, West Side and all around Downstate. The lowest legislative bow to the crime syndicate in 1963 came not from the West Side Bloc at all, but from the three top leaders of the state House of Representatives. These three, all non-Chicagoans, are minority leader Paul Powell, Majority Leader W. J. 'Bingo Bill' Murphy and Speaker John W. Lewis, Jr. They were part of a successful move to kill a bill that would have made syndicated gambling a felony. It was probably the most brazen embrace the legislature could give the crime cartel."

These syndicate paladins in legislative togas have been so successful in scuttling anticrime legislation that it took Chicago a century to pass a bill extending the term of its grand jury from thirty to ninety days—consequently, Chicago never had an effective grand jury investigation or a "runaway" grand jury. Experts in logrolling, vote-swapping and back-scratching, the blocsters, as one legislator put it, "sit on their hands all year long, never introducing any legislation, just waiting for someone to come and ask them to support a pet measure. 'Sure,' they reply, 'and some time I'll be around for your vote for something.' That's the way the bloc builds credits—putting in its debt any number of lawmakers who are not part of it."

Fortified by Republican turncoats, the Bloc is a powerful arm of the Democratic machine, relying for its strength on control of a huge patronage system, fear, favors, vote buying and fraudulent vote-counting. "The bloc," said the *Daily News,* "not only can elect its men to the Illinois Legislature and even to Congress—but has great power in close citywide and even national elections. In 1955, for instance, Richard J. Daley's victory edge in the Democratic mayoral primary came largely from the West Side river wards, citadel of the bloc."

There is little doubt that hoodlums control a major share of the patronage, which runs anywhere from six hundred to a thousand jobs in each bloc ward. The blocsters' only problem is to scare off worthy opponents in primary elections. Under Illinois voting procedure, each of the fifty-nine House districts elects three members to the legislature. The trick is to effect a bipartisan power alliance to guarantee that only three candidates are nominated—which assures all three of election regardless of the vote count. The voters are disenfranchised by default, which explains the longevity of many blocsters.

For example, Peter C. Granata, First Ward Republican committeeman, has been a state representative since 1933. In 1930, he was elected to the Congress of the United States, scoring a Republican triumph in the midst of a Democratic landslide. His opponent, Stanley H. Kunz, charged that Granata's success had been the result of bombing and violence by the Capone gang. After a recount, Granata was unseated in 1932, and immediately shuttled to Springfield to fill a vacancy, where he has remained ever since. (The Illinois Blue Book credits him with serving in the 72nd U.S. Congress but neglects to mention he was ousted.) He was also vice-chairman of the Republican State Central committee in 1963.

Serving from the same West Side district with Granata are Sam Romano, elected for his sixth term in 1964, and Andrew A. Euzzino, who has been in the legislature since 1941—he was Assistant Attorney General from 1937 to 1941. A thoughtful attorney, Euzzino helped Tony Accardo fill out his draft questionnaire. His thoughtfulness also benefited Joey Glimco. "At Glimco's request, this lawmaker [Euzzino] did not hesitate to go to police headquarters to ask and obtain the destruction of the record of Glimco's arrests, together with the photographs and fingerprints that might be useful in identifying him," the *Tribune* disclosed in 1959. "Euzzino stood around until he had seen the papers torn and scattered. The lawmaker, Euzzino, put the matter in these revealing words: 'Glimco asked me to get his record pulled and I agreed to do it. I've done the same thing for quite a few people.'" Sam Romano was once a business partner of Leonard Caifano in a company called Personal Business Service. A brother of Marshall Caifano, Leonard was shot and killed in 1951 when he attempted to kidnap Ted Roe, a South Side policy operator —Giancana was sought as an accomplice in the kidnap attempt.

Anthony "Busy-Busy" DeTolve, who replaced Libonati in 1957, is the Bloc's new Clown Prince of the Senate. His forte is to irritate his fellow lawmakers into sudden adjournment rather than listen to his extended, pointless attempts at humor and dramatic oratory. Al-

189

though a modest talent, it has proved particularly effective in delaying action on anticrime bills.

Take, for example, his performance on April 26, 1965, before a packed Senate gallery of schoolchildren and a delegation from the League of Women Voters. DeTolve took the floor to speak out against a crime bill that would have permitted policemen to stop, search and question persons suspected of having committed a felony. "Three storm troopers," DeTolve shouted, "so-called policemen, were in the place [an unnamed strip joint] from one A.M. to five A.M. and propositioned every waitress. They offered up to a hundred dollars for the propositions but the girls would have none of it. [The] storm troopers [also propositioned] a tap dancer, and a go-go dancer and a toe dancer [but were rebuffed]." Swinging his arms and humming loudly, DeTolve danced a few steps of the Watusi. "Boy, did the toe dancer have a figure—and attractive too. In order to beat a hundred-dollar bill for food and drink they had run up, the cops herded the girls into a back room. These girls were harassed and questioned. They were restrained and not given their freedom. Finally they were placed under arrest." Upon hearing of their arrest, "I went there instanter and forthwith, and I really mean instanter. I went through two stop lights. I'm a very busy, busy man, you know, I defend women because I think we need them, including the dancer, who's a good tap dancer, toe dancer and she does the Watusi." DeTolve paused and provided another demonstration of the Watusi. "This law would make a police state," he shouted. "A young man who walks the streets in my neighborhood and doesn't wear a $200 suit is picked up by the police" (which would probably include everybody but gangsters and politicians).

Once when referring to the Illinois Crime Commission, DeTolve suggested that the "stool pigeon" be substituted as the official state bird.

Political control of Cook County very often includes the state of Illinois. Since Governor Otto Kerner's election in 1960, Daley has governed the Statehouse from City Hall. The General Assembly is Dick Daley's legislature. The mayor's control derives not only from the fact that he approved nominations and supported campaigns, but from something a great deal more convincing. Of the forty-seven Democratic candidates from Chicago who were elected state representatives in 1964, twenty-seven held full-time jobs with the city or other local governments.

According to State Senator Paul Simon, a Downstate Democrat,

190

the theme song of precinct workers during election campaigns is, "Never mind the issues, how many jobs can you get us?" In an article in *Harper*'s (September 1964), Simon wrote: "Legislators often collaborate to satisfy this [patronage] hunger," he wrote. "The results are sometimes peculiar. Occasionally, for instance, a Republican legislator turns up on a Democratic payroll. Thus, in 1961, two Republicans who held Democratic spoils jobs in Chicago announced that they were too ill to vote, and a third GOP member voted with the Democrats at our organizing session. As a result, the Republicans failed to elect a Speaker though they held a one-vote majority in the House."

The Republicans who engineered the coup were two West Side blocsters, both employees of the Sanitary District in Chicago. Walter "Babe" McAvoy, who cast the vote that elected Democrat Paul Powell as Speaker of the House, received $803 a month and was the district's highest paid laborer foreman. Peter L. Miller, who was too ill to vote, was the district's paymaster at $11,508.16 annually.

Many legislators—as many as one-third (Simon told this writer it was as high as one-half)—were taking payoffs disguised as legal or public relations fees, or as campaign contributions in return for helping or hindering certain bills. Some payoffs were in cold cash, passed directly from one hand to the other. The going price for votes ranged from $200 to $700 each. Rumor, said Simon, estimated the under-the-table take of one House veteran at $100,000 a year, with others not too far behind.

"A few legislators go so far as to introduce some bills that are deliberately designed to shake down groups which oppose them and which will pay to have them withdrawn," Simon said. "These bills are called 'fetchers,' and once their sponsors develop a lucrative field, they guard it jealously."

Except for a weak law that requires lobbyists to register—for five dollars—with the Secretary of State, Illinois places no restrictions on their activities. Whatever they spend to influence legislation is their own private business. And legislators are protected by not having to account for campaign contributions or disclose their source. As to conflicts between the public's and the legislators' private interests, a statute calls for legislators to declare only when they own more than 7½ percent interest in a firm engaged in state business.

The Illinois Crime Investigating Commission, a project which was defeated by the West Side Bloc in session after session, became a reality in 1963 following the widely publicized slaying of Alderman

Benjamin Lewis. When the time came to name the members of the commission, the House sponsor of the bill, Anthony Scariano, was passed over. Instead, the Speaker chose one legislator who had voted against it and one who had been Chief Deputy Sheriff of St. Clair County at a time when it was so wide open that the Kefauver committee held a special probe into its affairs. Asked later by newsmen if the West Side Bloc was responsible for keeping him off his own commission, Scariano replied: "It wasn't the YMCA."

Two months after the publication of Simon's article, the commission—composed of twelve members: four each from the House and Senate, and four public appointments by the governor—voted to investigate the General Assembly, but only if the legislators failed to investigate themselves. "There is a cloud on both the House and Senate," a commissioner complained. "This has embarrassed everybody."

Late in January 1965, Simon and Scariano met with the commission's executive director, Charles Siragusa, and presented him with the names of fifteen legislators and six lobbyists suspected of corrupt practices. Four days later, Siragusa announced a probe of his own: "I have a lot of other allegations about a lot of legislators that should prove startling."

The *American* was overjoyed: "We keep rubbing our eyes, but the image is still there, and we feel a dawning, delighted suspicion that maybe it's for real: State officials seem to be getting seriously disturbed about graft in the legislature, and to be mounting determined action to stop it."

Daily News columnist Royko was not as optimistic: "They [commission members] would believe there is corruption in Springfield only if Scariano could bring them signed confessions, which are hard to come by. . . . The result will be that Siragusa will do what he can—but it won't be much. . . . And everybody in Springfield will eventually forgive Scariano and Simon. You can't get too angry if you don't get caught."

After interviewing 133 witnesses under oath and investigating 70 cases of alleged misconduct, the commission reported one month later that it found no substance to the charges of corruption in the General Assembly. For a while the commissioners debated the propriety of naming seventeen legislators charged with various corrupt practices in its report, but the General Assembly was threatening noisily to dissolve the commission if it "named names."

The original report (not published) was forty pages long and contained the names of fifteen accused legislators, two former legislators, and ten accusers, including Simon and Scariano. In the second version, the names of the accused were omitted, but the names of the accusers remained. The third version excluded all names. The fourth and final version was a nameless six-page apologia.

14

If ever a city had an opportunity to demonstrate the awesome power of a machine society, the presidential elections of 1960 provided that moment. Richard M. Nixon carried 93 of the state's 102 counties and lost Illinois to John F. Kennedy by 8,858 votes. If Nixon had received two more votes in each of Cook County's 5,199 precincts, he would have carried the state's twenty-seven electoral votes. This fact was not lost on the Republicans, who had been reduced to their lowest ebb of power since 1936—the only surviving GOP state official was Secretary of State Charles F. Carpentier. The most lamented Republican defeat was the office of State's Attorney where the incumbent, Benjamin S. Adamowski, lost to Daniel P. Ward by only 26,000 votes out of 2.4 million cast.

Charges and countercharges flew in the aftermath. The Republicans alleged that hundreds of thousands of votes had been spirited by ghosts and brazenly stolen by devious thieves in judges' clothing; Democrats countered that it was "a lie" propagated by "sore losers." Republicans decided to prove their vote fraud claim by contesting the defeat of Adamowski. A partial "discovery" recount of about five hundred paper-ballot precincts indicated that the former state's attorney had been cheated out of 8,875 votes. Contempt charges were subsequently brought against 677 election officials and precinct workers. It was then that the Democrats summoned their in-fighters to the game.

Daniel P. Ward promptly disqualified himself from the investigation and Morris J. Wexler, a Democrat, was appointed special prosecutor in the case by Richard B. Austin, chief justice of the criminal court (now a federal judge).

Judge Thaddeus V. Adesko, the county judge, also a candidate in the election, disqualified himself and appointed Judge John Marshall Karns, a city judge in East St. Louis, who wasn't responsible to the people of Cook County.

Within forty-five days, Judge Karns disposed of all the cases without requiring the election judges or the persons cited to respond and

193

describe what had occurred on November 8. As far as Frank Durham, chairman of the Chicago Recount committee, was concerned: "Anyone with an ounce of sense knew from the very beginning that nothing would come of the investigation. From the moment they appointed Judge Karns, that was apparent. They were looking for a way out, and they found it."

"The last act has been played in the legal farce which purported to be an investigation of wholesale frauds in the Nov. 8 election," said the *Tribune*. "Nobody is going to be punished. Nobody is even going to be censured. The net result of the judicial mummery is that election officials have received further assurance that stealing votes is no crime in Chicago. . . . Notwithstanding the Adesko-Karns whitewash, Republicans have no reason to withdraw their charges that they would have won both elections [Adamowski and Nixon] if the count had been honest."

There never was an official recount and the original election figures remained on the books. However, a GOP check of only 699 paper-ballot precincts showed net gains of 13,360 votes for Adamowski and 4,539 for Nixon.

When the Board of Election Commissioners reappointed 112 election judges from among the group cited for contempt in 1960, the mayor rebutted Republican attacks by contending the judges had been the victims of "scattergun charges. It's one thing to put a lot of allegations against people and another to prove them." Many of the judges cited had only committed unintentional errors, Daley asserted, or were charged by mistake.

Then came the primary election of April 10, 1962. Testimony by members of the Joint Civic Committee on Elections before the Illinois Election Laws Commission provided lively reading: "I never believed all the talk about voting irregularities," Dom Doherty testified, "that's why I wanted to see for myself. By golly, it's true." Doherty had watched the 30th Precinct, Forty-second Ward. "It was a big family affair," he said. "Ninety percent of the voters were illegally instructed. The judges told the people how to vote and went into the machines with them and told them which levers to pull." One of the two "Republican" judges marked judicial ballots for the Democratic judges. Judges stood outside polling booths and initialed thirty to forty ballots at one time before handing them out and instructing the voters to mark for the Democratic candidate. "I complained to the police sergeant," he said, "telling him the election

194

judges were marking the ballots for Democratic candidates. The sergeant replied, 'Yes, I know it's irregular but you can't fight City Hall.' "

Alfred Civa testified that of the 198 voters in the 30th Precinct, Twenty-seventh Ward, all but 12 required assistance. After the first ten or fifteen votes were cast, the judges raised the curtains on the voting booths and thereafter everyone voted in the open. Some of the illegal acts cited by Civa included judges instructing voters and pulling levers, and voters coming in with printed cards, handed to them just outside the polling place, which read: "I want to vote for Yates. I want to vote the straight Democratic ticket. Please assist me." Of the 186 voters given assistance, only 10 signed affidavits as required by law.

Donald Peacock testified that of the more than three hundred votes cast in the 41st Precinct, Twenty-seventh Ward, "not more than ten votes were cast in private. The Democratic precinct captain opened the voting machine when we arrived at 5:25 A.M. and after the first voter fumbled in the booth for seven or eight minutes, the captain threw the curtain back. After that nearly everyone was told which levers to pull and how to vote." The "Republican" judges, he said, instructed the voters to pull the Democratic levers.

Ray H. Greenblatt testified that voting in the 44th Precinct, Forty-second Ward, was "chaotic." The Democratic precinct captain, Vincent Salamoni, sat at the election judges' table and ran the show through the head judge, Dorothy Jefferson. "Salamoni would call off the names. Either Mrs. Jefferson or one of the judges would enter the voting machine and pull the levers for the voters. The voters were constantly instructed not to disclose their names to the poll watchers."

Greenblatt's testimony was corroborated by David R. MacDonald, who said he called the Board of Election Commissioners and the state's attorney's office. Both responded. After the judges were warned of illegal voting, they would desist for a while, then resume. Finally, the election judges called police headquarters. A squad car answered and Greenblatt and MacDonald were ushered out of the polling place. Greenblatt said he warned Mrs. Jefferson once that the votes were running far ahead of the applications for ballots. She replied, "Don't worry. We'll catch up."

Terrell Schwartz testified that the Democratic captain in the 26th Precinct, First Ward, took charge of the polling place and instructed judges. "Ninety-five percent of the voters were given assistance and told how to vote without aid of affidavits. Most of the time only one judge went into the voting machines but once there were two."

In the United States Senate, Paul H. Douglas clashed with John J. Williams (R. Del.) on April 27, 1965, during a senate debate over the federal voting rights bill. Williams lit the fuse when he referred to "the famous incident in Chicago in the 1960 elections" when eighty-two votes were cast in a South Side precinct in which only twenty-two qualified voters lived on election day.

"I object to Chicago being made a whipping boy when it is not justified," said Douglas. "I object to our being pilloried unfairly." The report of vote fraud was "a lie which has long been laid to rest. . . . At one time we had election frauds, in the period from 1915 to 1931. During twelve of those years William Hale Thompson was mayor and he was a Republican. Sam Insull represented the upper world and Al Capone the lower world. There was collusion, and William Hale Thompson's forces were the middlemen. . . . We Democrats in Chicago don't have to steal ballots to win elections. We showed that in the last election. . . . We had a cleaner election than usual last time."

"What's usual?" Williams inquired.

Douglas did not reply.

A month before the 1964 election, Sheriff Richard B. Ogilvie decided to ferret out Democratic ghosts, which he estimated at more than 150,000 on Chicago's election rolls.

Sidney Holzman, chairman of the board of Election Commissioners, promised all the cooperation "authorized by law" when Ogilvie asked to photostat voter verification records. But, said Holzman, "After giving due deliberation and consideration to your request of October 1, the members of the board have determined that there is no legal ground upon which your request can be justified in the election code of Illinois and, therefore, the board denies your request."

The sheriff was working against a legal deadline which stipulated that a political party could request a special canvass "not less than twenty days and not more than thirty-one days before an election." October 20 was set as the last day for challenging registrations.

Harassed but undaunted, Ogilvie and four hundred volunteers set

196

out on October 10 with poll lists printed before the April primary. Meanwhile, the sheriff's legal aid, Reginald Holzer, filed for a writ of mandamus before Judge Cornelius J. Harrington in Chancery court to compel the election board to honor their request for photostating the verification books. Judge Harrington dismissed the suit and the Appellate Court seconded the ruling.

Although the canvass was narrowed from eleven to six wards, the sheriff ferreted out some four thousand ghosts from such likely haunts as vacant lots, taverns, social clubs, churches and even a psychiatric hospital. The wards involved were the First, Second, Twenty-fourth, Twenty-fifth, Twenty-eighth and Twenty-ninth. A total of 3,806 challenges were mailed, and then the fireworks began in earnest. Mayor Daley expressed concern over the inconvenience caused to persons challenged, especially after the Democrats had worked so hard to convince the good people of Chicago of the importance of voting. And then, said the mayor, "along come a private organization [the Republican Party] and makes a lot of outlandish general charges against them [the voters]. This forces citizens to come downtown in order to protect their vote just because they happen to live in a certain area."

State Senator Bernard Neistein, who was charged with intimidating members of the sheriff's posse, attended the election board hearings on the challenged registrations. Surrounded by his usual "bunch of tough-looking precinct captains," the Democratic committeeman set the tone of the hearings by poking a stiff finger in the face of a woman volunteer canvasser and shouting "Shut up!" when she attempted to present evidence against sixty voting ghosts in Neistein's Twenty-ninth Ward. One of Neistein's captains, Lee Smith, then proceeded to offer eleven affidavits, all unnotarized, as evidence that eleven challenged voters were legally registered. Although the voters did not appear at the hearing, Smith testified that he had personally visited them the night before after his normal 9 A.M. to 5 P.M. working hours as a city employee.

Ogilvie's legal aid, Reginald Holzer, objected to the fact that the affidavits were not notarized, and asked to copy them for later investigation. His request was denied, and he was also refused permission to bring in a handwriting expert who, he said, could sit "quietly by" and examine the signatures without disturbing the proceedings. "All right," Holzer called to Smith, "then describe these people." "Well," said Smith, holding up an affidavit, "she's not big and not small. I'd say she's average size. It depends on what you call

197

big." Smith's description of the residence proved equally enlightening.

"I'll do the interrogating here," Stanley Kusper, the hearing attorney, interrupted.

"You're trying to keep me from my right to represent these challengers," said Holzer.

"One more derogation and you're not going to be around to be a part of these proceedings," Kusper warned.

"If you're going to continue to listen to everything these precinct captains say, why don't you save some time and do everything they say?" Holzer angrily retorted.

"Leave, leave the room," Kusper shouted.

"Don't forget to say goodby," piped in Holzman, waving. "Be courteous."

"These are star chamber proceedings," Holzer cried, rushing indignantly from the room.

Eventually, of course, there was a Democratic purpose to the madness of the proceedings. Of the 3,806 voters challenged, 843 were qualified to vote even though only some 300 had appeared before the board—the others were qualified on unnotarized affidavits presented by precinct captains. Still, Ogilvie had proved his point. Referring to the sheriff's original estimate of 150,000 ghosts in Cook County, the *Daily News* observed that "It's barely possible that Sheriff Ogilvie has overstated the issue. But, Chicago elections being what they are, it would be difficult indeed for him to overstate it to any important degree."

Reginald Holzer charged that voters in river wards lived in fear "lest they lose their political jobs." The voters feared being dropped from public assistance rolls or ejected from public housing "if they don't do the bidding of the precinct captains. These threats are made every day. It's time someone talked about these things. It's just like sex. Nobody wants to talk about it."

If nothing else, the 1964 election provided a postgraduate course in democracy—Chicago-style—for college students assigned to watch West Side polling places.

"Vote buying, illegal 'assistance' to voters, and repeated voting by the same persons marked yesterday's election in Chicago wards where the Democrats have little or no opposition," the *Tribune* summarized the next day. "The boldness of the illegal activities and the numerous complaints received . . . indicated the Daley machine was operating with its usual high efficiency."

"Chicago," said Holzman, chairman. of the board of Election

198

Commissioners, "has witnessed the most orderly election I can recall in my forty-five years of public service."

Police Superintendent Orlando W. Wilson, who had assigned nearly four thousand policemen to polling places, complained that "the day must come when police are not needed for this job."

"If Wilson is such a straight cop," one official told this writer, "why doesn't he find out how his men are assigned to precincts? It's not exactly a secret that cops receive gratuities from precinct captains. And it's not a secret that the same cops invariably turn up in the same precincts at every election. It's rather obvious that they've been sponsored by their respective committeemen. I've yet to hear of a cop reporting a voting violation. And you can bet the cops are there early in the morning, helping the captains twist the arms off those machines to record the votes of people previously intimidated into signing ballot applications, mostly welfare cases and people in public housing. The captains visit them before election to point out how fortunate they are to be living in a democracy where precinct captains devote their entire existence to their well being. And the cops are there when the judges follow voters into the booths to help pull the levers. That's to make sure that when they buy a vote it stays bought. It's called assistance voting, but it's actually the modern counterpart of the chain ballot. If all those voters are illiterate, then Chicago has to have the highest illiteracy rate in the world. In many precincts, the assistance runs as high as ninety percent. Even Holzman proudly admits he used to buy votes when he was a precinct captain. It's a sickening business without any apparent remedy. It's like a bad stench. The longer you live with it, the less noxious it becomes."

15

Recognized nationally as one of the Seven Wonders of American Engineering, and locally as Boodlers' Heaven, the Metropolitan Sanitary District of Greater Chicago was legislated into being in 1889 for the purpose of reversing the flow of the Chicago River, which emptied into Lake Michigan and polluted the city's greatest natural resource.

What proved to be a solution for Chicago soon became a problem for downstream communities, and the district began its second phase of construction before World War I by opening the first of three giant sewage treatment plants. The West-Southwest works at Stickney is considered the world's largest of its kind. Millions of gallons of sewage are processed daily and returned in water form—over 90 percent pure—to the waterways. Solids are removed and disposed of as fuel to generate power for other sewage treatment operations which convert wastes into fertilizer.

The district gained its popularity in the Whoopee Era. Wholesale disclosures of payroll padding, contract rigging, kickbacks, payoffs, hoodlum connections, expense account orgies and overall larceny were estimated at $5 million for prosecutive purposes, which was perhaps 10 percent of the total plunder of that decade.

From 1958 to 1966, the district was under the aegis of Frank W. Chesrow (nee Caesario), president of the nine-member board of trustees. Although some trustees have managed to springboard themselves into political orbit (no one has forgotten Kelly's grand exit from chief engineer to mayor), the board has historically been a dumping ground for political hacks, clownish knaves and low-caliber friends of the Outfit.

When Chesrow was first elected to the board in 1948, the *Tribune* described him as a forty-five-year-old "unassuming pharmacist" with a chain of three drugstores, and a former army major (now a reserve colonel) with "an outstanding record in sanitation work in Italy . . . largely responsible for beating a typhus epidemic" and a "frequent traveler, usually in search of new drugs." Other stories told of Chesrow's numerous unspecified military decorations—one suburban sheet placed the number at twenty, which must top Audie Murphy. He is also a Knight of Malta, a Knight of St. Maurice and Lazarus, and a private chamberlain of the Sword and Cape, an honor bestowed by the late Pope John XXIII in the summer of 1960. As the owner of three neighborhood drugstores, Chesrow has found the time and money to dabble in the arts, acquiring a rare collection of Italian and Western European Renaissance paintings—including the works of such masters as Tintoretto, Van Dyck, Poussin and Michelangelo.

While Colonel Frank was galavanting about in Italy, purchasing paintings and drugs, his brother Colonel Eugene J., medical superintendent of the Oak Forest Hospital, a patronage job, was covering Los Angeles and Las Vegas with Tony Accardo and Michael Mancuso, later identified as Sam Giancana. Unfortunately for Colonel Eugene, Los Angeles is not like Chicago—police there do not take kindly to peripatetic gangsters. The trio arrived in Los Angeles on TWA Flight 93 at 8:15 P.M. (January 15, 1953) and were met at International Airport by Anthony Pinelli and Frank Ferraro. Intelligence agents of the Los Angeles police tailed the five men as they

200

drove to Perino's Restaurant in Beverly Hills, and tailed them back to the airport three hours later. There, the hoodlums were taken into custody and interrogated singly. At first, Accardo denied that he knew Chesrow or Mancuso (Accardo, Mancuso and Chesrow were booked on the flight as S. Mann, S. Stanley and S. Whate—which meant that Giancana was using an alias to cover an alias). When the officers refused to accept Accardo's story, he admitted they were traveling as a group on their way to Las Vegas, and that Colonel Chesrow was his personal physician, stating he had known him for some twenty years. Chesrow, who admitted to having been Accardo's personal physician for fifteen to twenty years, said he made the trip at Accardo's invitation. After interrogation, they were handed the usual Los Angeles floater: "Get out of town and fast." The bankrolls carried by the trio were indicative of their status: Accardo $7,000, Giancana $5,000, Chesrow $250. (Thirteen years later, Dr. Eugene became indignant when Frank "Porky" Porcaro told sheriff's police that "When any hoodlum wants to take a rest or hide, they go out there [Oak Forest Hospital] and hide." "That's a lie," Dr. Eugene replied. "There has not been a gangster out here in all my twenty-eight years in the job.")

Elected district president in 1958, Frank Chesrow was a product of D'Arco's First Ward political machine. He also has been involved in real estate ventures with Tom Keane, the mayor's city council leader.

The vice-president of the Sanitary District is Vincent D. Garrity, a disk jockey by happenstance and a political batboy by choice—his boyhood dream was of becoming an alderman. Of the nine publicity-happy trustees, Garrity is perhaps the only one who would walk on his elbows with his thumbs in his ears to get his picture in the newspaper. To get his face on television, there is no telling what he would do. Consider this *Daily News* item, under the byline of John Justin Smith, of November 29, 1963: "A number of persons have been puzzled about the heavyset man who popped up several times on television screens during the vast coverage of the funeral of President John F. Kennedy. Once his face appeared on screens coast to coast as he leaned over the shoulder of Rep. John W. McCormack, speaker of the House. Twice he walked between Mr. McCormack and the television cameras. This was in the rotunda of the Capitol in the moments just before the President's body was borne first to church and then to Arlington National Cemetery for burial. He was there—horned-rimmed spectacles and all—as Mrs. Kennedy walked from the Capitol to begin her day of ordeal. Well, a little investigation shows that this was no mystery man. It was Vincent D. Garrity, Sanitary trustee and longtime Chicago political hack." Within an hour of President Kennedy's death, Garrity was on the telephone to newspapers with the story that he and the trustees had held a minute of silent prayer. "I was President Kennedy's favorite announcer in Chicago," he added. "I would appreciate anything you can do for me."

But to federal agents, Garrity is more than a ludicrous clown, as noted in one secret report: "Advised in December, 1961, that Chicago hoodlum Sam Giancana, Vince Garrity . . . and Peter C. Granata were considering Giancana's choice of candidates for the office of sheriff of Cook County. . . . These men place considerable importance on Giancana's desires."

The newspapers' favorite trustee was Marshall Korshak, brother of Sidney Korshak, the Syndicate's topflight advance man on the West Coast and a Chicago celebrity in his own right. (During the movie extortion trial, Willie Bioff testified that he had been introduced to Sidney Korshak by Charles "Cherry Nose" Gioe, a top lieutenant of Nitti, as "our man." "Pay attention to him [Korshak]," Gioe had warned. "Remember, any message he may deliver to you is a message from us.")

As Democratic committeeman of the Fifth Ward (Hyde Park—which includes the University of Chicago), Marshall Korshak wields hefty clout in machine circles. He served as a state senator from 1950 to 1962, when he became a Sanitary District trustee. He resigned in April 1965 to become State Director of Revenue, succeeding Theodore J. Isaacs, Governor Kerner's political manager, who was indicted for conspiracy and collusion in rigging bids for contracts on purchases of $1.2 million of envelopes by the state. The charges were later dropped.

Scandals in the Sanitary District come in bunches like bananas, the big ones shielding the little ones. It is not unusual to have a half-dozen scandals going full blast at the same time. No one has the slightest inkling of how many there have been in the past fifty years. The number is infinite. But not all scandals are of major proportion —by Chicago standards. Like the St. Valentine's Day massacre, scandals have to keep topping one another to gain attention.

One acceptable scandal in recent years was uncovered by *Ameri-*

can reporter Ted Smart. "The first time I became interested in the Sanitary District was in early December, 1961," Smart told this writer. "It was strictly a fishing expedition. There were all those rumors of graft and corruption and I decided to go over and see if I could find something on my own. At the time there was an $18 million project nearing completion called the Zimmerman process at the main works in Stickney. First, I went over and talked to William Dundas, who had been the district's superintendent for several years. I had heard that his son or son-in-law was a vice-president of Sterling Drug, the parent company for the Zimmerman firm, which was constructing this plant. I confronted Dundas with this information and he explained that it was simply coincidental. I took him at his word but I still asked to look at the contract. There were a number of contracts, of course, and I picked the electrical portion of it. I just pulled it out of the air for no reason. Dundas then introduced me to Byron Carter, the engineer in charge of electrical design and the man responsible for drafting electrical contracts. Carter told me there were actually two electrical contracts, an inside and an outside contract, titled YYD and YYE. The two totaled approximately $4 million. I noticed that the YYD contract had been awarded to Garden City Engineering Company. The president of the company was Maurice T. 'Mossie' Cullerton [a cousin of County Assessor P. J. Cullerton]. As you know, this is a rather prominent political name here in Chicago. They have been in local politics for seventy-five or eighty years. So, I thought, well this is where we should start then. This is the contractor, let's look at it."

Byron Carter then explained how the district protected itself against collusive bids and padded charges by preparing a secret estimate to be compared with the bids. "Okay, I said. Let me see your estimate and let's compare it with this contract." Carter hastily explained that the estimate had been prepared by Ralph R. Pinkerton, his former boss who had retired a few months after the two contracts were awarded in December 1960, a year before Smart began his investigation. The Pinkerton estimate was a hand-written document of some fifty pages. The first thing Smart noticed was the cost for stenciling numbers on 141 electrical motors. The labor estimate was two hours at $7 an hour per motor, and the stencils were listed at $2 each.

"Knowing that it takes a dab of paint and a piece of paper with the numbers stamped into it, I thought the cost a little high. So then I really dug into the contract. I took 422 items, just as they came, and compared them with the catalogue prices. I found that Pinkerton's estimates were 25 to 30 percent higher than the catalogue. Then I noticed there were asterisks beside the catalogue prices. I asked Carter what they meant, and he said, 'Oh, it's probably nothing important.' Well, I thumbed through the catalogue and saw where it said 'subject to discount.' So I went back and did it all over again. It was fantastic. Some of the discount prices were 50 percent lower than the listed prices. The labor cost estimates were just as out of whack.

"After going through all the entries, I projected the findings and discovered that the two contracts totaling $4 million should actually have run in the neighborhood of $2 million. Carter, I must say, was painfully defensive about Pinkerton's estimates. The next thing was to have an auditor go over my findings, but Chesrow called in Burton A. Scheidt, the chief engineer, a very shrewd gentleman who went from $7,200 a year to $27,000 a year in a relatively short span of time. In the presence of Chesrow, even before I announced my findings, Scheidt rejected my request to photostat the book of estimates, and Chesrow agreed with him. So I made candid copies of the pages and took the whole thing over to State's Attorney Dan Ward and laid it on his desk."

Pinkerton, who had contemplated an extended cruise of the South Pacific, was located in a San Francisco hotel by state's attorney investigators, and brought back to his $60,000 home in Chicago to appear before the county grand jury. He took the Fifth Amendment and subsequently disappeared, this time to tour the southwest. FBI agents found him six months later in a Phoenix motel.

The investigation was assigned to Assistant State's Attorney Robert Cronin, who hired Franklin D. Troxel, an electrical engineer, to verify Smart's figures. His findings were that $2.2 million went as profit on the contracts over and above a normal profit of approximately 10 percent.

In continuing his own investigation, Smart discovered that since 1946 only five companies had been favored with electrical contracts by the district. Upon analysis, a definite pattern emerged. The companies had virtually allocated the work among themselves. That is, contracts for certain installations were always awarded to the same companies. After checking through contracts totaling some $25 million, Smart concluded that an illegal profit of at least $12.5 million had been siphoned off by the five companies. His findings were again reported to State's Attorney Ward, whose grand jury

204

probe was slowly coming unglued. A federal grand jury, investigating the antitrust angle, was not faring much better.

"Cronin was a real tiger on this investigation. He really wanted to go all the way on it. But suddenly he was gone. Fired. His replacement was Louis B. Garippo, who was very cooperative for several weeks. I would come to him with further information, and he would act enthused and say things like 'Boy, we've got a real winner here, these dirty thieves' and so forth. Gradually our relationship changed. Mr. Garippo became a little tight-mouthed. He no longer uttered little cries of joy at the sight of new clues. The federal grand jury began its investigation around February 1962, and I would go to Garippo and say, 'Lou, how is it going?' He'd say, 'Well, all the books and records have been subpoenaed by the federal grand jury and our investigation is continuing but kinda at a standstill.' Well, it just fizzled out. Nothing further developed. The grand jury term expired and the people went home. So here we are years later and the statute of limitations, which is only eighteen months for conspiracy in this state, has run out. The thieves are home, free and clear of any local prosecution.

"Now the federal side of it was equally enlightening. The investigation was assigned to federal prosecutors Harry Farris and Dorothy Hunt, and they too were very enthused by what I had dug up. I testified before the grand jury and they were off and running. Further investigation revealed that Byron Carter was on Northern States Company's payroll—they had the YYE contract—as a consultant and was paid through an affiliate called M. C. Clark Company. Clarence Crager, the district's senior electrical plant engineer, was also on Northern States' payroll at $160 a week. Pinkerton, Carter and Crager had each more than thirty years' service with the district and were retired with full pensions.

"Well, the leaves of the calendar flew like they do in the movies, and first thing I knew winter had turned into fall. Farris and Hunt would hint that I could expect indictments in two months. The two months would turn into four, and the four into eight, and still nothing. Then a third party, a federal official who shall remain nameless, came to me and said, 'You've got to do something. They're trying to kill the case.' I said 'Who is they and what do I do?' He said, 'Well, they, specifically, is Earl A. Jinkinson [Midwest chief of the Justice Department's antitrust division]. He's been opposed to the case all along. In fact, he went before the grand jury and said you were a convicted thief. That you were fired from the *Daily News* and convicted and jailed for stealing money from your employer. He is trying to impeach you.' And I said, 'Yes, and with lies because none of it is true.' Actually, I spent a week in the House of Correction once for a series of articles on an assignment for the *Daily News*. And I might add, a highly successful series, but it earned me the enmity of certain people. Frankly, I couldn't imagine a federal prosecutor, and in this case the boss of the division, deliberately impeaching his own witness even if the charges had been true.

"There's another element to this story I should bring in at this point. Back in January 1962, Mayor Daley sent a press agent by the name of Charles C. Smith to the district as Chesrow's administrative assistant with orders to tone down the growing scandal. Smith, a former press agent for Bishop Sheil, now works for Paul Powell, our new Secretary of State. Anyway, Smith was a busy little man for a while. He was all over the federal building, talking to Jinkinson and to Chief Judge William Campbell, who was in charge of the federal grand jury. Of course, I don't know what they talked about. It could have been personal business. I might add, though, that Judge Campbell has a reputation in this town for being a very political guy. I know that Smith wrote to Campbell, charging that I was tampering with the jury. And it came back to me from many sources that Smith was spreading that story about my fictitious criminal record. Here we had a case involving millions of dollars and an obvious violation of the antitrust act as far as the collusive bidding was concerned, and all of a sudden everybody was terribly worried about my week in the House of Correction.

"The intrigue was not only in Chicago. It was buzzing in Washington, too. I heard from my third party a few months later that 'it's all fixed now. There are not to be any indictments. Two men from Washington will appear before the grand jury. They will say there have been apparent violations of federal laws, but not antitrust violations, and that the jury should return no bills.' This third party, who knew how good a case we had, said 'For God's sake, go to the foreman of the grand jury and tell him this.' So I went to the foreman and gave him the particulars. He asked me to repeat my story before the jury and I did. Two months later, the two men from Washington arrived and that was the end of that investigation. Meanwhile, Dundas and Scheidt have retired with pensions, and Jinkinson has left the government for a job with Winston, Strawn, Smith and Patterson, a law firm with plenty of City Hall clout."

It is basic arithmetic in Chicago that whenever big money is involved, it inevitably follows that a hoodlum is in the woodpile. In this instance, it was John F. Scanlan, former owner of Mid-West News, a wire service supplying racetrack information to Syndicate bookmakers. According to the Kefauver report, Scanlan had once "participated in the Guzik-Accardo-[Harry] Russell maneuver to take over" a wire service in Florida. With the demise of Mid-West News, Scanlan became a "front" for Syndicate bosses, particularly Ralph Pierce, overlord of Marshall Korshak's Fifth Ward. For several years, Pierce reported substantial income from E&J Construction, a company operated by Edward Joyce and John Scanlan. Known as the "mystery man of influence" in district affairs and a frequent visitor at its headquarters, Scanlan had long been an object of curiosity to federal agents. Following his visits with district trustees and officials, Scanlan invariably met with Murray Humphreys.

In June 1960, Scanlan borrowed $20,000 from a bank and formed Structural Maintenance Service, Inc. A short time later, he invested $10,000 in a joint venture with the Garden City Engineering Company, which held the $1.4 million YYD electrical contract. While Garden City put up all its assets in the contract and performed all the work, Structural Maintenance did nothing more tangible than put up the $10,000. Its reward was a 50 percent split of the $641,000 illegal profit reaped through the padded contract.

Trustee Garrity received a smidgen of publicity when he was identified during the federal grand jury probe as a friend of Scanlan. Otherwise, the revelation that hoodlums were involved did not stir too much curiosity.

Meanwhile, *Tribune* reporter George Bliss was busily digging into the district, writing a series of eighty stories (it earned him a Pulitzer Prize) about timesheet faking, loaded and padded payrolls, inflated wage scales, insurance kickbacks, rigged contracts and real estate lease payoffs that were costing the taxpayers at least $5 million a year. Of the 2,300 employees, nearly half were patronage workers, sponsored by politicians and labor leaders. Bliss wrote of the gambling, drinking and sleeping clubs—employees brought their own blankets and pillows to be more comfortable. He told of a district engineer who admitted having padded a payroll with $50-a-day "ghost" workers because he was promised reimbursement for doing so. He uncovered a large Syndicate bookmaking ring at the Stickney

207

plant, and bumper crops of marijuana, as much as 150 acres of it growing wild on district land, some of it as high as twenty feet. Marijuana has been growing on district land for years. Occasionally, police arrest trespassers in the act of picking the narcotic weed. (Some twenty years ago, one pusher, who admitted planting a marijuana field on district land, protested that he was only trying to raise $15,000 to buy a tavern so he could retire.)

A legion of ex-convicts were on the payroll, and in most cases their police records and fingerprint cards were missing from employment files. Richard B. Ogilvie, who was running for sheriff in 1962, charged that the district was a "rest home and haven for relatives and friends of the Chicago crime syndicate." Ogilvie had a list of thirty-six employees with Syndicate connections. Chesrow accused Ogilvie of playing politics and refused to read the reports, stating categorically that he knew of no Syndicate figures on the payroll. Ogilvie countered by naming Joseph Laino, an investigator working out of Chesrow's office. Pointing out that Laino had just received a raise, Ogilvie said: "I wonder how many Cook county taxpayers received a $74-a-month pay raise such as Laino received. Of course, most of them probably haven't been arrested in a Beverly Hills hotel with the brother of the late Al Capone, as was Laino."

When the kitchen stove began to melt before the 1962 election, the trustees named a blue-ribbon citizens committee to find a new general superintendent for the district. This strategic move, dictated by Daley, had worked beautifully for the mayor during the police scandal of 1960. The idea was to find someone with a soothing image like O. W. Wilson. The committee's choice was Vinton W. Bacon, a West Coast engineer and water pollution expert.

Not long after Bacon reported for work, he was invited out to dine with several of the trustees. After a couple of friendly drinks, one of the trustees leaned toward Bacon and whispered that everything was all set. Bacon chose to ignore the connotation. A moment later, the trustee again leaned forward to whisper: "She's a dish and clean. Nothing to worry about there, believe me." Without uttering a word, Bacon stood up and walked out of the restaurant. "That's an old gangster trick," one official explained. "You pull a man's pants down and make a bum out of him." Since that night, Mrs. Bacon is always at her husband's side when he attends trustee-sponsored dinners.

One of Bacon's first acts was to hire the firm of A. C. Kirkwood & Associates of Kansas City, Missouri, to make a complete study of all electrical contracts awarded since 1946. The firm's report substantiated Smart's projected estimate of $12.5 million in overpayments to five companies: Northern States Company with its two affiliates, Northern States Construction and M. C. Clark Company; Harmon Electric Company; Divane Brothers Electric Company; Garden City Engineering Company; Meade Electric Company and its subsidiary, Monroe Electric Company.

On March 19, 1964, two years after the federal grand jury investigation was initiated, Bacon filed suit against the above companies (Structural Maintenance Service, Inc. was not included), seeking treble damages totaling $37 million. The suit accused three former engineers with taking payoffs from the firms to fix prices, bids and cost estimates. Included in the suit were the eight bonding companies that had insured the electrical firms. The defendants were accused of violating the Sherman and Clayton Anti-Trust laws. The suit was filed by the law firm of McConnell, Curtis, and McConnell.

Two months later, Judge Campbell dismissed the grand jury, concluding the government's case. What followed was a long, futile effort by Attorney Francis McConnell to impound the defendants' books and records then in custody of Judge Campbell. On October 15, after seven months of attempting to subpoena the records under discovery procedure, McConnell learned that Judge Campbell had ordered the records returned in bulk to the various companies without itemization or receipt and without notice to plaintiff.

McConnell's next surprise came from George A. Lane, the district's chief attorney, who ordered him to drop the case. All nine trustees, sitting as members of the district's judiciary committee, approved the dropping of the suit on the grounds that it could not be won since a federal grand jury had failed to return indictments. Korshak informed the press that federal prosecutors had advised him against continuing with the suit. McConnell angrily countered that three federal prosecutors had recommended that the grand jury return criminal indictments but were overruled by Jinkinson. Also, said McConnell, "the burden of proof in a civil case is significantly less than in a criminal case." For one thing, defendants could not invoke the Fifth Amendment against self-incrimination.

Chesrow's reason for dropping the suit was that it would have cost "at least $250,000 to handle all the litigation involved."

Ted Smart, who had since left the *American* to join NBC-TV, had the final word when he interviewed Louis Pacheco, an architect and foreman of the federal grand jury, on WMAQ-TV on February 27, 1965. Smart asked Pacheco to explain what had happened after

209

government prosecutors, with the approval of the grand jury, drafted indictments and submitted them to justice department officials in Washington.

"We had officials come from Washington with instructions to the jury as to what their views were and they discussed this with me outside the jury room and outside the court," Pacheco replied.

"What did they tell you?"

"Well, they felt in their own minds . . . that the case was very weak."

"What was the attitude of the prosecutors toward the case outside the jury room as they may have expressed their opinions to you?"

"Well, they didn't think it was weak at all. In fact, I didn't, from a personal viewpoint, seem to feel that way."

In fact, the jurors had voted three times—twice unanimously—to indict six individuals and seven companies. When the government had refused to accept the grand jury's judgment, Pacheco had voiced his objections to Judge Campbell. "Well," replied the judge, "if Mr. Jinkinson says there isn't a case, then I suppose there isn't one."

To prove that they were not spoilsports, the trustees approved the final payment to the Garden City Engineering Company.

In the next three years, Bacon slimmed the budget from $74 million to $67 million, and slashed away at patronage with civil service examinations. Then, in April 1966, Bacon committed what the *Daily News* termed "the unforgivable political sin": He uncovered and exposed "some of the hidden wiring that links politicians, trade union leaders and the crime syndicate."

The scandal erupted when Bacon followed through on a hunch and impounded 224 test sheets for the civil service position of operating engineer, a $10,038-a-year job. Convinced that some of the exams had been rigged, he hired Forbes E. McCann, a Philadelphia consultant, to investigate. McCann's report concluded that scores had been fraudulently boosted for 39 of the 47 test papers with passing grades, while four who should have passed were cut to a failing grade by changes in correct answers.

Four months later, just as this scandal was beginning to subside, Bacon impounded a thousand test sheets involving twelve more sets of civil service examinations and asked the trustees for money and authority to continue his investigation. He estimated that the total payoffs involved in a single examination could run as high as $200,000. The board flatly rejected his request.

"I'll tear the place up and down in order to get at those other

210

twelve examinations," Bacon vowed. "I'm going to ask for the money to investigate, and I'll get it or else."

A few hours later, Bacon became the latest target of Chicago's favorite instrument of violence—the bomb. Four sticks of dynamite, rigged to explode when he turned on the ignition of his car, failed to detonate because a wire had slipped off a spark plug. The device was discovered by a service station attendant.

"I thought I was exempt from that kind of thing," Bacon said, his face pale and drawn. "I thought that if I was honest and did my job and didn't let them buy me, I was outside of that. I honestly never thought anything like that could happen to me."

The day following the bombing attempt, Chesrow enthusiastically embraced Bacon when they met in the presence of newsmen. "It's a dastardly thing to do to a man," he said. "He has been doing such a wonderful job."

A week later the mutilated body of Louis "Gigi" Pratico was found in a roadside ditch. A henchman of Frank LaPorte, the Syndicate's south suburban rackets boss, Pratico had been shot twice in the head and severely beaten. Police theorized that Pratico, a former Chicago Heights policeman and a known underworld bomber and strongarm thug, could have been slain for botching the attempted bombing of Bacon's car. (Bacon's new car is armor plated and "bombproof"— any tampering sets off a siren.)

Fresh from a fishing trip in Wisconsin, Mayor Daley blandly supported both sides in the controversy. "I take Mr. Bacon's word that the Sanitary District is being administered better today than at any time in its history thanks to Mr. Bacon." As to the trustees: "I don't think it's fair to blame the trustees. Is anyone charging that they did this [rigged the tests]? The grand jury is investigating. If there is any evidence against the trustees, the grand jury will turn it up. I've never subscribed to this idea of general accusations against a lot of people. We've gone through that before."

The "patsy," according to Bacon, was Ronald E. Huston, the district's assistant personnel director, and the only one indicted in the case. To Bacon, Huston "was taking orders from somebody above him." "There are a hundred reports and rumors crying to be tracked down," the *Daily News* charged, "of cozy and profitable relationships between district bosses, union officials, big-shot politicians, and hoodlums. . . . The state's attorney's office waded in boldly—but we are told it was Bacon who gave the grand jury practically all it had of substance, and that after 48 hours the investigation ran out of gas."

211

The Better Government Association pointed out that Thomas Hett, the assistant state's attorney in charge of the grand jury, was sponsored by Simon A. Murray, the venerable "coach" of the West Side Bloc.

Among those questioned in the probe were officials of Local 399, International Union of Operating Engineers, which had been linked numerous times to hoodlums and First Ward politicians. All test applicants with passing grades had to join the union before being placed on the district's payroll. One point of interest was the report that Local 399 officials had sent a list of top scorers to the district even before the list was posted.

Two weeks after Huston was indicted, the grand jury ground to a halt—one month before election day 1966—because, said Hett, there was not "sufficient evidence" to give them a full day's work. When jurors suggested that perhaps Chesrow might possibly fill a day, they received a "cool reception." It was a particularly busy month for State's Attorney Ward, who was a candidate for a seat on the Illinois Supreme Court, and for Chesrow, who was seeking reelection— Chesrow was defeated but Ward was elected.

Back in the summer of 1966, Bacon had introduced another vexing problem when he requested emergency funds to investigate "serious construction defects" in a three-mile-long sewer in south Cook County. Built at a cost of $3 million and serving 10,000 persons, the sewer was not only operating below par, but sand and water infiltrating it had caused $5 million in damages to the East Chicago Heights Treatment Plant. Already, more than 10 percent of the original installation had been removed and replaced. Ultimately, the entire sewer would have to be rebuilt at a cost of $2.5 million.

The original contract, Bacon disclosed, was awarded to Anthony Pontarelli & Sons, who submitted a bid of $1,562,850, the lowest of eight bids, and was recommended for acceptance by Frank Chesrow, then chairman of the engineering committee. Pontarelli subsequently was awarded two lump sum "extra" payments of $1,512,553 and $113,675, thus bringing the final payment to more than twice the original bid figure.

For years, Anthony and Michael Pontarelli have dominated sewer construction in Cook County, and for an even longer period, Chicago police have been trying to uncover their hidden ties to the upper echelon of the Syndicate. For example, a car registered to Michael Pontarelli was observed at the wake and funeral of Frank Russo in 1963, and again at the wake and funeral of Thomas Fratto in 1965,

212

both high-ranking mafiosi. Anthony Pontarelli was prominent in the operation of the National Cuba Hotel Corporation, owner of a chain of hotels, including the Blackstone and Drake in Chicago and Cuban hotels in pre-Castro days that were bossed by the notorious Meyer Lansky, former partner of the late Bugsy Siegel and highly touted member of the East Coast branch of the national crime cartel.

16

Attorney Harry Booth is Chicago's most formidable dragon slayer. Frail, myopic, rumpled and no taller or heavier than a jockey, his favorite mount is a monolithic public utility. The bigger they are, the faster they run when the diminutive attorney gets that riding gleam behind his thick-lensed spectacles. In the past forty years, he has filed more suits in behalf of consumers of natural gas, electricity, telephone, water and transit than all other lawyers in Chicago combined.

"Harry is a gadfly, a troublemaker, a misdirected knight on a white charger," say his detractors. "Harry often sees the devil in actions which are merely part of the routine operation of a large utility. . . . Harry makes us a little impatient sometimes when we have to spend money defending suits we feel are invalid. . . . Harry has no understanding of big corporations."

It was only natural that Harry's pulse would quicken whenever he read stories about the scandal-ridden Sanitary District. By late 1962, Smart and Bliss were concentrating on the district's real estate department and the leasing of its land at bargain prices, complete with payoffs and kickbacks. Booth knew that along the banks of the district's waterways were some two hundred million square feet of the most valuable commercial and industrial property in the metropolitan area—land that had been leased for up to a century to politicians, favored contractors, land speculators and other Brahmins of the Machine.

By October 1963, after months of diligent homework, Booth was ready to fight. But unlike the newspapers, which were satisfied with headlining minor violations, Booth presented the Circuit Court with a 66-page complaint, charging abuses to the public in the leasing of 2,800 acres of district land in a hundred long-term leases to twenty-three corporations since 1948, and that "substantially all such leases represent a gift of eighty to ninety percent" of the land value. His "conservative estimate" of total loss to the public was placed at $25

213

million. Included in the complaint was Material Service Corporation, owned and operated by Colonel Henry Crown, and two of its subsidiaries, the description of which occupied ten pages of the brief.

Of all the colonels in Chicago, there are none with more prestigious rank than Colonel Henry Crown, the home-grown, multimillionaire owner of Material Service Corporation. Compared to Crown's local press clippings, the writings of Horatio Alger were bitter satires. Born of indigent immigrant parents on Chicago's West Side on June 13, 1896, the incipient Midas paved the road to success with his own building materials in an era of such flagrant political corruption, labor racketeering and cutthroat competition that sheer survival aroused suspicion of capitulation.

"Well," says Crown, who today has as many aphorisms on the virtue of hard work and honesty as he has dollars, "honest politicians far outnumber the dishonest ones. The same is true of labor leaders. There are ways to avoid the crooks. A man does not have to pay bribes to operate a business successfully."

All great men are the subject of apocryphal stories that heighten the irony of their success. Albert Einstein, we are told, flunked math in the fourth grade. Henry Crown lost a $4-a-week job at the age of fourteen when he dispatched two loads of sand (or gravel—reporters are fairly evenly divided on this point) to a customer who had ordered one of sand and one of gravel.

Crown was to grow up to become the greatest exponent of sand and gravel in the world—virtually transforming sanitary district sand piles and quarries into gold mines.

"Henry Crown," said Booth, "views the Sanitary District as a small subsidiary of Material Service Corporation."

From the mid 1920s to the early 1940s, Crown purchased nearly 1,000 acres of district land through nominees—Benjamin Z. Gould, general counsel of MSC, and one Clarence R. Serb—without competitive bidding, paying an average of $64 an acre. These vast holdings, plus another 420 acres held under long-term leases negotiated mostly in the 1950s, literally formed the foundation of MSC. These properties had mountains of earth and rock deposits on their surface (spoil banks rich in limestone used for crushed rock and cement) which were the residue from channel widening and deepening at the turn of the century. They saved MSC the expense of quarrying for years.

214

In his complaint, Booth pointed out that "none of the leases approved by the Trustees authorized Material Service Corporation to engage in excavation of sand, gravel, or other materials from below the surface of the ground. On information and belief Material Service Corporation has engaged in extensive excavating operations and removed enormous quantities of sand, gravel, limestone and other materials from below the surface of the ground which it has sold . . . [obtaining] large revenues . . . and has unjustly and unlawfully enriched itself thereby. . . . All such acts and operations . . . are illegal and beyond the power granted to it by the district . . . under the laws of the State of Illinois. . . . From time to time Material Service Corporation has also been granted sub-leases and short-term leases also at inadequate rentals as well as buy the right to take other spoil banks at nominal prices. . . . Material Service Corporation operates over 10 docks on the waterways of the district, ships several million tons of gravel, sand, and stone over such waterways by a large fleet of tow boats and barges. . . . The land leased . . . has a frontage of more than 5 miles on the Main Channel. . . . Material Service Corporation in obtaining control of more than 400 acres of district land under long-term leases at total annual rentals of only $18,700 has dominated the Trustees and wrongfully induced such Trustees to favor [it] to the great loss and injury of the plaintiff and other taxpayers of the district or persons residing within the area served by the district."

MSC has always enjoyed good business relations with the district. For example, in 1951 the district paid MSC $456,499.32 to buy back some of its land in the form of sand and gravel. From 1951 to 1960, MSC supplied the district with nearly $2 million worth of building material and coal. Its rent for that period was less than 10 percent of that amount.

Long-term leases to MSC and its two subsidiaries, Marblehead Lime Company and Producers Supply and Engineering Company, comprised more than 15 percent of the total industrial real estate leased by the district. The approximate value placed by the district on its property leased to MSC was $740 per acre, about 2,000 percent below the value appraised by real estate experts. The yearly rental was based on 6 percent of the district's valuation. The total yearly rental received by the district from all its leases was $250,000, which was an average of four cents per square foot (even that nominal rate was more than double what MSC paid) for land appraised by experts at from a dollar to a dollar and a quarter a square foot. Booth's

215

contention that rentals paid by MSC were so "grossly inadequate as to constitute a fraud" was in itself a gross understatement.

Any clear picture of Crown's business involvement at any given time is subject to change. The Colonel has jumped into scores of profitable ventures, skimmed off a profit, and jumped out again without attracting public notice. However, recent holdings have included: Material Service Corporation (board chairman); General Dynamics Corporation (executive committee chairman); Hilton International Hotels Corporation (vice-president, director and second largest stockholder); Chicago, Rock Island, and Pacific Railroad (finance chairman and major stockholder); Liquid Carbonic Corporation, division of General Dynamics (stockholder); Chicago, Wilmington and Franklin Coal Company (owns substantially all the stock) and Freeman Coal Mining Corporation (a subsidiary of MSC)—combined, these two coal companies comprise the largest output of coal in Illinois; United Electric Coal Company, subsidiary of MSC; City Products Corporation (director); Baltimore and Ohio Railroad (director); Columbia Pictures Corporation (director); Madison Square Garden Corporation, New York City (director); Waldorf-Astoria Hotel, New York City (board chairman); West Indies Sugar Corporation (director); Hertz Corporation (director), and Marblehead Lime Company and Producers Engineering and Supply Company, subsidiaries of MSC.

As a sand-and-gravel man, Crown achieved the equivalent of *The Diamond as Big as the Ritz* when he purchased the Empire State Building in 1954. Here he played host to Queen Elizabeth, Fidel Castro and Nikita Khrushchev, delighting in their admiration of the wonders of sand and gravel.

"How could a poor, uneducated boy, who started as a clerk at the age of fourteen, rise so rapidly, particularly in recent years when other old companies were failing?" the Rev. Elmer L. Williams inquired in the February 1940 edition of *Lightnin'*. "Only Mr. Crown himself could give a complete answer. But we know some of the answers."

The year Henry Crown was born, a fire burned out the family business and home on Ashland Avenue, a block north of Milwaukee Avenue. His father, Arie Crown, a weaver of men's suspenders, had branched out into the match business with the resulting catastrophe.

After working at a number of jobs, Henry and his brothers, Irving and Sol, incorporated MSC in 1919 with a capital of $20,000, mostly in borrowed money. To economize, they shared an office with John

216

Gutknecht, who became attorney for the new company and a lifelong friend—thirty-three years later, Crown's sponsorship of Gutknecht led to his election as State's Attorney and four years later to a seat on the Circuit Court bench.

When Sol died of tuberculosis in 1921, Henry became president of MSC, then the smallest of the eighty-odd firms in the sand, stone and concrete business in Chicago. MSC was further hampered by being only a brokerage company without ownership of its sources of supply —the Colonel had not as yet discovered the Sanitary District. It did not remain the smallest very long: sales jumped tenfold—from $215,000 to $2,144,000—by 1923.

Of all the colorful stories that have attempted to explain Crown's initial success, the *Daily News*' takes the prize: "In 1922, Crown and a friend casually met on the street a man introduced to him as Anton Cermak. The name meant nothing to him then, although Cermak had just been named president of the County Board [of Commissioners]. A few days later, Cermak phoned Crown and asked about the price of stone. Crown thought it was a gag. When it was straightened out, Crown had another fat contract. The history of Material Service Corp. from then on belongs to the financial editors."

Although not a financial editor, the Rev. Williams, a contemporary of Crown, offered a different version in *Lightnin':* "Tony Cermak's friendly interest in the MS Corp. is too well known to need comment. Henry Crown has the run of Tony's office. 'Let's see what A. J. says about it,' is Mr. Crown's favorite saying. There is only one kind of 'sand' that Tony likes better than that of MS Corp. That is the sand brought in by the Morton Construction Co. from Canada. These 'vessels' dock at Goose Island at MS Corp. dock. My, what sand they had!"

Other politicians were also interested in MSC. State Senator John Dailey, then chairman of a legislative committee investigating the malpractices of Illinois contractors and materials companies, became a director of MSC in 1924. Dailey "bought" 10 percent of the company's stock for $25,000. State Senator Frank Ryan, later involved with Libonati and Paul Powell as a stockholder in Sportsman's Park, was placed on MSC's payroll as a vice-president. Another vice-president was Arthur J. Lindheimer, brother of Ben Lindheimer, chairman of the Illinois Commerce Commission and a close friend of Samuel L. Nudleman, State Director of Finance, and of Ernest Lieberman, State Highway Engineer.

On the other side of the ledger was Mike Carrozzo, regional satrap

217

of the Hodcarriers' and Common Laborers' Union, with some twenty-five Chicago locals, mostly Italian pick-and-shovel workers loyal to the padrones. A former procurer for Big Jim Colosimo, who first organized the Street Laborers' Union, Carrozzo's police record included arrests for mail theft, bank robbery and murder. One of his early associates was Big Tim Murphy, a slugger and assassin for the Building Trades Council, who was slugged fatally in 1928.

Carrozzo's dictatorial rule of labor unions gave him tremendous power over contractors and material firms. Contractors not acceptable to Carrozzo, or those using materials he had not endorsed, were forced to employ hand labor, mostly incompetent or inexperienced, to perform work usually accomplished by machines at great savings in time and cost.

As boss of the paving inspectors' local, he exercised control over asphalt, sand, gravel, crushed-stone and cement. Carrozzo's immediate superior was Anthony D'Andrea, bodyguard to Al Capone and a cousin of Louis "Little New York" Campagna. D'Andrea was responsible for keeping ready-mixed concrete out of Chicago for twenty years by refusing to let union paving workers handle it.

Among Carrozzo's favorite contractors was Sam Nanini, owner of Rock Road Construction Company and a close friend of Henry Crown. Nanini was also the beneficiary of Sanitary District land. Crown and Nanini were a powerful team: Crown with his political connections and Nanini with his contacts in Syndicate-operated unions. Crown furnished the materials and Nanini did the construction.

Soon a man of considerable wealth, Carrozzo bought five farms in Lake County, Indiana, near Hobart, and combined them into his Villa C. Grateful contractors and material purveyors aided the labor czar in erecting buildings and modernizing houses and barns on his large estate. Rock Road Construction built a patented multicolored tennis court, valued at $20,000, and a $17,000 swimming pool—government agents never were able to discover whether money exchanged hands. Carrozzo's Northern Illinois Agrolith Company was incorporated by Michael L. Rosinia, an assistant Corporation counsel, who also appears as the incorporator of Rock Road Construction Company. In 1933, Nanini formed the Bell Oil Company to deal in fuel, road oils and asphaltum products. A few years later, merchants at the Fulton Street Market charged that Joey Glimco's thugs were pressuring them to favor Bell Oil. This was only natural since Nanini had supported Glimco's second citizenship application.

218

Nanini's ties to the Syndicate were again revealed in 1947 when he wrote a letter to the federal parole board advocating an application by Louis "Little New York" Campagna (the gangster who had terrorized Cermak) for release from the United States Penitentiary at Atlanta, where he was serving a ten-year sentence as one of the seven mob chiefs convicted in the Browne-Bioff movie extortion conspiracy.

When Carrozzo died in 1940, Nanini filed suit seeking recovery of $11,547.11 from the estate, which was dismissed shortly afterward by agreement of both parties. Upon Carrozzo's death, the price of paving dropped a dollar a square yard.

(In April 1966, Rock Road Construction, then under the guidance of Nanini's son, William, became the subject of a lawsuit when Republican Alderman Edward T. Scholl revealed that Chicago had been overcharged as much as $1 million for asphalt over a three-year period. Scholl disclosed that while Rock Road Construction charged the city $13.20 a ton for cold patch asphalt, it sold the same grade paving material to suburbs for as low as $7.50 a ton; the state highway division paid $9.55 and Cook County $11.00. After considerable prompting by the press, the City of Chicago filed a breach of contract suit against Rock Road seeking $502,172 in damages.)

At the height of the Sanitary District's Whoopee Era, Crown (through a nominee) purchased his first of a series of large tracts of district land near Lockport for the usual pittance. But the fact that MSC often lacked ownership of its own source of supply never noticeably interfered with its ability to obtain public contracts. For example, in November 1931 MSC had no coal mines, coal trucks or coal yard facilities. Yet contracts for five of the seven school districts ($1 million worth of coal to more than four hundred schools) were awarded to nominees of MSC. All five bids represented the fuel as having exactly the same heat units and percentages of ash and moisture, a rather remarkable coincidence. To further accommodate MSC, the School Board revised its specifications to permit strip coal—the only type offered by MSC—to be included in the bidding even though there had been previous objections to the heating quality of strip coal in the schools.

When James McCahey, chairman of the School Board, was accused of favoring MSC, he announced that in the future the board would split up the business among several companies. A man of his word, McCahey then bought bricks for six new schools from three different firms: MSC; Howard-Matz Brick Company, owned by MSC; and Garden City Sand Company, a subsidiary of MSC. The bricks,

219

worth $28 a thousand on the open market, were sold as low as $33 a thousand.

A versatile entrepreneur, Crown was awarded the contract to supply soft drinks (Royal Crown Cola, Nehi Orange, Nehi Root Beer, Still Orange) to the schools at prices higher than charged to taverns.

Crown's penchant for leaning a little too heavily on a lead pencil caused some lively debate in the City Council, which by 1933 was struggling to keep the financially crippled city from going under permanently. Placed on the firing line by Republican members of the Council, Public Works Commissioner Oscar Hewitt explained that he had asked for bids three times on a paving contract, and each time the Consumers Company, the Moulding-Brownell Company and MSC had submitted identical bids: "I called the companies in and asked why the identical bids. They told me they had lost money last year on the city business because they fought for it, and admitted they got together on the bids. Cement was $1.28 a barrel last year and this year it's $2.10 a barrel."

"Well, cement is $1.57 a barrel in Indiana," said Alderman O'Grady, focusing his wrath on MSC. "Everybody knows the stock of this concern is owned by politicians."

"Democratic politicians who control the purchase of materials for public buildings, roads, sewers, sewage plants, pumping stations, etc.," Williams observed, "have made themselves rich and have enhanced the fortunes of their favored allies by the simple formula of 'addition, division and silence.' . . . An eminent engineer was brought to Chicago, from Wisconsin, to investigate some of the public construction under Cermak. After a cursory survey, the engineer said: 'Gentlemen, you do not need an engineer. You need a grand jury.' "

The quality of materials can sometimes be a relative thing, as one rash supplier learned when he underbid MSC on a public works contract. The contractor, who shipped gravel and crushed rock in from Wisconsin, was informed by city inspectors that his aggregate was below acceptable grade standards. Faced with costly return shipping charges, the contractor sold the shipment to Crown for the freight charges. A few days later, the contractor went out to the construction site and found his material passing every inspection.

Although MSC grossed $9 million in 1928, the company's credit expansion was moving at an even faster clip. By 1931, at the nadir of the Depression, Crown owed his bank, the Foreman-State, nearly $2

220

million without a dollar of collateral. Meanwhile, Cermak had sweetened Harold Foreman's disposition with large deposits of public funds. When Cermak withdrew the funds in 1931, the Foreman bank folded and was absorbed by First National.

Melvin A. Traylor, president of First National, happened to be a devoted Cermak booster. The first thing Traylor knew, he was Cermak's choice for favorite son in the 1932 national presidential convention—Mike Igoe had the honor of nominating Traylor.

"Mr. Cermak made a shrewd political play," Williams noted in *Lightnin'*. "He groomed . . . Traylor for President of the United States. Mr. Crown still owes his bankers a very large sum." The move was not too shrewd as far as Roosevelt was concerned—it precipitated the Florida meeting.

Building was at a standstill and Crown could not even raise the $10,000 monthly payment on $500,000 worth of MSC debentures exercised by the Consumers Company, its collusive competitor. Traylor's first act was to get Consumers to halve MSC's monthly payment. Then, believing in Crown's "ability . . . integrity . . . imagination," Traylor began advancing the additional millions Cermak's protégé would need in his climb to fame and fortune.

In 1939, Williams noted that "the big graft in the state is the material business, $86,000,000 appropriated for roads, etc. Henry Crown has extended his control of the material business in city and county since the days of Cermak by ways that make Bret Harte's Chinee a simpleton."

MSC's sales had climbed to $10.8 million. The next year, Crown began broadening the base of his operation by acquiring (with a First National loan) the Freeman Coal Mining Corporation for $1.5 million. Nine years later, Crown bought an abandoned mine on twenty-six thousand acres, near Farmersville, from the United States Alien Property Custodian for $150,000. After mechanizing the operation, the Colonel delivered his first million tons of coal to Commonwealth Edison in 1952. Public utilities, whose margin of profit is dependent on the good will of politicians, have always enjoyed doing business with Colonel Crown. The demand for Crown coal was so overwhelming that the Colonel paid $12.5 million for the Chicago Wilmington & Franklin Coal Company in 1954. For a while there was almost enough Crown coal to satisfy the clamoring customers. But not quite. So, in 1959, the United Electric Coal Company was added to the long list of MSC subsidiaries. Immediately, something very pleasant happened to the company: After years of unsuccessful

221

bidding for a portion of the Sanitary District's 1,000-ton-a-day business, it broke the hex in 1961 with an 80,000-ton order. Then, in 1962, it limited its bid to 100,000 tons and again received the contract. The balance, some 260,000 tons, was awarded to the District's chief supplier, the Truax-Traer Coal Company.

Vinton Bacon had already ordered an investigation into coal buying procedures when, in May 1963, the *Sun-Times* revealed that a "hoodlum-infiltrated" company had collected more than $500,000 in "expediters" fees on $7 million worth of coal contracts awarded to Truax-Traer from 1959 to 1962. The self-styled expediter was Edwin C. Roth, Sr., president of the Roth-Adam Fuel Company and owner of a string of race horses. Roth classified himself as a "watchdog," offering the press various explanations for his fees: service charges, handling charges and "checking things through." A spokesman for Truax-Traer thought Roth was more of a troubleshooter: "We were having trouble on our contracts with the Sanitary District until we began paying commissions to Roth. He is our troubleshooter. . . . We use him so we don't have to deal directly with the district." Roth's knack for troubleshooting was suddenly acquired in 1958 when he placed Nick Bravos* on the payroll at $1,000 a month. Police have since linked three other hoodlums to the firm's operation: Bravos' brother, George, and Charles and Sam English, who "have the run of the place" and "drive company cars all over town" and to the racetracks. The 8 percent "expediter" fee (thirty-eight cents a ton) was thoughtfully added to the coal firm's bid and passed on to the taxpayers. That United Electric was able to crack this rather formidable monopoly (Truax-Traer was the District's sole supplier) was another tribute to the Colonel's competitive spirit.

The Alien Property Custodian in 1947, the year the Colonel purchased the Farmersville mine, was David L. Bazelon, formerly an assistant U.S. Attorney in Chicago (1935–1940) and a senior member of the Chicago law firm of Gottlieb and Schwartz (1940–1946). In both positions he worked with Paul Ziffren, later a law partner of Jake Arvey, who represented Chicago interests in Southern California. Considered close friends, Ziffren and Bazelon joined in several multimillion-dollar ventures across the country.

A number of alien properties passed into the hands of investors,

* See Appendix.

222

who at times included Ziffren, Bazelon and Jake Arvey. Some of the properties were the Franklin Hotel in Chicago, the Rohm-Haas Corporation of Luxembourg and the Resinous Products and Chemical Corporation of Philadelphia, in which Rohm-Haas owned a big block of stock—it was described as a $12 million deal. Los Angeles interests included the Los Angeles Warehouse Company, United Credits Corporation and a whole string of hotels. In one hotel, police discovered that listed with Ziffren on the hotel's liquor license was the wife of Fred Evans, the late partner of Humphreys and Glimco. Another principal was Samuel Genis, a financial wizard who fronted for Alex Louis Greenberg, who in turn fronted for the Chicago mob's top hierarchy.

At the time, Genis held all the outstanding stock in Store Properties, Inc., which according to its incorporation papers had been founded for the purpose of "holding real property for investment in California, Arizona, Utah, Colorado, Oklahoma, Florida, Illinois and New York." An examination of Greenberg's tax records disclosed that he and Ziffren were partners with Store Properties in a parcel of developed real estate worth about $900,000 in San Bernardino, California.

Acting as a vice-president for Store Properties in its Arizona ventures was Harold Rado, business manager for a group of firms specializing in union insurance and owned by James Roosevelt. The Roosevelt enterprises were housed in the Spreckles Building in Los Angeles, which was owned jointly by Store Properties, Webb & Knapp and Ben Swig, who later became statewide finance chairman for Pat Brown in his campaign for governor.

This group held titles to more than $100 million worth of real estate in California alone. By his own estimate, Genis' holdings elsewhere in the country were valued at $180 million, which was not bad for a man whose police record included arrests for bad checks in Florida, embezzlement in New York, mail fraud and securities law violations in Georgia and four bankruptcies. Among his known underworld associates were Abner "Longie" Zwillman, rackets boss of New Jersey; Joseph Stacher, a lieutenant of Zwillman who masterminded the building of the Sands Hotel in Las Vegas; Frank Costello, then prime minister of organized crime; Joey Adonis, a New York gangster later deported to Italy, and Meyer Lansky, currently the national syndicate's chief gambling representative in England and the Bahamas.

But as in all underworld high finance, Genis' fortune mysteriously vanished in 1955 upon his death in an automobile accident. For probate purposes, his vast holdings dwindled to a mere $5.4 million, which was incumbered almost entirely by an outstanding loan held by a Chicago financial firm. Genis' heirs received less than $250,000. The probate was handled by Ziffren and the City National Bank of Beverly Hills, an institution controlled by Glencoe Distilleries and Alfred Hart, a business associate of Joseph Fusco.*

The year 1955 also proved unlucky for Greenberg. Four gangland bullets, administered in the forehead, chest, left arm and groin, were his final payoff. His autobiography, the Chicago *Tribune* suggested, might have been called "My 46 Years With Chicago Gangsters." The title could have included politicians as well. For example, back in the early 1930s, Greenberg (fronting for Nitti) had founded Lawndale Enterprises, Inc., along with Jake Arvey, Louis Mantynband (a law partner of Arvey) and Moe Rosenberg. In later years, Lawndale, which operated theaters and places of amusement and produced exhibit attractions, also enjoyed the sagacious advice of such officers as Arthur X. Elrod, Samuel B. Epstein (a law partner of Arvey) and Joseph G. Engert, a partner with Joseph Aiuppa in the Towne Hotel in Cicero.

Another Greenberg-Syndicate enterprise was the Roosevelt Finance Company, which made substantial loans to Manhattan Brewery, operated by Dion O'Banion and Hymie Weiss in the early years of prohibition. When the two gang bosses were killed by Capone gangsters in the mid-1920s, creditor Greenberg changed the name to Canadian Ace Brewing Company in an effort to deodorize its reputation. Arthur C. Lueder, Republican candidate for mayor in 1923 and a former postmaster, became the company's new president. When Lueder ran successfully for State Auditor in 1940, Greenberg contributed $20,000 to his campaign. At the time of Greenberg's gangland execution, Canadian Ace was grossing $10 million a year.

Ziffren's financial success in California involved scores of businesses linked to Chicago mob interests. By 1949, after only five years in his adopted state, Ziffren turned his considerable talents toward politics. Not one for starting at the bottom in any endeavor, he became money-raiser for Helen Gahagen Douglas' campaign against Richard M. Nixon for the United States Senate in 1950. Although she failed in her bid, Ziffren's meteoric rise astounded even the experts.

In 1953, he was elected Democratic National Committeeman for

* See Appendix.

224

California, a post that had taken his mentor, Jake Arvey, a lifetime to attain in Illinois. During Ziffren's seven-year reign, California Democrats climbed back into power, capturing both houses of the state legislature for the first time in seventy-five years. Said Paul Butler, chairman of the national committee, in 1960: "Paul Ziffren has been the greatest single force and most important individual Democrat in the resurgence of the Democratic Party in California." Yet Ziffren's public career was cut short that same year when a magazine unveiled some of his shadowy ties. His business career continues, of course, and his sagacious tax advice is sought by many movie greats. Bazelon's future was more propitious. On October 15, 1949, President Truman nominated him to the federal bench. Today he is Chief Justice of the United States Court of Appeals for the District of Columbia.

At the midpoint in World War II, while MSC was striving to whip the Axis through numerous war construction jobs, Henry Crown, commissioned a lieutenant colonel, became chief of procurement for the Great Lakes Division of the Army Engineers in Chicago. He was later awarded the Legion of Merit for having supervised the purchase of a billion dollars' worth of materials. A month before his discharge in August 1945, the Office of Price Administration filed suits of more than $1 million against MSC and Consumers Company, charging violations of OPA price ceilings on sand, gravel, cement and other building materials. Victims of the alleged overcharges were listed as the City of Chicago, State Highway Division, Chicago Park District, Chicago Surface Lines, Commonwealth Edison, Peoples Gas, Light & Coke Company and a number of Catholic cemeteries.

The Colonel faced another crisis in 1949 when the *Sun-Times* disclosed that "Jacob M. Arvey . . . had a substantial but hidden interest in property condemned for the Congress Street super-highway. He shared in a $1,206,452.62 judgment entered by Circuit Court Judge Stanley Klarkowski on September 21, 1948. Arvey was a key man in a syndicate that purchased the property secretly after Cook County had filed its condemnation suit in April 1946. . . . The price paid by this group for the square block of property and 27 buildings was approximately $900,000. . . . The county took a strip of property 207 feet wide out of this block for the super-highway. . . . A county appraisal dated March 1, 1946, set the value of the strip at $300,000. . . . The Arvey group was left with

225

the remainder of the block—including two good office buildings and smaller structures."

The financier of Arvey's syndicate was identified as Henry Crown. "Crown," said the *Daily News,* "put up about $1,000,000, the bulk of which was considered as a loan and has been repaid. Crown is interested in many businesses and is the head of several large ones. Best known is his material company, which sells to all kinds of public bodies in Illinois. It seems to be agreed that he volunteered his way into this deal by assuring [Arvey, *et al.*] in general terms that he would like to be helpful sometime. The time happened to be opportune. He may have been grateful for past favors. Perhaps he anticipated favors in the future. Arvey is probably not the only public man who has cause to be grateful in turn to Mr. Crown, or who anticipates future favors."

In recent years, Crown's interest in real estate has become national. In March 1959, he purchased, site unseen and in cash, a square mile of land at the north edge of Tucson for $1,280,000 from Sam Nanini, who had extended his operation to Arizona in the early Fifties.

Another real estate associate was Del E. Webb. In February 1959, they plunked down $5 million for the 3,000-acre Arrowhead Ranches, Inc., in Dear Valley, Arizona. Along about the same time, they purchased two California tracts: the 4,100-acre Bishop ranch near Santa Barbara, and 1,400 acres south of Riverside.

From 1954 to 1961, the Colonel had sole ownership of the 102-story Empire State Building. He paid $49.5 million and sold it for $65 million to Empire State Building Associates, a general partnership syndicate organized by Lawrence A. Wien, a New York real estate operator who specialized in syndications. On the same day, Wien sold the building to the Prudential Insurance Company of America with a leaseback arrangement that returned the property to the syndicate for 114 years. In 1959, Desert Inn Associates, another Wien syndication, purchased the Desert Inn in Las Vegas for $10 million and leased it back to its original owners until the year 2022. The Desert Inn boys were so happy with the tax-saving maneuver that they donated $50,000 to Wien's tax-exempt foundation.

If Crown ever lost any money on a business deal, it has not been recorded. But he came harrowingly close to it on December 31, 1959, when he merged MSC with the monolithic General Dynamics Corporation. At the time, MSC's estimated worth was set at $120 million, with annual sales in excess of $110 million. The merger was brought

about by an exchange of stock. Crown acquired convertible prefer-
ence stock, representing approximately 20 percent of the equity,
which in corporate language gave him a dominant influence—even 5
percent can often mean control in many American corporations. In
other words, Crown's 20 percent was the largest single bloc of stock
represented at a board of directors meeting. During the next two
years, 1960 and 1961, General Dynamics not only lost $425 million,
but became involved in an antitrust suit—the government charged
that the company required those from whom it purchased to recipro-
cate by buying its carbon dioxide.

Then, in 1962, the Defense Department awarded General Dynamics its $6 billion TFX (fighter plane, now called the F-111)
contract—the largest contract in the history of a government. This
reversed an eighteen-month-old unanimous recommendation by military experts to award it to Boeing.

A later investigation by the McClellan committee to determine the
motivation behind the administration's last minute switch involved
ten volumes of testimony from everybody concerned—everybody
except Colonel Crown. (In testimony before the Senate Rules Committee during its investigation of Bobby Baker, Don B. Reynolds
alleged there had been a $100,000 payoff on the controversial TFX
contract, and alluded to a "big sex party" in a New York city hotel.
When the Justice Department charged that Reynolds' testimony was
"unworthy of belief," Senator Carl T. Curtis, the top-ranking GOP
member of the committee, countercharged that it was an attempt to
prejudice the public against those "who testify against the politically
powerful.")

The year 1963 was rather active legally for the Colonel. Besides
the actions of McClellan and Booth, an $8.6 million suit on behalf of
stockholders was filed in federal court against the Hilton Hotels
Corporation. The suit charged that the corporation bought back
300,000 shares of its common stock from twenty of its officers who
had "insider's knowledge that the market would drop." Among the
defendants named were Conrad N. Hilton and Henry Crown. At the
time of the purchase, the shares were priced at from $28 to $29.50.
A few months later, the market value had dropped to $15.50 to $16
a share. Crown and members of his family, the suit claimed, sold
more than half of their holdings, through Hilton, to the corporation,
and Hilton unloaded 85,847 of his own shares. Consequently, the
purchases reduced the working capital by more than $8 million and
enriched the defendants by a total of $2,890,000. Judge Julius J.

227

Hoffman dismissed the case, and the ruling was upheld by the United States Court of Appeals in Chicago. On March 7, 1966, the United States Supreme Court reversed the Chicago ruling. The decision, announced by Justice Hugo Black, went on to say that suits by stockholders "have played a rather important role in protecting shareholders of corporations from the designing schemes and wiles of insiders who are willing to betray their company's interest in order to enrich themselves. . . . The serious fraud charged here, which, of course, has not been proved, is clearly in the class of deceitful conduct which the federal securities laws were passed to prohibit and protect against." Justice Black concluded by saying that dismissal of the case was in error and that the high court was sending it back to the District court in Chicago "for trial and merits." (Action is pending at this writing.)

When Mrs. Dora Greiver Stern appealed to the Illinois Appellate Court in 1963, her case had already been bouncing about the lower courts for fourteen years. After holding the case for six years, one judge threw it out in fifteen minutes. Judge Thomas E. Kluczynski dismissed it in 1961 on grounds that whatever rights Mrs. Stern may have had she lost by waiting too long to assert them.

Simple in language but startling in content, Mrs. Stern's contention was that she owned 21¼ percent of MSC. The legal briefs, in offering a version of how MSC was founded, said that Mrs. Stern, her brother, Simon Greiver, and their widowed mother, Bessie, lived at Division and Wood Streets and were neighbors of the Crown family. Simon Greiver and Sol Crown attended elementary school together and were close friends. When the Crown brothers decided to form MSC in 1919, they approached the Greivers for financial support. Bessie Greiver, who could neither read nor write, bought 170 shares of the 800 original shares for $4,250, which represented her life's savings and the insurance left by her husband. Mrs. Stern asserted that she signed her mother's name to the certificates as "B. Greiver." As secretary of the new company, Simon also signed his name to each certificate as "S. B. Greiver."

Incorporation papers filed with the Illinois Secretary of State, dated January 16, 1919, show S. R. Crown subscribing to 360 shares of stock for $9,000, H. Crown subscribing to 270 shares at $6,750 and B. Greiver subscribing to 170 shares at $4,250.

Crown told Drew Pearson that he was more worried over the

228

Stern suit than the Senate investigation of the TFX contract. He conceded that the Greiver family figured in the founding of MSC, but only to fulfill a law requiring three incorporators. Simon Greiver, said the Colonel, had carelessly intertwined the initials S and B so that they came out looking like B. It was merely a clerical error. None of the Greivers, however, ever had invested any money in his firm.

In 1963, Mrs. Stern's attorney, Nathan Kahn, argued that Illinois law in 1919 did not require a third original subscriber.

"I remember Sol Crown came over to our home very enthusiastic about going into the building material business," Mrs. Stern recalled in a conversation with Drew Pearson. "He said Henry had 'connections' with the city and would get all the city contracts. When we signed the papers, Sol put his arm around me and said 'Dora, if this goes through you'll never have to worry.' I signed for my mother because she couldn't write. My husband and my brother signed the incorporation papers. This $4,250 my mother put up was the only cash invested."

In his appearance before the Appellate Court, Crown's attorney, Albert E. Jenner, Jr., argued that the "mere passage of time, more than forty years, was enough to support the dismissal of the case."

Attorney Kahn attempted to explain the passage of time in his briefs. Mrs. Greiver, he stated, had frequently asked her son about her investment and each time he had assured her that it "was being taken care of." After her mother's death in 1938, Mrs. Stern also received the same assurances from her brother. Eleven years later, in 1949, Mrs. Stern, not having received satisfaction from her brother, petitioned Probate Court to name her administrator of the estate, asking also that a discovery hearing be held to disclose assets in her mother's estate. Her petition was granted by Judge George Schatz, who was summarily relieved the following day. The petition was subsequently reversed. Attorney Jenner explained to Mrs. Stern that Judge Schatz's removal was "just a coincidence. His time was up." At the moment, the judge was in the process of adjudicating seven other cases.

In his briefs, Kahn argued that Mrs. Stern's rights of possession were "as indestructible as the title of an owner of an inactive bank account of thirty or forty years or longer, and this title could not be destroyed or wiped out by any claim of" statutes of limitations.

Appellate Court Judges Ulysses S. Schwarz, John V. McCormick and John T. Dempsey upheld the lower court decision to dismiss the suit. It was, they said, a "question of laches"—undue delay. "Bessie

229

slept on her alleged rights for practically twenty years," the opinion stated. The judges refused to believe that a woman, even though illiterate, could be unaware of the phenomenal growth of MSC.

Although determined to renew her legal battle against the Crown empire, Mrs. Stern's campaign was further complicated in April 1966 when the Colonel severed all connections with MSC and General Dynamics, cashing in his holdings valued at about $120 million so he could devote his "energy to other businesses and to philanthropies." Among the other businesses, he said, the family had interests "in a couple of hundred companies."

From 1960 to 1966, the Colonel's general factotum was Patrick H. "Pat" Hoy, who went from president of the Sherman Hotel in 1960 to president of MSC and senior vice-president of General Dynamics in one sudden bold leap. While Crown hobnobbed with Mike Igoe, Sam Nanini, Jake Arvey, Frank Chesrow, George Halas, *Tribune* Editor W. D. "Don" Maxwell, Louis Mantynband and other old-time cronies, Hoy made the nightclub scene with Sidney and Marshall Korshak, Ralph Stolkin, a former Chicago punchboard operator turned California millionaire, and the Las Vegas crowd of Jake Gottlieb, Louis Lederer and Charles "Babe" Baron, a close associate of Arvey and a Syndicate representative in Las Vegas. (Back in 1929, Baron, while accompanied by Joe Cota and Robert Emmet Ryan, two notorious Capone hoodlums, shot and killed gambler Jimmy Walsh in front of Henrici's restaurant [no indictment]; five years later, he was a prime suspect in the machine gun slaying of Gus Winkler, a West Side gambler [remains unsolved]. A brigadier general in the Illinois National Guard, he was cleared to handle secret communications in 1961, soon after he returned from Cuba, where he had worked in casinos bossed by Meyer Lansky. Later, he became the official greeter at the Sands in Las Vegas.)

A Daley favorite of long standing, Hoy served on some of the mayor's most prestigious committees—his most recent post was as chairman of the Chicago Commission on Youth Welfare.

In the summer of 1966, barely three months after Crown severed all ties with MSC and General Dynamics, Hoy petitioned the federal district court in Chicago to protect him from his creditors. In a detailed financial schedule, Hoy listed his assets at $500,394 and his liabilities at $8,517,901. At the root of Hoy's financial misadventures was the United Equity Corporation, an insurance group holding company in which Hoy was a major stockholder. Originally capitalized at $300,000 by Hoy, Frank Chesrow and other investors, the

230

company was kept afloat through bank loans guaranteed personally, jointly and severally by the corporation's officers. In addition to the twenty-five or so creditors listed in the court brief, Hoy was the guarantor of $2,611,400 borrowed from the American National Bank and Trust Company of Chicago, which was guaranteed up to $1.6 million by Burton A. Scheidt, former chief engineer of the Sanitary District, and John B. Huarisa, president of Standard-Kollsman Industries Inc. This loan was separately guaranteed by Henry Crown on June 20, 1963, more than a year after the first loans were made.

A clue to Crown's enormous campaign contributions came to light in 1964 when MSC filed suit for a tax refund of $2,575,263 for the period 1951 through 1959. The government brief, filed in 1965, asked that MSC identify the "persons or organizations" that had received cash gifts amounting to $360,000. These "cash contributions to certain political campaign funds" were deducted as ordinary and necessary business expenses, the brief said. "It's a rarely told story that suggests how deeply a giant company can become involved in political activity in a large city," the *Daily News* noted. "The lion's share of the company's admitted contributions went to the Democratic Party, although Henry Crown, founder and head of Material Service, is a registered Republican. The Democratic organization in the 11th Ward, birthplace of the last three mayors of Chicago and a bailiwick honeycombed with city and county patronage workers, received more of the company's admitted political contributions than any other ward. . . . Although trade sources estimate that Material Service supplies only about 25 percent of the total ready-mix concrete in Chicago, its proportion of public construction is believed to run way above that." The suit was assigned to Judge Igoe.

Meanwhile, the adventurous challenge of Harry Booth, Chicago's "dragon slayer," had been blunted on a few legal cornerstones. In dismissing Booth's suit against the Sanitary District, Judge Cornelius J. Harrington ruled that Booth lacked jurisdiction and that the suit was "multifarious"—too many defendants joined in the same legal action. Besides, said the judge, Booth should have sought remedy from law enforcement agencies or the district itself before filing a taxpayer's suit. Booth answered that as a taxpayer he was not required to seek remedies before filing suit and that the suit was not "multifarious" because the defendants were in a "common conspiracy." The Appellate Court agreed with Judge Harrington.

In 1965, Booth revived the suit, charging that Judge Harrington should have disqualified himself from hearing the case since the judge's son was a partner in a law firm representing one of the defendants. "The case presents issues of the highest public importance," Booth stated in his brief, "and the district has conducted illegal and fraudulent acts in giving away the public's valuable property."

Although the suit is still in the legal hopper at this writing, there is nothing moot about its final disposition.

BOOK THREE
THE LAWLESS LAW

We have made less progress in Chicago than anywhere. Our success in Chicago so far has been with minor hoodlums. . . . Our difficulty is getting people to testify.

—NICHOLAS KATZENBACH, United States Attorney General, in testimony before the Senate Judiciary Committee, February 8, 1965.

1

I guess the place to start this story is when I was working for Wesley's pizza at 1116 Bryn Mawr Avenue, because to the best of my knowledge that is where everything started with the cops of the Fortieth police district.*

I knew most of them cops because I lived in the district all my life and there were a few I went to school with, and at the time of June, 1958, I was on the bad side of them.

[Morrison, released from the House of Correction on September 14, 1957, after serving a four-month sentence for petty larceny, explained that he was "trying to go straight." He was holding two jobs, planning to be married and trying to pay off his bills.]

Everything was going along fine until one day when I was walking down Berwyn Avenue from Broadway and the policeman, Frank Faraci, came out of the corner saloon and says to me, "Well, if it ain't the little burglar, Richie."

I knew Frank from the pizza place and I seen he was a little loaded so I just said, "Hi, Frank, how are things with you?" And he said, "Well, they would be a little better if you would cut us guys in on some of your jobs. You know Al Karras and some of the other fellows, and we'd go along with the show. After all, we like nice things, too." Just then another cop came out of the liquor store and Frank introduced me to him. His name was Al Brinn, and Frank said to him, anything you need just see Richie here. So I said to him, I'll see what I can do.

To tell the truth, I don't know what made me say that to him because I wasn't doing anything wrong since I got out of the Bridewell [House of Correction]. I didn't know at the time what I was really letting myself in for, but after I told them I'd see what I could do, it seemed like everyone in Forty [Summerdale police district on Chicago's North Side] was asking me to get them one thing or another. . . .

* Extracts from a 77-page confession by Richard Morrison, a 23-year-old master burglar.

Now, the first job I did with the cops in Forty was the Western Tire and Auto Store. I knew a fellow named Robert Curley that used to work in there and I had Curley with me that night.

We started to load all the items from the front window and the most expensive items the cops wanted, the tires and television sets, the radios, electric shavers, shotgun shells, guns. Faraci was in 207 that night and he kept circling to see if everything was going all right too. I told them to keep away until they got the word from Brinn on the three-wheeler, then we would be gone and they could go in and clean up. . . .

So, from day to day I met the cops in a restaurant at one A.M. and we set up jobs every night. I was allowed to keep any cash I stole. The coppers gave me orders for stuff they wanted or their wives wanted. At World Series time, they all ordered portable TV sets. When the weather began getting cold, they hit a gas station for antifreeze. They were greedy. They went after anything from automobiles parked in the streets to gum-ball machines.

From time to time I kept meeting more cops that were burglars, and from time to time I kept getting more cases in the Criminal court building and needed an awful lot of money for lawyers, bondsmen, and cops, as the ones I went on jobs with sometimes let their friends at D-3 [North Side detective bureau headquarters] know I did it, but they wouldn't let them know about themselves.

So I had to pay guys in D-3 to forget about the cases and it cost quite a bit, too.

You see, the cops that let D-3 in on the business got a nice cut of my payoff to D-3, too. I didn't find that out until after I was arrested this last time [July 30, 1959], and it was hard to believe that the same guys I went on burglaries with would also let their D-3 pals squeeze me so they could get a few more hundred bucks out of the job. . . .

Another night they wanted to hit a food store. . . . There were five cops and me, and we drove over to the place in squad car 207. I opened the door with a crowbar. We were all running around in the store getting this stuff when I happened to think, who was listening to the calls in the squad? Faraci said, "Somebody's got to listen to them." I said, "This is all your stuff, I'll go listen to the calls in the squad." So I went to the squad car and I was sitting there. They were coming out with bacon and hams

236

and everything you could think of in the store—real expensive foods. They kept filling the back seat of the squad car.

All of a sudden a '57 Cadillac pulled in back of 207 in the alley. It was the sergeant of the North Shore Patrol. I figured if he sees me and all this stuff in the squad car everybody is dead. So I had to think fast. I took off in the squad car and when I came back they were still there. They said, "Where the hell you been?" I told them, I said, "The damn sergeant came up behind me!" They said, "Jeez, we almost had a heart attack ourselves. We had our guns on him. We all laid low in the store. But he was checking the door of a place next door. He must have missed us completely. We might have had to drop him if he'd seen us."

Spring was coming around and three of those cops, Pat Groark, Al Karras and Al Brinn, were real anxious to get some outboard motors for their boats. They wanted water skis and everything. "All right," I said, "we'll hit Marine Supplies." I went and got this Floyd Wiley. I said, "You got to do me a favor. I can't hold six bricks, but if we both throw a couple we'll knock the whole window out and we'll get away." Then I explained how the cops would pretend like they're shooting at us, then they'd open the door legally.

We knocked in the whole front window in just a matter of seconds. They came by and chased us and we went and got away. Before they went into the place, they waited fifteen minutes and then they went in and pretended like they were investigating. They walked in the front window and they took their own outboards. I wanted to see how they did it. So we hid in the bushes and we seen them coming out with the big outboard motors. I told Floyd we'd scare the hell out of them. We decided to walk down the alley like pedestrians. All of a sudden we saw them stop with the outboard motors in their arms. They said, "Don't move, somebody's watching us." So I busted out laughing and I said, "You crazy jerks, it's only us." So they bawled us out for staying around there. They told us we scared the hell out of them. One cop was really burned up later when he saw he had taken a second-hand motor.

. . .

Then when I was on this trip to Las Vegas I happened to come back and they told me about the burglaries they did when I was out of town. One was at the Azuma

237

Sukiyaki House. After that they broke into a tavern and took all the money from the register. At a furniture store, one cop got this big marble-topped table and had to tie it up on the roof of the squad car to get it home. His wife told me about it. She said the bell rang in the middle of the night and there he was with this big marble table. She had a fit.

[In the spring of 1959, Morrison was arrested by Secret Service agents for passing counterfeit money.]

After that I started going to the race track just to have a good time and try to enjoy the summer, as I knew it would probably be my last one for a while. So all in all, when I come right down, I have to say that no matter how many people you know or how many coppers you go on burglaries with, the law of average catches up with you and crime doesn't pay.

Crime ceased to pay for Richard Morrison on August 1, 1959, when central bureau detectives arrested him following a detailed study of the burglaries in the Summerdale district. The pattern of operation fitted his *modus operandi* and he was seized as a suspect.

Morrison promptly confessed, implicating himself in some fifty burglaries. Sprinkled throughout his confession were allusions to his police-burglar friends in the Fortieth district. No one, however, seemed particularly interested.

Morrison got his chance to "sing" in December when he was questioned by State's Attorney Benjamin S. Adamowski, a Republican and a fierce critic of the Daley machine.

On the evening of January 14, 1960, state's attorney's police directed secret simultaneous raids on the homes of eight Summerdale policemen and picked up four truckloads of stolen merchandise from seven of the homes. Of the eight policemen arrested, five—Frank P. Faraci, Allan Brinn, Allen J. Clements, Alex and Sol Karras (twins) —admitted they knew that some of the loot recovered from their homes was stolen. Two policemen—Peter Beeftink and Henry T. Mulea—made denials. Patrick J. Groark, Jr., in whose home no evidence was discovered, also denied knowledge of the burglar ring. Groark was the son of a late police captain.

With the scandal breaking in a national election year, it was inevitable that police corruption would become a major political issue.

"The whole department is blackened," moaned Police Commissioner O'Connor. "The work of ten thousand good policemen is undone. It makes you heartsick."

"This thing is a shocking indictment of the moral tone of law enforcement in Chicago," Adamowski complained. "There are too many unsolved crimes. It is my opinion that the mayor better start looking through the whole department."

Time being of the essence, Mayor Daley did the next best thing— he fired O'Connor and appointed his chief assistant, Kryan V. Phelan, acting commissioner.

(On June 26, 1961, the eight police burglars were brought to trial before an all-woman jury. Two months later, all eight defendants were convicted as charged. Henry T. Mulea and Peter Beeftink were fined $500 each, and Patrick J. Groark, Jr. was sentenced to six months in jail. But for the other five defendants, the ones who had previously acknowledged possession of the stolen property, the sentences were somewhat more realistic. Frank P. Faraci, Alex Karras and Allen J. Clements were each sentenced to a term of two to five years in state prison; Sol Karras, two to three years, and Allan Brinn, one to two years.)

Renowned as the city's most celebrated police scandal, the 1960 exposé was little more than a magnified keyhole glimpse into one minute segment of an enormous kinky shadow-world which for a century had been subordinated to the will of greedy politicians for the protection of ruthless gangsters.

"It is a world," said the *Tribune,* "in which wrong is right—in which all incentive for honor, justice, suppression of crime, and even fundamental discipline has disappeared from broad divisions of the police department, the courts, the all-pervading Democratic political party machine that has a strangle hold on Chicago proper."

Encouraged by the public's sudden clamor for reform, a number of policemen began appearing at the offices of the state's attorney with "reports of rottenness in the department." In many instances, the inside information they volunteered was of far greater consequence than the larcenous antics of burglar cops. One such report named high police officials who had a working alliance with politicians and Syndicate moguls.

For example, one of Chicago's highest police officials was "strictly devoted to the Syndicate and is a personal tool of John D'Arco." When this captain was in command of a First Ward police district, he "sanctioned the largest crap game in the city" to operate at the 15th Street market. "All the books, and there were plenty of them, were operated by Fifi Buccieri." The captain's bagman, a policeman who was still in his employ, collected from all the "fruit joints, striptease shows, pornographic movies and peep joints, prostitutes, and the tavern and hotels the prostitutes used." While in command of a North Side district, the captain and Botchie Connors had divided the "take equally between them, which was collected from the usual vice joints by two other police-bagmen." At the time, there was a total of "thirty-nine wide open gambling rooms." One of the bagmen, saved in a scandal, was later assigned to the state's attorney's office, "and he did some collecting and organizing for him."

A police captain, who was an attorney and a silent partner in a law firm, ran prostitution from a hotel he owned in the Twenty-seventh Ward. His bagmen were the three policemen assigned to the Commissioner's office. They collected from vice joints all over the city. When they got into trouble, the captain conducted the investigation, and "what a farce it turned out to be." The captain spent his time "on Rush Street, drinking and being in huddles with known hoodlums and prostitutes."

Another police captain, a licensed pilot, used to take Monk Allegretti and his wife for rides in his private plane. His favorite hangout was Allegretti's Valentino's restaurant in the Berkshire Hotel, where he "often sat around with Allegretti, DiVarco, Bill Gold and Benny Goldberg."

While working as a "detective in a West Side district," one captain had been the "protector of saloons and vice joints for various captains and ward heelers." His first marriage was to a madam, and one of his closest friends was Julius "Juju" Greico. When he made Chief of Detectives, his collectors worked the queer and strip joints on Division, Clark, Rush and Madison streets.

One enterprising captain used to check the message book for the names of hoods who had been arrested in other districts so he could call their lawyers to let them know what station or bureau was holding them.

The report listed eleven captains, two lieutenants and several detectives and patrolmen. And that was not the end. Others sought out sympathetic ears to unfold their tales of wholesale corruption. After listening to scores of complaints, the *Tribune* summarized its findings: Powerful Democratic politicians wield the clout within the department like a club. They have, in five years, almost wrecked the department. Examples follow:

—A patrolman who was Mayor Daley's campaign chauffeur became the unofficial and most powerful commissioner of police after Daley's election in 1955. This man, from an office in City Hall, arranged transfers and appointments to virtually all levels of police jobs until he died in 1958.

—A chief of detectives made the disgusted observation that sponsorship of a Democratic politician was essential before a policeman could be transferred to the detective bureau.

—Appointment of patrolmen to the rank of detective [plain clothesman] in precincts became a part of the Democratic city administration's political patronage. Sponsorship of a committeeman, an alderman or a party organization chief of some kind was mandatory before a patrolman could make the $600-a-year jump in salary that goes with a detective rating.

—"I can't make a detective or dump him," one captain told the *Tribune*, "and this means I have no control over my own men. They know it. A man doesn't have to give a damn about me. He listens to the politician who helped him get his rank."

—Politicians, the policemen predicted, are not going to step out of the Chicago police picture because of the burglary scandal. The stakes in power and money are too high and the "fix system" is too well-established by the crime syndicate that is willing to come up with a steady and substantial stream of dollars to get the protection it requires.

—Chicago's crime syndicate operations are traditionally based on "cash clout"—that is, the straight money payoff for freedom from interference. Sometimes this even includes the "pushing around" by policemen of citizens who want to cause trouble for syndicate gambling places, handbooks or slot machines, a veteran policeman told the *Tribune*.

—"But in recent years," this police veteran added, "the syndicate has elected some of its own politicians—a regular syndicate bloc [West Side Bloc] well-known in the city *Tribune*], "have no doubts that the regular syndicate ball at all times, but are not at all slow about getting into the collecting on their own. No matter what is said about crime organization—aside from the top level of it—practically everybody who is kinky is on the make for himself, and is not to be trusted with money or opportunity for shakedowns. This is what causes some of the hoodlum murders—fights right inside the syndicate for power and money."

—"About this business," [one police captain told the *Tribune*], "have no doubts that the regular syndicate payoffs are going right along while the scandals are on page one. The syndicate is too big and too entrenched to be worried about a few stupid policemen who teamed up with a punk burglar. The syndicate payoffs are big time, involve the whole city enforcement system, extend into the courts and state legislature, and perhaps higher. Everybody who is anybody wants to forget the hysteria over the burglar scandals—but don't, for heaven's sake, upset any apple carts involving the real payoff."

2

Of the thousands of Chicago scandals that have inspired headlines in recent years, the story of the "little red notebook" is a contemporary classic. It contained all the elements of a post-Kefauver Hollywood crime-and-corruption thriller—except, of course, for the typical Chicago happy ending.

It began in the spring of 1953 when the City Council Emergency Crime Committee—known dramatically as the "Big Nine"—became interested in the personal finances of Captain Redmond P. Gibbons, then chief of the uniformed forces and a former commander of the Hudson Avenue police district on Chicago's North Side.

Created originally by the Republican faction of the city council to investigate charges of an alliance between crime and politics, the Big Nine was already the focal point of a raging controversy when it voted to ask Police Commissioner Timothy O'Connor to order Captain Gibbons to disclose his personal financial status. "I don't see how the commissioner can do anything but say 'yes' on this," Alderman Robert E. Merriam told the press. "After all, Mayor Kennelly told the Senate [Kefauver] crime investigating committee a couple of years ago that if there were even the shadow of a doubt concerning the honesty of a policeman he would demand that he reveal his income."

Summoned to testify before the committee, Gibbons refused to reveal his income and wealth. A few days later, a small package, addressed to the city room of the *Sun-Times,* arrived in the mail. Inside the package was a little red notebook which contained lists of gambling dives, saloons, nightclubs, bookie wire centers, payoff spots and the private telephone numbers of Syndicate hoodlums, politicians and police officers. A subsequent anonymous telephone call identified the notebook as the property of Captain Gibbons.

The story of the little red notebook became headline news on March 23, 1953, when the *Sun-Times* revealed part of its content along with the findings of a handwriting expert, who concluded that the "handwriting in the book was similar to the signature of Captain Redmond P. Gibbons' currently on file at the Chicago Civil Service Commission." When shown the book by a *Sun-Times* reporter, Gibbons refused to comment. "I don't want to discuss anything about anything at all," Gibbons said.

A number of entries in the notebook coincided with testimony before the Big Nine by Robert Butzler, an undercover agent who had spent six months in the Hudson district as a committee sleuth. Butzler testified that Alderman Mathias "Paddy" Bauler, Bill Gold and Syndicate boss Ross Prio were "the boys to see" about vice and gambling in the Hudson district.

On one page of the notebook appeared the listing: WH 4-9270. That telephone number was traced to a drug store at North and La Salle. In this store, committee investigators learned, Gold had set up "payoff headquarters each month, handing out cash to detective bureau squads." Around the first of each month, neighborhood people told investigators, there would be as many as three or four police cars parked outside the drug store, while Gold busily paid off inside.

On the following page appeared Gold's unlisted home telephone number. There were two telephone numbers in the book for Bauler— one for his palatial Miami Beach home on Biscayne Bay and the other for his Chicago residence.

Another telephone number was checked out to the 2249 Club. At that location, Butzler testified, red-haired, 250-pound Bess Burlin, queen of the poker games, operated highly profitable gambling.

On one page was the entry "Mr. Lee," and under it "SU 7-4971" and "WH 4-9248." The numbers were traced to Jason Lee, a Korean gambling boss who operated 24-hour-a-day games for Orientals at 1358 North Clark Street. One witness, Peter Patras, told the Big Nine he complained to police about Lee's racket. As a result, he got a warning from "Buck" Loftus, secretary to "Botchie" Connors. Patras was instructed to "forget" his complaint.

Hand-printed ink entries in the notebook listed twenty-nine hand-books, wire rooms and card games, together with the names of operators and more unlisted telephone numbers. The initials "B. G." appeared after three addresses. Butzler testified that those three places had gambling under the supervision and protection of Bill Gold while Captain Gibbons commanded the district, and that they had operated without any apparent interference from the law. Next to each entry in a handwritten list of twenty-five taverns there appeared figures ranging from 10 to 100.

"There is nothing I cannot explain," Gibbons promised the press. "I've always done my work. You fellows know that."

State's Attorney John Gutknecht was of the opinion that grand jury action "of any kind" based on the notebook alone was unlikely since the information was more than three years old and therefore automatically ruled out by the statute of limitations.

On March 26, the *Sun-Times* disclosed that Ross Prio and Fred A. Romano, an assistant state's attorney, shared an office at 134 North LaSalle, and that the two men had been associated in various business ventures since 1938 when they first appeared as incorporators of the L and P Milk Company, shortly after Prio was questioned, and released, on charges of wrecking rival dairy firms. Their next venture came in February 1940, when along with Thomas Neglia they organized the Publix Parking Company. The next year, Romano, Tony Paterno and Gabriel Spataro founded the Grande Cheese Company, for the purpose of "owning, leasing and managing dairies, dairy farms and creameries" on a national scale. Two years later, Neglia was murdered "Mafia-style" while being shaved in a barber shop. Following the murder, Romano was elevated to the presidency of Publix Parking. That same year, Prio replaced Spataro as a director of Grande Cheese. It was about this time that James D'Angelo, who had evidenced an interest in Grande Cheese, was found stuffed in a car trunk. The management of Grande Cheese changed in 1946. Prio was replaced by Giuseppe Uddo of New Orleans, who was succeeded in 1949 by Eugene Taormina of Long Island, New York. Neither Romano nor Prio appeared in Grande

244

Cheese after that time. But in 1953, Romano and Prio were still in control of L and P Milk. (Another incorporator of this firm was Marcus Lipsky, who in the past forty years has fronted for the Syndicate in scores of enterprises, including Reddi-Whip and Grid-L-Rich.)

State's Attorney Gutknecht's reaction was to blast the *Sun-Times* for "yellow, irresponsible journalism." In a written statement to reporters, Gutknecht said that Romano had offered to produce his income tax returns for the past ten years and to submit to a lie detector test.

"Are you going to give him the test?" asked a reporter.

"For what?" said Gutknecht, angrily. "I have no evidence against him. I have found no evidence of anything unethical and, of course, no criminal conduct on his part." Romano and Prio, he explained, had gone to school together and were old friends. It was that simple. As far as Gutknecht was concerned, Prio had not been convicted of any crime, and all that talk about the Capone mob did not alter the situation.

The next day, the *Sun-Times* revealed that back in January of that year, Gutknecht was almost persuaded by Barnet Hodes (law partner of Jake Arvey and Fifth Ward Democratic committeeman) to appoint Gibbons as chief investigator for the state's attorney's office—the same post that earned Dan Gilbert the title of "the world's richest cop." Aaron Kohn, former chief investigator for the Big Nine (he was fired when he charged that certain politicians and administration aldermen were plotting to turn the inquiry into a whitewash), told the *Sun-Times* that he had blocked Gibbons' appointment when an alderman came to him with a confidential inquiry as to whether the captain would be mentioned unfavorably in crime committee testimony and reports. "I told the alderman to inform Gutknecht that Captain Gibbons certainly would be involved in my investigative reports. In fact, I sent word that I would recommend that the case against Gibbons be presented to the grand jury."

The little red notebook, meanwhile, was turned over to O'Connor and Gutknecht. Gibbons was dropped from active service and went on voluntary leave of absence pending the outcome of what Mayor Kennelly termed "a swift and unsparing investigation."

As to the figures ranging from 10 to 100 opposite the names of tavern owners, Gibbons offered this explanation: "The list of names and the numbers indicated behind these names could very well have been a list of purchasers of football tickets, the sale of which is evidenced by a receipt now in my possession. . . . Any reference to

245

addresses of gambling establishments was compiled strictly in the performance of duty for ready reference when away from the police station. . . . The casual manner in which this document was compiled and permitted to remain in public places renders quite clear, and I herewith state the fact to be, that its contents were never regarded as of any great importance and certainly in no manner indicated any derelictions of duty on my part."

A few weeks later, the Big Nine was declared illegal by Judge Walter R. O'Malley when he granted Gibbons' petition to dismiss the committee's suit to force him to reveal his income records.

After one of the longest—and most predictable—civil service trials, Captain Gibbons was cleared of all charges, restored to duty with back pay and assigned as special assistant to the Commissioner. At the time of his death in 1957, he was in command of the West North Avenue district. Commenting on his death, Mayor Daley observed that Chicago had lost "an outstanding police officer and a dedicated and devoted public servant."

3

The appointment of Orlando Winfield Wilson to the newly created post of police superintendent in the spring of 1960 was considered a powerful antidote to the poison loosened in the body politics by the police burglary scandal. As dean of the school of criminology at the University of California at Berkeley, Wilson had gained a national reputation in the field of police organization and administration. Although nearing retirement at UC, Wilson could not resist the challenge of Chicago. "This was an opportunity that would never come again," he has said, "an opportunity to demonstrate to the world the simple truth of the police theories that I had spent a lifetime teaching and talking about."

Wilson's appointment was heartily endorsed by the press and the various reform groups. There seemed to be no strings attached. Wilson was given a two-year contract and a free hand to overhaul the badly demoralized, scandal-shaken department. At the same time, the city council created a five-man police board to act as a buffer between the mayor and the new superintendent—with the mayor selecting the board members. The office of the superintendent (formerly commissioner) was moved from City Hall to police headquarters (two miles away) at 1121 South State Street; this was the first time a Chicago mayor had permitted the head of the police department to leave the political sanctuary of City Hall.

Enlisting the aid of recognized experts from the International Association of Chiefs of Police and the Public Administration Service, Wilson proceeded on all fronts simultaneously. The archaic police structure, both physical and administrative, was streamlined to modern needs. One of Wilson's first innovations was a $2 million communications center (considered one of the finest in the world) which directs the movement of police cars and guarantees assistance within five minutes from the time a telephone message is received—a rather novel improvement from pre-Wilson days when it took anywhere from an hour to a lifetime. IBM computers were installed in the record and statistical department, and $250,000 was spent updating the laboratory, including the latest neutron activation analysis methods. The vehicle fleet was increased almost 100 percent, all the cars were painted a striking blue and white, and the traditional red dome lights were replaced by large blue flashers.

At the time of Wilson's appointment in 1960, there were thirty-eight police districts in Chicago, each with a station house and complement of men under the command of a captain who owed his allegiance to the ward bosses in which the district was located. Long recognized as a political anachronism—as antiquated as the city's fifty-ward structure—the system had been tailor-made to the specifications of the Machine. To the astonishment of the oligarchy, Wilson closed seventeen police districts in a consolidation move designed for greater efficiency. Alderman Paddy Bauler, who believed that "Chicago ain't ready for reform," threatened to march on police headquarters to protest the closing of the old Hudson Avenue station.

One of Wilson's first moves was to create a police public relations section to offset the bad publicity of the police scandal and to enlist public support. The cost of this operation was $198,000 in 1965—more than all the rest of the city departments combined spend on public information. However, in the past five years the change in the public's attitude toward policemen has paid off handsomely for the administration.

The consensus of opinion in Chicago is that Wilson has sharply improved the general efficiency of the department. He increased the size of the force by hiring civilians to relieve policemen from clerical duties, raised salaries, lowered traffic fatalities and more than doubled the motorized patrol system. And according to his new statistical division, major crimes have decreased. Some policemen, however, have charged that they are encouraged to falsify crime statistics to make Wilson look better. Wilson has denied the charge, stating that his investigators have not found this to be the case. The police budget, meanwhile, has soared from $72.8 million in 1960 to $91.3 million in 1965—it was $40 million in 1955.

Writing in the April 1964 issue of *Harper*'s Wilson summed up the police reorganization in these words: "I am pleased, of course, with our progress in rebuilding the Chicago Police Department. However, I must frankly admit to a major disappointment. We have made little progress in our efforts to prosecute the higher-ups in organized crime."

The Syndicate is as inviolate today as it was five, fifteen or thirty years ago. Kinky (crooked) cops, sponsored by clout-wielding politicos, are as prevalent as ever in the department. Wilson's chief administrative assistant, Sergeant Paul Quinn, was linked to the Syndicate in a secret federal report on organized crime and politics in Chicago. The report, compiled in 1964 on orders from former Attorney General Robert F. Kennedy, was the result of a coordinated effort involving all federal law enforcement agencies operating in the greater Chicago area.

The appointment of Quinn in May 1961 was the first visible sign that the old political *status quo* had not been unduly disturbed by "the perfesser"—as Wilson is colloquially known in the wards.

According to the federal report, Quinn was on the payroll of near North Side hoodlums for many years. At the time he joined Wilson's personal staff, he was receiving $200 per month on direct instructions from Ross Prio. In May 1962, federal agents observed Quinn in conference with DiVarco, Allegretti and Pete Speren in the Curve Lounge of the Maryland Hotel on Rush Street. That same month, he was again observed in conversation with Speren at the Candystick Lounge on the near North Side. Speren was "payoff man to Quinn, who acted as a tip-off man for near North Side hoodlums." Considered by the government to be one of the highest Syndicate contacts in the department, Quinn used his influence in the assignment of certain detectives friendly to the Mob.

Wilson sharply denied the federal charges. "I am confident he [Quinn] has not collected any payoff since I have been superintendent of police," Wilson said in defense of his aide. "I want it plainly understood I'm not inferring I have any derogatory information about Paul Quinn antedating my coming here." The truth of the matter,

248

Wilson explained, was that he had asked Quinn to conduct a vice investigation for him of a type "in which you can't get information from Sunday school teachers."

Wilson admitted that it was "not impossible" for the Mob to get to a man in his office. "However, I don't think the Mob would pass out money to anyone who can't produce and Paul Quinn is in no position to deliver anything." He had picked Quinn for his aide because "he was the best man I could find [out of 10,360 strong] and he still is."

Quinn's explanation was that he had met with the hoodlums to get information on the operations of the Syndicate on the near North Side. "I have never taken money from Speren," Quinn said. "He has never offered me any money. Nobody has offered me money through him." Quinn said his acquaintance with Speren went back twenty-five years. "We worked at the Drake Hotel together before I was a policeman. Pete became associated with crime syndicate hoodlums in the last seven years. Superintendent Wilson was interested in crime syndicate operations in near North Side establishments and I sought out the answers to how to curtail the crime syndicate in these establishments."

In an appearance before the McClellan committee in October 1963, Wilson spoke bluntly about the frustrations inherent in his job. "The picture which I have painted is one filled with frustrations. It is a picture of a handicapped and somewhat feeble effort on the part of a well-intentioned municipal police agency to cope with a problem of gigantic and overwhelming proportions. It is frankly a picture of failure and impotence. . . . As a municipal police administrator, I have often maintained that organized crime threatens the very existence of our society; that it is a far greater threat internally than is communism. I feel it is essential that we recognize . . . that local police agencies are no better equipped to stage a successful fight against a nationwide network of organized crime than they are equipped to cope with the nationwide web of Communist infiltration."

The infiltration of the Syndicate into the police department was demonstrated vividly in the secret federal report—a report which Wilson denied receiving over the government's insistence that it was forwarded through "unofficial" channels.

The report itself was a testament to Wilson's "picture of failure and impotence." Quinn was not the highest Syndicate contact named in the report. The highest was a member of the newly created police board. This man and a member of the Cook County Board of Commissioners were observed in conference with Murray Humphreys, Frank Ferraro and Sam Giancana in a private car near O'Hare airport in March 1960—only a few weeks after Wilson became superintendent.

Excerpts from the 1964 federal report follow:

—The Central Police District, which encompasses the Loop, is one of the worst in the city. The Syndicate makes monthly payoffs to a central fund which is distributed to various members of the district force ranging from Captain——down to certain sergeants. Payoffs total as high as $4,200 which was amount paid in February 1963. Gus Alex, who controls gambling in the First Ward, was cautioned by [this Captain] to be extremely careful in view of Wilson's desire for strict law enforcement. Favorable treatment was promised but agreement was reached to the effect that [the Captain] would conduct raids and enforce laws pertaining to strip joints on occasions in order that his reputation not be tarnished and in order that his superiors would consider he was performing his functions efficiently and honestly. This is why raids have been made on occasions but strip operators continue to flourish.

—During the late fall and early winter of 1960, Murray Humphreys instructed his associates, namely Gus Alex, to maintain liaison with a member of the Intelligence unit of the Chicago police force, who at the time was furnishing information to Alex regarding investigations of Chicago hoodlums by the Intelligence unit. On several occasions Alex was able to obtain information from this police source which included the lines of information and makes of the automobiles being utilized by the Intelligence unit, the identity of hoodlums under surveillance by the unit, the locations of meeting places of hoodlums known to the unit, and the identity of the hoodlums who had been observed by the unit to be in contact with each other. The hoodlums were able to have these investigative reports destroyed.

—Humphreys and his associates, notably Ralph Pierce, were apparently able to corrupt Captain——during the time when he was a lieutenant and acting captain of the Summerdale district on the North Side. The subject later was placed in charge of a unit of the Bureau of Inspectional Services and at one time was Chief of Detectives.

250

The subject meets every month, between the 1st and 5th, with Humphreys. The meet in March, 1963, was in the Roosevelt Club, a coffee shop in the 800 block of West Roosevelt Road. Sometimes it takes place in the Bismarck Hotel. Sole purpose of the meet is to chat and make a drop. This captain was apparently sponsored in the department by Jake Arvey.

—Informant advised that he has operated a gambling house on the South Side of Chicago with the knowledge and consent of the Fifth Police District. . . . The informant's gambling operation, a comparatively small one, cost about $500 a month to the district. All other gambling operations made similar payments, the larger ones paying up to $1,000 a month.

—In late 1960, Humphreys was very satisfied with the fact that State's Attorney Daniel Ward accepted Lieutenant——on his staff of investigators. Humphreys enjoyed a relationship with [the Lieutenant's] uncle and father, also Chicago police captains, and was pleased to form a similarly pleasant relationship with the subject.

—Ross Prio was reportedly acquainted with Captain ——, who at one time was in charge of the Intelligence unit of the Chicago police department. The subject reportedly accepted money in the past from Prio, Allegretti and others, and once accepted a loan of $1,400 from Allegretti just prior to the time he was promoted to captain.

—Humphreys and associates were able to corrupt Captain——several years prior to the time he was placed in charge of a South Side district. When a captain in charge of a First Ward district announced his retirement, Humphreys wanted [this Captain] to replace him, and asked D'Arco to determine whether the subject wanted the position. At first it did not appear that he wanted it, but he subsequently changed his mind. D'Arco then contacted Mayor Daley and advised the mayor that he wanted the subject to command this district. The appointment was later announced by Commissioner O'Connor.

—Captain——, one of Chicago's highest police officials at the time of the police scandal, received payoffs from associates of Giancana and Humphreys for a substantial number of years and was once in command of a First Ward district. Humphreys was quite concerned when he learned from D'Arco that information had been re-

251

ceived by the department from a federal law enforcement agency that the possibility existed that [the Captain] was a homosexual. D'Arco was given orders by Humphreys to do what he could to protect him so that he did not lose his newly acquired position.

—Advised in February, 1962, that two detectives, who are now with the Intelligence unit of the department, are handling policy payoffs, hotel prostitution and other gambling payoffs. Advised that Allegretti will take care of the police district in which a madam or prostitute operates for a ten to twenty-five percent payoff of the establishment's take. If a tavern or hotel in the North Clark Street area uses B-girls or prostitutes, they have to pay Allegretti or his men $200 a month for the privilege and that part of this money goes for police protection.

—Advised on January 21, 1961, that during the past eight years the estimated Outfit payoff to police in one area was a half-million dollars. The money was left in numbered envelopes for the various police officers to pick up at a certain location. The envelopes were numbered to indicate the specific policeman to receive it. One Julie Epstein always dropped the envelopes at a certain restaurant. Epstein is a very trusted aide of Gus Alex and his associates and formerly operated the gambling activities of the J and J Picnic Grove. Policemen receiving envelopes included six captains [one a top-ranking staff official], one lieutenant, one sergeant, and one patrolman.

—Sergeant——is on the payroll of the English brothers, who are pleased with his services. He performs favors without even being asked. They frequently meet at 5th Jacks, a known hoodlum hangout. Information indicates that in March, 1963, just prior to the murder of Alderman Benjamin Lewis, the subject was closely associated with him, and they were doing "a lot of business." The sergeant has been a protector of organized crime interests in the Fillmore area and receives a cut from various gambling activities and from prostitution. Once when he received instructions from the Syndicate to keep an individual from running a competitive policy wheel in the Twenty-fourth Ward, he stopped it within a week's time.

—Advised during the fall of 1960 that Giancana was making grandiose plans for the replacement of individuals

252

holding state political appointed jobs, particularly with the state police, in view of the recent election in which the incumbent Republican administration in Illinois was defeated. It was indicated that Frank LaPorte, a Syndicate representative in Southern Cook County, was well situated with the state police organization in that area, particularly through Captain——of the Blue Island state police district. It was indicated that [this Captain] received a considerable amount of money on a monthly basis for his services to LaPorte, Giancana, *et al.* Another state police captain, covering the northwest section of the state, was also placed on the payroll and performed services for Joe Amato and "Willie Potatoes" Daddano, hirelings of Giancana and LaPorte. In the fall of 1960, LaPorte found it necessary to pay off all the way down the line from captains to patrolmen. Although this cut considerably into the profits, it was considered a necessary evil. [Another captain] received $1,850 per month from Vogel, LaPorte, and Robert Ansoni, who was Giancana's representative in gambling enterprises in Cicero. LaPorte intimated that extra income could be derived by sharing the payoff [this captain] was getting from overweight trucking operations in Northern Illinois, which amounted to an estimated quarter-million dollars per year. [The captain] later transferred one lieutenant because he believed that he was not getting his fair share of the payoffs collected by the lieutenant.

—When Rocco Potenza reported to Giancana that he was getting "rough treatment" from a committeeman in Wheeling Township, Illinois, who was supposed to be on the Syndicate's payroll, Giancana recommended the committeeman be taken out of office.

Of the forty-nine persons named in the federal report, four were state policemen, two were Cook County deputy sheriffs and the others were all members of the Chicago police force—twenty-three captains, five lieutenants, five sergeants and ten patrolmen. To date, nothing has been done to intrude on the careers of these patently kinky cops. Five captains and one sergeant have since retired for age, and one captain has died of natural causes. The rest, it may be assumed, are still doing what comes most naturally and profitably.

"I would be surprised if it had any validity," Daley told newsmen. "If it is what they say it is, I have too many things of a constructive nature to do rather than to read this. It's a police matter and it's up to Mr. Wilson and I have great confidence in his judgment and ability. It's a vicious document."

"We absolutely do not have any evidence against them," Wilson said. A few days later, he announced that "at least two" Chicago policemen were suspected of having crime syndicate connections. "But we are not able to make a case against them."

The two suspected policemen were later identified as Robert Hopkins and James Apostol, West Side vice control detectives. Apostol was named in the federal report as a "courier" for Fifi Buccieri and as a bagman for ranking West Side police officials and politicians.

Both detectives were accused of demanding a $200 bribe to allow a policy wheel to operate. The wheel operator was John J. Gallagher, an undercover agent for the Illinois Crime Investigating Commission. Gallagher testified before a county grand jury investigating the policy racket that he was approached by Hopkins who said that Apostol had ordered him to collect $200 when the policy wheel opened for business. Gallagher also testified that Attorney Robert J. McDonnell had obtained the Syndicate's permission for the wheel's operation and had introduced him (Gallagher) to James "Cowboy" Mirro, the Syndicate's representative in that district. McDonnell, who admitted having about twenty-five conversations with Gallagher, denied the introduction was for the purpose of obtaining Syndicate clearance.

Hopkins was suspended after he refused to sign an immunity waiver and to testify before the grand jury. (On October 21, 1965, Hopkins was indicted by a federal grand jury on charges of bootlegging 80 proof moonshine at $10 a gallon on the West Side.) Apostol spent twenty minutes before the grand jury and reportedly took a lie detector test, the results of which were not disclosed. He was then demoted to patrolman and transferred to another West Side district. The police order demoting Apostol was noncommittal. It said he was "reduced in rank on the basis of monthly detective performance ratings made by supervisory personnel and reviewed by command personnel." It was signed by Superintendent Wilson.

In the course of researching this book, this writer interviewed many knowledgeable policemen concerning Wilson's methods versus the Syndicate's machinations. The consensus was that Wilson was dollar-honest but too politically naive to cope with a system as complex as the Machine. To point up this strange dichotomy between the real world of Machine politics and the imaginary world of

Orlando Wilson, and to add that extra dimension of sinister intrigue which attends all that is political in Chicago, a brief pastiche of these interviews follows:

—James B. Conlisk, Jr., is the real power behind Wilson's throne. His father was the unofficial police commissioner, I'll say for twenty years. He was a deputy commissioner under O'Connor and was very close to the Democratic party. He was one of the nine old men who retired when the police scandal broke in 1960. He's dead now but his son is as big as he ever was. Junior went from patrolman to captain in something like seven years. A year later, Wilson made him a deputy superintendent. Now he heads the Bureau of Field Services which is the largest branch in the department with something like nine thousand men under his command. This man takes orders only from the mayor. Conlisk makes and breaks all the men. When political changes are made, he's the boss. I'm not talking about administrative changes like painting the squad cars blue or ordering green paper to write on. I'm talking about high echelon changes which affect the System itself. Let me give you an example. When they were making the district commanders after Wilson came here, each one got certain choices. Conlisk got some choices, other deputy commissioners got some choices, and Wilson got a couple of choices. Frank Kreml [chairman of the police board] got a couple of choices. Conlisk's choices were all the mayor's choices. Conlisk's clout is big in the Catholic Church. His choices included two Irish cops whose brothers are monseigneurs.

—Captain John J. McDermott was put in the Eighteenth police district (near North Side honky-tonk area) because he was not hip. He spent most of his years in the record division of the traffic section. What would he know about heading a district like this? They thought they could work right around him. Later they took him out because it was going cheap and they had to show a change. Besides, the Outfit couldn't get along with him. At the end he was starting to get smart. So the Outfit sent Richard Cain [chief investigator in the sheriff's office, later convicted for perjury] and he made a lot of noise, made all kinds of mickey mouse pitches and the press wrote it up like they'd pinched Al Capone with a fork or something. And this got rid of McDermott. The mayor said, "We don't need this

255

heat, get rid of him. Put someone else in there." So they put in Captain Walter A. Maurovich. His four new guys that were going to clean up the district pinched twenty-six Negro whores on Wells Street. This is their clean-up of the district. You and I could go out without a gun and pinch forty-five white whores, let alone twenty-six Negro ones. But in the papers, with these stories, to the guy with the lunch pail, it looks like the man is cleaning up the district. They are cleaning up overt things. You know, things that people can see when they ride by.

—There are as many rackets in the police department as in the Outfit. Let me tell you something. [At this point, the informant mentioned two high-ranking police officials.] You think these guys are straight cops? They used to be partners in the Hudson Avenue district. They were the bagmen for Redmond Gibbons, who was the captain in charge of the district—you know, the little red notebook scandal. And they were in charge of the tavern detail. Now taverns for policemen are very lucrative. Let me put it this way. You can't work for a venal police captain unless you're venal. I mean you can't work for him on vice and remain straight. It's impossible. It's just like trying to get on a swimming team and you don't even know how to swim. Now there's a fellow at headquarters who takes $200 a month from each district commander in the city of Chicago. There are twenty-one districts. That means his take is $4,200 a month. This money moves right up the line. But he keeps some of it. You ought to check captains around here. They make $10,300 a year and they send their kids to the best schools, they live in $40,000 homes and they have new cars every year. Captain Frank Pape has been paying the taxes on a twenty-three acre island in Pistakee Lake and he's trying to get the place deeded to him by the state. It's known as Hook Island and it was given to him in 1960. He uses it to hunt ducks with his Dago friends. This guy Pape has killed more men than the Outfit's top assassin. But he gets medals for it. He once cut a guy in half with a machine gun. My advice to you is that you better watch out who you talk to in the department. Some of those guys will set you up real quick. They don't play around. There's too much at stake.

[Often called Chicago's toughest cop, Pape joined the force in 1933 and spent twenty years in the detective

256

bureau. During that time, he engaged in fifteen gun battles in which nine persons were killed. In 1966, he nearly became a candidate for sheriff of Cook County when supporters obtained the pledges of ten thousand registered voters. Asked whether he was seriously seeking the nomination of either party, he replied: "Well, I guess it would be a fine way to round out my police career." Pape was named in the federal report as an associate of Syndicate bosses.]

—It's a matter of policy versus procedure. The policy of the department is to suppress crime and whatever else it is supposed to do. The district commander does not set the policy in the sense that the superintendent does. But he sets the procedure by which the policy is executed. So we will have rigid enforcement of the gambling laws. And he lets everybody know about it. Or we won't have rigid enforcement. He doesn't say, we won't. It is just the way he says it. Let's say a commander was on the take for policy. He would say, "I want a little bookmaking ventures in this district"; then he wouldn't have any arrests for policy. He didn't say, "don't get policy." It's the way he said it. He then calls the three watch commanders into his office and levels with them. You must remember that the district commander is only a captain. And his title is just honorary with $3,000 added to his salary. He could be dumped tomorrow morning. So he wants to be friends with these three captains because next week he could be working for one of them. Nobody gets hurt. They don't get suspended and they don't get in trouble. All they have to do is go along and play the game. Everybody looks fit and polished, everyone smiles and wears a clean shirt. And it is all coming in the back door.

—The going rate for promotion to sergeant today runs around $3,000 to $5,000—depends on how much they think they can take off the man. Lieutenancies are in the neighborhood of $10,000 and captaincies anywhere from $15,000 and on up. It depends on who you are and how big your clout is with the Party or the Outfit. Some cops come up with the money on their own, but mostly it is from sponsors. There is only three ways you can become a captain of police. You can pay the money yourself; the Party or the Outfit can pay it for you; or you can cause so much trouble, make so much publicity for yourself, that they'll have to make you or else people are going to ask

257

and find out why. Some good cops have made it this way. There are fifty wards in the city of Chicago, and the alderman or committeeman, depending on who's boss, is allowed to pick two men for each promotional examination. They get the first hundred on every list. After that everybody submits a name. A judge, anybody with clout. He'll say, "I want to go for this man." All right, but now they pick the smartest ones. They don't want to be embarrassed like in the old days. Then they would sponsor anybody. They are a little more choosey these days. "Here's a man," they say. "Let's check and see. He's a college graduate. That's good. We'll go for him. But the Outfit wants to make this Giovanni Jones. Let's look at him. He went through eight years of grammar school. He's got a good police record; he hasn't been in any trouble. Oh, boy, he's a thief. He's been caught a couple times but it was kept off his record. Oh, no, we can't go for him. But the Outfit says they want this man made anyway. Well, it's going to cost a little bit more to make him." So the price goes up on this one. But the other men, the ones with average intelligence and good police records, clean, decent fellows, they've got to use this system or they aren't going to get anywhere at all.

And the worse thing is that the Civil Service Commission isn't worth a damn. It's run and controlled by Daley and that's it. He makes the appointments. Didn't he make three of his bodyguards sergeants at one crack. There was a big squeak about that among the patrolmen. Let's say Daley keeps a couple of promotions for himself, then he gives one to Seymour Simon [then president of the board of County Commissioners], one to Big Bill McFetridge [member of the police board and a labor leader], he gives a couple to the governor. Remember, though, at the time of the scandal, before Wilson came here, everything was up for grabs. They made a lot of people they now regret making because they've had a lot of trouble with them. They can't control them; they have no sponsors, and they can't get rid of them without bringing more heat.

Let me give you a case in point on how promotions are made. There's an Outfit hood by the name of Mike Glitta, who owns the Shore Club on North Clark Street. His brother-in-law is Vince Serritella. Old Dan Serritella was the City Sealer under William Hale Thompson. Vince made sergeant a while back and Glitta bragged that it had cost him five grand. Glitta said he was going to put Vince in the state's attorney's office where he could do him the most good. I went down to Intelligence and raised hell. I told them I'd go to the newspapers and blow this Serritella and his brother-in-law off the face of the map if he got into the SA's office. Now I know this kind of corruption. I gave Intelligence the names of two other Outfit-connected cops in the SA's office, but they're still there. Another Outfit-connected cop was made a captain by his father-in-law who's a big shot in the Steel Workers Union. Another Italian. Believe me, there are a lot of sleepers in the department. I mean policemen who are Outfit connected, hoodlum related. They are left strictly alone. Nobody bothers with them. They make them and they let them go on their merry way.

Actually, there is more information gathered about kinky cops with Outfit connections than anything else. But nothing is ever done about it. This is the province of the Internal Investigation Division, the IID. And let me tell you, the size of the IID is the biggest secret there is. If some of their men grab you, you've got to come up with money, and I mean big money. I know of one cop who was grabbed for committing three acts of armed robbery. He stopped a traffic violator, handcuffed him, took him home, shook him down for $75 and then released him. The citizen complained, but the cop is still on the job. Another cop in the Youth Division had eight young boys come and point him out as committing the act of oral copulation upon them. He was transferred to the Seventeenth district and did not get a single day's suspension. There were two cops from the Vice Control Division who were big shots in the policy racket on the South Side. The Treasury boys found out they were building a $150,000 bowling alley. They were transferred to the Fourteenth district. I could give you a hundred similar cases in just the last year alone.

—The Intelligence Division has been in operation just a few years. At first they didn't have any information at all. There was nothing in the general files. In the old days, nobody ever made a written report on a hood because if they did it would be stolen from the files and sold to the hood within an hour. In the beginning, Intelligence got their background stuff on the Outfit from the Chicago Crime Commission. They spent months photostating news clippings and secret reports. A lot of their information now comes from anonymous letters and telephone calls, from the Better Business Bureau, the Better Government Association, the Civic Federation and other public organizations. All policemen are now supposed to report any information they learn about organized crime directly to Intelligence. So in this period of time, Intelligence has been able to pick up a great deal of stuff, a great deal of knowledge about the Syndicate. This information could be a benefit to all law enforcement agencies, but as such, other law enforcement agencies cannot get it, not even the federal government. If they come into the captain's office with a request for the file on Paul Ricca, they don't get it. They have to ask for some specific item, like what happened on a certain date. Then Intelligence will check its files and report just on that one item. They won't generalize and they won't volunteer anything. They won't say, "Here Mr. FBI, here is the file on Paul Ricca. Now everything on the yellow paper is supposition and everything on the blue paper is actual fact. Here's his record. Here are his activities, his associations, his rackets, his legitimate enterprises." Everything this hoodlum has done as such is public record. His arrests, his convictions, his associations, everything else. A lot of it has been in the newspapers. They're not violating anybody's civil rights by sharing this information. But they won't do it. They will not come up with it. They will not tell you anything. Not even their own policemen. "Why do you want to know?" they ask. "Huh, that's none of your business." You get no cooperation. But they'll trade information, except most of the time it's a one-sided deal.

The sad part of it is that they were set up specifically to fight organized crime. And the way they act, you'd think they were protecting it instead. Everybody in the department is in competition. Everybody protects his own little domain. IID trades with Intelligence. They exchange dope on kinky cops for dope on Outfit hoods. A few years back the Treasury department had eight secret indictments brought up against police captains in a federal grand jury, but it was never pushed. Nothing came of it. Somebody up there, you might say, looks over kinky cops. Intelligence has about 140 investigators checking on the Outfit around the clock. They can tell you what Accardo had for breakfast, what Caifano had for lunch and what Alderisio had

260

for dinner. They know who's queer and who's sleeping with whom. But that's all they know. The files are jam-packed with this nonsense. Everybody is drowning in paper work. They're paralyzed by it. Still nobody knows anything important. Some of their mug shots of top-ranking hoods are twenty and thirty years old. They didn't even have a picture of Gussie Alex until the Los Angeles police bagged him and snapped his picture a few years ago. They don't know where or when half of those guys were born, how many kids they've got, who they're related to, what businesses they own, who fronts for them, how much money they take in or how they get it out of the country. While they're watching the kingpins eat, the underlings are bombing some other restaurant down the street or knocking off some stubborn competitor. Intelligence spends its energy theorizing about who's who in the crime hierarchy. It's all guesswork based on who dines with whom. They learn more from reading the newspapers than anything else. You want to know how many cases Intelligence has made against the Outfit in all this time? One word. None. They've got a lot of license numbers and street addresses, but you can't convict anybody for owning a home or driving a car.

It's all a big game. I know. I've played it long enough. It makes you ashamed of being a cop. I truly mean it. The worst of it is that Intelligence has a first-rate staff. They've got some of the sharpest guys in the department. They're sharp and crafty, and they all get plenty of promotions. Now and then they give stuff to the press. Tiny morsels of gossip that the reporters blow up into a big noise and splash without hurting anybody. And that's what they want most of all. They all want publicity. They all want big action, a lot of movement, but don't do anything foolish. Don't hurt anybody that can come back and knock your brains out. Play it cool and wait for the next promotion.

—In the districts, some of the captains go to the hoods and ask for a pinch. So they give them a stick-up team or something. One that's not Outfit connected. Or they'll pinch some free-lancing whore or knock over a little Negro-operated policy wheel. But the cop on the street is a lot smarter than he used to be. He isn't going to take any chances when he goes on the take. There's no meeting a guy on the street or at a tavern. They get the money right there and then. "Give it to me now. I'm not meeting you any place. You're not putting me in the middle. I'll make my money right now any way I can make it and that's all." Even patrolmen are making more money today. Before a patrolman would never take a chance on making a dollar from a tavern. If the sergeant or captain caught him, he would be transferred so far out it wouldn't be funny. Now he walks in a tavern and says, "I'll put you down on report that you're running whores out of here, or that you're running gambling in here. I'll give you more heat than you can carry." So they give him a five or ten dollar bill and everything is fine.

Wilson has made this possible. If the captain gets a call from Alex, say, about the patrolman putting the bite on him, and the captain transfers him out, the patrolman writes to Wilson and says I'm being transferred for this reason: "I went in there and found whores drinking champagne in darkened booths"—boom, boom, boom. Here's a lousy patrolman making trouble for Gus Alex. This is unheard of. But this is the power Wilson gave the young patrolman. On the other hand, a sergeant can walk into a strip joint and say something like this to Alex: "I was at a staff meeting the other day, Gussie, and they are hot on your strip joints. They want them down. They want me to submit a daily report. Now what am I going to say? Am I going to say that I see you and Ralph Pierce going into Binyon's all the time? Am I going to say that the whores are running around here? What do you want me to put down on the report? I want to be fair with you." "Jesus, thanks, sergeant. Listen, make it as easy as you can. Tell them we've got strippers here but they don't hustle the bar or anything like that. Here's a couple bucks and stop in to see me the first of every month."

You figure it out. Say the sergeant covers a hundred taverns in his area at ten bucks each. So now we have the patrolman getting five bucks, the sergeant gets ten and the lieutenants and captains get a lot more. And they're getting it from the same places. And there are thousands of taverns in Chicago. This is just one racket. One out of hundreds.

In an interview with this writer, Wilson explained how the department kept pressure on the "seedbed of organized crime," which he

262

described as prostitution, narcotics, gambling and liquor law violations.

Q. Has there been much progress in these areas?

A. Certainly. But I would be the last person to claim that there are no violations in those areas. But this has cut into the profits of the Syndicate. It may have forced the leaders to seek other areas of revenue. Taking their ill-gotten gains and investing them in what people would ordinarily take as legitimate enterprises. But using the same techniques in these businesses they use in organized crime. We've made a little progress in this area. But we have not succeeded in convicting any of the really top-level people in organized crime.

Q. What do you need to accomplish that?

A. Well, we need legislation to empower us to wiretap. We need a law which would make syndicate gambling a felony [enacted in 1966].

Q. Would this stop them from going into legitimate business?

A. This would not. Except this. All these people had their beginnings in narcotics or prostitution, gambling and liquor violations. This is how they got their power [and] money. They developed their techniques and methods of control. While it's a long-term operation that won't bear fruit immediately, if we can keep recruits from coming up and amassing wealth, these old boys are going to have to die off one day and this may provide some promise.

Q. Do people generally get the kind of government they deserve?

A. Yes, this is true, I believe this implicitly. This department was a corrupt department when I came here and I don't mean that there aren't elements of corruption still remaining. But it was the citizens of Chicago who corrupted their own police department. . . . It starts in such a subtle way. Some wealthy man has his limousine parked in some convenient place and he gives the policeman a gratuity for not molesting him in parking. Then there are Christmas gifts and the officer making himself readily available to receive them. And in some cases actually soliciting. Then there is the practice in traffic violations of giving the officer some money. You see, the citizen justifies what he does in cases like that. He says, "I was wrong; I was speeding and I shouldn't have been. I saved myself from going to court and I gave the money to a badly underpaid public servant who is providing protection to our community." This then leads to the officer who arrests a felon who has a thousand dollars in his pocket. The felon says, "Here, take the money and give me a pass." And the officer rationalizes and says, "Well, if I bring him in, a bondsman and shyster lawyer are going to get the thousand. Why shouldn't I?" Then, in the case of the Summerdale scandal, they were actually working as burglars. The citizens of Chicago were responsible for the corruption of their police force.

Q. What about policemen who are reportedly in the employ of the Syndicate?

A. I have heard of no reports of any policemen who are in the employ of the Syndicate.

Q. Or knowing Syndicate hoodlums and getting money from them, payoffs in the districts and so forth?

A. Well, what about it?

Q. There is the federal report.

A. It was just a lot of unsupported allegations. They have not been able to prove that any of the people named in this report were corrupt.

Q. Has there been much change in personnel in the past four years?

A. We are under the civil service law and I'm not free to dismiss civil service employees. I can bring charges before the police board and this requires that we have a pretty tight case. There are cases, however, where I know that we are dealing with a corrupt policeman, I can suspend him for thirty days if we haven't enough evidence to get him before the board. This means that we still have the man.*

The parade of corruption in the police department supplies the local press with an endless source of copy material. Chicago newspapers print more stories on wayward cops in a month than New York does in a year. Policemen still regularly commit burglary, robbery, felonious assault, bribery, auto theft, extortion, larceny, brutality and murder. They still moonlight for the Syndicate as

* Wilson retired on August 1, 1967, and was succeeded by James B. Coolisk, Jr., who retained Sgt. Paul Quinn as his administrative assistant.

procurers, narcotics peddlers, bootleggers, collectors and assassins. Cases are made against policemen in nearly all these categories monthly. In the majority of incidents, they are exonerated by the courts and continue on the police payroll.

Supervision within the department continues to falter despite Wilson's highly praised reorganization. In pre-Wilson days, it was common practice for switchboard operators to protect (for a fee) officers who left their post of duty. It was not unusual for as many as a hundred cops on a single shift to fail to make the required hourly pulls of police boxes and be automatically reported as "present and accounted for."

Although Wilson's $2 million communication center has antiquated the police boxes, collusion between radio operators and policemen continues unabated as revealed in a recent investigation by the *Tribune*. As a result of this probe, forty-three supervisory personnel up to the rank of captain and thirty-four patrolmen were called before a special police disciplinary board. Twenty-three patrolmen were suspended and two others reprimanded. Although they had called the communication center to report they were going off duty hours before their shift ended, records in the various traffic headquarters showed they had worked a full tour of duty. The deception could not have succeeded without the compliance of supervisors, since the cheating policemen had to return to their headquarters to file reports on traffic cases and turn in their squad cars.

As to the quality of police personnel in the Machine society, polygraph expert John E. Reid, whose firm screens for a dozen suburban police departments, found in one recent study that 57 percent of all police applicants admitted "gross criminal behavior," including burglary, use of narcotics, bribery, molestation and assault.

The department is mired down hopelessly in corruption, and no amount of administrative reorganization is going to alter the situation. Until the thieves and thugs that have braced the political backbone of every administration since the days of Long John Wentworth (Chicago's first mayor) are weeded out, it will take more than words and resolutions to eradicate the Syndicate.

4

Since the day Al Capone captured Cicero some forty years ago, a generation of Cook County sheriffs, prodded by militant reformers, have promised—at election times—to liberate this hustling little burg from its legacy. To date no one has succeeded. In fact, no one has seriously attempted it.

Traditionally, the office of sheriff is considered the next step to the political graveyard. As a result, it has been occupied by a horde of political hacks who took what they could in the four years allotted them before gracefully bowing out into affluent obscurity.

The late Thomas J. O'Brien was one of the few politicians to survive the onus of the office—his term, 1938–1942, came after he had served three terms in the United States Congress. Tagged as "Blind Tom" by the press during his four years as Cook County Sheriff, O'Brien was reelected to Congress in 1942 and remained in Washington as the people's choice until his death in 1964. Attacked repeatedly for the widespread gambling and vice that flourished in the county during his term as sheriff, O'Brien succinctly summed up his law enforcement philosophy when asked about a proposal to allow Illinois sheriffs to succeed themselves: "Hell, no," he replied. "If he can't make it the first time, don't give him a second chance."

The sheriff from 1962 to 1966 was Richard B. Ogilvie, a former federal attorney who convicted Tony Accardo for income tax violation in 1960—later reversed by the U.S. Circuit Court of Appeals in Chicago.

Ogilvie's campaign was directed against the Outfit—which again illustrates its pervading importance in the community. "I soon found that the crime syndicate had not overlooked my activity in the investigation which I had directed against them," Ogilvie observed in a speech. "Hardly had the slatemakers begun their deliberations when I received word from an unimpeachable source that Sam Giancana, the operating leader of the Syndicate, had passed the word that 'Ogilvie was to be stopped.' A few days later, again from an unimpeachable source, I learned that Giancana had passed the word to his associates that, indeed, 'Ogilvie had been stopped' and would not be slated for sheriff."

At last, it appeared that the people of Cook County had elected a sheriff with a proven track record against the indomitable Outfit. Characterized as an "implacable foe of organized crime," the sheriff promptly lived up to his reputation with a series of lightning blitzes against Cicero vice dens. Photographed with ax in hand in a manner reminiscent of New York's "Little Flower," the "implacable foe" battered down steel doors like tenpins. (Arthur Bilek, Chief of the Sheriff's Police, fell headlong after battering down one steel door and broke his right arm—to Ogilvie it was "the last straw.") Unfortunately, the grapevine traveled faster than the sheriff's mechanized "western style" posse. No one of importance was grabbed in any of the raids. In most cases, both patrons and proprietors had long before vacated the premises. A number of bartenders were booked, and an even greater number of deserted slot machines were mercilessly reduced to rubble.

When this program failed to produce the desired results, Ogilvie's deputies began a regular patrol of Cicero. This unprecedented move drew strong protests from Cicero Town President Jerry F. Justin and Police Chief Erwin J. Konovsky. But Ogilvie was adamant. He promised to continue the patrol as long as his budget would permit it. Seymour Simon, president of the Cook County board of commissioners, described Ogilvie as a "vigilante," and ventured the hope that the patrol would not be of long duration. Simon was the man who set Ogilvie's budget. One week later the patrol was abandoned, and the sheriff announced a five-point program that was designed to obliterate the Syndicate from its quaint stronghold.

In essence, the entente was based on Chief Konovsky's promise to execute forthwith and with vigor the laws of the State of Illinois as they related to gambling and vice. Chief Konovsky was to establish a vice control unit composed of "exceptional" policemen. Even firemen would be alerted to the menace of crime.

Tranquil months passed, and then one morning in April 1964 Chief Konovsky found himself seated before the Illinois Crime Investigating Commission.

"How many men do you have on your force?" he was asked.

"One hundred and seven," he answered.

"And how are they assigned?"

"About forty are assigned to traffic," said Konovsky. "We have a lot of traffic in Cicero with our compressed size and industry."

"Is it possible that all the traffic is from the gambling patrons coming and going?"

"No," he answered. "No, I don't think so."

But before long Konovsky was agreeing with the commission that his policemen were not very good at finding gambling. The reason, he submitted, was that gamblers were smart enough to recognize the faces of Cicero cops. And by the same token, the police of the sheriff and state's attorney had been more successful because their faces were unfamiliar to the gamblers.

"Has it ever occurred to you, Chief," asked one interrogator, "to hire outside undercover men that the gamblers don't know?"

267

"I just didn't think of it, I guess."

"Would you care to comment on a report . . . that Cicero police-men pay $500 to get their jobs."

"I never heard of that."

"Have you heard of reports that Joe Aiuppa pays off policemen in or around the village hall?"

"If he does, I don't know about it."

"You have had trouble as police chief, haven't you?"

"I was, uh, I was indicted in 1951 for denying Negroes civil rights. And I was indicted for gambling. They were dismissed."

In the barrage of questions and answers that followed, Konovsky admitted that no arrest for gambling had been made by his department in 1963, and only one arrest had been made up to that time in 1964. Prior to 1961, he said, gamblers "had open rooms and I guess that's what's called wide open." But as to the present, "There is no open prostitution or narcotics in Cicero and gambling is on a sneak basis."

Ogilvie had pledged to staff his own office with investigators and deputies a hundred percent dedicated to the war on crime. "If we can't produce 175 honest law enforcement officers," he said, "then this county is in worse shape than I think it is." Former Sheriff Joseph D. Lohman had his doubts. "They can make a joke of him," he said.

And "they" did exactly as Lohman predicted before Ogilvie had a chance to complete half of his four-year term. The "they" in this instance were Richard B. Cain (nee Scalzetti), head of the sheriff's Special Investigations Unit (SIU), formed to combat organized crime, and three investigators from that ten-man unit popularly known as "Cain's men": Lieutenant James Donnelly and Sergeants John Chaconas and William Witsman. All four men were indicted September 25, 1964, by a Cook County grand jury on charges of conspiracy to commit perjury and conspiracy to obstruct justice in connection with a $250,000 drug burglary at the Zahn Drug Company warehouse in Melrose Park. If the public was shocked at the prospect of another major police scandal, insiders were not even mildly surprised —they knew too much about Cain's oblique methods of operations and dubious connections.

Ogilvie's appointment of Cain was opposed by the Chicago Crime

Commission, Wilson's IID and at least two federal agencies. Even a perfunctory rundown of his newspaper file should have been sufficient to discourage the new sheriff.

For example, Cain's suspension from the Chicago police department in 1960 was preceded by a number of "unusual" experiences. A year earlier, Cain and Gerald Shallow had shot and killed an ex-convict named Harry Figel, allegedly in the heat of a gun battle. Figel's family attorney charged that he had a witness who would prove that Figel was seized on the South Side and taken to the Loop and murdered. The charge was subsequently dropped. A few months later, a 68-year-old prostitute, Grace Van Scoyk, complained that shortly after her arrest by Cain and Shallow, an attorney, David Landau, recommended by the officers, visited her at the lockup and persuaded her to surrender her keys to a safety deposit box. Following her release, she found the box empty and $30,000 missing. Confronted by Mrs. Scoyk, Landau said he had used part of the money to pay off the policemen involved in the case. Then, in April 1960, while on furlough from the police department, Cain and Shallow, posing as employees of Accurate Laboratories, a private-eye agency, were arrested for electronically eavesdropping on Irving N. Cohen, City Commissioner of Investigation, who worked directly for the mayor. Suspended for thirty days, Cain announced he would take a $20,000-a-year job as general manager of Accurate Laboratories, which was operated by John Scherping, a former police captain. Scherping was also president of the Frontier Finance Corporation, a juice operation bossed by vice-president Frank "The Horse" Buccieri. Other investors at $20,000 each included Postmaster Carl A. Schroeder and Edward F. Moore, former Republican County Chairman and a board member of the Chicago Transit Authority. Among Frontier's celebrated clientele was Joseph Siciliano, the horsemeat king who made millions in the early Fifties by peddling nag-burgers as beef. Joe Spadevecchio, a mob terrorist and collector, was on Frontier's payroll, and Anthony Eldorado, a mob enforcer, occupied office space in the rear of the building.

For Louis Zahn, owner of a multimillion dollar wholesale drug business, the story behind the burglary of his warehouse "reads like a Grade-B movie plot. There are secret meetings with underworld characters, private detectives arranging secret deals, mysterious recovery of loot too hot to handle, and all the trappings of a melo-drama."

It began on Friday, October 4, 1963, when a 35-foot aluminum-covered trailer was backed into Louis Zahn's new $2 million ware-house in Melrose Park, a nearby Chicago suburb. Because it was late in the day, the driver uncoupled the tractor and drove off, leaving the loaded trailer "safely" behind burglar-proof doors protected by an alarm system so sensitive that "even a cat walking across the floor would set it off."

Sometime between that evening and Monday morning, the trailer disappeared, and with it some $250,000 worth of drugs, including sleeping pills, tranquilizers and amphetamines. Three days later the trailer—empty except for a few cartons of drugs valued at $7,000—was found behind a building at 1150 West Jackson Boulevard in Chicago.

Three months later, Cain's men, armed with submachine guns, descended upon the Caravelle Motel in Rosemont. They burst into Room 31 and found forty-six cartons containing $43,000 worth of the stolen drugs. Since the fearless raiders were accompanied by reporters and photographers, the affair received wide publicity.

An anonymous tipster had telephoned on January 6, 1964. "That tipster was someone in the burglary gang," Cain said. "After we got the tip, [Sergeant John] Chaconas and other detectives went to the motel on a stakeout. When they didn't see anyone around the room, we entered it and found the drugs."

It all appeared so uncomplicated and routine at the time. Room 31 had been rented by a man giving the name of John J. Matheos of 190 East 9th Street, Peoria. He signed registration card number 6927 and indicated that he represented the Holland Furnace Company. He was driving a blue Cadillac sedan bearing Illinois license plates number KL-5354. As expected, the license plates were stolen and the Peoria address was false.

Cain seized the registration card before raiding the room. How-ever, he failed to perform certain basic police functions: He neglected to dust the room for fingerprints and he did not take an inventory of the loot or set some of it aside as evidence in case the burglars were apprehended. These oversights were to count heavily against him in the trial that followed ten months later. (As a point of historical interest, the Caravelle Motel was formerly owned by Sam Giancana under the name of River Road Motel. Subsequent to the gangland-type murder of banker Leon Marcus, who held a $150,000 mortgage on the motel, Giancana changed the name to Thunderbolt. Charles Giancana, a brother, operated it until February 1963, when it was sold to Donald Stevens, village president of Rosemont.)

As these events were gradually unfolding in the spring and summer of 1964, State's Attorney Daniel P. Ward was in the midst of a heated political campaign for reelection. His Republican opponent was John H. Bickley, a former assistant United States attorney who had gained a modicum of fame in 1957 by successfully prosecuting the government's denaturalization case against Paul "The Waiter" Ricca. Following in the footsteps of Sheriff Ogilvie, his GOP mentor, Bickley aimed his big guns at the Syndicate—particularly at the prospect it would face if he became state's attorney while Ogilvie was sheriff. The implication was that Ward's calculated indifference was hampering the sheriff in his concentrated drive against organized hoodlums.

Ogilvie could not have agreed more. In campaigning for the Republican ticket, the sheriff laid the blame for the Syndicate's success directly at the doorstep of the Democratic party, which in his opinion controlled the largest policing agency—the Chicago Police Department, the state's attorney's office and the U.S. attorneyship through federal patronage, as well as 90 percent of the judiciary, both local and federal.

Then Bickley and Oglivie posed an embarrassing question: What about the assistant and the former assistant on Ward's staff of prosecutors who were the sons of high-ranking Syndicate hoodlums? The former assistant—he had resigned the previous month—was identified as Stewart Katz, son of Phil Katz, a notorious North Side gambling boss. The son, interestingly enough, had been assigned to try gambling cases. When Bickley demanded that Ward publish Katz's trial record in the gambling division, one of Ward's assistants quoted another assistant to the effect that "Mr. Katz did an exemplary job." The other assistant was Arthur Zimmerman, a member of Ward's staff for more than two years. His father, Frank Zimmerman, had a long police record (including armed robbery) and was regarded as a Syndicate overseer on the West Side.

Bickley and Ogilvie barely had time to congratulate each other on the Katz-Zimmerman coup before Ward announced that his office was investigating the circumstances surrounding the recovery of Zahn drugs from the Caravelle Motel. Chief Investigator Richard Cain,

Lieutenant James Donnelly and Sergeants John Chaconas and William Witsman were to have an opportunity to explain their "irregular" conduct before the September grand jury.

The probe had been initiated in August after the state's attorney learned that Cain and Donnelly had relayed "sell-back" offers from the thieves to Louis Zahn only a few hours after their widely publicized raid. The two officers met with Zahn in a Melrose Park steak house and there presented him with a list of unrecovered merchandise taken in the burglary. The list, they affirmed, was genuine since it was provided by the same informant who had tipped them on the Caravelle cache. They thought they could get the stolen drugs back for $20,000. Zahn took the list, but later mailed it back to Cain with the notation that he could not make out the listed items. Cain sent him a new list which itemized some $80,000 worth of unrecovered drugs. In a subsequent conference, Zahn declined the offer, but asked if it could be submitted to the insurance company. The two officers agreed; the insurance company also rejected it.

Following the Caravelle raid, Ward's office had obtained detailed depositions from Cain, Donnelly, Chaconas and Witsman in which *all four men* claimed to have participated in the Caravelle raid. This was to become the basis for the "conspiracy to commit perjury" indictment later returned by the grand jury.

The announcement of the state's attorney's probe on September 3 came just three days after the shotgun slaying of Guy "Lover Boy" Mendola (nee Mendolia, Jr.) in Stone Park. A professional thief with an impressive yellow sheet, Mendola was a charter member of the notorious Peanuts Panczko burglary mob.

One of the first officers to reach the murder scene that night was Cain, the sheriff's chief investigator, who quickly theorized that the Mendola murder signaled "either the opening of a war between two rival gangs or the extermination of a band of burglars who crossed the crime syndicate." Cain disclosed that two other associates of Mendola had suffered severe beatings in previous weeks. Asked how they might have "crossed the crime syndicate," Cain suggested that perhaps "it might be retribution for burglary or robbery of the home of a crime syndicate figure or a mob-operated restaurant or business enterprise." (This was a highly unlikely theory since Mendola was a godson of Sam Giancana.)

When a palm print was found on Mendola's Cadillac, Cain said, "The palm print will enable us to identify the killer—if we can find him." Cain then arrested three alleged suspects, and promptly re-

272

leased them when their palm prints failed to match the one found on the automobile.

If State's Attorney Ward had a theory on the Mendola murder, he did not submit it to the press. Yet he did have one secret item of curious information: Guy Mendola had been Cain's well-informed "informant"—the tipster who had offered to return some of the stolen loot for $20,000. In fact, his murder coincided with Ward's initiation of an investigation to explore Mendola's connection with the Zahn burglary.

On September 25, the grand jury returned six indictments against the sheriff's four investigators. Each man was named individually in indictments charging perjury and obstructing justice; a fifth indictment charged all four with conspiracy to obstruct justice, and a sixth accused them of conspiracy to commit perjury.

Here briefly are some of the vital points established by the prosecution in a two-week trial:

> —Sergeant John Chaconas was identified by Caravelle Motel employees as the mysterious John J. Matheos who had registered in Room 31 six hours before the raid. A police handwriting expert identified the writing on the motel registration card and samples of Chaconas' handwriting as having been "executed" by the same person. The registration card identified by the handwriting expert was a carbon copy obtained by Ward's investigators two days after the raid. It was the prosecution's contention that Cain had confiscated the original card in an effort to shield Chaconas, but had overlooked the carbon copy. The prosecution established that Chaconas *could not* have participated in the raid (as testified to by all four defendants before the grand jury) because motel personnel would have immediately recognized him. The grand jury testimony was further contradicted by the two newsmen who accompanied the raiders. They testified they did not see Chaconas that evening.
>
> —The day clerk at the motel, who identified Chaconas as the fictitious John J. Matheos, testified that he had arrived in a blue Cadillac sedan bearing Illinois license plates number KL-5354. The state then introduced evidence that Chaconas owned a blue Cadillac sedan.
>
> —As the first witness for the defense, Chaconas testified that on the evening of the raid he obtained the name and address of the owner of license plates KL-5354 by a

273

radio call from his squad car. "I went to that address. The guy was a Greek." "You say you went there?" "Right. We met this guy—he was at work—we met this guy later that evening." "[Was his name] Angelatos?" "It was something like that."

—Angelo Angelatos, in whose name the license plates were registered, had died on October 5, 1963—three months before his alleged conversation with Chaconas.

—A clue to Cain's investigative genius was gleaned in his grand jury testimony. Asked why he failed to dust the motel room and the forty-six cartons for fingerprints, he replied: "One would assume the burglars would be wearing gloves." But in his deposition to Ward, his reason was that it would have entailed too much work. "I have to point out," Ward said, "that the agency which would have done the job was the Chicago Police Crime Laboratory which has a substantial organization." And when Ward had ordered the room dusted two days after the raid, a nice clean fingerprint was lifted from a wall—it belonged to Sergeant Chaconas.

On December 8, 1964, Cain, Donnelly and Chaconas were found guilty on the conspiracy to commit perjury indictment. The jury was unable to agree on Witsman and the indictments were nol-prossed. (According to state's attorney's records, Witsman had a police sheet: held for investigation in Lafayette, Indiana, in 1946, and arrested in Danville, Illinois, on May 8, 1957 and charged with being an inmate of a gambling house. No dispositions indicated.) Judge Walter P. Dahl imposed sentences of one to three years on Cain, Donnelly and Chaconas, which they immediately appealed. They were released on bond. On motion of the State, a nolle prosequi was entered and allowed as to all remaining indictments.*

Many questions remained unanswered—as is so often the case in Chicago. "It is a little difficult to tell who are the cops and who are the robbers in this script," the *Tribune* concluded, "but the bemused citizen will not be in deep error if he concludes that justice has a somewhat strange way of manifesting itself in Cook county." Asked the *Sun-Times:* "How did it happen that Ogilvie, a knowledgeable

* The perjury conviction was reversed by the Illinois Supreme Court, which held that Judge Dahl had failed to conduct a "meaningful examination" of a woman juror who claimed to have seen a newspaper headline about the case during the trial.

Recent press reports have placed Cain in Mexico, where he is the "official bodyguard for Sam Giancana."

274

law enforcement officer who as an assistant prosecutor built a reputation as a foe of the crime syndicate, hired men such as these as his own policemen?"

As a final note of intrigue, Ward disclosed that Cain, Witsman and Moran once had been employed by the Burns International Detective Agency, the company which had installed the "burglar-proof" alarm system in the Zahn warehouse.

Deputy Jack Moran had the last word. On hearing of the sentence levied against his boss, Moran remarked: "Well, that's show business."

Ogilvie's headless Special Investigations Unit, already depleted by four, was about to suffer other casualties. Exactly one week after the Cain trial ended, Ward announced that his office would seek a grand jury indictment against Sergeant Camille Wilson, a female member of Cain's original group, who was charged with obstructing justice by concealing a missing witness from a grand jury investigation in an attempted abortion case (Sergeant Wilson was indicted, tried and acquitted).

By then six of the original ten SIU members were out of action: Cain, Donnelly, Chaconas, Witsman, Wilson and Jack Moran, who resigned because "I don't feel I could function to the maximum of my capacities under any other police officer except Chief Richard Cain." But the purge was not yet over. Ward was hot on the trail of two other SIU deputies accused of attempted extortion.

Captain Thomas Mahon, then acting head of SIU, explained that a seventeen-year-old girl had been used by the two deputies as a decoy in purported shakedown efforts. Two Northlake tavern operators had complained of being solicited for money by the sheriff's men after the teen-age girl—looking much older—bought drinks in their places. "I ordered the two men out of the SIU to avoid any recurrence," Mahon told newsmen.

Questioned by the same newsmen before he had an opportunity to confer with Mahon, Ogilvie shrugged off the charges. "These were allegations, not accusations. They were checked out as a matter of routine and proved to be completely unfounded. That's the end of it." Apprised of Mahon's incriminating comments, Ogilvie snapped back: "I don't know what Captain Mahon is talking about. I'm going to have to speak to him."

A few days later Ogilvie disbanded the Special Investigations Unit.

In the months following the conviction of Richard B. Cain, political analysts hinted strongly that Ogilvie might quit politics when his term expired in 1966.

"Holding public office is not all it's cracked up to be," Ogilvie told one interviewer. "These last two years have been a real eye opener." (He was elected governor of Illinois in 1968.)

5

A secretly taped conversation between Donald Shaw, a 26-year-old sheriff's patrolman; Joseph "Joey" Aiuppa, Mafia vicelord of Cicero, and Jacob "Dutch" Bergbreiter, a former vice squad lieutenant with the sheriff's office, provided a rare insight into the Syndicate's recruiting program. Six months preceding this recording session, Shaw and his partner, Patrolman James P. Bredican, "accepted" (with the knowledge of Sheriff Ogilvie) a $500 bribe from John Carr (nee Casper Ciapetti), a Syndicate underling and police bagman. Indicted by the grand jury for bribery, Carr was awaiting trial when Bergbreiter approached Shaw and confided that Aiuppa had a special interest in the case. The next evening (July 3, 1965) Shaw was wearing a concealed miniature radio transmitter when he met Aiuppa in Bergbreiter's real estate office in Palatine. As the three men walked to a hot dog stand, the conversation was recorded in a police squad car parked a block down the street:

AIUPPA: Would you have any objection to helping John Carr off the hook in court for a consideration and, if in doing so, it wouldn't hurt your position as a police officer?

SHAW: I wouldn't mind helping if I didn't hurt myself as a police officer and I didn't perjure myself in court.

AIUPPA: You won't hurt yourself and you won't have to be in court. Just give the lawyer a loophole in our prosecution. Now you wouldn't want to see them put him [Carr] in the pen for ten years.

SHAW: I don't know him. I heard rumors that the guy has been an assassin.

AIUPPA: What?

SHAW: An assassin.

AIUPPA: Never.

BERGBREITER: Don't believe all the stuff you hear. Who told you he was an assassin?

276

SHAW: I don't know. I just heard.

AIUPPA: Excuse me, do you think there's such a crime as playing a slot machine or a pinball machine?

SHAW: By the law, there is.

AIUPPA: Wait a minute. The laws are flexible, they are made to bend, just like a big tree standing here, it's made to flex. I agree with this. I am a servant of the law and a citizen. (*Then he launched into an obscene tirade against Sergeant Michael O'Mara, head of the sheriff's police vice squad.*)

SHAW: Like I say, it's the law. I get paid to do it.

AIUPPA: All right. All right. Fine. We understand each other. There is several ways to do things. Take this man like O'Mara. He's a nice guy. He's going to try to break the Syndicate. He's going to try to get with the state's attorney. He's building up his stature, you understand, on your work. He's brainwashing 'all you young guys. Then [after the election] he dumps you. (*He assures Shaw he will take care of him when Ogilvie's term expires.*) . . . You just can't hurt people. . . . You have to use good common sense. You really do, reasoning. When the saturation point comes, you're saturated. You're through. Our machines aren't taking money away from children, their milk money, or the money they go to school with. When you find out about me, you will see I am a pretty nice guy. All I am interested in is the gambling and night spots in Cicero. It would be different if I sold broads, if I sold junk, if I sold counterfeit money. But I can go into a bar or a drugstore and someone might even sit down and have a cup of coffee with me. We have nice people here. You will find out as you travel in Cicero that it is really a nice town. I'll guarantee you that my mother, sister, my daughter could walk down the residential streets with no problem. I've been there [Cicero] for forty years.

BERGBREITER: And he will still be there when others are gone. I know that he will stand up, what he says, he will do.

AIUPPA: I expect you to stand up, too. If you can't stand up, I don't want to talk to you. We're men, we're friends, we try to help each other. Do you want to go along?

SHAW: Tell me what you want me to do.

AIUPPA: Let's say you were in court now and you were asked, "Could this man [Carr] have offered you this

277

money as a bond for Mr. Doyle?" Isn't it possible it could have been that way? (*Shaw is fearful that his rigged testimony might conflict with the account he gave the grand jury.*) . . . You would like to read the transcript [of the grand jury hearings]? Is that what you want? All right, we'll do that. (*Shaw points out that his partner, James Bredican, will also be a witness against Carr.*) . . . Forget about Jim. I know what you said before the grand jury, and I know what Jimmy said. I know more about it than you think I do. This is yours. Two big ones. (*He holds up two fingers to indicate a payoff of $2,000.*) For yourself. Don't tell anybody.

BERGBREITER: Don't even tell your wife. Believe me.

AIUPPA: If you tell anybody, I want no part of it. (*Pauses and stares hard at Shaw before making his next pitch.*) . . . Every month I will see that there is a C-note or some worldly goods in your mail box. You'll be on the roll.

SHAW: What do you want from me to be on the roll?

AIUPPA: All I want from you is the information, so that they will not be kicking me with the point of the shoe but the side of the shoe. If you find something out, see something you think I should know about, I'll give you a number. You follow me?

SHAW: The thing of it is, I would suddenly be out of a job if I stopped making pinches.

AIUPPA: You will never stop making pinches. If you haven't got an out, you go ahead. I paid for these pigeons [set-up raids].

BERGBREITER: He will give you some good ones.

AIUPPA: Do you follow me? All I'm interested in is the gambling and the night spots in Cicero. I'm not interested in the residential areas.

BERGBREITER: Shaw, can I give you a little advice, being a boss like I was out there?

SHAW: In vice and gambling?

BERGBREITER: That's right. I used to be the captain in charge of vice and gambling under [Joseph] Lohman and the Outfit always took care of me after I got smart and got on their payroll. Do this on your own. This is between the three of us. Don't trust your partner, nobody.

SHAW: Say the intelligence unit had a game under surveillance and then gave it to us and suddenly it wasn't there any more? They would get wise.

AIUPPA: Fine. The tables would be there. The game would be there, but the money wouldn't be on the table. Do you follow me? I'll never embarrass you, never hurt you. I can be nice to you. I can help you. If you have any problem, I can be nice to you. I can decorate the mahogany a little bit. You know what I mean? . . . If you walked into a place and saw me in there and your superior said, "pinch him"—I never even met you. Go ahead and pinch me. I go along with the show.

SHAW: I kick you with the side of the shoe?

AIUPPA: Now you're catching on. . . .

(*Later that evening Bergbreiter comes to Shaw's home to deliver a $500 down payment on the $2,000 bribe offered by Aiuppa. In the ensuing days, Shaw talks to Bergbreiter on several occasions, and each time the conversation is recorded. Then, about three weeks after his meeting with Aiuppa, Shaw is confronted by a distraught Bergbreiter as he arrives home late one night.*)

BERGBREITER: Listen, I hear you were wired for sound when you met Joey.

SHAW: You crazy? Not me.

BERGBREITER: Joey learned that there was a guy under your crawl space.

SHAW: You're kidding.

BERGBREITER: And Joey learned that a helicopter was used for surveillance on him when he met with you.

SHAW: Well, they must be watching me. They wouldn't be watching you.

BERGBREITER: Joey don't want to see you again until he gets a chance to test you.

The next time they saw each other was when Joey was being fingerprinted and mugged by sheriff's police. Bergbreiter was apprehended a few days later in a hideout in Wisconsin.

As is so often the case in Chicago, the good work of the sheriff had a reverse effect on the image of his department. "I'm not going to cover up this thing," he said. "We may lie test six, twelve or even fifty policemen. If the mob has spies on my police force, I want to know who they are."

"At one point," said one Ogilvie aide, "it appeared that Aiuppa knew more about our investigation than Shaw did."

Because of the security leak, Ogilvie had no choice but to halt the investigation. "After the first meeting," he said, "we believed we had enough evidence to convict Aiuppa and Bergbreiter of bribery. But we wanted to find out whether Aiuppa could make good on his boast that he has access to secret grand jury testimony and even can supply verbatim accounts of it."

"We located every copy of the transcript that was made in that case," Ward reported. "We keep very tight security on all grand jury transcripts. We naturally will pursue this, but my first thought is that Aiuppa was bluffing." Ward then referred humorously to the Syndicate mogul as "Professor Aiuppa," dismissing his claim to "inside" information with "it sounds like a typical con artist bragging."

At first, four of the six men who constituted the entire vice control unit of the sheriff's police force balked at the idea of taking lie tests. Finally, everyone consented except Detectives Donald L. DeVriendt and David S. Meyers, who were suspended for thirty days and subsequently dismissed.

On March 30, 1966, Carr (alias Casper Ciapetti was acquitted in a bench trial by Judge Edward F. Healy. Ciapetti testified that the $500 was bond money for Edward Doyle, owner of the Cicero tavern raided by Shaw on gambling charges. Doyle also testified that he, too, interpreted the money as a bond. The judge thought that perhaps Doyle's testimony "could be counted on." However, he was pretty sure that policeman Shaw's version was full of discrepancies.

Aiuppa and Bergbreiter were indicted on two counts of bribery on October 1, 1965, and brought to trial in the summer of 1966. Bergbreiter was convicted and sentenced to two years in prison. His boss was freed in the same case by Judge William S. White, who discovered a lack of evidence in the state's case against the Cicero vicelord.

It was not Aiuppa's first escape. For example, there was the case of Duane S. Seavey, a former steel company salesman, husband and father of four, who was suddenly metamorphosed into a small blue index card in the police department's missing persons file. Like hundreds before him, Seavey went from gambling man and bon vivant, to police informer and patsy, to mob victim and police statistic.

Seavey's troubles began with a raid by State's Attorney's police on a gambling operation in the Towne Hotel—Aiuppa's headquarters (formerly the Hawthorne Inn, it was Capone's Cicero stronghold back in the mid-1920s). The first mistake, described as inadvertent, occured when a clerk typed Seavey's real name into the body of the warrant instead of the alias "David Smiley" which was used in the signature blank to protect his identity. When the raiders struck on

280

November 1, 1962, Seavey was in the gambling room posing as a patron. Aiuppa was one of the thirty-five persons arrested.

Six weeks later, Seavey wrote a letter to a *Daily News* reporter whom he had known in high school: *"In case you can print this story which is so important to my safety, and reputation, here are the important points: (1) That I was the undercover informant in the raid on the gambling room in the Towne Hotel in Cicero, for the State's Attorney's police, on Nov. 1, 1962. (2) That I had laid out, diagrammed, and planned the entire raid for the State's Attorney's office, and the raid itself was very successful. (3) That I have in the past two years done undercover work for the FBI, Federal Narcotics, and the United States Attorney. (4) That I was asked (for what reason I don't know) to be in the place as a patron at the hour it was raided. (5) That, unfortunately, the TV cameras got only me in the story of raid, and I appeared on 10 a.m. news November 1st as a patron (CBS). (6) That I was placed in jeopardy by a mistake made on the search warrant. . . . Subsequently a State's Attorney's police guard was detailed to protect me 24 hrs. per day. (7) That Dan Ward suggested that I relocate and asked for cost. When he got cost, he accused me of attempting to blackmail the public. He wanted to pay my furniture moving expenses, and family and self transportation, and dump me. (8) Also, that I subsequently had a meeting with Joe Aiuppa, at the suggestion of one of State's Attorney's investigators. Both Joe and Geo. Crane, his attorney, said I had nothing to fear. (9) That by letter, I have finally gotten rid of police guard. There are other bits, but the important points are listed above. Sure hope you can help. Thanks. Duane."*

After his meeting with Aiuppa, Seavey turned up with a certificate from a doctor stating that a heart condition made it impossible for him to testify before the grand jury hearing the case. But even without his testimony, the grand jury returned indictments against Aiuppa and five other persons on gambling charges.

The trial on March 7, 1963, did not last very long. Judge F. Emmett Morrissey ruled that the search warrant was faulty because of the mixup in using both Seavey's name and the alias "David Smiley," and dismissed the charges.

Nothing happened for thirteen months. Then, on April Fool's Day, 1964, Seavey's wife telephoned Sheriff Ogilvie and reported her husband missing. Six months later, Seavey's car was found in a parking lot at O'Hare Airport. The key was in the ignition and Seavey's brown leather briefcase was still in the car. But the regular matting was missing from the floor of the trunk, which led police to thoughts of mayhem and bloodstains. Seavey, they conjectured, was "probably part of the expressway, buried under tons of concrete."

"This is the sad—and frightful—story of Duane S. Seavey," wrote one reporter, "and what can happen to a customer who crosses the syndicate."

On October 9, 1964, exactly one week after Seavey's car was found, the Appellate Court reversed Judge Morrissey's ruling, and the gambling charges against Aiuppa, *et al.*, were reinstated. During the new trial, three witnesses (gambling patrons), who had previously identified the defendants before the grand jury, were suddenly unable to recognize anybody. "The parade of witnesses who testified were guilty today of loss of memory," Judge Walter P. Dahl noted as he acquitted Aiuppa and two codefendants. Two patrons were found guilty of gambling and fined $250 each.

6

For those who know the name of the game, crime is Chicago's most popular and profitable local sport. It is a spirited contest between crooks and cops, coached by lawyers, refereed by judges, fixed by politicians, advertised by newspapers and financed by the world's largest and most enthusiastic captive audience.

High among the sport's stellar attractions are the Panczko brothers —Joseph, Edward and Paul—three ugly thieving bums who have been affectionately tagged Pops, Butch and Peanuts by an army of enchanted Boswells. Accomplished burglars, the Panczkos also dabble in robbery, aggravated assault, rape and murder. For nearly three decades, the saga of this larcenous trio has kept millions of Chicagoans laughing while driving thousands of other to the brink of bankruptcy.

If the Panczkos possess one distinguishing trait, it is their unique disregard for their public image as great thieves. In their individual hard-working careers, they have indiscriminately lifted everything from a cement mixer to an unplucked chicken to $1.7 million worth of gems to a handful of S&H Green Stamps. Pride in their professional status is secondary to opportunity. Their greatest singular accomplishment has been their almost invincible skill in defeating the opposing team. To date, they have collected an enviable score of literally hundreds of arrests and only a handful of convictions,*

* Police statisticians admit they have lost count in the welter of records that include as many as thirty court continuances on each charge.

282

mostly federal or out-of-state raps—their batting average slumps badly on the road.

Their record becomes even more remarkable when one considers their innate weakness to score in the clutch. In any other league, the Panczkos would have been farmed out for life early in the season. The credit for their perennial success belongs in great measure to their devoted coaches, attorneys George Bieber and Michael Brodkin, otherwise professionally known as The B & B Boys or The Habeas Corpus Twins. The B & B Boys are strictly major league, having coached such hall-of-fame champions as Jake "Greasy Thumb" Guzik, Murray "The Camel" Humphreys, Tony "Big Tuna" Accardo and Momo "Sam" Giancana.

Products of the near Northwest Side "badlands" where so many of their teammates got their start, Pops (Joseph) and Butch (Edward), when not otherwise vacationing at the state's expense, still work and play in the old neighborhood—near California and North, along Division Street and Milwaukee Avenue; Peanuts Paul was more interested in travel.

The oldest and once the captain of the team, Pops, born about 1915, had a modest enough beginning at the age of 12. "I used to steal chickens on the Fulton Market," he says. But even in those early days Pops was fascinated by the unlimited possibilities of a simple screwdriver. He gradually increased his skills and with it his take-home pay. Everything went along larcenously until 1940, when Pops took his first fall. But even then a charge of burglary was reduced to a misdemeanor. Pops served six months in the House of Correction.

Back on the street again, Pops picked up another screwdriver and went back to work. Almost immediately he was arrested in Oak Park for attempted burglary. The next day the charge was reduced to disorderly conduct. He was fined $100 and costs. Five months later, Pops was back in court, this time charged with burglary. He was acquitted. Then in January 1942, while fleeing from a burglary, Pops' souped-up car ran over a pedestrian in full view of pursuing cops. Charged with manslaughter, Pops' luck held out once more. The case was nol-prossed.

Pops took his second fall in the spring of 1942. Caught with a friend in a stationery store with the lights on and burglary tools lying beside a "cracked" safe, Pops had a ready alibi: "We was only walking along, and needing a bathroom. Seeing the door was open, we just dropped in to borrow the john."

This time the jury was not convinced, and the judge sentenced him to two-to-five years. Pops indignantly appealed and the conviction was reversed on a technicality. Almost a year later, Pops was retried and again convicted, receiving a sentence of one-to-life. Pops spent three years in Joliet before being paroled in 1946.

Pops' next caper was more painful. It was New Year's Day, 1948, and Pops and a friend were happily transferring cases of liquor from a restaurant to their automobile. Pops, who by this time was used to "making bail" at the scene of a crime, quickly reached into his pocket when officer Walter Dietz materialized in the darkness. "Here's $400 to forget all about this," he said, moving toward the policeman. The next thing Pops knew there was a bullet in his shoulder and he was flat on his back. Police records do not indicate the disposition of this incident, but whatever it was it did not even interfere with his parole. A few weeks later he was again arrested for investigation.

Another New Year's Day rolled around, and Pops, who perhaps had been delinquent with his Christmas shopping, spotted a Railway Express truck which was conveniently parked in the downtown area. But he took too long window shopping. He aroused the interest of Carl Ohlin, a company guard stationed inside the truck. Pops only had time to break open the lock and grab a box containing a fur coat before Ohlin drilled him in the groin.

This time Pops had more to worry about than his wound. The truck was ruled an interstate shipment and that meant a federal rap. Even the magic of Bieber & Brodkin proved fallible. Sentence: two years plus three years' probation.

While Pops languished at Terre Haute federal prison, brothers Butch and Peanuts continued with the family enterprise. Peanuts, the precocious baby brother, had already collected forty-eight arrests without spending a day in jail. Two of his best friends were Martin "The Ox" Ochs and Paul "Needlenose" Labriola, notorious Capone mob plug uglies, who were both murdered in the mid-Fifties. Both Peanuts and Butch have chummed around with Syndicate thugs, and police have frequently linked them to gangland slayings. Bigger and tougher than Pops, the brothers have demonstrated a greater capacity for violence. In 1948, a garage mechanic was nearly slugged to death after he allegedly overcharged Peanuts for "souping up" a getaway car. Brodkin extricated him from that jam.

Butch has tended to direct his violence toward women. On December 22, 1942, Butch and two pals were charged with robbing two homes and beating and choking three elderly women. No conviction. On August 2, 1947, Butch was arrested for molesting two young girls. No conviction. On October 6, 1948, Butch and Charles Szelog

284

were tried for rape and contributing to the delinquency of a minor. Under cross-examination by Bieber, the 15-year-old victim admitted sexual relationships with several men. No conviction. The next day, Szelog was found dead with four .38 slugs in his back. Unsolved.

Although the Panczkos had confiscated more than a million dollars in merchandise by 1949, Peanuts became disenchanted with diversified looting and began specializing in jewelry. For a while his brothers were proud of him. Even when he was identified by a redcap at the North Western railway station as one of two thieves who had lifted two sample cases containing $50,000 in diamonds, Bieber had him out within two hours on $10,000 bond. Municipal Judge Joseph A. Pope cheerfully interrupted a fishing trip to sign the bond. Under cross-examination by Bieber at the trial, the redcap suffered the usual lapse of memory. He could no longer identify Peanuts as the man who had lured him away from the jewelry bags. Case dismissed.

Encouraged by his phenomenal success in Chicago, Peanuts decided to expand his territory. Accompanied by Guy "Lover Boy" Mendola and Walter Jedynak (a prime suspect in the Szelog slaying), Peanuts headed for the hills of Tennessee. A few days after the trio arrived in Nashville, a cab carrying a jewelry salesman was forced to the curb by three men in another automobile. One jumped into the cab and grabbed $100,000 in diamonds, leaving behind a hat bearing a Cicero clothing store label. Luck, as Peanuts sadly discovered, was a relative thing. The charge was robbery—a far cry from simple burglary—and the sentence was five-to-fifteen years in the Tennessee State Prison (the gems were never recovered). For the next eight years and ten months, he and his companions became good cotton choppers.

For a while, Butch was the only Panczko out on the street. Worthy of the family name, he also managed to compile an impressive record. By 1950, he could brag of fifty-four arrests, covering a wide variety of crimes, and only six minor convictions: five separate burglary charges reduced to disorderly conduct with fines of $1.00, $2.00, $100.00, $5.00 and $5.00, and a ten-day county jail sentence for a motor vehicle violation which he never served—the stiffest penalty ever levied against him.

Butch's success in eluding the law was not entirely happenstance. His Syndicate connections brought him to the attention of people of far more importance than The Habeas Corpus Twins.

For example, when Butch was caught in the act of burglarizing the B & B Novelty Company, a juke box enterprise owned by Bert

Biondioti, a competitor of Eddie Vogel (once, on Vogel's order, Sheriff "Blind Tom" O'Brien turned all of Biondioti's machines to the wall), the Syndicate rushed to his rescue. Within an hour of his arrest, Biondioti received a message from Fred "Jukebox" Smith (a Vogel henchman and a power in electrical unions) to go easy on the boy. A short time later, State Senator Robert "Happy" Petrone telephoned to plea for leniency because he "had watched the boy grow up" and he knew his family well. This was followed by a visit from Roland V. Libonati and Joseph Porcaro, which in turn was followed by the appearance of John "Bananas" DeBiase and Phillip Mesi. Biondioti relented and Butch paid a $2 fine on a reduced charge of disorderly conduct.

A hazard of the burglary business is the risk presented by frightened, trigger-happy cops. Butch nearly became a statistic on the actuarial tables on February 24, 1951. Assisted by four eager partners, Butch was loading the second of two safes into a souped-up sedan when two officers from the Traffic Division appeared from out of a heavy fog behind the National Currency Exchange in Cicero.

Ordered to stand still, all five men naturally raced to escape. Butch caught the first slug in the chest before he could move a half dozen steps. Another bandit, James Murray (with a record of thirty-three arrests), was captured, but three others escaped.

The job was the kind you can see nightly on the late late show. To circumvent the burglar alarm, the burglars had forced entry into an adjoining restaurant and then smashed a hole in the wall of the currency exchange. But they made so much noise tunneling through that a resident nearly a block away telephoned the police to complain of the racket.

Butch survived not only the wound but the trial as well. A jury freed the two men after their attorney argued that police could not be certain of their guilt because of a heavy fog. And besides, when captured they had nothing in their possession (i.e., they were not holding the safe) to associate them with the burglary.

Meanwhile, Pops was transferred from Terre Haute to Joliet to complete his one-to-life sentence since authorities felt that the robbery of the Railway Express truck constituted a breach of his parole. A year later, Joseph D. Lohman, then chairman of the Illinois Parole and Pardon Board, decided that it was in the "best interest of the inmate and the community" to parole Pops for the second time. "We examined his record on its merits," said Lohman, "and we felt the time was ready to see if Panczko had made a successful adjustment.

286

He gave evidence of being inspired by his continued incarceration."

Just a glance at Pops' subsequent record indicates that Lohman may have confused hunger with inspiration. In the next four years, Pops collected a score of arrests and had so many cases pending that he had to consult an appointment book to keep court dates from conflicting.

Again astride the old treadmill, Pops had to step up his work schedule to meet the various bail bonds and attorney fees which he once estimated at between $75,000 to $100,000 a year. And being a local celebrity, he was always cooperative when a newsman needed a feature for the Sunday supplement. At such times, he would reminisce about the old days when the scores were good and the sentences painless.

Pops was particularly proud of the fact that he had contributed the "three-minute crash" to the burglary profession. "We'd really plan those [clothing store] jobs," he said. "We'd look the place over, figure out which way each of us would move once we were in, and then take the joint the next night. By planning, we wouldn't be stumbling over each other in the dark. And we got assorted sizes. It worked like a charm. We grab the clothes, pipe racks and all, load up two or three cars, and be gone in three minutes flat."

Pops' favorite hangout was an ice cream parlor on West Grand Avenue. He enjoyed mesmerizing the kids with tales of his big scores. Sometimes he even mesmerized himself into confusing the future with the past. These lapses have seriously handicapped his performance in recent years.

Take, for example, the T. J. Cullen jewelry store caper in suburban Wilmette. Some stool pigeon—perhaps a disenchanted member of Pops' teen-age fan club—tipped the cops that the place was to be burglarized by Pops and Ralph Campagna when its owner locked up for lunch that day.

Ten minutes after the owner left that noon, there was a knock at the back door of the jewelry store. Policeman Harold Graf, who was staked out in a small room at the back of the store, tells what happened next: "I didn't answer. I picked up my shotgun and waited. I saw the door handle turn and then the door was forced open with a crowbar. The two men came in, each carrying a cardboard carton. I pointed my shotgun at them and said I was a police officer and would shoot if they made another move. One of them—the one that got away—threw the box in my face."

Graf took up the chase, firing the shotgun as he ran. One of the men screamed and staggered into a vacant store, where Graf found him leaning over a basin in the washroom. "Get an ambulance," Pops cried. "I'm dying."

Doctors at Evanston Hospital plucked five shotgun pellets from Pops' skull and one from his brain. But in no time he was out of bed and back on his busy schedule of daily court appearances and nightly burglaries.

Assisted by attorneys George Bieber and Harry Busch, another Syndicate specialist, Pops was able to forestall the moment of truth for ten months with fifteen continuances from six different judges. But, finally, Pops found himself before a jury of his peers. The prosecution put on seventeen witnesses while Bieber had only one—Pops. "That day I was out looking for a nice house to buy for my mother," Pops said wistfully. "I got hungry. I seen that shopping center and stopped, thinking to get a sandwich and a cup of coffee. I was getting out of the car and somebody shot me in the head and just about killed me." Verdict: not guilty.

"I'm at a loss for words," said Graf. "It sort of hits you low—you do your best, then this."

Meanwhile, charges against Pops and Butch were continued in another case. These charges included one against Pops of attempted bribery, while he and Butch were charged with assault and battery, aggravated assault, assault and resisting arrest. A few months earlier, Butch had beat a burglary and murder rap resulting from the attempted looting of the Mandel Brothers fur vault. Like Pops in the jewelry store caper, Butch and two companions had walked into a police trap. In the ensuing chase, one of the burglars was shot to death and Butch was charged with felony murder—based on the premise that a man is responsible for what happens when he conspires to commit a felony. (The case against Pops and Butch also washed out.)

Regardless of size, nothing is safe from a Panczko when opportunity strikes. Consider, for example, one mild February afternoon when Butch and James Panos spied a two-ton concrete mixer mired down in mud in a vacant lot. After three and a half hours of steady pushing and tugging, they managed to get it out of the lot and to a junk yard, where they sold it for $36 cash.

Hours later, Hans Martin found his property in the process of being chewed up by the junk yard's steelcutting saws and sledge hammers. Brought to trial, Butch had a ready answer. "I didn't steal it," he said. "I asked a man in the lot if we could have it and he said,

288

'Sure, take it.' " Asked how he knew the generous bystander was the legal owner of the mixer, Butch replied, "How would I know? I never saw him before in my life."

After this performance, Bieber made a motion for a directed verdict which Judge Henry W. Dieringer promptly granted. "The state," concluded the judge, "has failed to prove felonious intent."

Pops' popularity in the press became a sore point with a growing number of Chicago policemen. After a while, it got so they were putting the arm on him the moment he stepped out of his house. And since the profession entails the possession of certain cumbersome implements, the adventures of Pops began appearing in the local press with the regularity of a comic strip.

"The cops are driving me goofy," Pops complained in one interview. "They're tailing me so I can't make a living. Gee whiz, so I like tools. I like to have them around me. I use them all the time." Asked to elaborate on his occupation, he gave a simple answer: "I'm a teef." As to the cops who did not arrest him, Pops provided a clue: "Usually I'm good for half a hundred every time they stop me."

Sometimes, of course, nothing seemed to work. There was the night Edward Koniecki peered out his bedroom window and spied Pops at work on his garage door. Moments later police found Koniecki on top of Pops on the garage floor. And there, still in Pops' hand, was a screwdriver. Lying near him were a brace and bit as well as an open combination lock.

A prosecutor would have to spend many sleepless nights to concoct a better prima facie case. Or so it appeared. About seven o'clock that same evening, the telephone rang in the Koniecki household and a policeman answered stating he was Mr. Koniecki.

"Well," said the caller, "this is a friend of Panczko. He's a nice guy and maybe if you lay off, it might be worth your while." The policeman invited the caller to hurry over. Within minutes the doorbell rang. The policeman opened the door, and before anyone could get a word in edgewise, arrested Butch and William Heneghan. The case was swiftly disposed of in Felony Court when Butch denied having made the telephone call and insisted that they had just happened to "drop in."

At Pops' trial, Koniecki refused to testify, stating that he feared for his safety and that of his family. "Besides," he added, "I've got a heart condition." The judge was less than sympathetic. He sentenced him to a year in jail for contempt, but pressure from the press and civic groups saved Koniecki from serving the sentence. Pops was later convicted for possession of burglary tools, but the Illinois Supreme Court reversed it on a technical error.

It seems the consensus among Panczko buffs that Peanuts was spoiled by his older brothers. This, as psychiatrists tell us, can lead to sibling rivalry, which inevitably leads to thumb sucking, resentment, contempt or hostility. Where Butch was happy with a cement mixer and Pops quite often with a lot less, Peanuts wanted more.

The Pompano Beach caper in February 1962, for example, was a score worthy of any thief—nearly $2 million in gems. Pops had devoted his whole life to looting stores and popping car trunks to aggregate that much. And Butch had earned perhaps less. Now Peanuts could eclipse them both in one bold stroke.

When Peanuts and four other bandits left Chicago's O'Hare airport for Florida, FBI agents were there to wish them a silent farewell. And when they landed in Miami Beach, other federal agents were there not only to express a silent greeting but to tail the quintet to their motel.

On the day of the robbery, two men—one calling himself John Kennedy—rented two outboard motor boats at a waterfront marina. Later in the day, four men (all wearing identical golf caps so they would not attract attention) casually strolled into the Leonard Taylor jewelry store in Pompano Beach. In no time, nickel-plated gun barrels were glinting in the sunlight. Before the manager could object, he and the store's porter were herded into a backroom closed off by an iron grillwork gate. As the robbers feverishly tied up their captives, the gate slammed shut, locking everyone in. The manager obligingly supplied a ring of keys, but after ten minutes of struggling with the keys, the dauntless bandits were begging the manager to let them out. Not in a position to debate the issue, the manager soon obliged them.

For the next few minutes, the caper went according to plan. They filled a suitcase with 521 pieces of jewelry worth $1.7 million, virtually emptying the shop. Then they dashed out the front door— nearly trampling a bystander who watched in amazement as the robbers attempted their "getaway." The driver, who was parallel-parked at the curb, suddenly slammed the car into reverse and nearly ran over a colleague who was dashing around behind the car. Then, just as they were ready to drive off, another automobile slipped in behind, wedging them into the parking space. After some frantic maneuvers, the bandits were on their way as a gathering crowd of tourists watched in astonishment.

290

They abandoned their stolen car at the south end of Pompano Beach and boarded the two speedboats awaiting them at the marina. One refused to start. They tied a rope to the stalled boat. The rope broke when they started too fast. An exasperated Peanuts squatted on the bow of the stalled boat, holding the tow rope as the other craft pulled it across nine miles of water in a blizzard of spray to Fort Lauderdale. From there they drove without incident to Miami Beach.

That evening, on a bulletin from the FBI, the Miami police stopped a rented car and hit the jackpot. Inside was the drip-dried Peanuts, two burglar companions and two gang molls. They also found a key that unlocked the trunk of a car at Peanuts' motel. The suitcase with its precious baubles had been carelessly tossed against the spare tire. (How happy it would have made Pops to pop that trunk.)

In less than forty-eight hours, Peanuts was released on $50,000 bond and was airbound for Chicago.

"Hold on to your hats—and anything else movable with a potential market value," the Chicago *American* warned its readers. "Peanuts is back in town."

At the moment, Peanuts was more interested in $75,000 worth of television sets stowed away in a chicken house in Chicago Heights than in hats. But lo and behold, the G-men had beat him to that, too. Not only had they recovered the loot, but they had bagged six of his buddies in the process.

Peanuts was frantic. He needed big money and fast for attorney fees, bail bonds and perhaps a little grease here and there. The first trial ended in a hung jury. The second was sheer disaster: guilty and a life sentence.

The Chicago *American* offered a little advice: "[Peanuts] Panczko, the youngest, most ambitious, and clearly the most inept of Chicago's three burgling brothers, was sentenced to life imprisonment in Fort Lauderdale, Fla. . . . The story doesn't exactly prove that crime doesn't pay—it has paid pretty well for the Panczkos who stayed in Chicago—but it does point up a few other morals. . . . (a) Don't think big unless you have the equipment for it, and (b) For a Chicago crook who can afford the right lawyers, there's no place like home."

While out on bond pending a motion for a new trial, Peanuts took the *American*'s advice and did not wander from home. But judging from what happened next, he would have been safer in Milwaukee— noted for its quick frontier-style justice.

It began when Peanuts tried to run interference for a stolen pickup truck. The truck had been stolen from the Powers Electrical Appliance company when its driver had stopped to make a delivery. It contained two washing machines and a hot-water heater. A description of the vehicle was broadcast, and within minutes two policemen in a squad car spotted the truck ahead of them. There was only a sedan between them and the truck, but every time they tried to pass it, its driver sounded the horn, swerved and slowed down, blocking the pursuing squad. Suddenly, the truck was abandoned in the middle of the street as its driver took to his feet. This left the squad car and sedan trapped behind the truck which completely blocked the street.

Peanuts had to made a quick decision under stress—which apparently is a mistake for a Panczko. In his pocket were two keys stamped "U.S. Mail" (the type used to open street storage boxes) which, as anyone knows, only a mailman can possess. So Peanuts did the first thing that popped into his head. He tossed them out of the car. (Pops once tried to swallow an auto trunk key when he was apprehended. It was wrapped in a piece of paper bearing the owner's name. Pops could not even swallow the paper.)

Four young boys playing nearby were attracted by all the excitement. One of the boys courteously returned the keys to Peanuts, who muttered "Thanks." A moment later, out flew the keys and again the boy politely returned them: "Here, mister, you lost your keys again." "Get outta here, kid," Peanuts snarled as he unlimbered his pitching arm and flung the keys into a vacant lot seconds before the cops reached his car.

This time the boy returned the keys to the officers just as Peanuts was in the process of explaining that he was not running interference for the truck, but was only trying to get out of the way of that "crazy" squad car and got "confused." "Here, sir," said the boy, "this man keeps losing his keys."

Indicted by a federal grand jury, it took fourteen months to get Peanuts to trial, and his attorney, George Callaghan, another Syndicate mouthpiece, was not overlooking any possible technicality. As it happened, Peanuts had been arrested over the weekend during a fur burglary investigation, and Callaghan was fearful that the news might have "infected" the jury. The federal judge disagreed. Callaghan then asked for a mistrial when one of the potential veniremen asked, "Is that the guy I've been reading about all these years?" Again the judge disagreed.

The verdict was guilty and the court imposed the maximum sentence: ten years in federal prison and a $500 fine.

And there was more bad news for Peanuts. While the mail-key trial was in progress, ten Secret Service agents, armed with shotguns and submachine guns, broke into his $30,000 bi-level home in Melrose Park. They were looking for counterfeit money, but found instead three fully loaded .38 caliber revolvers, three hydraulic jacks used to smash through walls or force open stubborn doors, an automobile key code book for all General Motors cars with key blanks and key-cutting equipment, two cloth hood-type masks with slits for eyes and mouth, canvas gloves, bolt cutters, lock pullers, two walkie-talkie radios, a collection of black jackets, sweaters and top coats described as his "work clothes," and enough electronic eavesdropping devices to bug a fair-sized hotel.

Charged with conspiracy to possess and pass more than $32,000 in counterfeit $10 bills between September 1960 and August 1963, Peanuts was released after posting a $5,000 surety bond. One of his alleged coconspirators in the bogus money plot was Guy "Lover Boy" Mendola, his Tennessee cellmate who was murdered during the Zahn investigation. (Years ago, Mendola lost his girl friend to Butch in a dice game. When he tried to recoup in another game, he lost the furnishings in his love nest. Mendola's wife, Donna, was formerly Butch's wife.)

And then there was good news. Arrested on a murder warrant charging him with the slaying of a salesman during a $52,000 holdup of a Sears store, the grand jury refused to indict after one witness gave contradictory testimony. The other witnesses recalled that one of the three bandits—all of whom wore plastic masks—had the "same red neck, general build, and peculiar shuffle" that mark Panczko. The dissenting witness thought the killer had walked with a limp.

For a while the news was mixed. The Florida conviction was reversed on a technicality and the case was remanded for a new trial. Peanuts was convicted of counterfeiting and sentenced to fifteen years in federal prison. The ten-year sentence for possession of stolen mailbox keys was set aside by the U.S. Court of Appeals, which held that Judge Abraham L. Marovitz committed reversible error when he permitted the jury to go home after it had begun its deliberation. Marovitz, said the Appeals court, violated a principle which "has long existed and was binding on the District court." By this time, of course, Peanuts was used to judges making reversible errors.

Judge Bernard M. Decker denied bail in the counterfeiting case, but the Appeals court ordered him freed on a $50,000 bond. Another $25,000 bond was required on the pending retrial of the mailbox keys. And then, when Florida authorities tried to extradite him on charges of burglarizing a King Korn trading stamp center, Peanuts posted a $5,000 bond.

On May 12, 1966, Peanuts and three companions were arrested as suspects in a $30,000 robbery of a jewelry salesman. The salesman, Irving Cohan, told police he was hit in the mouth with a gun by robbers wearing plastic masks. Cohan and his driver were forced to lie on the floor of the car for about ten minutes before their captors departed with three sample cases of jewelry and Cohan's wallet.

Nine hours later, the four suspects were arrested in a garage behind the home of one of the suspects. Three women's wigs, four plastic masks, two revolvers, two walkie-talkies and Cohan's wallet were seized by police, along with Peanuts, who was found hiding in a dog house on the premises. (That was pretty much the situation in Peanuts' adventures at this writing.)

The last time Butch, the most elusive Panczko, was convicted was in 1961. He pleaded guilty to two charges of receiving stolen property—6,254 S&H Green Stamps—and drew a $1 fine and a suspended one-day jail term.

Thomas J. Regan, assistant state's attorney, said: "I almost fainted. I was quite surprised. I was worried about our chances of a conviction. We were well satisfied to take the guilty plea. Among other things it saved five days in court."

Although professionally sliding downhill in recent years, Pops still managed 119 court continuances on five felony cases in a period of three years. In his spare time, he enjoyed playing tribal chief of the clan. When police confiscated $500 worth of belts, twenty-five rings, seven wrist watches, umbrellas, cotton dresses, a fur coat and forty books of trading stamps valued at $140 in a raid on Butch's apartment, Pops marched right down to the station house. "He's clean," Pops shouted. "He went straight six years ago. Stick me with this one." Since Pops was so willing to be stuck, the police searched him. They found forty auto keys in his pockets. But nobody got stuck with anything. Attorney Bieber got Butch off on a motion to suppress the evidence because the items found were not identical with those itemized in the search warrant. And the charges against Pops were never officially filed.

294

Pops' most recent fall came in 1965 when he found himself without the solicitude of George Bieber. "I've been arrested two hundred times," Pops reminisced, "and I've spent a total of five years in the pen. After all that I haven't got a dime. I had to plead guilty because I had no more money for legal costs." Pops pleaded guilty on charges of possessing burglary tools and driving with a revoked license; he pleaded not guilty on a charge of attempting to bribe two policemen with forty-four wrist watches, but he was found guilty. He served eleven months of a one-year-and-a-day sentence.

Although not esteemed as highly as Syndicate czars, the Panczkos have achieved considerable admiration for their prankish role in the game of cops and robbers.

7

Chicago justice is as real as foxfire—it glitters in the darkness, but only from a distance.

"You must see the whole army marching through the municipal courts, facing indictment by a grand jury, bargaining all along the way for freedom, low bail, 'no bills,' exchange of 'felony' for 'misdemeanor,' acquittals, new trials, probation—the number of defendants growing less and less and less—you must see all of these before you can fully realize that each month the state's attorney and certain judges add to their personal following, enlist political workers, some who are free only on condition: 'stricken with leave to reinstate.' . . . Add to this the lowering standards of young lawyers appointed to prosecute and who soon see the 'system at work.' And more, see the unscrupulous defense attorneys who also enlist for the officials who give them a 'break.' The whole legal fabric becomes moth-eaten and eventually is a menace instead of a protection."

These words are as valid today as they were forty years ago, when the Rev. Elmer L. Williams wrote them. Even Orlando Wilson, who is known for his reticence to criticize the judiciary, could not resist the opportunity offered by the McClellan committee in 1963: "We today engage in a daily treadmill operation in which petty offenders charged with gambling, prostitution, and narcotics violations are dismissed without punishment. Such is the case despite the fact that evidence is legally obtained, admissible, and sufficient to establish guilt. In most instances, failure to convict results from invoking trumped-up legal technicalities. . . . Rules of evidence designed to protect the weak, the oppressed, and the indigent are, at the level of the trial court, being perverted and exploited to the benefit of the gangsters, the hoodlums, and the murderers."

One would have to be hopelessly naive to think that the attorneys representing the Syndicate are better forensically endowed than their less fortunate colleagues. The primary talent of a Syndicate mouth-piece is political clout that guarantees the cooperation of machine-controlled judges.

Another secret federal report reached some specific conclusions on the condition of the Cook County judiciary, the largest court system in the nation. "The most important function through the years of the First Ward," said the report, "has been its ability to obtain the cooperation of judges. Attorneys representing crime leaders contact politicians who in turn do their utmost to see that cases are assigned to judges who will render a favorable verdict.

The report went on to name sixteen Circuit Court judges, who "have at one time or another been contacted by various representatives of the crime syndicate to handle specific cases. . . . Ninety percent of all cases within the past year of persons arrested in Loop strip joints have been brought before either [the report named five judges]. Very few, if any, guilty verdicts were rendered from the bench in any of these cases."

The report named several other judges, many of whom were observed in direct contact with Murray "The Camel" Humphreys. Concerning one judge the Syndicate was "grooming" for the federal bench, Humphreys warned John D'Arco to curtail his requests for favorable treatment from the judge so that his friendly relationship with the Syndicate would not become publicly obvious. A few months later, D'Arco, accompanied by Jake Arvey, Frank Chesrow and Tom Munizzo (reputed to have great influence with Daley) visited the mayor to back the appointment of Humphreys' candidate for a federal judgeship in the Northern District of Illinois.

Humphreys masterminded the successful court fight to recover $89,284.75 confiscated by State's Attorney Adamowski in a gambling raid on the Viaduct Lounge in Cicero. Among the hoodlums seized in the raid were Rocco Fischetti, a cousin of Al Capone and a gambling boss in his own right before his death in 1964, Leslie "Killer Kane" Kruse and Gus Leibe. Realizing that the court would suppress the evidence on some phony technicality and thus automatically return the money to the hoodlums, Adamowski instituted a civil suit involving the contraband money and nol-prossed the criminal charges.

Presiding over the case was John Marshall Karns, Sr., a municipal judge in the city of East St. Louis, Illinois, the same judge who had so efficiently dispatched the vote fraud cases following the general election of 1960.

In the gambling action, Judge Karns ruled against the People and in favor of the hoodlums on the grounds that the state did not present any (admissible) evidence that the money had been used in a gambling operation. Therefore, the money was not subject to retention by the state.

Then there was the murder trial of George Ammirati (nee Ammeratto), forty-five-year-old son of the late "Big Jim" Emery, onetime Capone mob boss of Chicago Heights. Indicted in December 1962 for the murder of Stanley Tomaszek, he was provided with the legal services of Julius Lucius Echeles, which automatically assured him of a dozen continuances in the quest for a sympathetic judge. When Ammirati finally came to trial (without a jury—at his request) ten months later, the judge was George B. Weiss.

The facts, as presented by prosecution witnesses, established that in the early morning hours of December 3, 1962, Ammirati, who had been drinking with his twenty-six-year-old wife in a tavern on South Cicero Avenue, became noisy, vulgar and abusive, making insulting remarks to a woman friend of another tavern patron identified only as "The Swede." In the ensuing argument, The Swede struck Ammirati, who angrily stormed out of the tavern to return momentarily with a revolver. When Ruth O'Connel, the owner of the tavern, asked for the weapon, Ammirati slapped her on the side of the head with the gun barrel, knocking her unconscious. Then, brandishing the revolver and shouting obscenely, Ammirati ordered everyone to line up along a wall as he searched for The Swede. It was then that Stanley Tomaszek attempted to disarm him and was promptly shot in the chest. The wounded man staggered out of the tavern and collapsed in the parking lot, face down. Ammirati, who had followed him outside, fired a second shot into Tomaszek's back, killing him instantly.

Arrested by state troopers later that evening, Ammirati listed his occupation as a "self-employed bookie," and boasted that he was the son of the late "Big Jim" Emery and a close friend of top Syndicate hoodlums.

The bench trial lasted one day. Judge Weiss dismissed the charges of murder and voluntary manslaughter. The verdict was guilty of involuntary manslaughter (which carries a penalty of one to ten years) and the sentence reduced to probation for five years with only ninety days in jail.

In defending his decision to newsmen, Judge Weiss, who had been on the bench twenty-nine years, explained that a probation report on Ammirati showed him to be "a good family man," and that he had not been in trouble with the law since 1951—at that time he was arrested for carrying concealed weapons but the charge was dropped. "I try to do the best I can with what I get," Weiss added. "Ammirati has been leading a clean life. . . . I don't think he meant to shoot him. I believe that shot [the one in the back] was accidental, too. I believe both shots were on the accidental side."

In a bench trial before Judge Burton M. Bergstrom in 1959, John Sortino (brother of Frank Sortino, alias Frank "Strongy" Ferraro, who before his death in 1964 was recognized as one of the top leaders of the Syndicate) was charged with assault with intent to murder his two teen-age sons, Joseph and John Jr., aged fourteen and thirteen.

In a deathbed (they ultimately recovered) statement to the state's attorney's office, John Jr. said that shortly before nine o'clock on the morning of May 12, he was in the bathroom brushing his teeth when his father entered and shot him twice in the abdomen. Joseph said that he remained in his bedroom when he heard the shots, but that a moment later his father came into his room and Joseph asked him, "What did you do?" The father, whom Joseph stated was not drunk, replied, "This is what I did," and shot him twice in the chest. As the boy fell on the bed, the father asked, "Do you want some more?" Both boys stated that their father, who had often threatened their recently estranged mother with a gun, instructed them to say that their mother had shot them.

On cross-examination by the defense, the boys recanted their earlier statements and testified that their father was drunk when he shot them. Judge Bergstrom did not even wait for the defense to present its case. Since the defendant was drunk, Bergstrom concluded, he could not have had a criminal intent to murder. Finding: not guilty.

Assistant State's Attorney Frank Ferlic was dumbfounded. "This

298

decision," he said, "gives anyone the license to go out and get drunk, then rob, rape or kill with every right to expect to escape punishment."

Of course, not all defendants are treated this magnanimously. For example, five demonstrators who were picked up during one of the protest marches around Mayor Daley's home were convicted on two counts of disorderly conduct—taking part in an unauthorized march and creating a disturbance—and were fined a maximum $400 each. The *American* was intrigued by the court's interpretation of the phrase "creating a disturbance." "If the words meant what they mean in ordinary English, the charge was pretty well shown to be false," the editorial concluded. "The marchers were under strict instructions to make no disturbance, and even the arresting police testified that they had made none. The disturbance was caused by Daley's angry neighbors, who had gathered to jeer at the marchers and were threatening to break thru police lines to get at them. . . . Can a person be convicted for creating a disturbance, when it is plainly someone else who is making the noise? At the least, this case calls for some clarification of language."

8

The frequent courtroom adventures of Sam DeStefano, the mad-hatter of the Syndicate, have been described by the Chicago Crime Commission as "the most disgraceful 'trials' in judicial history"—a rather conservative opinion.

A professional terrorist and a practicing lunatic, DeStefano never fails to make his day in court a memorable occasion. Cited for driving the wrong way on a one-way street, DeStefano refused to pay the $10 fine and insisted on a trial before Municipal Judge Cecil Corbett Smith. When the trial began on May 16, 1963, DeStefano announced that he would serve as his own attorney although his lawyer, Robert J. McDonnell, had accompanied him to court. Also at DeStefano's side was Leo S. Foreman, a swindler and confidence man with more than twenty arrests for passing worthless checks, forgery, confidence game, embezzlement, swindling and perjury. It was later discovered that Foreman was a personal friend of Judge Smith.

Because of DeStefano's status in the Outfit and his popularity in the gossip columns, the trial played to standing room only. Even the Chicago Crime Commission dispatched an investigator to observe the proceedings.

DeStefano began with a series of motions, including one to prohibit the press from taking pictures in the courtroom, and another to exclude all witnesses. Then he charged that a newspaper article contained prejudicial statements and asked for a mistrial.

The first witness was the arresting officer, Detective Lee Gehrke, who recited the facts leading to the traffic citation. He testified that when he and his partner stopped the defendant, DeStefano emerged from the driver's side of the automobile while Willie "Potatoes" Daddano alighted from the right side of the front seat.

"I'll not have the names of any gangsters mentioned during my trial," DeStefano shouted. When Attorney McDonnell leaned over to whisper something to DeStefano, he abruptly turned on him and yelled, "Shut up!"

DeStefano's cross-examination of Detective Gehrke consisted of a barrage of personal questions with no relevancy to the issues in the case. Then, when the court finally sustained an objection to this line of questioning, DeStefano shouted, "I want to know his background. Joe Stalin may have sent him. Birmingham, Alabama, here I come."

Following the noon recess, Judge Smith instructed the defendant to confine himself to the issues and avoid questions on irrelevant matters. "Please don't handcuff me, your honor," DeStefano replied, simultaneously making a motion for a mistrial which was denied. "Are you trying me or persecuting me?" he demanded, successively requesting a mistrial, a jury trial and a continuance, claiming that he was in physical agony and under a doctor's care.

With these motions denied, DeStefano unsuccessfully tried to have Gehrke held in contempt of court. "I see we're still in Birmingham," he shouted at Judge Smith.

Before court convened the next morning, DeStefano took advantage of the capacity audience. Waving a handful of thousand dollar bills, he asked, "Who says it's wrong to have money?" Then "Castro and I are pals. He tried to get me in the juice business." Turning to a young lady in the front row, he offered to set her up in the juice business, suggesting that she "peddle juice in the traffic court" where judges would be her best customers. Ignoring a "No Smoking" sign, he lit a cigarette and puffed away. Upon accidentally overturning a glass of water, he began wiping with a piece of paper, exclaiming, "I have a million dollars and I'm scrubbing your stinking courtroom."

When the prosecutor pointed out that the defendant did not know the rules of evidence and was turning the case into a circus, DeStefano referred to himself as an eminent attorney who had received

300

extensive knowledge of the law at that great institution at Waupum, Wisconsin—the Wisconsin State prison where he served from 1933 to 1944 on a bank robbery conviction. Judge Smith ruled that DeStefano could continue to represent himself.

On DeStefano's motion, the case was continued to May 20, at which time it was continued to May 27. On that date, Judge Smith found him not guilty of the traffic violation, but fined him $200 for contempt of court, a small price to pay to avoid a violation notation on his driver's license. However, DeStefano cursed and ranted for days, obscenely berating Judge Smith and his boss, Judge Augustine Bowe, on the telephone. Even his close friend, Leo S. Foreman, feared for his life. "If you find me in a trunk," Foreman told police, "DeStefano is the man who put me there."

Six months later, Foreman's mutilated body was found in the trunk of his automobile by a garbage truck driver. Besides suffering a severe beating, Foreman had been stabbed eight times and shot in the right forearm and left buttock. Except for one leg of his trousers and an undershirt pulled over his head, the deceased was nude.

Foreman had been engaged in a precarious business. As head of the LeFore Insurance Company, he had used the business as a front for a juice operation specializing in the bankrolling of criminals in need of cash to finance burglaries, robberies and hijackings. In addition to the repayment of the loan, Foreman took a percentage of the score.

A few weeks before his death, Foreman opened a new office in Carpentersville (in Kane County some forty miles from Chicago) which also offered an emergency towing service with bail bond privileges to members. To promote his new agency, Foreman gave a "get acquainted" steak dinner for forty-three guests, including Kane County Circuit Court Judge Neal Mahoney, Chief of Police Robert Puffpaff of East Dundee, Chief of Police Richard Karolus of West Dundee, Chief of Police James Klinkhamer of Carpentersville and Police Magistrate James Scott of Carpentersville, who had been retained as Foreman's Kane County office manager. The master of ceremonies was Judge Cecil Corbett Smith, who told jokes and reminisced about their many years of friendship. The judge had even visited his good friend while he was in Joliet serving time for embezzlement. Foreman described Smith as his "father confessor."

Then on October 22, 1963, while investigating Foreman's murder, police found a diary he had maintained from January 1963 until his death. It contained the names of Sam DeStefano, Anthony Accardo,

Jr., Robert J. McDonnell, and an impressive list of assistant prosecutors, defense attorneys, judges and police captains. And topping the list was Judge Smith.

As the central character in a full-scale scandal, Judge Smith denied having accepted any bribes from either Foreman or DeStefano. He consented to a polygraph test. When asked, "Have you ever taken anything to fix a case?" he replied, "I have been given things afterward." The judge, who had been on the bench since 1932, resigned on January 15, 1964, on a pension equal to one-half his $26,500 annual salary.

In recent years, DeStefano's court appearances have multiplied and his performance (if possible) degenerated. Charged with voting illegally in 1964 (ex-convicts are not entitled to vote unless their civil rights have been restored), Sam arrived in court dressed in a red silk dressing gown over silk pajamas and reclining on a wheeled stretcher. As he rode through the corridors of the Criminal Court Building, he roared profanities through an electronically amplified bullhorn. "We are now living in a Gestapo country," he thundered. "We have lost our civil rights." He denounced justice, the courts, prosecutors, police, reporters and Charles Siragusa, who had initiated the court action: "Snaky Siragusa is a hundred percent imported stool pigeon." He ordered newsmen to refer to him as an "alleged juice racketeer" rather than as a rapist, bank robber, ex-convict, terrorist and murder suspect. Then he rode to the fourth-floor courtroom of Judge Daniel J. Ryan on an elevator reserved for the use of judges and jurors.

When instructed by Ryan to put down his horn, he pointed to the prosecutor and roared in tones almost as loud as the horn: "Who the hell are you?"

Obviously ill at ease, Judge Ryan abruptly continued the case and DeStefano was wheeled out of the building. As he was gently lifted into a waiting ambulance, DeStefano pointed to the fifth-floor windows of the Cook County Jail and again bawled over the horn: "Hello to all the stool pigeons in the witness quarters. You are all stool pigeons paid by the state's attorney's office."

Judge Ryan denied that DeStefano had received "preferential treatment" in court. Asked why he had not held DeStefano in contempt for shouting through the bullhorn, Ryan said: "The important thing was to get DeStefano in and out of the courtroom as fast as possible. He was not permitted to do anything that would merit a contempt citation. When he came into the courtroom using the bullhorn, I ordered him not to use it. I have dealt with Sam De-

Stefano before. If I challenged his use of the stretcher on the ground that his illness was an act, I would have been playing right into his hands. It would give him a chance to bring a doctor into court and put on another act. He'd love to make a judge look foolish. So I was determined to conduct the hearing as swiftly and judiciously as possible."

In his twenty years in United States and European courts, Siragusa, a former federal narcotics agent, explained that he "never saw or heard of a guy addressing a court with a bullhorn. DeStefano's court appearance was another of the surprises that have contributed to my higher education in the Chicago underworld."

"If DeStefano uses his bullhorn anywhere in the court building when he comes back Wednesday," Sheriff Ogilvie warned, "he will be arrested."

DeStefano was back on Wednesday with his bullhorn, bellowing invective in the corridors. Instead of arresting him, sheriff's deputies made Sam more comfortable on his wheeled stretcher, propping up the hoodlum so he could sip coffee. One deputy even assisted him in lighting the cigarette he smoked in a long holder. Nevertheless, Sam cursed Ogilvie as a "numskull" and his deputies as "Gestapo agents." He bawled obscenities at newsmen in the courtroom and predicted the death of one reporter. "I predict he [the reporter] will commit suicide," DeStefano shouted.

When Judge Alexander J. Napoli took the bench, he asked De-Stefano: "What's that you've got in your hand?"

"That's my bullhorn," DeStefano replied.

"I'm going to confiscate it. I'll order a deputy sheriff to impound it."

"Say, this horn is my property."

"Well, make sure you don't bring it back in this building," the judge relented. "You will be in contempt of court if you use it anywhere in this building."

"You don't have that authority," DeStefano challenged.

"Well, you can test it."

"We'll test it, possibly."

"I am directing you not to use that horn in this building at any time."

"I take exception to the court's ruling."

At this point, Judge Napoli cut off further defiance by ordering sheriff's deputies to remove the mobster from the courtroom. But DeStefano had the last word as he was being wheeled out of the courtroom. "They can't stop me with their stinking court orders of contempt," he shouted in a voice that proved beyond doubt that the bullhorn was unnecessary.

DeStefano's most recent courtroom debacle involved three jury trials on a charge of conspiracy to commit perjury. The charge originated in a case involving Frank Santucci, a burglar and robber whose record for "beating raps" even surpasses that of Pops Panczko.

It began on the night of October 5, 1962, when Santucci and two companions stole $1,500 at gunpoint from Ben's Place, a tavern operated by Ben and Norma McCluskie and Patrick and Henrietta Burns. As the robbers were leaving, Norma McCluskie grabbed a revolver from behind the bar and fired six shots, wounding Santucci in the left shoulder. All four owners identified the three robbers when they were apprehended by the police. But in typical Chicago style, the witnesses failed to identify the robbers in court, and Judge Irving Landesman directed verdicts of not guilty for each defendant.

But a clue to Santucci's phenomenal success in court came to light a few months later when Henrietta Burns, brought before a grand jury on perjury charges, told the panel that all four owners had been bribed by Sam DeStefano. "Sam told us he had been contacted by Santucci," Mrs. Burns testified, "and Santucci had offered to give us $1,000 of our money back if we would not positively identify any of the men involved in the robbery. . . . Sam told us that Santucci was a desperate man and that he didn't want to go to prison." But, they insisted, DeStefano had no personal interest in the case. He was merely being a good samaritan. He just did not want to see them harmed by Santucci.

Their bartender, Charles Gramaldi, had arranged the meeting in the tavern between the owners and DeStefano. When informed that they had already identified the robbers, DeStefano advised that it would be all right to say that they looked like the men but to refrain from a positive identification. DeStefano later summoned the owners to his home, where an unidentified third party gave them a thousand dollars.

On October 21, 1964, a few weeks after DeStefano was indicted on the conspiracy to commit perjury charge, Ben's Place mysteriously burned to the ground, killing the McCluskies' five-year-old son and a twenty-seven-year-old bartender who tried to save the boy.

"It must have been an act of God," said Mrs. McCluskie. "They say that hoodlums are lower than animals, but I don't think anybody could be that rotten. He [DeStefano] was always a friend to us."

"You never heard of even the meanest of them [hoodlums] ever hurting kids yet," said her husband, trying desperately to reassure himself. "I don't know anything about these hoodlums. All I know is that I woke up in a nightmare." The McCluskies and their four children lived in an apartment over the tavern.

A witness told the police that he saw the arsonist from his bathroom window, which viewed the alley behind the tavern. He noticed a car with three men drive slowly down the alley. The car stopped and one man got out. For a moment, the witness lost track of the man in the darkness, but spotted him again as he tossed an object to the second floor porch. Sparks, as if from a "lighted fuse," came from the object. Seconds later the porch burst into flames as the shadowy figure fled.

Police cast doubt on the witness' story, identifying him as a former mental patient. An arson expert predicted it would be difficult to prove a fire-bomb was used to start the blaze—and, of course, he was absolutely right.

Although the McCluskies had received threatening phone calls from DeStefano warning them not to testify at his pending perjury trial, the police had assigned only one officer to guard the family, and he was stationed in front of the tavern. The fire came as a complete surprise to him.

DeStefano resented being mentioned in the newspapers in connection with the fire. "Why do they link me with everything?" he protested. "I'm no mobster. They're just destroying my family."

On January 12, 1965, DeStefano was convicted in a jury trial before Judge George N. Leighton. Defended by Julius Lucius Echeles, DeStefano had discarded the histrionics for a bored, yawning attitude which he maintained throughout the proceedings. Even the conviction did not alter his complacence. A few days later, Judge Leighton ruled that certain remarks made by himself and the prosecutors were prejudicial to the defendant, and granted a new trial.

(Following his election to the bench in 1964, Leighton, a former attorney for Sam Giancana, created a nationwide controversy when he freed two defendants charged with resisting arrest and assaulting one officer with a broken beer bottle—requiring twenty-eight stitches on the policeman's face. "I found nothing in the law that says carrying a broken bottle is against the law," Leighton reasoned in defending his ruling. For all his Honor knew, the defendants might have been intending to deposit the bottle in a trash bin. Leighton refused to admit the testimony—ruling it as hearsay—of the two policemen that they approached the defendants only after being warned by a citizen that "a crazy guy is walking down the street with a broken beer bottle threatening people." In approaching the defendants in an alley, the police officers identified themselves and called, "Drop that bottle." One of the defendants responded, "Come and get it, you fucking cops." The policemen drew their guns and one of them attempted to strike the defendant who was holding the bottle. According to Leighton's summation, "As he [the officer] did so, the defendant lifted up his right hand in which he held the broken bottle and as a consequence the bottle struck [the officer] in the face." In the judge's opinion, the police had used excessive force and so the defendants were "justified in resisting them." "This decision," said Senator John L. McClellan, "and the reasons assigned therefore . . . are reprehensible beyond description and contemptible under any civilized standards of justice and human conduct." J. Edgar Hoover found Leighton's reasoning and judgment "disturbing." "In this particular instance," Hoover said, "the judge placed the law enforcement officer in an untenable position. If the officer had refused to respond when faced by an apparent law breaker, he would have been neglecting his duty. He responded, risking his life and incurring serious personal injuries, and was told he acted improperly and deserved what he got.")

DeStefano's second trial in February ended in a hung jury—the jurors stood eight to four for conviction. Sam merely blinked sleepily.

(Meanwhile at least one columnist was keeping her readers informed: "The word is that Sam DeStefano's prognosis at the Mayo clinic was—'seriously ill.'" And, "Word is he is sicker than anyone realizes." And, "Some police officials have confided to us that Sam used to be very, very brainy and could have been a top executive in any industry or business—if he had only gone that route.")

Brainy Sam struck out the third time up. On September 10, 1965, a jury brought in a verdict of guilty, and in keeping with his new courtroom personality, Sam smiled and yawned as Judge Nathan M. Cohen sentenced him to three to five years in prison. That evening he reverted to type as he dashed for a telephone to conduct his own personal poll of the jurors. They interpreted Sam's loud inquisition as threatening and reported it to Judge Cohen, who then refused to set an appeal bond, which meant that Sam was forthwith escorted to Joliet to begin serving his sentence.

DeStefano was in the prison's diagnostic center just long enough for a shave and a Joliet-style crewcut. In fact, it took lawyer Echeles just six days to find a jurist on the Illinois Supreme Court who was cooperative enough to free Sam on a $10,000 appeal bond. "It was the discretion of the court to set bond," Justice Harry Hershey said after granting the motion, refusing any further comment on his ruling.

9

As a top defense attorney for Syndicate hoodlums, there is little Echeles will not do to keep his clients from prison. Once in pleading for leniency for a client, Echeles told the judge, "I've been in prison and I know what it's like." And it was true. Back in 1954, he was sentenced to twenty-eight months in the federal penitentiary at Terre Haute, Indiana, for selling jobs and promotions in the Chicago Post Office. The sentence later was reduced to twenty-two months by the U.S. Court of Appeals. Despite the stretch in prison, Echeles continued with his law practice. He was not disbarred because he voluntarily withdrew from practice. When he got out of prison, the Illinois Supreme Court graciously readmitted him.

At this writing, Echeles is free on bond awaiting appeal on another federal conviction, this time for procuring perjured testimony in a narcotics trial. Flamboyant in dress and speech, the fifty-year-old Echeles has skillfully defended such Mob savages as Frank "Hot Dogs" Lisciandrello, Gus Liebe, Jimmy "The Monk" Allegretti and Sam DeStefano.

In the narcotics case, Echeles tried a little too hard to establish an alibi for his narcotics-peddler client. He represented that at the time the offense was committed, his client, Broadway Arrington, was registered in a motel in Hot Springs, Arkansas. To support this alibi, Echeles introduced two witnesses, Patrick Carr, owner of the motel, and Mrs. Lucille Smith, a former motel clerk, who submitted motel registration cards which purported to establish Arrington's presence in the motel on the date in question. There was just one hitch. The government proved that the motel registration cards had not been printed until after the date which appeared on them. Once exposed, the witnesses recanted their testimony and admitted their guilt in the forgery plot.

Subsequently indicted by a federal grand jury for subornation of perjury, obstruction of justice and conspiracy to suborn perjury, the resourceful Mob mouthpiece armed himself with a dazzling lineup of character witnesses.

Testifying to his "good reputation for truth and veracity" were

307

Chief Justice Wallace C. Schaefer and Associate Justice Ray I. Klingbiel of the Illinois Supreme Court; United States District Judge Michael L. Igoe; Appellate Judge Joseph Drucker; Circuit Court Judges Daniel A. Covelli, F. Emmett Morrissey and Alexander J. Napoli; attorneys Barnabas Sears and George N. Leighton, who was then a member of the board of managers of the Chicago Bar Association. "There were those of us who had faith in Mr. Echeles' rehabilitation," Leighton testified. "The case for his rehabilitation was impressive and persuasive."

Although defended by attorney Frank Oliver, Echeles delivered his own final summation. In a dramatic and impassioned forty-five minute plea, Echeles sadly informed the jurors that a conviction would mean the end of his professional life, "the only thing worth anything to me."

The eloquence and heady list of character witnesses were not enough to save him. Ironically, the prosecution caught a key defense witness in some embarrassing contradictions in his testimony. On May 6, 1964, the jury found him guilty on four counts and U.S. District Judge Edwin A. Robson sentenced him to serve five years on each count, the sentences to run concurrently.

An expert at obtaining continuances, jaunty Julius continues to entrance juries as he prances about in his tight continental suits, spilling rhetoric in his high-pitched voice which is so appealing to juries.

The courtroom antics of Mob mouthpieces are more often staged than spontaneous. Witnesses experience lapses in memory, policemen make reversible slip-of-the-tongue errors, prosecutors ignore valuable evidence, judges rule improperly, and jurors are bribed, intimidated or just plain hate to commit their childhood heroes to prison. Echeles once won acquittal for a client by challenging the sex of the marijuana involved in the case. The bewildered prosecutor admitted he did not know whether the marijuana was male or female. This, as incredible as it may seem, created enough doubt in the jurors' minds to free the defendant.

Judge Samuel Leibowitz, a noted New York jurist, observed in his testimony before the Kefauver committee that "there are criminal lawyers and lawyer criminals." It was one thing, Judge Leibowitz believed, for a criminal lawyer to defend his client honestly and squarely and to see that he got his day in court according to our laws and our Constitution, but it was "another thing to be in the hire of some gang to advise the gang how to operate, and to be at the beck and call of the gangster or act as his right-hand man."

Eugene Bernstein, who received his training as a federal attorney with the Bureau of Internal Revenue, has been the Outfit's income tax expert for more than thirty years. At one time or another, he has prepared income tax returns for just about every hoodlum in the higher income brackets. Acting coy before the Kefauver committee, Bernstein engaged chief counsel Rudolph Halley in semantic nonsense:

> BERNSTEIN: The word "gangster" has a different connotation to me than it may have to other people. A gangster is an individual who goes out and, by means of force, duress, obtains sums of money. If you and I go out and do certain things legally, and place funds in his possession without duress, at our own direction, and then he does something with that, that would not be gangsters. Gangsterism is very definitely a form of violence.
> HALLEY: A gangster is a man who belongs to a gang, isn't he?
> BERNSTEIN: Then you and I are gangsters . . .
> HALLEY: What gang do I belong to?
> BERNSTEIN: We belong to the human race. We belong to a political party. That may be a gang.

In an age of specialization, the Syndicate also wants its lawyers to specialize. The Syndicate retains income tax lawyers, real estate lawyers, union lawyers, corporation lawyers, criminal lawyers for state cases, lawyers for federal raps and lawyers who excel in appellate work.

Some of the top talent in the federal bullpen include Anna R. Lavin (Accardo's appeal attorney and a close friend of Judge Nathan M. Cohen), Edward J. Calihan, George F. Callaghan, Maurice Walsh and Richard E. Gorman—all former prosecutors in the United States attorney's office.

Gorman, however, had even more going for him when he switched his allegiance to the bad guys. Years ago he was chief of the polygraph section of the Chicago Police Department, and had been a member of the old Scotland Yard unit, formed to fight organized crime in pre-Wilson days. In fact, Gorman was so well-equipped for his new vocation that even Giancana and Prio sought his services.

309

Like all successful Syndicate lawyers, Gorman was particularly brilliant in the field of loopholes. In one case, for example, he argued that his client, Eugene C. James, could not be guilty of income tax evasion since the $900,000 item in question had been embezzled from the Laundry Workers Union and thus was not taxable as income. The U.S. Supreme Court concurred and Congress moved swiftly to plug the loophole. Jubilant over his victory, Gorman submitted his $15,000 fee not to James but to the union.

But in 1962 Gorman had to hire an attorney of his own when he was indicted by a federal grand jury on charges of bribing a juror in a whisky hijacking case. The facts in the case go back to December 1957 when a truckload of whisky valued at $44,000 was hijacked as it was moving interstate from Louisville to Chicago. Four months later, FBI agents traced thirty-four cases of the stolen booze to three syndicate joints—Cafe Continental, Silver Domes, Flame—operated by Gerald Covelli in partnership with other syndicate hoodlums. Once a business associate of Paul "Needlenose" Labriola and James Weinberg, Covelli's police record included four convictions for auto theft, burglary, robbery and strongarm robbery.

Brought to trial before Federal Judge Joseph Sam Perry for possession of stolen whisky, Covelli was defended by attorney Gorman. The jury deadlocked at eleven to one for conviction.

Six months later, FBI agents arrested Robert Saporito, the hold-out juror in the Covelli case, and his brother Michael Saporito, a Chicago policeman, on charges of tampering with a federal jury. Robert Saporito, a free-lance artist, copped out the moment an FBI agent pointed a finger and accused: "You got $500 for holding out for an acquittal, didn't you?" In his confession, Robert Saporito implicated his brother by quoting him as saying: "The boys have approached me on this. If you vote not guilty and prevent a guilty verdict, there is $500 in it for you and a job with the [police] Narcotics detail for me." But Robert had collected only half of the $500 bribe from his brother.

When the brothers were arraigned before U.S. Commissioner C. S. Bentley Pike, bond was set at $15,000 for Michael and $10,000 for Robert. However, a few hours later, Federal Judge Michael L. Igoe reduced Michael's bond to $10,000 and Robert's to $5,000. They were represented at the hearing by attorney Joseph Green, who had been dispatched by Bieber and Brodkin. Another link to the Syndicate was revealed that evening when bondsman Pat Cerone, a cousin of "Jackie The Lackey" Cerone, posted bail for the brothers. To no one's astonishment, Michael Saporito, the only link between the hoodlums and his brother, was soon among the missing. Police theorized that he was executed and his body permanently disposed of by his assassins—perhaps under one of Mayor Daley's new expressways.

Meanwhile, Gerald Covelli was in federal custody in Houston, Texas, as the central figure in an international stolen car ring which had disposed of $165,000 worth of automobiles stolen in Chicago to customers in Guatemala and Mexico. Indicted with Covelli was his top lieutenant, Max Olshon, who had been brought to Chicago several months earlier to identify two lawyers, Seymour Kurtz and Harold Turner, as members of the ring.

It was Olshon, a former bartender, who first leaked the bribery plot to FBI agents. Faced with the ominous prospect of long federal prison terms for crimes in Houston and Chicago, Covelli also decided to switch sides and turn government informer.

A year later, federal indictments were returned against Gorman, Joseph "Little Caesar" DiVarco and Charles "Chuckie" Hudson on charges of conspiring to bribe a juror. It took another two years to get the defendants before Federal Judge Hubert L. Will (a former law partner of Mayor Daley) and a jury.

(Robert Saporito, meanwhile, entered a plea of no defense before Federal Judge Joseph Sam Perry, receiving a suspended sentence of two years and probation.)

As the prosecution's star witness, the tall, sad-faced Covelli calmly unfolded a tale of intrigue as familiar to Chicagoans as pollution in Lake Michigan. Here, wrapped in a single thread, was the whole sinister ball of yarn: police, judiciary, politics, business, crime—The System.

Covelli testified that at the end of the first day in his 1959 trial, Attorney Gorman gave him a list of the twelve jurors, with the name of Saporito marked by a cross. "Gorman told me to give the list to Mr. DiVarco and to be careful." The witness said he went directly to the Sterile Glass Company at 405 North State Street and found Joseph DiVarco and Charles Hudson:

Q. (*by Assistant U.S. Attorney William O. Bittman*).
What happened then?
A. Mr. Chuckie Hudson walked with me to a back room. Mr. DiVarco came in and asked: "Where's the list?" He pointed to a name and said: "That's our boy."
Q. And then?

311

A. Mr. DiVarco instructed Chuckie to get in touch with Mr. [Alderman Mathias "Paddy"] Bauler's office. Mr. DiVarco said we must reach the sponsor of the policeman [Michael Saporito]. The call [to Bauler's office] was made. I don't know what was said. Mr. DiVarco then asked Mr. Hudson if he knew the captain's man [bagman] at the Cragin Station and Chuckie said he did not. (*Michael Saporito was assigned to the Cragin Station on the city's West Side.*)

Q. Was anything else said?

A. Mr. DiVarco told Mr. Hudson to get in touch with Mr. [Jimmy "The Monk"] Allegretti, that we had to get in touch with his [the policeman's] sponsor. (*Allegretti could not be reached, and DiVarco went out and came back with oatmeal cookies and coffee.*) When DiVarco came back he said that it was very possible that, [Policeman Saporito] being from the West Side, Jackie Cerone had sponsored him. (*Covelli and Hudson then drove to Cerone's home in Elmwood Park.*) Hudson went into the house for fifteen minutes. He came out and told me that I had nothing to worry about; that everything would turn out in my favor. (*Their next stop was at the home of Policeman Saporito, and again Covelli waited in the car.*)

Q. Did Hudson say anything to you in the car?

A. He told me at no time to repeat what was being done for me, not even to tell my mother.

Q. Was anything else said?

A. He told me I had nothing to worry about, just to relax. . . . (*On January 18, when the whisky trial was recessed for the weekend, Covelli said he talked to Gorman in a bedroom of the attorney's home.*) Gorman said he had talked to DiVarco, and I had nothing to worry about; that the outcome would be in my favor. (*In the bedroom that Sunday afternoon, they rehearsed perjury for an hour.*) My attorney instructed me to lie. We rehearsed it. . . . (*On January 19, the day the jury was deadlocked by Robert Saporito, Covelli said he reported to DiVarco that the jurors "looked odd."*) I said: "I don't think we can trust that person [Saporito]." DiVarco said: "He [Saporito] is a good talker. The only way you can change that man's testimony is by cutting off his head." Later that day, Gorman told me, "You've got nothing to worry about. The worst you can get is a hung jury."

The next day, after the jury deadlock ended the trial, Covelli and Olshon returned to DiVarco's headquarters. "Gerry walked in with a big smile on his face," Olshon told the court. "Caesar embraced him and said: 'When I tell you something, you can rely on me. These things cost a lot of money but we don't care.' " Covelli's ex-wife, Jeannie, testified with apparent reluctance as a "court's witness." She recalled having seen a list of names, scrawled on yellow paper, her husband brought home during his 1959 trial. But she could not "honestly recall" any "marks" on the list next to Saporito's name. She disputed Covelli's statement that DiVarco was his associate. Her husband saw DiVarco only "rarely," she said. "I'll tell you why," she added. "Mr. DiVarco is more of a business man. My husband was— how can I put it?—he wasn't substantial; he was jumping here and there."

(At a private hearing in Judge Will's chambers three weeks earlier, Mrs. Covelli disclosed that DiVarco had threatened her and the children with death. On DiVarco's orders, she had gone to the office of attorney Anna Lavin to sign a prepared affidavit which she signed without reading. She later denied the death threat or the existence of the affidavit.)

The defense based its strategy on the testimony of two character witnesses: Federal Judges Michael L. Igoe and Joseph Sam Perry. Igoe testified that Gorman's reputation for honesty, integrity and veracity was "excellent."

Judge Perry, in whose court the jury fixing took place, was equally generous: "I want you to know," he said, looking at Gorman, "I did not order this investigation because I believed you were guilty. I did not believe it then, and I do not believe it now." Perry said he had known Gorman for many years, both as a former federal prosecutor and as a highly successful defense attorney, appearing many times in his court.

> Q (by defense attorney). Do you know his reputation
> for truth and veracity in that field?
> A. It is the very best—excellent.
> Q. Would you believe him under oath?
> A. I would, I would.

The jury took forty-five minutes to acquit all three defendants. If convicted, they each would have been eligible for prison terms of twenty-two years and $32,000 fines. Although the jurors admitted they were much impressed by Judge Perry's testimony, they insisted the "testimony was strong for the defense from the start."

Covelli, who was sentenced to three years for his part in the bribery conspiracy, summed up his feelings on the Syndicate: "I got tired of carrying someone else's load. I covered completely for those guys. But they threw me down the river." Covelli had languished in a Texas jail eight months because they would not post a $25,000 bond. "During all that time I kept my mouth shut even when I was put in isolation. Instead of helping me, they protected themselves. They got rid of the policeman [Saporito]. I finally figured out that the others were looking out only for themselves. That's when I opened up. I put $25,000 of my own money in Cafe Continental, and then the Outfit muscled me out. They gave me credit. And when I got jammed up and took that fall in Houston with the stolen cars, they told me that they were my partners and my share was 25 percent. I never got a dime out of it." His self-proclaimed partners were Allegretti, DiVarco and Jackie Cerone.

Was he worried about what would happen next? "Certainly. I'm concerned about the possibility of getting hit. I'm going to have to disappear. I'll have to think of where to run before I get out. They got to me in Leavenworth." A Syndicate lawyer had dispatched one of Covelli's relatives to Leavenworth to deliver a message: "Tell Gerry he has signed his death warrant."*

In Covelli's world, fixes were daily occurrences. In one case, "a buddy of mine was on trial and the fix was in with the assistant state's attorney. But the defense lawyer was so drunk he was blowing the case. The prosecutor had to keep making mistake after mistake to make sure there'd be a not guilty verdict and he could collect his money." (On September 27, 1966, Attorney Gorman was convicted on five counts of income tax violations—failing to file income tax returns for 1959 through 1963—and sentenced to two years in federal prison.)

10

On April 16, 1965, his eightieth birthday, Judge Michael L. Igoe, after twenty-seven years on the federal bench, announced that he would fade gradually into semiretirement.

In his tenure as a federal judge, Igoe, who is more commonly known in legal circles as "Ego" and "Iago," has epitomized all that is "desirable" in a machine politician disguised in ermine. Shortly after leaving the U.S. Attorney's office in 1938 for a seat on the federal

* Covelli managed to delay the "death warrant" five years. The end came in Encino, California, on June 18, 1967, when a time bomb—planted under the driver's seat of his car—exploded, killing him instantly.

bench, two of his former prosecutors were indicted and placed on trial for fixing cases. Igoe descended from the bench to testify that he had instituted daily conferences with his staff and knew all that was transpiring. In spite of this reassuring testimony from their former chief, the defendants were convicted and sentenced to prison.

In his interminable career, Igoe has made frequent court appearances in the defense of Party cronies. Although highly successful in local judicial arenas, his road record is questionable. For example, Igoe ventured to Cincinnati in 1927 to sell George Remus (on trial for murdering his wife) as a "man of peace and quiet, with a reputation for truth and veracity as a man and lawyer." Remus, a disbarred lawyer who served time in the Atlanta penitentiary for prohibition violations, had amassed a fortune estimated in the press at between $7 million and $10 million.

Igoe told the court that he was a South Park Commissioner in Chicago, a former assistant United States attorney, for years a member of the Illinois legislature, and for six years Democratic leader of the house. Before the prosecutor finished with his cross-examination, Igoe admitted that Remus had contributed $9,000 to his (Igoe's) campaign fund for state's attorney in 1920, and had given him numerous expensive gifts along the way. The jury found Remus insane.

Frank Richardson, prohibition director in Illinois during the early Twenties, was threatened with arrest by special Internal Revenue agent Joseph A. Tatro for attempting to release four bootleggers arrested by Tatro as members of a nationwide ring. Richardson said he acted on request from Michael Igoe, a "good friend." Tatro told him he was "crazy," which put him in a class with Remus.

In 1915 Igoe was vice-president of a million-dollar insurance "trust" which had no assets except some office furniture, and which sold $100,000 worth of stock before going into bankruptcy. One of its top salesmen was S. E. Smith, an ex-convict who made the mistake of going into Wisconsin—where they punish criminals—to sell stock. He was extradited from Chicago and lodged in a Wisconsin jail. The firm, known as the National Operating Company, promptly went into receivership. No one, however, visited Smith in Wisconsin.

Igoe, who early in his career was an honorary pallbearer at the funeral of Big Jim Colosimo, was also attorney for Dennis Cooney, chief whoremaster under Capone.

For a brief period in the late Twenties and early Thirties, Igoe became a light heavyweight contender on the political machine scale. When George Brennan died in 1928, it was his deathbed wish that

Igoe be elected national committeeman—which to some Irish Democrats made Igoe the heir apparent. But Brennan was dead and Anton Cermak had plans of his own. By 1930 even the Irish faction had hitched their political wagons to Cermak's coattails. As the Democratic candidate for state's attorney, Igoe had been defeated twice, in 1920 and 1924, which cast him in the role of a loser in popularity contests that involved more than his West Side Irish domain. He was later to lose in primary elections in which he sought nominations for governor in 1932 and for United States senator in 1938. In quick order, Igoe became a political hack who survived only as a patronage appointee in jobs where he could do the Party the most good: U.S. Attorney and federal judge.

But even in semiretirement, Igoe continues to add laurels to his "distinguished record as a judge," as illustrated by his dismissal of the seventeen-count indictment against labor racketeer Joey Glimco in 1965.

Whether federal, state, county or municipal, every judgeship is a political party selection. The idea that federal justice is impartial is nothing more than a popular myth, a myth that is soon exploded when one realizes that federal judges in Chicago are Chicagoans just as federal judges in Mississippi are Mississippians. In a practical sense, the sovereignty of the state is equated to the sovereignty of the political machine in power.

Nobody gets to be a judge in Chicago unless somebody with clout puts him there. Candidates are passed upon by Daley, Keane, Simon, Bieszczat, Danaher, Marzullo and other party potentates. Qualifications are assessed strictly along Party lines: service, loyalty, indebtedness, gratitude, connections, sponsorship, financial contribution, vote-pulling potential, overall clout and nationality. Legal ability is an accidental bonus.

Through the years, Syndicate lawyers have held the inside track not only in nominating candidates but in achieving the ultimate station for themselves. One of the most recent appointees to the federal bench was Abraham Lincoln Marovitz, former attorney for Willie Bioff. Marovitz, whose popularity in the gossip columns rivals that of Sam Giancana, is a showbiz-oriented swinger and a Party favorite with clout tentacles reaching back to his West Side days with Jake Arvey and Artie Elrod.

Igoe's resignation sent the political in-fighters into a frenzy. New

316

candidates appeared daily in the press, complete with detailed analyses of the political waves forming in the wake of each appointment. Two highly touted candidates—circuit court judges who qualified in all departments including nationality—were also candidates on the secret federal report. The appointment, however, went to William J. Lynch, former law partner of Mayor Daley and the general counsel for the Chicago Transit Authority and Chicago Thoroughbred Enterprises, Inc., which owns Arlington Park and Washington Park racetracks. When another opening was created in 1966, Mayor Daley's choice after another long behind-the-scenes struggle was Alexander J. Napoli, reportedly a leader of the Italian community, and a judge whose sixteen-year record of leniency toward Syndicate hoodlums speaks for itself.

In theory, federal judges are nominated by the President with the approval of the Senate. But almost without exception the appointment is based on the personal wishes of the senator from the state involved, and the senator in turn goes along with the wishes of the local party chieftain.

Incumbent judges were virtually assured lifetime tenure when the Illinois court system was "modernized" in 1964. The purported intention of the legislature was to make judges as free as possible from political affiliations and pressures. Once a judge has been elected on a partisan basis, his name is periodically placed on a "retention" ballot. Instead of running against a political opponent, he now "runs against his record." All he needs to survive is a majority of "yes" as opposed to "no" votes.

The *raison d'être* behind the judicial act to separate candidates from party labels, and *ipso facto* from political pressures and influence, presupposes that judges, unlike other patronage favorites, could survive in a political and social vacuum. It overlooks the fact that the judiciary is merely an extension of the political robot, and that security is seldom a substitute for ambition, "friendships" and greed.

"Associate Judge Louis W. Kizas of Cicero seems to be one of those embarrassing types who just don't know when to stop, and who are always spoiling a neat little arrangement by going too far and attracting attention," said the *American* on May 13, 1967. "Kizas has apparently landed all kinds of people in hot water by an incredible abuse of his judicial powers."

Kizas' *faux pas* came about as "a matter of courtesy" to a lawyer friend when he freed without bond—on their own recognizance—two men charged with robbing a Catholic church—they escaped with

317

$1,760 after shooting at one nun and tying up two others, two priests, and an altar boy.

When the storm of public indignation broke, the System shifted into high gear. John S. Boyle, chief judge of the circuit court, asked Kizas to resign. "I won't resign," Kizas replied. "There are other judges that have done things that should be scrutinized. What am I, a devil? . . . This church that was held up didn't happen to be a tavern. If it had been a tavern, this wouldn't have happened. . . . I just did it as a favor. I don't think it's so unusual. A judge is required to make bonds. When I'm called upon to make them, I go out and make them."

And he certainly did: over a thousand in a seventeen-month period. To facilitate the procedure, Kizas allegedly distributed pre-signed pads of bonding slips to attorney friends so they could free defendants without his having to make a personal appearance at the jail.

In no time at all, a half-dozen investigations were on the way. The state's attorney's office began looking for "irregularities" in the bail bond cases. The Chicago Bar Association was anxiously awaiting the names of the 10 to 15 lawyers who most frequently obtained bonds from Kizas. The Chicago police were checking into the possible collusion of lockup-keepers and other policemen in notifying Kizas' attorney friends when prisoners had no attorneys of their own. Judge Boyle suspended Kizas and impounded his bond records, promising to forward them to the state's Supreme Court, which he hoped would convene a judicial commission to hear charges against Kizas. The Internal Revenue Service was ready to audit the income of all persons involved in the probe. They were particularly interested in attorneys who had obtained bond money from defendants Kizas had released on their own recognizance.

"I'm no hood," Kizas pleaded. "It was an honest mistake. The hatchet fellows are out to get me." One of Kizas' more celebrated bond beneficiaries was Peanuts Panczko.

A former Cicero town judge before he was absorbed into the new state-operated judicial system in 1964, Kizas managed his busy bonding service while sitting in small claims court, where court observers described him as "friendly and inclined to talk about his real estate investments in the western suburbs and in Florida."

Meanwhile, the bonded church robbers did not cooperate. They defaulted on their bonds and police charged they had engaged in two subsequent robberies.

318

"The important thing," said the *American,* "is to investigate this whole situation right down to the ground and find answers to all the questions that Kizas unintentionally brought up: Are other judges providing their friends with the same service, as Kizas has broadly hinted? If so, who are they, who are their friends, and what must be done to break up this buddy system once and for all?" (Judge Kizas was awaiting a hearing before a Supreme Court commission at this writing.)

The Bar Association is also welded to the Machine. Hundreds of its members staff the offices of the state's attorney, U.S. attorney, corporation counsel and Illinois attorney general. Hundreds more are on political payrolls or receive major portions of their income from political fees or appointments. Association officers head powerful law firms that have prospered through city patronage and court-awarded receiverships. Monotonous Democratic victories in judicial elections have convinced distinguished attorneys (outside the political orbit of the Machine) that judgeships are rewards for work in the precincts rather than for distinction within the profession itself. Occasionally there are exceptions—exceptions which make the rule more palatable to would-be reformers and low-keyed critics.

Few reformers are stalwart enough to attack a corrupt judge for fear that the effort may prove unsuccessful. As Emerson once said to Justice Oliver Wendell Holmes, "If you shoot at a king, you must kill him." Even President Johnson's own crime commission, convened in 1965 with the mandate to conduct the most extensive study of U.S. crime ever attempted, failed to be specific in any area of corruption. For example, a 63-page special report on the links between Chicago hoodlums and public officials, prepared by Notre Dame Professor G. Robert Blakey, was reduced to four innocuous footnotes in the commission's final report. Among the censored items was Blakey's thesis that "The success of the Chicago group [Mob] has been primarily attributable to its ability to corrupt the law enforcement processes, including police officials and members of the judiciary. . . ."

11

The police and courts are the grease that keep the wheels of the Machine in motion. Without this lubricant, the elaborate machinery would soon come to a screeching stop. Nobody appreciates this fact more than the gangster. So long as the wheels keep turning, his position will be secure and his power and wealth will continue to multiply, regardless of newspaper crusades, crime commissions, elections, stronger laws or books such as this one.

This is not only Chicago's problem, but, in various degrees, America's. The question is what are we going to do about it.

APPENDIX
THE ANTISOCIAL REGISTER

The following biographical sketches are based on material from the files of several federal bureaus and agencies, and the Chicago and Los Angeles police departments. Other sources include the McClellan and Kefauver hearings, the Chicago Crime Commission and Chicago's four daily newspapers: *American, Daily News, Sun-Times* and *Tribune*.

ABBREVIATIONS AND EXPLANATIONS

AKA: Also Known As; aliases and cognomens
CIR: Chicago Identification Record
CLPD: Cleveland Police Department
CPD: Chicago Police Department
EDU: Education; total years of schooling
FBI: Federal Bureau of Investigation
FH: Family history only as it relates to intermarriages and relationships within the orbit of the Syndicate
FIFTH: Subject invoked the Fifth Amendment, a constitutional privilege against self-incrimination
FPC: Fingerprinting code classification
HC: House of Correction
ISPJ: Illinois State Penitentiary, Joliet
ISPM: Illinois State Penitentiary, Menard

321

ISPMC:	Indiana State Penitentiary, Michigan City
ISPP:	Illinois State Penitentiary, Pontiac
ISRP:	Illinois State Reformatory, Pontiac
LAPD:	Los Angeles Police Department
MS:	Military Service
OSRM:	Ohio State Reformatory, Mansfield
RO:	Racial Origin
SPPI:	State Penitentiary, Pendleton, Indiana
USPA:	United States Penitentiary, Atlanta, Georgia
USPL:	United States Penitentiary, Leavenworth, Kansas
USPM:	United States Penitentiary, Milan, Michigan
USPS:	United States Penitentiary, Springfield, Missouri
USPTH:	United States Penitentiary, Terre Haute, Indiana
WSPW:	Wisconsin State Penitentiary, Waupun

Accardo, Anthony Joseph

AKA: (nee Antonio Leonardo Accardo) Tony Accardo, Arcado, Joe Batters, Big Tuna, Joe Batty.

DESCRIPTION: Born April 28, 1906, Chicago; 5 feet 9½ inches, 190 pounds, brown eyes, black hair, dark complexion, tattoo of "Dove" base of right thumb outer, several irregular scars back of left hand; Edu: 6th grade; MS: rejected; RO: Sicilian; FH: son, Anthony Ross; brother, Martin Leonardo; sisters, Martha (Mrs. Dominick Senese), Maria (Mrs. Tarquin Simonelli).

FREQUENTS: Singapore Steak & Chop House, Armory Lounge, Mike Fish's and Fritzel's restaurants, and other favorite hoodlum hangouts in Loop, Near North Side and western suburbs. Resides at 1407 Ashland Ave., River Forest.

RECORD: FBI No. 1410106. CPD No. D-83436. FPC No. 31-W-MO/4-W-OI. Record dates back to 1922, more than 27 arrests: carrying concealed weapons, gambling, extortion, kidnaping, murder. Convicted of income tax evasion, sentenced to 6 years in prison, fined $15,000—reversed on appeal, acquitted in second trial. Prime suspect in several murders. Cited as one of 28 Public Enemies by Chicago Crime Commission in 1931, where he was listed as a suspect in the murders of Joe Aiello, Jack Zuta and "Mike de Pike" Heitler, and a suspected gunman in the St. Valentine's Day Massacre. Never spent a night in jail. Cited for contempt of Congress in Kefauver hearings; took Fifth 144 times before McClellan Committee.

BUSINESS: In everything from baking to trucking, from coal and

322

lumber to hotels and restaurants, and from currency exchanges to travel agencies. Has substantial investments in Florida, Arizona, Nevada, California and South America.

MODUS OPERANDI: Former bodyguard of Al Capone, he came to power following suicide of Frank Nitti in 1943. Ruled Syndicate until 1956, when Giancana became chief enforcer. Presently chairman of the Syndicate's board of directors, and one of the top mafiosi in the nation.

Aiuppa, Joseph John

AKA: Joey O'Brien, Tom O'Brien, J. Buonoma, James Spano.

DESCRIPTION: Born December 1, 1907, Chicago; 5 feet 6½ inches, 200 pounds, brown eyes, brown-gray hair, dark complexion, scar on right wrist, lobe of right ear missing; Edu: 3d grade; MS: 4-F; RO: Sicilian; FH: brother, Sam, works as a front in legitimate businesses under various aliases.

FREQUENTS: Towne Hotel at 4827 Cermak Road (formerly the Hawthorne Inn, it was Capone's Cicero stronghold back in the mid-1920s), the Turf Club and numerous Cicero nightspots which he owns through fronts. Resides at 4 Yorkshire Drive, Elmhurst.

RECORD: FBI No. 951184. USPTH No. 15404. Record dates back to 1935, more than 10 arrests: assault with intent to kill, gambling, bribery, questioned in several murder investigations. Convicted of contempt of Congress in 1951 (Kefauver hearings), later reversed. Convictions: failing and refusing to register as a dealer in gambling devices, 1 year and 1 day in USPTH, $1,000 fine and costs; illegally possessing and transporting 563 mourning doves from Kansas to Chicago, 3 months in federal prison and $1,000 fine. Took Fifth 56 times before McClellan Committee.

BUSINESS: Scores of taverns and strip-joints in Cicero and neighboring communities; also in advertising, real estate and taxicabs.

MODUS OPERANDI: Began as muscleman in old Capone organization; presently Mafia chieftain of Cicero; overlord of all vice activities. Chartered Local 450, Bartenders, Waiters, Waitresses and Miscellaneous Workers Union in 1935; still in control through Anthony Spano.

Alderisio, Felix Anthony

AKA: (nee Felice Antonio Alderizo) Milwaukee Phil Aldonese, Phil Alderisio, Phillip Aldi, Phil Gato, Felix Alerise, Alderist, Aldresse, Aldrise, Phil Elderise.

323

DESCRIPTION: Born April 26, 1912, Yonkers, New York; 5 feet 9½ inches, 190 pounds, brown eyes, black-graying hair, ruddy complexion, 1½ inch scar on right cheek; RO: Sicilian; FH: cousins, Frank "One Ear" and Rudolph Guy Fratto.

FREQUENTS: Valentino's Restaurant, Pepito's, Armory Lounge, Hickory House, Eros Lounge, Playboy Club and numerous other Rush Street taverns. Resides at 505 Berkley Drive, Riverside.

RECORD: FBI No. 1021382. CIR No. 32180. CPD No. D62062. FPC No. 16-JOO-0/24-WOI. Record dates back to 1929, more than 36 arrests: auto theft, extortion, mayhem, narcotics, loan sharking, burglary, gambling, vagrancy, assault and battery, conspiracy in murder threat, murder; a prime suspect in at least 14 murders. Convictions: Federal tax violation, 1 year probation; attempted extortion, 4½ years in federal prison, $7,500 fine, free on $10,000 bond pending appeal.

BUSINESS: A scam operator, he has been in and out of hundreds of enterprises.

MODUS OPERANDI: Boss of the 44th and 46th wards. Alleged to finance Mafia associates in large-scale narcotics deals and juice. A top Mob enforcer in labor unions; one of many named as "contract" killers. A Syndicate gambling representative in the Caribbean Islands and Las Vegas. Controls prostitution in Milwaukee. Known as the "king of scams" for his technique of moving in on legitimate businesses to run "controlled" bankruptcies for vast profits.

Alex, Gus

AKA: Mr. Ryan, Sam Taylor, Paul Benson, Gus Johnson, John Alex, Gussie, The Muscle, Shotgun, Slim.

DESCRIPTION: Born April 1, 1916, Chicago; 5 feet 11 inches, 175 pounds, brown eyes, black hair, dark complexion, wears huge sunglasses in public; Edu: 10th grade; MS: 4-F; RO: Greek; FH: brother, Sam; sister, Dorothy (Mrs. Frank Glimco); brother-in-law, Frank Tournabene.

FREQUENTS: Fritzel's and Mike Fish's restaurants, Bismarck's Swiss Chalet, Postl's Health Club, Italian Village, Singapore Steak and Chop House, Playboy Club, Covered Wagon Restaurant & Cocktail Lounge, Celano's (custom tailors), John D'Arco's First Ward Democratic organization at 100 N. LaSalle. Makes annual trips to Europe; declared *persona non grata* by Swiss police. Resides at 1150 N. Lake Shore Drive.

RECORD: FBI No. 4244200. LAPD No. 495650-A. Record dates back to 1930, more than 25 arrests: fugitive, bribery, assault with intent to kill, manslaughter, kidnaping; prime suspect in at least 6 murders—two gave deathbed statements naming Alex as their slayer, 3 received death threats from Alex shortly before their murder. No convictions. Took Fifth 39 times before McClellan Committee.

BUSINESS: Hidden interests in various honky-tonks, real estate ventures, service organizations, retail establishments, amusement centers; substantial interests in California and Nevada.

MODUS OPERANDI: Syndicate boss in Loop, protégé of the late Jake "Greasy Thumb" Guzik. Political fixer and power behind First Ward politicians. Ruthless, vicious killer, described by police as "one of the wiliest and slickest crooks" in the city. Suffered several mental breakdowns in recent years.

Allegretti, James

AKA: The Monk, James Millo, John Adams. Arrived in U.S. May 16, 1906, as Vincenzo Rio, stepson of Lucia Rio; registered as alien under name of James Policheri and for Selective Service as James Allegretti, both in 1940.

DESCRIPTION: Born May 31, 1905, Naples, Italy; 5 feet 8 inches, 195 pounds, brown eyes, gray hair, ruddy complexion; diabetes has left him blind in one eye; habit of scratching hands and arms won him nickname "The Monk"; Edu: 7th grade; MS: 4-C; RO: Italian; FH: stepbrother, Benny Policheri.

FREQUENTS: Valentino's Restaurant, Regency and Berkshire hotels, The Living Room, Playboy Club, Pepito's, Eros Lounge, Rush Street area. Resides at 20 E. Cedar St. (now in USPTH).

RECORD: FBI No. 1500264. CIR No. E-50620. Record dates back to 1933, more than 20 arrests: narcotics, counterfeiting, bootlegging, bribery, loan sharking, conspiracy to bribe juror, morals charge, bombing, murder. Conviction: hijacking, presently serving 7-year sentence in USPTH. Took Fifth 23 times before McClellan Committee.

BUSINESS: Hotels, restaurants, taverns, strip-joints and nightclubs; meat and produce firms.

MODUS OPERANDI: Vicelord and fixer on Near North Side. Bagman for bookmaking collections, handles police contacts, payoffs and complaints, controls union activities in his area. Business fronts of

325

Near North Side night spots bring their cash-register tapes to Allegretti's Valentino's restaurant after closing each night.

Aloisio, William

AKA: Smokes

DESCRIPTION: Born October 9, 1906; 5 feet 7 inches, 140 pounds, hazel eyes, brown hair (balding); MS: draft dodger; RO: Italian.

FREQUENTS: Calewood Barber Shop, Blue Moon Cocktail Lounge, Tom's Steak House, all in Melrose Park. Resides at 2434 N. Lorel Ave.

RECORD: FBI No. 4040530. CIR No. D-73100. USPL No. 62328. Record dates back to 1928, more than 10 arrests including murder. Conviction: Aiding and abetting the evasion of the Draft Act, 5 years in USPL.

BUSINESS: Congress Arcade Bowling Alley, Rite-Lite Neon Sign Co., taverns, and labor and interstate trucking interests.

MODUS OPERANDI: Former old Capone mob lieutenant. Boss of 34th ward, controls gambling, vice and police payoffs in his district. Was key figure in horse-meat racket. In 1936, "Machine Gun" Jack McGurn was slain in Aloisio's bowling alley. Muscleman and reputed killer.

Arnold, Joseph

AKA: Joseph Aranyos, Jerome and/or Jerry Voltaire, Big Joe.

DESCRIPTION: Born June 1, 1917; 6 feet 2 inches, 244 pounds, hazel eyes, gray hair, fair complexion; RO: Italian.

FREQUENTS: Pepito's, Eros Lounge, the Berkshire, Regency and Maryland Hotels. Resides at 426 W. Briar Place, Skokie.

RECORD: FBI No. 211015. CPD No. 5-62203. OSRM. No. 23586. Record dates back to 1929. Convictions: auto theft, 1 to 20 years in OSRM; operating stolen auto ring (interstate), 3 years in USPA; extortion, 10 years in USPL.

MODUS OPERANDI: Bodyguard and chauffeur of James Allegretti, now works as lieutenant in Near North Side gambling and vice operations while Allegretti serves his prison term. Boss of 38th ward.

Bacino, Philip

AKA: Tony Bacino, Tony Cello, Tony Bello.

DESCRIPTION: Born January 4, 1902, Ribera province of Palermo, Sicily; RO: Sicilian.

FREQUENTS: John's Pizza. Resides at 14 63rd St., Calumet City.

RECORD: FBI No. 2020359. CLPD No. 32767. Record dates back to 1928, arrests include bootlegging, tax evasion, murder. Conviction: moonshining in 1940, 6 years in USPTH, paroled in 1943.

MODUS OPERANDI: Seized in Mafia meeting in Cleveland, 1928, gave name as Tony Bello, was not identified until 34 years later. Although ostensibly inactive in recent years, he is believed to be an important "sleeper" in the Syndicate and "probably" a member of the Syndicate's board of directors.

Battaglia, Sam

AKA: Teets, Sam Batagly, Battaglea, Joe Rock, Sam Rice.

DESCRIPTION: Born November 5, 1908, Chicago; 5 feet 9 inches, 170 pounds, brown eyes, gray hair (balding), ruddy complexion; RO: Sicilian.

FREQUENTS: Casa Madrid, Armory Lounge, North Avenue Steak House, Twist Lounge and Moor's Mud Baths in Waukeshaw, Wis. Resides at 1114 N. Ridgeland Ave., Oak Park; owns a large race horse breeding farm in Pingree Grove, near Hampshire, Ill.

RECORD: FBI No. 320614. CPD No. D-20339. Record dates back to 1924, more than 25 arrests; burglary, larceny, robbery, possession of fire arms; prime suspect in at least 7 murders. Convictions: attempted burglary, 5 months; assault with intent to kill, 1 year; attempted murder (plea of guilty to assault with deadly weapon), 1 year; interstate extortion, 15 years, $10,000 fine, pending appeal. Took Fifth 60 times before McClellan Committee.

BUSINESS: Real estate, construction, dairy farms, finance companies, restaurants, taverns and hotels.

MODUS OPERANDI: Believed heir-apparent to Giancana's gangdom empire. Controls gambling and policy on West and North Sides. Overlord of narcotics traffic. Connected with juice, extortion, hijacking, burglary, fraud, murder. Sits as "judge" in "debtors court" held in basement of Casa Madrid for delinquent juice victims; penalties meted out include severe beatings and death. Casa Madrid was closed recently by authorities, but it is business-as-usual in the basement.

Blasi, Dominic

AKA: Dominic DeBlase, Blase, Joe Bantone.

DESCRIPTION: Born 1911, Chicago; 5 feet 6 inches, 158 pounds,

327

hazel eyes, dark chestnut hair (balding), sallow complexion, scar right side of chin, wears glasses; RO: Italian.

FREQUENTS: Resides 1138 Park Ave., River Forest.

RECORD: FBI No. 635770. CPD No. E-8187. USPL No. 48512. Record dates back to 1932, more than 13 arrests: unlawful transportation of machine guns and ammunition, robbery. Convictions: auto theft, 1 year probation; counterfeiting, 5 years in USPL.

MODUS OPERANDI: Chauffeur and bodyguard for Sam Giancana.

Brancata, Dominick

AKA: Nags, Dom.

DESCRIPTION: Born February 26, 1906, New Orleans, La.; 5 feet 8 inches, 175 pounds, brown eyes, brown hair, fair complexion, bridge upper-front teeth, part of left ear missing; RO: Italian.

FREQUENTS: Valentino's and Milano's restaurants, Commonwealth Hotel, Subway Poolroom, Rush Street area, local racetracks. Resides at 444 W. Goethe.

RECORD: FBI No. 732118. CIR No. C-26383. FPC No. 17-1-00/3 —00. Record dates back to 1924, more than 41 arrests: burglary, robbery, vagrancy, larceny, carrying concealed weapons; prime suspect in at least 10 murders. Convictions: vagrancy, 6 months, reversed; larceny of auto, probation.

BUSINESS: Alpine Construction Co.

MODUS OPERANDI: Considered a very dangerous and vicious gangster. Strongarm thug in the old Capone mob. As one of the "Three Doms" (Brancata, Nuccio, DiBella), collects tributes from North Side gamblers and prostitutes, and active in their (three Doms) own vice operations.

Bravos, Nick

AKA: (nee Nick Pravos) M. Brado, Nick Bravas.

DESCRIPTION: Born July 22, 1913, Romania; 5 feet 7 inches, 185 pounds, brown eyes, brown-graying hair, swarthy complexion. RO: Romanian; FH: brother, George.

FREQUENTS: Sportsman's Park. Resides at 8831 Kathy Lane, Des Plaines.

RECORD: FBI No. 680995. CPD No. E-36804. ISPJ No. 8370. Record dates back to 1932, more than 7 arrests: investigation, robbery, larceny. Convictions: larceny of auto, 1 year probation; armed robbery, 10 years in ISPJ, paroled 1940 after serving 7 years.

328

BUSINESS: A-1 Industrial Uniforms, poolroom and expediter for Roth-Adams Fuel Co.

MODUS OPERANDI: A Syndicate gambling lieutenant, also active as a loan shark.

Buccieri, Fiore

AKA: Fifi, Bucceri, Puccieri, Bucciri.

DESCRIPTION: Born 1904, Chicago; 5 feet 9 inches, 195 pounds, hazel eyes, dark chestnut hair, fair complexion, partial upper dental plate, tattoo of "heart and wreath," wears glasses; RO: Italian; FH: brother, Frank.

FREQUENTS: Armory Lounge and Playboy Club. Resides at 3004 S. Maple Ave., Berwyn. Has large estate at Lake Geneva, Wis., equipped with rifle and skeet range where Syndicate gunmen sharpen their aim.

RECORD: CIR No. D60488. Record dates back to 1925, more than 16 arrests: receiving stolen property, "muscleman" for Embalmers Union, bribery, carrying concealed weapons, larceny, murder. Convictions: burglary reduced to petty larceny, 6 months in HC; disorderly conduct, 10 days in HC. Suspect in bombing of 3 gambling establishments in 1954.

BUSINESS: Finance companies, meat and produce, taverns and nightclubs.

MODUS OPERANDI: An arsonist, bomber, terrorist and professional assassin, he has been identified with labor union rackets, juice and gambling. Boss of the 25th and part of the 27th and 1st Wards. In 1966, federal authorities named him the lord high executioner of the Chicago Syndicate.

Buccieri, Frank

AKA: The Horse, Frank Bruno.

DESCRIPTION: Born 1919, Chicago; 6 feet, 215 pounds, dark hazel eyes, dark chestnut hair (wavy), fair complexion, upper dental plate; RO: Italian; FH: brother, Fiore.

FREQUENTS: S.A.C. Club, Playboy Club and Rush Street area. Resides at 2020 Arthur, Park Ridge.

RECORD: FBI No. 1378635. CIR No. E-4652. CPD No. C-84057. Record dates back to 1936. Conviction: petty larceny, 6 months probation.

329

MODUS OPERANDI: A loan shark and lieutenant in West Side gambling and legitimate business for his brother, Fiore.

Buonaguidi. Lawrence

AKA: Larry the Hood, Lawrence Bradi, Brady, Buonaguida, Bounaguide.

DESCRIPTION: Born December 15, 1915; 5 feet 6 inches, 200 pounds, blue eyes, black hair, fair complexion; RO: Italian.

FREQUENTS: Valentino's Restaurant, Subway Poolroom, Athens Restaurant and Lounge, Eros Lounge and Rush Street area. Resides at 2618 N. Francisco.

RECORD: FBI No. 1599701. CPD No. E-50234. CIR No. 38072. USPTH No. 1317. ISPJ No. 24283. Record dates back to 1933, more than 20 arrests: burglary, gambling. Prime suspect in several gangland murders. Convictions: larceny, 60 days; violation of Internal Revenue laws, 1 year in USPTH; armed robbery, 1 to 3 years in ISPJ.

BUSINESS: Vending machines and strip-joints.

MODUS OPERANDI: A terrorist and enforcer for Allegretti on Near North Side.

Caifano, John Michael

AKA: Marshall Caifano, Cafano, Califano, Shoes, Heels, Joe Russo, Michael J. Monette, Frank Robarto, Frank Roberts, John Roberts, Joseph Rinaldi, George Marini, Michael Heale, Johnnie Moore, John Stevens, Thomas J. Hynes, Joe Russell; legally changed name in 1955 to John M. Marshall.

DESCRIPTION: Born August 19, 1911, New York City; 5 feet 7 inches, 154 pounds, brown eyes, brown hair, dark complexion; Edu: 5th grade; RO: Italian; FH: brother, Leonard "Fats", murdered in 1951.

FREQUENTS: Pepito's, Eros Lounge, Armory Lounge, Playboy Club; represents Chicago Syndicate in Las Vegas and Los Angeles. Resides at 222 N. Marion, Oak Park.

RECORD: FBI No. 552863. CPD No. C-30104. CIR No. E-51771. Record dates back to 1929, more than 35 arrests: failure to register as an ex-convict, vagrancy, burglary, extortion, indicted for conspiracy to defraud (mistrial, acquitted in second trial). Prime suspect in more than 10 murders. Convictions: burglary, reduced to petty larceny, 6 months; larceny, 1 year, sentence vacated and 1 year probation granted; bank robbery, 1 to 3 years in HC; interstate extortion, 10 years; interstate fraud, 12 years to run concurrently with 10-year sentence he was already serving. Cited for contempt of Congress in 1958; took Fifth 73 times before McClellan Committee.

BUSINESS: Several nightclubs and taverns, auto agencies, apartment houses, restaurants, construction and engineering firms, aluminum products, meat and produce.

MODUS OPERANDI: Playboy and feared gunman, presently a bookmaker and Rush Street entrepreneur. One of eleven undesirable gangsters black-listed by the Nevada Gaming Control Board.

Capone, Ermino John

AKA: Mimi, Miami, John James Capone, Phil Cohen, Jack Martin, John A. Martin, Arthur Colby.

DESCRIPTION: Born April 12, 1904, Brooklyn, N.Y.; 5 feet 10 inches, 200 pounds, brown eyes, gray hair (balding); Edu: 8th grade; RO: Italian; FH: father Gabriel; mother, Theresa Rialo (both from Naples, Italy, deceased); brothers, Vincenzo (changed name to James Hart, deceased), Salvatore (killed by police in gun battle during 1924 elections in Cicero), Alphonse "Scarface" (deceased), Umberto (changed name to Albert Rayola), Matthew "Matt the Mooch" (deceased), Ralph "Bottles"; sister, Mafalda (Mrs. John Maritote); nephew, Albert "Sonny" Capone (son of Alphonse); cousins, Rocco, Charles (both deceased) and Joseph Fischetti, Rocco, Frank and Vito De Stefano.

FREQUENTS: Conrad Hilton Hotel in Chicago and Bel Aires Hotel in Miami Beach. Resides at 5427 Hyde Park Blvd.

RECORD: FBI No. 282094. CIR No. D-93525. Record dates back to 1922, more than 7 arrests: gambling, vagrancy, murder. No convictions.

BUSINESS: Nightclubs and restaurants in Miami and Chicago, substantial oil and real estate holdings.

MODUS OPERANDI: A brother of Al Capone, supervises various Syndicate gambling activities in Chicago and Miami. Also a known contact man for loan sharks.

Caruso, Frank

AKA. Frank Spino, Skid.

DESCRIPTION: Born November 11, 1911, Chicago; 5 feet 6 inches, 165 pounds, brown eyes, brown hair (balding), dark complexion, tattoo of "heart" and "Viola" on left arm, tattoo of a rose on right arm; RO: Italian; FH: brother, Joseph; father-in-law, Bruno Roti (deceased).

FREQUENTS: Area known as "The Patch" on Near Southwest Side, Acorn Club, Kai Kai and Nick's restaurants. Resides at 215 W. 23rd St.

RECORD: FBI No. 1068090. CIR No. 56704. FPC No. 32-0-0/24 —01. Record dates back to 1935, more than 13 arrests: grand larceny, conspiracy, gambling.

BUSINESS: Caruso Plumbing, Hillside.

MODUS OPERANDI: Operates on South Side of First Ward, active in narcotics; runs dice, poker and policy inherited from Bruno Roti after his death in 1956.

Cerone, Frank

AKA: (nee Francesco Cironato), Skippy, Skip, Thomas Frank Cerone, Eddie, Rollings.

DESCRIPTION: Born April 12, 1913, Chicago; 5 feet 8½ inches, 178 pounds, blue eyes, brown hair, wears glasses; RO: Italian; FH: brother, Daniel (murder victim).

FREQUENTS: Show Tap Lounge, Blue Moon Lounge, Tom's Steak House. Resides at 1530 Broadway Ave., Melrose Park.

RECORD: FBI No. 4042028. CPD No. destroyed. FPC No. 17-WII-I/14-UOO. Record dates back to 1928, more than 10 arrests; vagrancy, robbery, assault to rape. Conviction: bribery and conspiracy to evade draft, two 5-year concurrent sentences in USPTH, $20,000 fine.

BUSINESS: Blue Moon Lounge, Century Enterprises, construction and real estate.

MODUS OPERANDI: Active in gambling and narcotics. Considered a "hit" man.

Cerone, John Phillip, Sr.

AKA: (nee Cironi) Jack Cerone, Jackie the Lackie Cerone, J. Arnold.

DESCRIPTION: Born July 7, 1914, Chicago; 5 feet 6 inches, 175 pounds, brown eyes, brown hair (balding), light brown complexion, slight scar on middle finger of right hand; RO: Italian; FH: brother, Anthony, (murder victim).

FREQUENTS: Twist Lounge, Armory Lounge, member of White

332

Pines and Riverwood country clubs. Resides at 2000 N. 77th Ave., Elmwood Park.

RECORD: FBI No. 92-1040. CPD No. C-41741. FPC No. 32-OII-I/32-OII. Record dates back to 1933, more than 19 arrests: loitering, vagrancy, bookmaking, keeper of a gambling house, robbery, armed robbery; prime suspect in at least 4 murders. Cited for contempt of Congress in 1958; took Fifth 45 times before McClellan Committee.

BUSINESS: Construction, real estate, liquor stores, taverns, aluminum products, apartment houses.

MODUS OPERANDI: Former chauffeur for Tony Accardo, referred to as Accardo's pilot fish. A master fixer and political sponsor of applicants to police force. Expensive dresser in old tradition of flashy gangsterism. West Side gambling boss who muscled his way into power; a feared gunman and Syndicate executioner. Boss of the 28th, 30th and 37th wards.

Coli, Eco James

AKA: James Aseco.

DESCRIPTION: Born February 15, 1922; 5 feet 8½ inches, 150 pounds, brown eyes, black hair; RO: Italian.

FREQUENTS: Northwest Side. Resides at 5808 W. Lake St. and 2216 N. 75th Ave., in Elmwood Park, and 22 S. Lavergne, Northlake.

RECORD: FBI No. 4505973. CPD No. E-80437. Record dates back to 1945, more than 12 arrests: assault, sex offense, attempted hijacking and a prime suspect in numerous murder investigations. Convictions: contributing to delinquency, 1 year probation; armed robbery, 8 to 12 years at ISPJ, released in 3 years (1955) by order of Illinois Supreme Court.

MODUS OPERANDI: Secretary-treasurer and business agent of Teamsters Local 727, Funeral Drivers, Directors, Embalmers and Miscellaneous Union. Associates with burglars and hijackers. A terrorist and strongarm thug in labor unions and a Syndicate assassin.

Daddano, William, Sr.

AKA: Doddomo, Daddeno, Dado, Dr. Miller, William Russo, Willie Potatoes, Blinky.

DESCRIPTION: Born December 28, 1912, Chicago; 5 feet 5 inches, 150 pounds, hazel eyes, brown hair (balding), fair complexion, one-inch scar left side of forehead, occasionally assumes identity of deaf-mute, converses fluently in sign language; MS: 4-F; RO: Italian.

FREQUENTS: Armory Lounge, Moon's Restaurant, Riviera Lanes. Resides at 8109 W. 26th St., North Riverside.

RECORD: FBI No. 1922776. CIR No. D-030878. ISPJ No. 21923. USPTH No. 3899. Record dates back to 1936, more than 9 arrests: bank robbery, larceny; prime suspect in at least 7 murders. Convictions: in 1945, burglary, 1 to 14 years (served 1 year) in ISPJ; 1946, attempted bank robbery, 1 year in USPTH. Indicted in May 1966 in $1 million hijacking of silver bullions, acquitted.

BUSINESS: Scavenger services, automobile agencies and restaurants.

MODUS OPERANDI: Assassin and torturer. Active in gambling in Cicero and Berwyn, also active in juice. Controls distribution of jukeboxes and pinball machines in DuPage County. Considered a top-echelon Syndicate hoodlum.

DeBiase, John

AKA: John DeBiesio, DeBaise, DeBiesio, Johnny Banana, Bananas.

DESCRIPTION: Born January 1, 1901; 5 feet 5 inches, 160 pounds, brown eyes, black hair, dark complexion; RO: Italian.

FREQUENTS: Roasa Nova Tailor Shop, Valley Farm Market. Resides at 638 N. Euclid, Oak Park.

RECORD: CPD No. D-36753. Record dates back to 1954, several gambling arrests.

BUSINESS: Taverns and jukeboxes.

MODUS OPERANDI: Activities directed toward gambling, juice and narcotics on West Side; known to bankroll stables of robbers, burglars and hijackers.

DeGeorge, James

AKA: (nee Vincenzo DeGiorgi), Don Vincenzo.

DESCRIPTION: Born about 1898; RO: Sicilian; FH: both sons suffered violent deaths; daughter, Louise (Mrs. Anthony Pinelli, Jr.); brother-in-law, Frank Tallo (murder victim); brother, Charles.

FREQUENTS: Resides at 3716 N. Kedvale Ave. (mysteriously destroyed by fire on Jan. 7, 1966); Triple D Ranch, Route 2, Hancock, Wis.—a 6,000-acre black Angus cattle ranch, protected by watchdogs, private guards and alarm system.

RECORD: First arrested in 1922 with his brother, Charles, for the gang-type murder of Frank Fondanetta, no indictment returned; also arrested as an accessory to murder in 1933.

334

BUSINESS: Extensive national interests in the Italian olive oil, grapes, cheese, bread and macaroni industries.

MODUS OPERANDI: Got his start in the early 1920s in the Italian bread industry. A power in the grape business in Chicago, which he buys in carload lots in California and sells to Italians for home wine making. Dominates Wisconsin rackets, and credited by local and federal authorities as the absentee ganglord of rackets in Lake County, Indiana. Ranks in the upper echelon of the Mafia. A member of the Syndicate's board of directors.

DeGrazia, Rocco

AKA: DeGrazio, DeGrasse, Robert DeGrazia, George Matter, Rocky, Gramps, Mr. Big.

DESCRIPTION: Born August 12, 1897; 5 feet 8 inches, 170 pounds, hazel eyes, dark-graying hair, fair complexion; RO: Italian.

FREQUENTS: Resides at 171 N. 25th St., Melrose Park.

RECORD: FBI No. .389499. CIR No. D-26847. ISRP No. 9569. USPL No. 46290. Record dates back to 1914, more than 14 arrests: fugitive, keeper of a book, conspiracy, robbery, narcotics. Convictions: burglary, 1 year in ISRP; larceny, 1 year in ISRP; income tax violation, 18 months in USPL.

MODUS OPERANDI: Old-line Capone hoodlum, active in gambling, narcotics and juice. Owns the Casa Madrid and lives on premises. Recently closed by authorities, Casa Madrid (see Battaglia's Modus Operandi) was often raided for gambling and liquor violations.

DePietto, Americo

AKA: Amerigo, America, Pete, Tony, DePieto.

DESCRIPTION: Born 1913; 5 feet 8 inches, 200 pounds, brown eyes, black-graying hair, dark complexion, fancy dresser; RO: Italian.

FREQUENTS: Formerly frequented Sportsman and Arlington race-tracks, North Avenue Steak House, Lido Motel. Resided at 104 Lavern, Hillside (now in USPL).

RECORD: FBI No. 1633923. CPD No. 41629. USPL No. 747262. Record dates back to 1935, more than 21 arrests: bootlegging, burglary, robbery, felonious assault, larceny, extortion, selling liquor after hours, narcotics, assault to commit murder. Prime suspect in bomb and arson attacks on Chicago restaurants, businesses and nightclubs. Convictions: possession of hijacked property, 4½ years in USPL; assault to rob, 1 to 10 years in WSPW; trafficking in narcotics and assaulting a federal officer, presently serving 20-year sentence in

USPL; interstate transport of stolen money orders, 5 years, pending appeal.

MODUS OPERANDI: A Syndicate narcotics boss, operating a $10 million ring. Feared enforcer and extortionist. Associated with fur and jewel thieves on West Side.

De Stefano, Rocco Nicholas

DESCRIPTION: Born June 28, 1913; 6 feet, 175 pounds, brown eyes, brown hair; RO: Italian; FH: brothers, Frank and Vito; a cousin of Al Capone and Joe Fusco.

FREQUENTS: Italian American National Union. Resides at 2912 N. Commonwealth Ave.; Conrad Hilton Hotel; Fontainebleau, Miami.

RECORD: CPD No. C-72492. Record ordered destroyed August 28, 1945, by Police Commissioner Allman. Record dates back to 1936, more than 5 arrests: hijacking, gambling, failure to pay state sales tax, conspiracy to spend $910,000 looted from treasury of Local 1248, Retail Clerks International Protective Association Union.

BUSINESS: Construction, land development, oil drilling, real estate, hotels, home subdivisions, home decorations, tobacco and beer distribution.

MODUS OPERANDI: Buys and sells motels, restaurants, taverns and nightclubs; connected with legitimate businesses financed by Syndicate.

DeStefano, Sam

AKA: Mike DeStephano, Mike DeStep, David Triner.

DESCRIPTION: Born September 13, 1909; 5 feet 10 inches, 165 pounds, brown eyes, black-graying hair, sallow complexion, wears glasses; Edu: 6th grade; RO: Italian; FH: brothers, Mario, Michael (murder victim).

FREQUENTS: Postl's Health Club. Resides at 1656 N. Sayre Ave.

RECORD: FBI No. 373004. CPD No. 48953. USPL No. 64185-L. ISPJ Nos. 57827 and 2089. Record dates back to 1926, more than 40 arrests: auto theft, fugitive (jail escape), assault to kill, carrying weapon, assault with deadly weapon, armed robbery, burglary, intimidating a federal judge, battery and intimidation, contempt of court (numerous times), rape (twice); suspect in several restaurant bombings and in at least 6 gangland slayings. Convictions: rape, 3 years in ISPJ; bank robbery, 15 to 40 years in WSPW; possession of counterfeit sugar stamps, 1 year and 1 day in USPL; assault with a deadly weapon, $200 fine; contempt of court, 30 days; illegally offering to vote, 1 to 3 years (reversed on appeal) 1 year to run concurrently plus $2,000 fine for contempt of court; conspiracy to commit perjury, guilty verdict set aside, convicted in new trial, 3 to 5 years in ISPJ, pending appeal.

MODUS OPERANDI: The mad-hatter of the Syndicate; a juice racketeer, extortionist, rapist, torturer and sexual psychopath. Known to finance hijacking, burglary, counterfeiting, narcotics and bank robbery. A member of Giancana's old "42-Gang," he is the gangster police elect as the most likely to be discovered in a car trunk.

DiBella, Dominick

AKA: DeBello, Bello, Bells, Ballow, Ballo and Frank Thomas.

DESCRIPTION: Born May 10, 1902, Franklin, La.; 5 feet 9 inches, 165 pounds, brown eyes, light chestnut hair (balding), fair complexion; RO: Italian.

FREQUENTS: Rush Street area, Papa Milano's Pizza, Sunshine and Valentino's restaurants, Pepito's, Cozy Claremont Club, Mark Twain Hotel Restaurant, Subway Poolroom, Berkshire, Regency and Commonwealth hotels. Resides at 2603 West Wright St., McHenry; business address, 1700 Greenwood Ave., Glenview.

RECORD: FBI No. 305340. CPD No. D-55939. CIR Nos. 24186 and E-54317. FPC No. 23-0-10/20-00. Record dates back to 1923, more than 22 arrests: carrying concealed weapon, extortion, burglary, robbery, larceny, vagrancy, booking bets, nonsupport, auto theft, assault and battery, narcotics, manslaughter, murder. Prime suspect in at least 10 gangland slayings.

BUSINESS: Vast real estate holdings in Illinois and southwestern United States.

MODUS OPERANDI: A major Syndicate hood operating vice and gambling on Near North Side; active in bookmaking and wire rooms. One of the "Three Doms" (with Nuccio and Brancata) reputed to be top gunman; a very dangerous, vicious gangster.

DiVarco, Joseph Vincent

AKA: (nee Placideo DeVarco), Joey Ceasar, Little Ceasar, Joseph DeVarco, J. Moran.

DESCRIPTION: Born July 27, 1911, Chicago; 5 feet 5½ inches, 170 pounds, brown eyes, brown hair, dark complexion, wears elevator shoes; Edu: 7th grade; MS: 2 years in army; RO: Italian.

FREQUENTS: A. Abbot Store Fixture, Valentino's Restaurant,

Pepito's, Snack Bar, Playboy Club, Sunshine Restaurant (Niles), Pittsburgh and Florida. Resides at 4275 Jarvis, Lincolnwood.

RECORD: FBI No. 1095466. CPD No. E-33232. USPM No. 4022. Record dates back to 1937, more than 10 arrests: conspiracy to bribe a juror, fraudulent voting, suspect in several gangland murders. Conviction: counterfeiting conspiracy, 1 year in USPM. Cited for contempt of Congress in 1958; took Fifth 45 times before McClellan Committee.

BUSINESS: Furniture and fixtures for taverns and nightclubs, vending machines, currency exchanges, poolroom, nightclubs, real estate and construction, connected with Las Vegas gambling.

MODUS OPERANDI: Active in vice, gambling, juice on Near North Side; an extortionist, considered a top Syndicate assassin.

English, Charles Carmen

AKA: (nee Englise), Chuck.

DESCRIPTION: Born November 7, 1914; 5 feet 10 inches, 180 pounds, brown eyes, dark hair; RO: Italian; FH: brother, "Fat" Sam; sister, Grace (wife of Carlo Urbinanti, a narcotics peddler).

FREQUENTS: 5th Jack Club, Maggio's Steak House, Armory Lounge, Playboy Club, Big Top Restaurant, Fresh Meadows Country Club in Oak Park. Resides at 1131 North Lathrop, River Forest.

RECORD: CIR No. G-40625. FPC No. 9-U-00/3-W-M. Record dates back to 1933, more than 8 arrests: robbery, extortion, hijacking and conspiracy, loan sharking, counterfeiting phonograph record trademarks, murder. Took Fifth 56 times before McClellan Committee.

BUSINESS: Phonograph records (Lormar Distributing Co.), jukeboxes, vending machines, real estate, taverns and finance company B & D Acceptance Co., Inc.

MODUS OPERANDI: Syndicate overlord of 29th Ward, rules politics and rackets. Active nationally in phonograph records and jukeboxes. Incorporated the Rim Rock Ranch in Phoenix, Arizona, as a multi-million-dollar enterprise to deal in real estate, contracting, construction, public works, loans, and as a base of operation to invade the Arizona jukebox industry. Spread used as a winter hideaway for Syndicate hoodlums and politicians.

Frabotta, Albert

AKA: (nee Fravatto), Albert DeMarco, Aeron Oberlander, Obie.

DESCRIPTION: Born August 24, 1911, Steger; 5 feet 7 inches, 195

338

pounds, brown eyes, gray hair (balding), fair complexion, small mole on right cheek; RO: Italian; FH: mother, Josephine Rienzi, once sentenced to 18 months for receiving stolen property; brothers, Joseph and Rocco (twins), James "Foxey"; sisters, Theresa (Mrs. Rocco Monico), Angelina (Mrs. William Fratto).

FREQUENTS: Armory Lounge, The Living Room, Pepito's and Rush Street area. Resides at 3950 N. Lake Shore Drive.

RECORD: FBI No. 521263. CPD No. E-48072. SPPI No. 21912. Record dates back to 1927, more than 45 arrests: gambling, armed robbery, extortion, attempted rape, murder. Prime suspect in at least 6 murders. Convictions: larceny, 90 days in HC; burglary, 1 year in HC; bank robbery, 10 years in SPPI.

BUSINESS: Meat and produce, real estate, aluminum products, food processing and by-products.

MODUS OPERANDI: Former member of old "42-Gang," active in burglary, auto theft and strongarm tactics. Benet test indicates a mental age of 13 years and 2 months and IQ of 82.3. A collector of gambling revenue for Marshall Caifano until 1962; recently assumed a supervisory position on West Side in gambling and vice; gambling interests in Milwaukee.

Fratto, Frank

AKA: Frank Frappo, One Ear Frankie, Half-Ear.

DESCRIPTION: Born March 24, 1915, Chicago; 6 feet, 185 pounds, brown eyes, brown-graying hair, sallow complexion, flesh mole on left cheek, deformed right ear; RO: Italian; FH: brothers, Carmen, Louis (aka Lew Farrell), Rudolph, William (married Angelina Frabotta); brother-in-law, Don Ross (nee Donald Rosenberg); cousin, Felix Alderisio.

FREQUENTS: Kool-Vent Awning Co., Courtesy Storm Window Co. and Near North Side area. Resides at 6300 N. Olcott.

RECORD: FBI No. 2890731. CPD No. D-82974. Record dates back to 1941, more than 10 arrests: fugitive, theft, assault to commit murder. Conviction: Interstate theft of whisky, 3 years probation. A suspect in the 1957 murder of Willard Bates and the 1963 murder of Alderman Benjamin Lewis.

BUSINESS: A half-dozen firms dealing in aluminum products and storm windows, a savings association and a disposal service.

MODUS OPERANDI: A Syndicate terrorist on North Side who muscled his way into the aluminum siding and storm window business. His brother, Rudolph, is known as the "garbage king" of the Rush Street saloon strip.

Fusco, Joseph Charles

AKA: Joe Long, Joe Carey, Joseph Sayth, Joe or E. J. Thompson.

DESCRIPTION: Born May 6, 1902; 5 feet 7 inches, 200 pounds, dark but graying hair (balding); RO: Italian; FH: brother-in-law, William W. Gamble; cousins, Rocco, Frank and Vito De Stefano.

FREQUENTS: Armory Lounge and Playboy Club. Resides at Conrad Hilton Hotel.

RECORD: FBI No. 854516. CPD No. D-29816. Arrest record prior to June 8, 1928, ordered destroyed. Numerous arrests including assault with a deadly weapon, receiving stolen property, conspiracy. Indicted with Al Capone in 1931 and charged with 5,000 violations of the federal prohibition laws. No convictions. Identified by the Chicago Crime Commission as one of 28 Public Enemies in 1930.

BUSINESS: Van Merritt Beer and Bohemian Brewing Co., plus several liquor and beer distributorships under various titles.

MODUS OPERANDI: Served apprenticeship as a beer runner in the old Capone mob. Supplies beer and liquor to taverns, liquor stores, nightclubs, motels and hotels controlled by the Syndicate across the U.S. One recent Fusco conquest was the Pacific Brewing Co. in California, operated by associate Alfred Louis Hart.

Gagliano, Joseph

AKA: Joe Gags, Galiano, Joey G, Joe Gay, Jack Gailo, Pip the Blind.

DESCRIPTION: Born July 21, 1914; 5 feet 8 inches, 185 pounds, brown eyes, black hair (balding), dark complexion, tattoo of "woman's head" and the word "Marge" on forearm, "Felix the Cat" tattooed on other forearm; RO: Italian.

FREQUENTS: American Legion Post 1056, Moon's Restaurant, Eros Lounge. Resides at 1731 N. Thatcher Rd., Elmwood Park.

RECORD: CPD No. D-23606. CIR No. E-36776. ISPJ Nos. 8906E, 14506, 29176. ISPM No. 15680. ISPP No. 17892. Record dates back to 1926, more than 9 arrests: tried for kidnaping and beating, acquitted. Convictions: bootlegging, $100 fine; larceny, 1 to 10 years in ISPM, later transferred to ISPJ; armed robbery (4 counts), 3 to 7 years each in ISPJ. Took Fifth 7 times before McClellan Committee.

BUSINESS: Commercial Phonograph Survey, which collects 90¢

monthly from each of 6,975 jukeboxes owned by 492 distributors; vending machines, taverns and restaurants.

MODUS OPERANDI: A muscleman for Joey Glimco and Chuck English in the jukebox racket, and a West Side loan shark, gambler and narcotics trafficker. Underboss of the 28th, 30th and 37th wards for overlord John Cerone.

Giancana, Sam

AKA: (born Gilormo Giangono, baptised Momo Salvatore Giangono), Momo, Moe, The Cigar, Sam Mooney, Sam Moonie, J. Mooney, Sam Gincani, Giancaco, Giacana, Gianenna, Gianeana, Giancane, Gincanna, Giancanna, Gincanni, Ginncana, Giancano, Giancona, Albert Masusco, Albert Manusco, Michael Mancuso, G. Stanley, P. Rosie, Sam Flood, Sam Volpe.

DESCRIPTION: Born May 24, 1908 (baptismal record says June 15, 1908), Chicago; 5 feet 9 inches, 165 pounds, brown eyes, black hair (balding), fair complexion, oblique scar 2 centimeters right front of nose; Edu: 6th grade; MS: rejected, classified as psychopath; RO: Sicilian; FH: daughters, Antoinette (Mrs. Carmen Manno), Bonita Lucille (Mrs. Anthony Tisci), Francine Marie (Mrs. James Perno); brothers, Joseph and Charles; nephew-in-law, State Senator Anthony DeTolve.

FREQUENTS: Fresh Meadows Golf Club, Armory Lounge, Airliner Lounge, Mike's Restaurant, Central Envelope & Lithographic Co., Maggio's Steak House, clubs along Mannheim Road, Fontainebleau Hotel (Miami), visits Mexico, Europe, Hawaii and Las Vegas. Resides at 1147 S. Wenonah Ave., Oak Park now in Cuernavaca, Mexico.

RECORD: FBI No. 58437. CPD No. E-27465. ISPJ No. 2807. USPTH No. 104. FPC No. 25-10-15/4-00. Record dates back to 1925, more than 70 arrests: contributing to delinquency, vagrancy, burglary, assault and battery, larceny, fugitive, assault to kill, damage by violence, conspiracy to operate a "book," possession of burglar tools and concealed weapons, bombing suspect, gambling, fictitious driver's license, murder; prime suspect in countless murder investigations, three before the age of twenty: indicted on one at 18, released on bail, charge stricken following the murder of key witness. Convictions: auto theft, 30 days; burglary, 1 to 5 years in ISPJ; operating a still, 4 years in USPTH. Served 1 year for contempt of federal grand jury, released June 1, 1966. Took Fifth 35 times before McClellan Committee.

BUSINESS: Nationwide investments in legitimate enterprises through fronts. Substantial interests in Florida, Nevada and West Indies.
MODUS OPERANDI: Boss of all bosses of the Chicago Syndicate and a member of the Mafia's National Commission.

Gianola, Leonard

AKA: Needles.
DESCRIPTION: Born November 19, 1910, Chicago; 5 feet 10½ inches, 195 pounds, blue eyes, medium-dark chestnut hair, fair complexion, false teeth (2 plates), wears glasses; RO: Italian; FH: brother, Sam.
FREQUENTS: Sportsman Park, Athen's Restaurant, Taylor Liquors, Seabrook Apartments in Miami. Resides at 7344 N. Tripp Ave., Lincolnwood.
RECORD: FBI No. 651234. CPD No. 62426. USPL No. 46288. FPC No. 15-R-0/30-U-0. Record dates back to 1932, more than 8 arrests. Convictions: malicious mischief, 6 months probation; vagrancy, fined $60, suspended; theft of interstate shipment, 3 years in USPL.
MODUS OPERANDI: A West Side labor racketeer; on payroll of Local 46, Laundry, Cleaning and Dye House Workers International Union. Active in narcotics.

Glimco, Joseph Paul

AKA: (nee Giuseppe Glielmi), Joey, Joe Glimico, Glinco, Glielmo, Giuseppe Primavera, John Murray.
DESCRIPTION: Born January 14, 1909, Salerno, Italy (entered U.S. in 1913); 5 feet 4½ inches, 160 pounds, brown eyes, black but graying hair (balding), dark complexion, prefers blue suits to accentuate silver at his temples; Edu: 7th grade; RO: Sicilian; FH: son, Joseph, Jr.; brother, Frank (married to Dorothy Alex).
FREQUENTS: Jim's Place and Rush Street area. Resides at 629 Selbourne Drive, Riverside.
RECORD: FBI No. 233623. CIR No. C-18336. Record dates back to 1923, more than 38 arrests: disorderly conduct, vagrancy, assault with auto, bootlegging, threats to do bodily harm, malicious mischief, auto theft, assault and battery, racketeering through terrorism, perjury (2 counts regarding application for driver's license), armed robbery, assault with gun with intent to murder, murder. Prime suspect in at least 4 murders. Tried for murder in 1928 after a deathbed statement by victim, acquitted. A 17-count indictment for

342

violations of Taft-Hartley Act was dismissed by Federal Judge Michael L. Igoe in August 1965. Convictions: larceny, 1 year probation; served 20 days in Waukegan County jail on a government charge of conspiracy to violate the Volstead Act. Applied for citizenship in 1932 and denied for lack of good character; again denied in 1938 due to extensive police record; citizenship granted in 1943 by Federal Judge Michael L. Igoe after State Representative Andrew A. Euzzino had subject's police record destroyed. Took Fifth 80 times before Kefauver Committee, and 152 times before McClellan Committee.

BUSINESS: (See Chapter 5, Book I for partial listing.)

MODUS OPERANDI: The Syndicate's top labor czar; boss of at least 15 Teamster locals; a power in the jukebox and coin machine industry, and a hidden owner of a wide variety of legitimate enterprises—a front for top Syndicate bosses, who in turn uses fronts. A Mafia don with a reputation as a vicious and brutal gangster who enforces his edicts with violence and murder.

Infelice, Ernest Rocco

AKA: Ernest Infelise, Henry Marks, Rocky.

DESCRIPTION: Born March 16, 1921; 5 feet 11 inches, 240 pounds, brown eyes, black hair (balding); RO: Italian.

FREQUENTS: Sportsman and Arlington racetracks, Big Top Restaurant, North Avenue Steak House, Americana Hotel in New York City. Resides at 1407 LeMoyne Ave., Melrose Park.

RECORD: FBI No. 308006. CIR Nos. D-91246 E-21213, E-57190. USPA No. 74035. Record dates back to 1952, more than 7 arrests: robbery, burglary, murder; prime suspect in many arson cases. Convictions: violation of National Firearms Act, 2 years in USPA; interstate transport of stolen money orders, 5 years, pending appeal; $1 million hijacking of silver bullion, 10 to 20 years; indicted in April 1966 for failing to file income tax returns for 1959, 1960 and 1962, case pending.

MODUS OPERANDI: A ranking figure in narcotics and gambling on West Side with Americo DePietto. Travels to New York, Hot Springs, Ark., and Florida on bookmaking business for Syndicate.

Inserro, Vincent Joseph

AKA: Vincent Incerro, Frank Tufano, Joe Carson, Joseph Carsoni, Joe DeFiore, Joseph DeFiano, Little Vincent St. Louis, The Saint, Frank Relli, Joe DeFranco, Vincent Perri.

DESCRIPTION: Born February 6, 1911; 5 feet 1 inch, 128 pounds, hazel eyes, dark hair; MS: Army, 3 years; RO: Italian.
FREQUENTS: Berkshire and Regency hotels, Mario's Pizzeria, Rush Street area. Resides at 2236 S. Northgate, North Riverside.
RECORD: FBI No. 1202410. CPD No. E-20458. ISPJ No. 6009. Record dates back to 1930, more than 15 arrests: auto theft, illegal possession of weapons, burglary, fugitive, labor racketeering, murder. Convictions: auto theft, 30 days; larceny, 6 months; armed robbery, served 11 years in ISPJ until pardoned in 1943 for induction in U.S. Army. Tried for murder, knife, in 1956 and acquitted; income tax evasion (admitted he had filed only 4 income tax returns in his life), 2 years, pending appeal.
MODUS OPERANDI: A Syndicate wheel-and-muscle expert on West Side; free-lances in burglary and robbery. Active in narcotics.

Kruse, Leslie Earl

AKA: Lester "Killer Kane" Kruse, Kid, Lee Kane, Lester Krause, Kelly Kove, Richard Burnas, Lee McCarthy, Lee Marshall, Joe Marshall, J. Sweeney, George Howley.
DESCRIPTION: Born October 5, 1906, Chicago; 6 feet 2 inches, 210 pounds, blue eyes, gray hair (balding), poor health, wears glasses, RO: Jewish; FH: cousin, Theodore Kruse.
RECORD: FBI No. 274989-B. CPD No. C-85179. CIR No. 25630. Arrested for conspiracy (gambling), twice for investigation of murder. Record ordered destroyed.
BUSINESS: Restaurant fixtures, pancake house, motels, construction, beer-coil cleaning service, real estate, automobile agency and interests in Las Vegas casinos.
MODUS OPERANDI: Former bodyguard for Jake Guzik and a gambling partner of the late Rocco Fischetti. Considered a high-ranking Syndicate hood with varied gambling interests in Lake County and Waukegan area. Reputed to run the town of Half Day with an iron fist. Receives special police protection for his home.

LaBarbera, Joseph Anthony

AKA: Joseph Labarbara, Joe the Barber, Joe Little New York, Joe Barone, Joe Villa, Tony New York.
DESCRIPTION: Born August 17, 1910; 5 feet 8 inches, 160 pounds, gray eyes, gray hair, medium complexion, wears glasses, uses pretext of being deaf when arrested; RO: Italian.
FREQUENTS: Subway Poolroom, Berkshire, Regency and Mark

Twain hotels, Rush Street area. Resides at 1432 N. Mohawk St., and 14 W. Elm St.

RECORD: FBI No. 383602. CPD No. 10386. Record dates back to 1929, more than 32 arrests: assault, fugitive theft from auto, attempted extortion, vagrancy, gambling, receiving stolen goods, robbery, grand larceny, possession of narcotics. Convictions: attempted robbery reduced to assault, 6 months; burglary, served 2 years in Buffalo, N.Y.

MODUS OPERANDI: Considered a heavyweight in upstate New York rackets before coming to Chicago in mid-1940s; a terrorist in Syndicate vice operations in Near North Side; active in narcotics.

LaPorte, Frank

AKA: (nee Francesco Liparota), Liperetto, Lipperatti.

DESCRIPTION: Born October 7, 1901, San Biose, Italy (entered U.S. in 1913, naturalized in 1926); 5 feet 5½ inches, 250 pounds, brown eyes, brown hair (balding), ruddy complexion; MS: 2 years in U.S. Navy; RO: Italian; FH: brother, Joseph; sisters, Natalie (Mrs. Theodore J. Bartusiewicz), Therese (Mrs. Ruggerio Luzi), Concetta Marie (Mrs. Anthony Franze), Rosina (Mrs. James Iaderosa—aka Ross), Victoria (Mrs. Mario Pulicini), Frances (Mrs. Frank Franze); nephews, Frank and John Luzi, Roger Franze.

FREQUENTS: South Cook County, Joliet and Calumet City. Spends considerable time in California, Nevada and Arizona. Resides at 1730 Cambridge Ave., Flossmoor.

RECORD: FBI No. 261150E. FPC No. 1-R-II/17-R-OI. No record listed. Prime suspect in at least 2 murders. Booked and held 2 days for murder in 1926.

BUSINESS: Outside investments include gold and silver mines in Calif., uranium mine in Colo., tungsten mine in Nevada, a gas well in Ariz. and real estate at Lake Geneva.

MODUS OPERANDI: Syndicate overlord in South Cook and Will counties—territory runs from Calumet City to Kankakee, and from Chicago Heights to Joliet. Operation recently extended to include Lake County, Indiana, where gambling and prostitution is a $50,000-a-day business, and a vice resort in Godley. Also operates in Central America. Controls gambling, vice, narcotics, juice, jukeboxes, extortion, vending and pinball machines, taverns, strip-joints, bail bond business (through F. L. Bail Bond Co. operated by nephew, Frank Luzi, who is also his chauffeur-bodyguard), and granting of liquor licenses in his vast domain. FBI indicates that payoffs to Chicago

345

Heights policemen are made from Cooperative Music Co. where officers pick up weekly envelopes. A top-ranking mafioso and member of the Syndicate's board of directors.

˙ Lardino, John

AKA: John Nardi, Edward Nardi, John Olcott.
DESCRIPTION: Born in 1908; 5 feet 10 inches, 198 pounds, brown eyes, brown hair (balding), ruddy complexion; RO: Italian.
FREQUENTS: North Avenue Steak House, Blue Moon, White Pine Country Club and Horvath's Lounges. Resides at 1201 Belleforte, Oak Park.
RECORD: CPD No. D-57251. Record dates back to 1927. Convictions: vagrancy, 6 months; robbery (reduced to petty larceny), 1 year probation. A suspect in several gangland slayings. Took Fifth 60 times before McClellan Committee.
MODUS OPERANDI: A former Syndicate gunman who posed as a respectable union official, he was boss of Local 593, Hotel-Motel Service Workers, Drug Store, Sports Events, and Industrial Catering Employees Union.

Mesi, Sam

AKA: Sam Messi.
DESCRIPTION: Born in 1900; 5 feet 6 inches, 145 pounds, hazel eyes, dark chestnut hair, sallow complexion, tattoo of flag "U.S.A.," wears glasses; RO: Italian; FH: brother, Phillip.
FREQUENTS: Sportsman Park, Moon's Restaurant, Phil's Lounge. Resides at 1430 N. Harlem Ave., River Forest.
RECORD: FBI No. 453495. CIR No. 90824. Record dates back to 1919, more than 8 arrests: cartage theft, moonshining, bookmaking, murder; prime suspect in at least 4 gangland murders. Conviction: armed robbery, 1 year in HC.
MODUS OPERANDI: A West Side bookmaker with a knack for violence. Comes from a family with Syndicate ties going back three generations. Yearly gross of $800,000 from one of his horse parlors set a precedent in tax court. Boss of the 26th ward.

Messino, William

AKA: Wee Willie Messina, Orlando Messina, E. Serpico.
DESCRIPTION: Born January 7, 1917; 5 feet 6 inches, 160 pounds, brown eyes, black hair (balding), medium complexion; RO: Italian.

346

FREQUENTS: Moon's Restaurant, Twist Lounge, Pussycat Lounge, the Colony House. Resides at 2037 N. 77th Ave., Elmwood Park.
RECORD: FBI No. 922367. CIR No. 36776. ISPJ No. 1350. Record dates back to 1935, more than 13 arrests: loan sharking, illegal possession of weapons, extortion. Indicted and tried on kidnaping and mayhem, acquitted. Conviction: armed robbery, served 5 years and 8 months in ISPJ; conspiracy-intimidation-assault-kidnaping, 10 to 30 years. Took Fifth 10 times before McClellan Committee.
BUSINESS: Liquor stores, jukeboxes, linoleum and tile.
MODUS OPERANDI: A Syndicate terrorist in juice and coin machines on West Side.

Mirro, James

AKA: Cowboy.
DESCRIPTION: Born December 29, 1913, Chicago; 5 feet 7 inches, 197 pounds, brown eyes, black hair, ruddy complexion, 1½ inch horizontal scar left side of face at ear; RO: Italian.
FREQUENTS: Cicero, Melrose Park and other western suburbs. Resides at 1547 S. 61st Ct., Cicero.
RECORD: FBI No. 4617657. CIR No. D-80631. USPTH No. 12025. Record dates back to 1932, more than 10 arrests: robbery, larceny, gambling, loan sharking. Conviction: transporting and concealing stolen goods, 3 years in USPTH; interstate transport of stolen money orders, 5 years, pending appeal.
BUSINESS: Restaurants and cartage service.
MODUS OPERANDI: Active in gambling and loan sharking in western suburbs.

Nicoletti, Charles

AKA: Chuck, Chuckie, Charles Nicoletta.
DESCRIPTION: Born December 3, 1916; 5 feet 10 inches, 180 pounds, brown eyes, dark but graying hair, dark complexion, gold front tooth; Edu: 8th grade; RO: Italian; FH: brother, Carl; stepfather, Paul Tergo, deported following prison term in ISPJ.
FREQUENTS: Caravelle Motel, Blackie's Pizzeria, Italian-American National Union No. 9. Resides at 1638 N. 19th Ave., Melrose Park
RECORD: FBI No. 1426506. CIR No. 1634. USPM No. 10113. Record dates back to 1934, more than 12 arrests: furnishing equipment to handbook operators, conspiracy, gambling, possession of auto rigged as "hit car," murder—questioned in most of the gang

347

killings involving top hoods and politicians in past 30 years (shot and killed his father in 1929 during an assault on subject and mother— ruled justifiable homicide). Convictions: burglary, 1 year probation and $5,000 fine; narcotics, 18 months in USPM.

BUSINESS: Several auto and insurance agencies, taverns, restaurants, variety stores.

MODUS OPERANDI: Gambling boss of Monroe Police District on West Side. A Syndicate enforcer in charge of planning and executing gangland murders; active in narcotics.

Nuccio, Dominick

AKA: (nee Domano Nuccio), Dommic, Dominic Nutcenio, Nutcchio, Mike Carlo, D. Nino, Joe Delano, Libby, Little Libby.

DESCRIPTION: Born April 9, 1895, Chicago; 5 feet 4 inches, 150 pounds, brown eyes, dark but graying hair, ruddy complexion, moles right side of face and nose, poor health; RO: Italian.

FREQUENTS: Walton Club, Loop and Near North Side. Resides at Webster Hotel.

RECORD: CPD No. D-15232. FPC No. 9-R—12/2-a-R. Record dates back to 1917, more than 24 arrests: gambling, attempted burglary, extortion, fugitive, robbery, larceny, tax evasion, carrying concealed weapons, assault with intent to murder, murder. Prime suspect in at least 10 murders. Convictions: vagrancy, 60 days in HO; burglary, guilty, reversed and remanded, stricken.

BUSINESS: Real estate, insurance and nightclubs on Near North Side.

MODUS OPERANDI: Once a member of the notorious Gloriana gang, a terroristic mob operating in the 1920s and composed chiefly of Italians engaged in bootlegging. An old Capone-mob gunman, now a North Side Syndicate boss with extensive gambling interests. Regarded as a high-level mafioso.

Patrick, Leonard

AKA: Lenny, Joseph Cohen, Pete Peonardi, Leonard Levine, Blinkey.

DESCRIPTION: Born March 23, 1913, Chicago; 5 feet 11 inches, 185 pounds, blue eyes, chestnut hair (balding), fair complexion, bad teeth, irregular scar lower left corner of left eye, mole on right jaw; Edu: 7th grade; RO: Jewish; FH: brother, Jack.

FREQUENTS: Black Angus Steak House. Resides at 2820 W. Jarlath Ave.

348

RECORD: FBI No. 635564. CIR No. D-31577. ISPMC No. 16629. Record dates back to 1932, more than 8 arrests: gambling, larceny, murder (held to grand jury without bail, no-bill in 1932), murder (nol-prossed in 1947). Conviction: bank robbery, 10 years in ISPMC.

BUSINESS: Hotels, restaurants, supermarkets, liquor stores, aluminum products, disposal service, vending machines, insurance, industrial uniforms.

MODUS OPERANDI: Syndicate overlord of 24th and 50th wards. A layoff bookmaker with Dave Yaras on national sporting events. Reputedly an expert on gangland executions; police credit him with masterminding some of the Syndicate's more important liquidations.

Pierce, Ralph

AKA: Robert W. Symons, P. R. Symmons.

DESCRIPTION: Born June 12, 1903, Newcomerstown, Ohio; 5 feet 10½ inches, 200 pounds, blue eyes, gray hair, medium complexion; Edu: 8th grade; RO: Jewish.

FREQUENTS: New Michigan Hotel and other hotels along South Shore Drive. Resides at 7743 S. Merrill Ave.

RECORD: FBI No. 768056. CPD No. 33057. Record dates back to 1926, includes arrests for gambling, extortion and prime suspect in several gangland murders. Held for grand jury in rape, no bill; auto theft, acquitted in bench trial; indicted for kidnaping and assault, nol-prossed; multimillion-dollar movie extortion (Browne-Bioff case), acquitted. Conviction: fictitious driver's license, fined $25 and cost, sentence vacated and found not guilty.

BUSINESS: Hotels, construction, restaurants, scavenger services, real estate, taverns, nightclubs, beer coil cleaning service, jukeboxes, vending machines, insurance, oil drilling and substantial investment in Las Vegas casinos.

MODUS OPERANDI: Former adviser to Al Capone, presently associated with Battaglia and Giancana in policy and gambling on South Side. Syndicate overlord of 5th, 6th and 7th wards, which includes Hyde Park, Woodlawn, Grand Crossing and other South Side communities.

Pinelli, Anthony R., Sr.

AKA: Tony or Joe Pinelli, Tony or Joe Legno, Frank Heisler, Mr. Tom, Joe Ferro, Tony Milton.

DESCRIPTION: Born October 28, 1899, Sicily (entered United

States in 1912, naturalized in 1933); 5 feet 5 inches, 180 pounds, brown eyes, black but graying hair (balding), scar left side of chin; RO: Sicilian; FH: sons, Anthony, Jr. (married Louise DeGeorge), Salvatore, married Concetta Amari—daughter of Phil Amari of New Jersey, a top-level mafioso); nephew, Anthony Gruttadauro.

FREQUENTS: Los Angeles, Las Vegas, Chicago. Resides at 481 Sierra Madre Blvd., Sierra Madre, Calif., and 6054 W. School St., Chicago.

RECORD: FBI No. 2678506. LAPD No. C-253957. FPC No. S-25—IIO-15/S-3—IIO-17. Record dates back to 1925. Indicted for income tax evasion. Convictions: bootlegging: 1926, $100 fine; 1927, 6 months in jail; 1930, $500 fine; 1932, 6 months in jail and $100 fine; 1932, $500 fine; 1933, 6 months in jail. Took Fifth 45 times before McClellan Committee. Pleaded guilty to one count of income tax evasion on May 23, 1966—2 years probation and $2,000 fine. Presently fighting deportation.

BUSINESS: Partner with DeGeorge in grape business (North Side Grape Distributors); food, oil products, motels (Movietown Motel), restaurants, vending machines, real estate in California and midwest.

MODUS OPERANDI: A member of the Chicago Syndicate's board of directors, he ruled vice, narcotics and gambling in Lake County, Indiana, in the 1940s, moving his sphere of influence to California in 1953 while maintaining his position in Chicago and Gary, Indiana.

Potenza, Rocco

AKA: Botenza, The Parrot.

DESCRIPTION: Born September 24, 1912; 5 feet 9 inches, 180 pounds, brown eyes, brown hair, dark complexion; sharp, pointed nose and constant flow of profanity earned him nickname "Parrot." RO: Italian; FH: brother, Thomas; son, Robert, placed under one-year court supervision after criminal assault charges were reduced to a misdemeanor.

FREQUENTS: Albion Grill, Retreat Lounge, Riviera Lounge, H & H Restaurant. Resides at 8857 N. Kildare Ave., Skokie.

RECORD: FBI No. 670308. CIR No. D-30737. FPC No. `13-U-IOO/21-R-000. Chicago police record destroyed: arrested numerous times for gambling, suspect in bombings. Conviction: violation of internal revenue, 2 years in federal penitentiary and 2 years probation.

BUSINESS: Taverns, strip-joints, motels and restaurants.

MODUS OPERANDI: Operates card and dice games; Syndicate over-seer in Northwest section of Cook County.

Pranno, Rocco Salvatore

AKA: Jim, Robert, Prano, Parnno, Pionno, Joe Martini, Judge Conway, Rocky, Joe Martell, Rocky Bretell, James Hartell.

DESCRIPTION: Born December 18, 1916, Chicago; 6 feet, 186 pounds, dark hazel eyes, black but graying hair, ruddy complexion; RO: Italian; FH: brother, Albert J; nephews, Anthony and Louis Pranno; cousins, Andrew P. Signorella (former chief of police in Stone Park), Daniel W. Provenzano (chief of police of Northlake, associated with Pranno in recent extortion case but not indicted).

FREQUENTS: Robert's Lounge, Red Lion Inn in Elgin. Resides at 1608 N. 39th Ave., Stone Park now in USPL.

RECORD: FBI No. 785212. CIR No. D-51378. ISPJ No. 1804. ISPP No. 10081. Record dates back to 1934, more than 12 arrests: armed robbery, gambling, threat to do bodily harm, extortion. Murder and bombing suspect; indicted for robbery, nol-prossed. Convictions: burglary and malicious mischief, finding of guilty for malicious mischief, 30 days; armed robbery, 1 year to life in ISPJ; assault and battery, 4 months, pending appeal; extortion and conspiracy in March 1966, 15 years in USPL. Took Fifth before McClellan Committee.

BUSINESS: Strip joints, taverns and vending machines.

MODUS OPERANDI: Syndicate overlord for vice and gambling in Stone Park, Franklin Park, Schiller Park, Melrose Park, Northlake and DuPage county village of Lisle. A wild and vicious hood, quick with threats and baseball bat.

Prio, Ross

AKA: (nee Rosario Fabricini and Rosario Priolo), Ross Brio, Ross Frio, Rossi.

DESCRIPTION: Born May 10, 1900, near Palermo, Sicily (born as Rosario Fabricini and adopted by Priolo family who brought him to U.S. about 1909); 5 feet 4 inches, 200 pounds, brown eyes, brown hair (balding), dark complexion, wears glasses; RO: Sicilian; FH: son, Ross, Jr.

FREQUENTS: Milano's, Valentino's and Mike Fish's restaurants, Berkshire Hotel, Playboy Club, Walton Club. Resides at 6485 Sauganash, Lincolnwood.

351

RECORD: FBI No. CG 92-737. CPD Photo No. 11227. FPC No. 9U-00-12/4-WI. Record dates back to 1929 (previous record destroyed by court order), more than seven arrests: assault with a deadly weapon, malicious mischief and intimidation by arson, bootlegging, murder. Questioned in several bombings, prime suspect in at least 12 murders. Cited for contempt of Congress, took Fifth 90 times before McClellan Committee.

BUSINESS: Subject owns several dairies, a string of parking lots, a half-dozen currency exchanges, finance companies, office buildings, hotels, motels, restaurants, nightclubs, key clubs, vending machines, real estate and realty companies, amusement centers, scavenger service and attendant services for nightclubs and hotels. Investments include oil wells in Southern Illinois, real estate at Lake Geneva and casinos in Las Vegas.

MODUS OPERANDI: Syndicate overlord of North Side and boss of the old multimillion-dollar Cadillac policy game. A political fixer and police corruptor, regarded as one of the most sinister hoodlums in Chicago. Respected and feared by underlings, has a reputation as a torturer and murder expert. Named by Joseph Valachi before McClellan Committee as one of seven "top-power" hoodlums in Chicago. His domain stretches northward from the Chicago River to Skokie, and from the lake to the western limits of the city.

Ricca, Paul

AKA: (nee Felice DeLucia), The Waiter, Paul Maglio, Anthony DeLucia, Paul Viela, Paul Villa, Paul Salvi, Paul Barstow, The Porter, Mops.

DESCRIPTION: Born November 14, 1897, Naples, Italy (entered U.S. in 1920); 5 feet 8 inches, 180 pounds, brown eyes, white hair (balding), ruddy complexion, wears silver-rimmed glasses, has diabetes and hypertension; MS: draft dodger in World War I; RO: Italian; FH: Al Capone and his sister, Mafalda, were witnesses at subject's wedding; son, Paul, Jr.; sister, Amelia (convicted of murder in Italy during a feud which resulted in 14 deaths).

FREQUENTS: North Avenue Steak House, Mike Fish's Restaurant. Resides at 1515 Bonnie Brae, River Forest.

RECORD: FBI No. 832514. CPD No. D-78267. USPA No. 63776. USPL No. 62118. Chicago record dates back to 1927, more than 13 arrests: conspiracy (indicted, nol-prossed), income tax evasion and conspiracy, extortion and postal fraud (indicted, nol-prossed), falsifying application papers for citizenship; questioned in scores of Mafia

352

murders, including 14 during a family feud in Italy. Convictions: murder (as 17-year-old in Italy), served 2 years—upon release from prison, he murdered the witness who had identified him in the murder trial and fled to the U.S.; tried in absentia for the second murder, he received a 22-year sentence. Multimillion-dollar movie extortion (Browne-Bioff) case, 10 years in USPA, later transferred to USPL and paroled within 3 years, an event which created a national scandal and led to a Congressional investigation—conclusion was that the Syndicate's influence had reached all the way to the Justice Department and White House. Income tax evasion and conspiracy to make false statement, 9 years and $15,000 fine, U.S. Court of Appeals reduced sentence to 3 years in USPTH and $5,000 fine with acquittal of conspiracy charge. Denaturalized and fined $500 for contempt of court, contempt charge later reversed; deportation first ordered in January 1959, freed on $20,000 bond pending appeal, still in U.S. in 1967. Took Fifth before Kefauver Committee and 47 times before McClellan Committee.

BUSINESS: Parking lots and real estate.

MODUS OPERANDI: An extortionist and labor racketeer, serves as an elder statesman of the Chicago Syndicate and as a member of the board of directors.

Salvatore, Rocco

AKA: Salvatore Rocco, Joseph Rocco.

DESCRIPTION: Born March 22, 1911.

FREQUENTS: West and Northwest suburbs. Resides at 1114 N. Ridgeland Ave., Oak Park.

RECORD: No criminal identification number. Record dates back to 1939: investigation for gambling and a prime suspect in at least 3 murders. Took Fifth 6 times before McClellan Committee.

BUSINESS: Jukeboxes, vending machines, real estate.

MODUS OPERANDI: Chauffeur for Sam Battaglia. Active in North Side suburban gambling. Trains race horses at Battaglia's farm.

Torello, James Vincent

AKA: Torrello, Turk.

DESCRIPTION: Born December 15, 1930, Chicago; 5 feet 7½ inches, 210 pounds, blue eyes, black hair, fair complexion; RO: Italian.

FREQUENTS: West Side suburbs. Resides at 1836 S. 60th Court, Cicero.

353

RECORD: FBI No. 4450441. CPD No. 3238. USPA No. 74036A. USPL No. 70736. FPC No. 25-I-M-14/27-I. Record dates back to 1945, more than 14 arrests: possession of burglary tools, robbery, burglary, auto theft; indicted for armed robbery, nol-prossed; robbery (2 counts), not guilty. Conviction: violation of firearms act, 2 years in USPA.

MODUS OPERANDI: Active in loan sharking on West Side and a Syndicate assassin.

Vogel, Edward

AKA: Big Head, Dutch, Five-by-Five, Eddie Brown, Guy Cahn, E. David, Eddie Miller, George A. Renn, George Crane, George Walters, Edward Wartenberg.

DESCRIPTION: Born July 16, 1895, Chicago; 5 feet 6½ inches, 180 pounds; Edu: 8th grade; RO: Bohemian.

FREQUENTS: Postl's Health Club, Playboy Club, Armory Lounge. Resides at 7730 N. Milwaukee Ave., Niles.

RECORD: FBI No. 4329702. CIR No. D-33254. Record dates to 1926, more than 7 arrests. Took Fifth 39 times before McClellan Committee.

BUSINESS: All manners and forms of coin-operated machines.

MODUS OPERANDI: A power in Cicero in days of Al Capone; one of gangsters who engineered the Syndicate's take-over of Cicero in 1924. Considered slot-machine czar of Cook County for the past 40 years.

Yaras, David

AKA: David Miller, Yarras, Yaris.

DESCRIPTION: Born November 7, 1912, Chicago; 5 feet 9 inches, 175 pounds, blue eyes, brown hair, sallow complexion; RO: Polish.

FREQUENTS: West Side and Miami, Fla. Resides at 3600 N. Lake Shore Drive.

RECORD: FBI No. 655697. CPD No. D-14360. Record dates back to 1930, more than 14 arrests: burglary, robbery, possession of burglary tools and a prime suspect in several gangland slayings. Indicted with William Block and Leonard Patrick for the 1947 murder of James Ragen, nol-prossed.

BUSINESS: Industrial uniforms, bath houses, jukeboxes.

MODUS OPERANDI: A West Side gambling boss; layoff bookmaker with Patrick on national sporting events; active in juice.

INDEX

A. C. Kirkwood & Associates, 208
A-1 Industrial Uniforms, 329
AMI Music Company, 40
Abata, Dominic, 37, 40
Accardo, Anthony Joseph: as Mafia chief, 3, 7; convicted of tax evasion, 5, 266; names Giancana successor, 8; not called by grand jury, 12-13; assigns "contract" of Big Jim Martin, 175; ordered out of Los Angeles, 200-1; biographical sketch, 322-23; mentioned, 6, 25, 27, 30, 31, 35, 38, 51, 58, 61, 62, 81, 88, 110, 131, 139, 143, 151, 172, 176, 177, 178, 189, 207, 260, 283, 301, 309
Accardo, John, 35
Accardo, Ross, 81
Accurate Laboratories, 269
Ackerman, Frederick P., 50-54
Acme Products Company, 115
Acorn Club, 332
Adamowski, Benjamin S., 193, 194, 238, 239, 296, 297
Adduci, James, 173-74, 181, 182
Adduci, Joseph, 33, 181, 182
Adesko, Thaddeus V., 193, 194
Adonis, Joey, 223
Airliner Lounge, 341
Aiuppa, Joseph John: conversation (taped), 276-82; biographical sketch, 323; mentioned, 19, 25, 29, 53, 151, 224, 268
Aiuppa, Sam, 35
Albion Grill, 350
Alderisio, Felix Anthony: "king of scams," 77-78; biographical sketch, 323-24; mentioned, 19, 41, 60-61, 64, 68, 76, 83, 87, 260
Alex, Gus: meetings with John d'Arco, 152; and police agent, 250; biographical sketch, 324-25; mentioned, 7, 22, 38, 43, 65, 87, 122, 138, 142, 252, 261, 262
Allegretti, James: and terrorist sales tactics, 83-84; and payoff racket, 252; biographical sketch, 325-26; mentioned, 87, 89, 240, 248, 251, 307, 312, 314
Allerton Hotel, 84
Allman, James P., 117
Aloisio, William, 5, 326
Alpine Construction Co., 329
Amato, Joe, 253
American Continental Insurance Company, 30
American Legion Post 1056, 340
American National Bank and Trust Company, 231
Ammirati, George, 297-98
Anco, Inc., 141, 153
Angelatos, Angelo, 274
Angeleri, Vincent, 40
Annenberg, Max, 110
Annixter, Julius, 124
Annunzio, Frank, 12, 139, 140-42, 148, 150-51
Ansoni, Robert J., 25, 253
Anthony Pontarelli & Sons, 212
Anticrime legislation, 188, 190
Apalachin Convention, 10
Apex Cigarette Service, 138
Apex Waste Company, 82
Apostol, James, 254
Arger, Louis, 43
Arlington racetrack, 335, 343
Armory Lounge, 322, 327, 329, 330, 332, 334, 338, 339, 340, 341, 354
Armour, Philip, 3
Arnold, Joseph, 122, 326
Arrington, Broadway, 307
Arrowhead Ranches, Inc., 226
Arson, 29
Arvey, Jacob M. (Jake): becomes alderman, 104; attorney for Moe Rosenberg, 105-7; sponsor of Elrod, 115; and Cermak election, 116; and Capone Bloc, 117; friend of "Jake the Barber" Factor, 122, 123; joins Illinois National Guard, 124; dumps Kelly for Kennelly, 125-26; as national kingmaker, 126-27, 133-35; on racketeering, 130; backs Lenny Patrick, 169; and Greenberg enterprises, 224; and Henry Crown, 225-26, 230; mentioned, 41, 42, 184, 222, 223, 245, 251, 296, 316
Associates Discount Company, 81
Astor, Vincent, 120
Athens Restaurant and Lounge, 330, 342

Atlantic Hotel, 84
Attendant Service Corporation, 89
Austin, Richard B., 9, 193
Automatic Music Instrument Company, 40
Automatic Phonograph Distributing Company, 40

B & B Novelty Company, 285-86
B-girls, 96
Babb, John E., 133
Bacino, Philip, 3, 327
Bacon, Vinton W., 208-12, 222
Baker, Bobby, 227
Bankhart, Basil, 132
Bankruptcy racket, 77-84
Barbarians in Our Midst, 46
Barker, George, 117
Barkowski, John, 33
Baron, Charles, 230
Barvitz, Frank, 16
Barzini, Luigi, 4
Bas, Marvin, 130
Battaglia, Florence, 81
Battaglia, Sam, 5, 11, 68, 69, 73, 83, 326-27
Bazelon, David L., 222-23, 225
Bauler, Mathias "Paddy," 135, 186-87, 243, 247, 312
Beasley, Clara, 121
Beck, Howard J., 13
Becker, Morris, 18
Bee-Gee Builders, 58
Beeftink, Peter, 238, 239
Bell Oil Company, 218
Bembenster, Edward, 81
Ben's Place, 304
Bergbreiter, Jacob, 276-80
Berger, Ralph, 90-91
Bergstrom, Burton M., 298
Berk, Robert, 78
Berkshire Hotel, 240, 325, 326, 337, 344, 345, 351
Bernstein, Eugene, 309
Berrell, Patrick, 19
Bertsche, Christian, 138
Best Sanitation and Deodorizing Company, 39
Best Sanitation and Supply Company, 42
Betar, Sam, 161
Better Business Bureau, 260
Better Government Association, 151, 176, 212, 260
Bickley, John H., 271
Bieber, George, 131, 283, 284, 285, 288, 289, 294, 295, 310
Bieszczat, Mathew W., 181-82, 316
Big Nine, 242-46
Big Top Restaurant, 338, 343
Bilek, Arthur, 266
Bioff, Willie, 5, 6, 34, 173, 202, 219, 316
Biondioti, Bert, 285-86
Bishop ranch, 226
Bismarck Hotel, 251
Bittman, William O., 311
Black, Hugo, 228
Black Angus Steak House, 347
Black Hand, 131-32
Blackie's Pizzeria, 347
Blackstone Hotel, 84, 213
Blair, Sam, 155-56
Blakely, James, 26, 27
Blakey, G. Robert, 319
Blasi, Dominic, 14, 162, 327-28
Bliss, George, 207-8, 213
Block, William, 122, 130
Bloom, Ike, 97
Blue Moon Cocktail Lounge, 326, 332, 346
Board of Election Commissioners, 194, 195, 196, 198-99
Bohemian Brewing Co., 340
Bolton, John, 173
Bombings, 29
Bonanno, Joseph, 9-10
Booth, Harry, 213-16 passim, 231-32
Bourne, Nancy, 68
Bowe, Augustine, 301
Bowler, James P., 100

357

"Boyd, Mr.," 56
Boyle, John S., 129, 130, 131, 318
Brancata, Dominick, 130-31, 328
Bravos, George, 58, 59, 76, 222
Bravos, Nick, 222, 328-29
Brazier, Arthur M., 171
Bredican, James P., 276, 278
Brennan, George, 105, 111, 116, 184, 315-16
Briatta, Joe, 157
Brill, Joseph E., 91
Brinn, Allan, 235-39 passim
Broadway Sheet Metal Works, Inc., 38
Brodkin, Michael, 131, 283, 284, 310
Brotherhood of Evil, 13
Brown, Lou, 78
Brown, Pat, 223
Browne, George, 5, 6, 23, 34, 219
Bruno, Sam, 33
Bruscato, Frank, 81
Buccieri, Carmen, 81
Buccieri, Fiore, 5, 53, 55, 60, 61, 62, 64, 69, 76, 87, 254
Buccieri, Frank, 55, 56, 87, 240, 269, 329-30
Buchalter, Louis "Lepke," 22
Building Service Employees International Union, 23, 43
Building Trades Council, 218
Bulger, Joseph I., 141
Buonaguidi, Lawrence, 84, 330
Bureau of Field Services, 255
Burlin, Benn, 243
Burns, Henrietta, 304
Burns, Patrick, 304
Burns International Detective Agency, 275
Burton, Richard, 149
Busch, Harry, 288
Butler, Paul, 225
Butzler, Robert, 243

C & B Meat Company, 83
C. & O. Restaurant, 183
CIO Political Action Committee, 139
Cafe Continental, 310, 314
Caifano, John Michael (Marshall), 5, 7, 64, 83, 189, 260, 330-31
Caifano, Leonard, 7, 189
Cain, Richard B., 12, 255, 268-75 passim
Cal-Neva Lodge, 11, 71
Cale, Frank, 187-88
Calewood Barber Shop, 326
Calihan, Edward J., 309
Callaghan, George F., 293, 309
Calumet Harbor Service Company, 41
Campagna, Louis, 23, 24, 34, 38, 39, 119, 124, 218, 219
Campagna, Ralph, 287
Campbell, William J., 13-14, 160-62, 164, 206, 209, 210
Canadian Ace Brewing Company, 224
Candystick Lounge, 248
Capezio, Tony, 25, 38, 39
Capone, Al, mentioned passim
Capone, Ermino John, 153, 331
Capone, Ralph, 78
Capone Bloc, 117, 136, 139. See also West Side Bloc
Cappelletti, Peter, 52
Capri Restaurant, 23, 24
Caravelle Motel, 270, 271, 272, 347
Caravello, Sandor, 58-59
Carbone, Mathew, 78
Carpentier, Charles F., 193
Carr, John, 276, 277, 280
Carr, Patrick, 307
Carrozzo, Mike, 23, 217-18, 219
Carter, Byron, 203, 204, 205
Cartwright, Howard, 85
Caruso, Frank, 5, 68, 331-32
Caruso Plumbing, 332
Casa Madrid, 327, 335
Castro, Fidel, 216
Celler, Emanuel, 149, 150
Central Casualty Insurance Company, 80
Central Envelope & Lithographic Co., 341
Central Police District, 250

Century Enterprises, 332
Century Music Company, 138
Cermak, Anton J.: as Insull "investor," 103; and Moe Rosenberg, 105, 106-7; as mayor, 116-17; assassination of, 118-21; and South Side policy racket, 171; and Henry Crown, 217, 221; mentioned, 3, 187, 219, 220, 316
Cerone, Frank, 64, 332
Cerone, John Philip, Sr., 41, 60-64 passim, 175, 310, 312, 314, 332-33
Cerone, Pat, 310
Cesario, Sam, 68
Chaconas, John, 53, 268, 270, 272-74
Champagne, Anthony V., 7, 14, 27-28, 141
Checker Taxi Company, 33, 37, 39, 40
Checkroom Attendants Union, 26
Chesrow, Eugene J., 200-12 passim
Chesrow, Frank W., 154, 158, 200, 212, 230, 296
Chez Paree, 48, 100, 125
Chiagouris, Albert, 58-59
Chiagouris, George, 58-59
Chiagouris, Jack, 58-59
Chicago American, 10, 12, 29, 49, 71, 77, 104, 115, 123, 154, 165-66, 172, 192, 202-3, 209, 291, 299, 317, 319, 321
Chicago Bar Association, 106, 151, 318, 319
Chicago Crime Commission, 26, 46, 53, 118, 128, 129, 140, 143, 184, 259, 268-69, 299, 321, 322
Chicago Daily News, 11, 12, 29, 43, 69, 76, 85, 98, 109, 112, 136, 144, 157, 172, 174, 179, 183, 187, 188, 192, 198, 201, 206, 210, 211, 217, 226, 231, 281, 321
Chicago Discount Center, 80
Chicago Federation of Labor and Industrial Union Council, 30
Chicago Guarantee, 72, 73
Chicago Heights Distributing Company, 88
Chicago Herald-Examiner, 20, 111-12
Chicago High School for Home Study, 80, 82
Chicago Park District, 42, 43
Chicago Recount Committee, 194
Chicago Restaurant Association, 23, 26, 28
Chicago Street Cleaning Union, 23
Chicago Sun, 141
Chicago Sun-Times, 56, 129, 222, 225, 243, 244, 245, 274, 321
Chicago Tribune, 106, 107, 108-12, 125, 127, 128, 156, 175, 181-82, 189, 194, 200, 207, 224, 230, 239-40, 265, 274, 321
Chicago Wilmington & Franklin Coal Company, 221
Chicken feathers, 37
Cicero, 266-68, 277, 278, 354, and passim
Cigarette tax stamp scandal, 72, 153
Circella, Nick, 34
Circus Cafe, 25
Citizen's Traction Committee, 106
City Council Emergency Crime Committee, 242
City National Bank of Beverly Hills, 224
City Savings Association, 72, 73
Civa, Alfred, 195
Civella, Nick, 151
Civic Federation, 260
Civil Service Commission, 258
Civil Service Protective Association, 144
Clark, Tom C., 14
Clark, William G., 41
Clay, John D., 19
Cleary Transport Company, 27
Clementi, Louis, 19
Clements, Allen J., 238, 239
"Clout," 12
Cohan, Irving, 294
Cohen, Irving N., 269
Cohen, Nathan M., 306, 309
Coli, Eco James, 64, 333
Collins, Robert, 161
Colony House, 347
Colosimo, Big Jim, 97, 100, 107, 137, 218, 315
Combined Industries, Inc., 80
Comforte, Victor, 69
Commercial Phonograph Survey, 40
Commonwealth Edison Company, 103, 106, 221
Commonwealth Hotel, 328, 337
Congress Arcade Bowling Alley, 326

358

Congress Hotel, 84, 119
Conlisk, James B., Jr., 255, 264 n
Connors, John, 183
Connors, William J. "Botchie," 183-85, 187, 240, 244
Conrad Hilton Hotel, 157, 331, 336, 340
Consumers Company, 220, 221, 225
Conti, Elmer, 148
Continental Press, 130
Continental West supper club, 167
Cook County Democratic Central Committee, 124, 134, 160, 181
Cook County Jail, 14-17
Cook County Licensed Beverage Dealers Association, 27
Cook County Trust Company, 106
Cooney, Dennis "Duke," 138, 315
Cooperative Music Co., 346
Cope, Amoth C., 174
Cordovano, Joseph, 68
Corngold, Joseph, 122
Corydon Travel, Inc., 79-80
Costello, Charles, 88
Costello, Frank, 88, 125, 223
Costello, Joseph, 19-20, 88
Costello, Josephine, 88
Cota, Joe, 230
Coughlin, John, 97, 98, 99, 100, 136-37
Courtesy Storm Window Co., 339
Courtney, Thomas J., 128, 129
Covelli, Daniel A., 308
Covelli, Gerald, 310, 311, 312-14
Covelli, Jeannie, 313
Crager, Clarence, 205
Crane, George, 281
Crib Diaper Service, 39
Crime in America, 93
Crime Without Punishment, 28
Crispino, Charles C., 177-79
Cronin, Robert, 204-5
Crowe, Dorsey R., 100, 184
Crowe, Robert E., 101
Crowley, James, 24, 25
Crowley, Wilbert F., 8
Crown, Henry, 214-22
Crown, Irving, 216
Crown, Sol, 216, 217, 228, 229
Cullerton, John, 89
Cullerton, Maurice T., 203
Cullerton, P. J., 203
Cunningham, Tom, 176
Curley, Robert, 236
Curran, Thomas J., 155
Curtis, Carl T., 227
Cutter, Oscar, 129

Daddano, William, Sr., 4, 5, 51, 64, 89, 178, 253, 300, 333-34
Dahl, Walter P., 274, 282
Dailey, John, 217
Daley, Richard J.: and "Daley Decade," 135-36; malapropisms of, 144; on Libonati, 148; and John D'Arco, 153; on Anthony DeTolve, 156; ultimatum to Mike FioRito, 158; on D'Arco and Marcy, 160, 163-64; on Edward Hanrahan, 162; on murder of Ben Lewis, 170; controls Illinois, 190; on election scandal, 194, 197; on Vinton W. Bacon, 208, 211; and police scandals, 239, 241, 251, 253-54, 255-56, 258; on Captain Gibbons, 246; and demonstrators, 299; mentioned, 16, 28, 30, 50, 175, 182, 184, 185, 188, 198, 206, 296, 311, 316, 317
Daly, Maggie, 77, 91-92
Damone, Vic, 56-57
Danaher, Matt, 181, 316
D'Andrea, Anthony, 218
D'Angelo, James, 244
Dann, Louis, 125
D'Arco, John, 12, 62-63, 139, 140, 141, 142, 151-65 passim, 185, 239, 251-52, 296
Darwyn, Jane, 167-68
Davis, Irwin, 78
Dawson, William L., 170-73
DeGeorge, James, 3, 38, 147, 334-35
DeGrazia, Rocco, 68, 71, 335
DeGrazio, Anthony J., 13

Dearborn Insurance Agency, 37, 38
Death Corner, 60
DeBiase, John, 68, 286, 334
Decker, Bernard M., 294
Del Prado Hotel, 21, 22
Democratic National Committee, 171, 225
Democratic National Convention, 125
Democratic Party, 105, 197, 198, 231, 271, and passim. See also Cook County Democratic Central Committee
Democratic Union Organizing Committee, Local 777, Seafarers International Union, AFL-CIO, 40
Demore, August, 143
Dempsey, John T., 229
Deneen, Charles S., 114
Dentlemen, Pete, 180
Depietto, Americo, 51, 53-54, 64, 68, 335-36
Desert Inn, 226
Despress, Leon, 136
De Stefano, Frank, 72, 74
DeStefano, Mario, 52, 54-55, 167-68
DeStefano, Michael, 54
De Stefano, Rocco Nicholas, 65, 69-76 passim, 336
DeStefano, Sam, 5, 16, 51-53, 68, 76, 167-68, 299-307, 336-37
De Stefano, Vito, 72, 74
DeTolve, Anthony, 148, 154-67, 189-90
Deutsch, Sidney, 169
Dever, Mayor, 179, 183
DeVriendt, Donald L., 280
Dewey, Thomas E., 126
DiBella, Dominick, 30-31, 337
DiCaro, Charles, 68
DiCaro, Joseph, 68
Dienhart, John, 121
Dieringer, Henry W., 289
Dietz, Walter, 284
Dimitri's Restaurant, 29
Dirksen, Everett M., 134
Ditlove, Meyer, 41
Divane Brothers Electric Company, 209
DiVarco, Joseph Vincent, 5, 65, 83, 87, 89, 240, 248, 311, 312, 313, 337-38
Dixon, Alan J., 57
Doherty, Dom, 194-95
Dolendi, Frank, 35
Don Marcie, Inc., 39
Donnelly, James, 268, 272, 274
Donovan, Edward, 27, 42
Douglas, Helen Gahagen, 224
Douglas, Paul H., 126-27, 130, 134-35, 196
Dowdle Brothers, 116
Doyle, Edward, 280
Dragin, Milan, 81
Drake Hotel, 125, 213
Drucker, Joseph, 308
Druggan, Terry, 100
Drugs. See Narcotics trade
Drury, William, 130
Duffy, William J., 58, 68
Dundas, William, 203, 206
Dunne, George W., 175, 185
Dunne, Robert Jerome, 25
Durham, Frank, 194
Durso, Thomas N., 51, 65, 68, 182
Dust and Tex Cleaning Company, 39

E & J Construction, 207
Echeles, Julius Lucius, 297, 305, 306-7, 308
Edelstein, Ben, 97
Edgewater Beach Hotel, 65
Edison, Thomas, 103
Edmier, Larry, 75
Edmier Inc., 75, 76
Egan, Edward, 45
Eisenhower, Dwight D., 126, 135
Eldorado, Anthony, 269
Election scandals, 11, 193-96
Eller, Emanuel, 114
Eller, Morris, 108, 114, 139
Elrod, Arthur X., 115, 124, 125, 169, 224, 316
Embalmers Union, 329
Emery, Big Jim, 88, 297
Emery, Ralph, 88

Empire Press, 47
Empire State Building, 216, 226
Engert, Joseph G., 224
English, Charles Carmen: and county furniture purchase, 166; gambling and jukebox operations, 166-67; biographical sketch, 338; mentioned, 28, 40, 51, 63, 87, 168, 178, 222, 252
English, Sam, 27, 166, 167-68, 222, 252
Enright, Mossy, 34
Epstein, Julie, 252
Epstein, Martin C., 90, 91
Epstein, Samuel B., 224
Erie-Buffalo, 45
Eros Lounge, 325, 326, 330, 340
Erwin, Alice, 59
Esposito, Anthony, 151
Esposito, Diamond Joe, 114
Esposito, Frank, 60-63, 141, 181
Essanay Electric Manufacturing Company, 35
Ettelson, Samuel H., 108, 109, 115
Eulo, Frank, 165
Euzzino, Andrew A., 189, 343
Evans, Fred, 23, 24, 39, 82, 223
Everleigh Club, 95-96
Exchange National Bank, 76
Extortion, 20, 78, *passim*

FBI. *See* Federal Bureau of Investigation
F. L. Bail Bond Co., 345
Factor, Jerome, 124
Factor, John "Jake the Barber," 122-24, 132
Faraci, Frank, 235, 236, 238, 239
Farris, Harry, 205
Federal Bureau of Investigation: charged with harassment by Giancana, 8-9, 149; first time ordered to investigate gangland slaying, 31-32; and Esposito plot, 60-63; and Manny Skar, 70, 72; and John D'Arco, 152, 154; mentioned, 4, 11, 12, 13, 14, 47, 155, 161, 162, 168, 204, 260, 281, 290, 291, 310, 311, 322-54 *passim*
Federal Communications Commission Act, 13
Federal Narcotics Bureau, 70
Federal Savings and Loan Insurance Corporation (FSLIC), 72
Feighan, Michael, 149
Feldman, Benjamin, 78
Ferlic, Frank, 298-99
Ferraro, Frank, 152, 200-1, 250
Ferri, Nicholas, 178
Fiesta Warehouse Center, 80
5th Jack Club, 166, 252, 338
Figel, Harry, 269
Finklestein, Henry, 117, 118
Fiorenzo, Leonard, 65-68
FioRito, Mike, 157-58
Firotta, Tom, 19
First Guarantee, 72, 73
First National Bank, 221
First National Life Insurance Company of America, 123
Fischetti, Charles, 20, 130, 131, 132-33
Fischetti, Rocco, 187, 296
Fisher, Harry, 113, 114
Fisher, Louis I., 114
Fish Handlers Union, 36
Fitchie, Robert G., 17-18, 21
Fitzmorris, Charles C., 101
Flame, 310
Flying Carpet Motor Inn, 59
Fontainebleau Hotel, 336, 341
Foreclosure cases, 107
Foreman, Leo S., 299, 301
Foreman-State Bank, 220-21
"42 Gang," 5, 6, 139
Foster, Frank, 112, 113, 114
Four Deuces, 100-1
Frabotta, Albert, 5, 65, 83, 338-39
Frabotta, Mrs. Albert, 81
Franchina, Dorothy, 55-56
Franklin Hotel, 222
Frantzius, Peter von, 113
Franze, Tony, 88
Franzone, Leonard, 81
Fratto, Frank, 41, 339-40

Fratto, Rudolph, 41
Freedman, Larry, 78
Freeman, William O., 114
Freeman Coal Mining Corporation, 221
Fresh Meadows Country Club, 338, 341
Fritzel, Mike, 48, 100
Fritzel's restaurant, 48, 100, 322
Frontier Finance Corporation, 269
Fullerton Metals Company, 83
Fulton Street Market, 38, 218
Fusco, Joseph Charles, 23, 87, 89, 224, 340
Fusco, Peter, 139

Gagliano, Joseph, 40, 58, 65, 68, 340-41
Galiano, Dominic, 81, 97
Gallagher, John J., 254
Gallagher, Thomas, 100
Galvin, Mike, 174
Gambling, *passim*
Garden City Engineering Company, 203, 207, 209, 210
Garden City Sand Company, 219
Gargano, Michael, 65-68
Garippo, Louis B., 205
Garrison, William, 174
Garrity, John J., 127
Garrity, Vincent D., 201-2, 207
Garydon, Charles E., 114-15
Gaylur Mercantile Corporation, 83
Gehrke, Lee, 300
General Dynamics Corporation, 226-27, 230
General Electric Company, 103
General High School for Home Study, 82
General News Bureau, 99
Genis, Samuel, 223-24
Genovese, Vito, 80
Giancana, Bonita Lucille, 145
Giancana, Charles, 271
Giancana, Sam: as Syndicate chief, 4-17; protests FBI surveillance, 8-9, 149; control of politicians, 148, 181, 202, 252-53, 266; and John D'Arco, 151-52, 154; freed from jail, 160, 161, 162, 164; ordered from Los Angeles, 200-1; biographical sketch, 341-42; mentioned, 27, 28, 38, 62, 68, 71, 87, 139, 142, 145, 155, 166, 176, 189, 250, 251, 270-71, 272, 274 n., 283, 305, 309
Gianola, Leonard, 5, 19, 68, 165, 342
Gibbons, Redmond P., 242-47, 256
Gigante, Pat A., 35
Gilbert, Allan T., 106
Gilbert, Dan, 25, 127-34, 245
Gill, Joe, 134
Gioe, Charles, 35, 39, 202
Gior, Anthony, 35
Girard, Charles, 172
Girolami, Anthony C., 148, 176
Glas, John, 70
Glazer, Ben, 125
Gleck, Herman, 169
Glimco, Joseph Paul: as labor czar, 36-43; has arrest records destroyed, 189; biographical sketch, 342-43; mentioned, 7, 33, 71, 75, 96, 166, 178, 218, 223, 316
Glitta, Mike, 258-59
Goddard, Calvin, 113
Gold, Bill, 240, 243, 244
Goldberg, Benny, 240
Gordon, Maurice, 20
Gorham, Sidney S., 106
Gorman, Richard E., 14, 309-10, 311
Gottlieb, Jake, 230
Gottlieb and Schwartz, 222
Gould, Benjamin Z., 214
Graf, Harold, 287-88
Gramaldi, Charles, 304
Grana, Gregory, 31
Granady, Octavius, 108
Granata, Peter, 139, 148, 174, 185, 189, 202
Granata, Ursula, 185
Granata, William John, 173-74, 185
Grande Cheese Company, 244-45
Graver, Clem, 174-75
"Gray Ghost," 34

360

Graziano, Rocky, 88
Green, Dwight H., 174
Green, Joseph, 310
Greenberg, Alex Louis, 223, 224
Greenblatt, Ray H., 195
Greenlease, Robert, 19, 20
Greico, Julius, 240
Greiver, Bessie, 228-30
Greiver, Simon, 228, 229
Grid-L-Rich, 245
Grieco, Donald, 55-56
Grieco, Joseph, 55-56, 57
Griffin, John, 100
Groark, Patrick J., Jr., 237, 238, 239
Gross, Charles, 180, 182
Guilfoyle, Marty, 180
Gus' Steak House, 165
Gutgsell, Ralph J., 28
Gutknecht, John, 216-17, 244, 245
Guzik, Jake, 7, 23, 38, 122, 128, 130, 131, 132, 138, 139, 172, 207, 283, 325
Gym Smoke Shop, 129

H & H Restaurant, 350
Haffa, Titus, 33, 117, 118
Halas, George, 230
Halley, Rudolph, 133, 309
Hanley, William, 36
Hanrahan, Edward V., 47, 160-64
Hansen Paper and Storage Company, 80
Harmon, Frank E., 126
Harmon Electric Company, 209
Harrington, Cornelius J., 73, 197, 231-32
Harris, George J., 78, 81, 82
Harrison, Carter H., Jr., 97-98, 99, 100
Hart, Alfred, 224
Hartman, Morton Don, 78
Harvey's Furniture Company, 80
Healey, Edward F., 280
Hefner, Hugh, 88, 89, 90
Helwig, Bruce, 82
Heneghan, William, 289
Hershey, Harry, 307
Hett, Thomas, 212
Hewitt, Oscar, 220
Hilger, George, 166
Hilliard, Raymond, 82
Hilton, Conrad N., 227
Hilton Carpet Company, 80
Hilton Hotels Corporation, 227
Hochstein, Harry, 158, 172, 175
Hodcarriers' and Common Laborers' Union, 218
Hodes, Barnet, 245
Hodge, Orville E., 72-73, 144
Hoellen, John J., 158
Hoffa, James R., 19, 33, 38, 40, 149, 150
Hoffman, Julius J., 227-28
Hogan, Frank, 89, 90
Holman, Claude, 136
Holy Name Cathedral, 140
Holzer, Reginald, 197-98
Holzman, Sidney, 196, 198-99
Hoover, Herbert, 120
Hoover, J. Edgar, 9, 31, 155, 306
Hopkins, Robert, 254
Horan, Al J., 125
Horner, Henry, 117, 171
Horvath's Lounge, 346
Hotel and Restaurant Employees and Bartenders International Union, 89
Howard-Matz Brick Company, 219
Hoy, Patrick H., 230-31
Hoyt, George, 79
Huarisa, John B., 231
Hudson, Charles, 311-12, 313
Humphreys, Murray: and kidnaping and terrorism, 17-22; deal with Factor, 123-24; and Congressmen Libonati and O'Brien, 145-47; and corrupt policemen, 250-52; mentioned, 7, 12, 24, 26, 38, 39, 122, 139, 142, 143, 152, 158, 185, 187, 207, 223, 283, 296
Hunt, Dorothy, 205
Huston, Ronald E., 211, 212

I.A.T.S.E., 34
IID. See Internal Investigation Division
IRS. See Internal Revenue Service
Idlewild Country Club, 88
Igoe, Michael L.: dismisses indictment against Glimco et al., 43; as Insull "investor," 103; nol-prosses Dowdle Brothers indictment, 116; reduces Saporitos' bonds, 310; character witness for Richard E. Gorman, 313; public record, 314-16; grants citizenship to Glimco, 343; mentioned, 100, 221, 230, 231, 308, 343
Illinois Crime Commission, 47, 190
Illinois Crime Investigating Commission, 15, 16, 50, 57, 59, 83, 191, 254, 267
Illinois Election Laws Commission, 194
Illinois Liquor Control Commission, 85
Illinois Retail Merchants Association, 57
Inciso, Angelo, 30-31, 33
Industrial Garment Service, Inc., 39
Infant Diaper Service, 39
Infelice, Ernest Rocco, 19, 51, 53-54, 65, 343
Inserro, Vincent Joseph, 45, 60, 65, 68, 343-44
Insull, Samuel, 3, 101-6, 196
Intelligence Division, 259-61
Interest rates, 57-58
Internal Investigation Division, 259, 260, 269
Internal Revenue Service, 5, 18, 21, 44-45, 47, 70, 80, 101, 123-24, 177, 309, 315, 318
International Alliance of Theatrical Stage Employees and Motion Picture Operators, 23
International Brotherhood of Teamsters, 19, 86, 147. See also Locals
Isaacs, Theodore J., 202
Italian-American National Union, 336, 347
Italian Welfare Council, 141
The Italians, 4

J and J Picnic Grove, 252
Jackson, William, 52, 60-61, 158-59
Jacobson, Benjamin "Buddy," 12, 139-40, 141, 142, 151, 152, 161, 162
Jacobson, Joey, 48
Jalas, Clarence A., 35
James, Eugene C., 310
Jazz, Ltd., 85, 89
Jedynak, Walter, 285
Jefferson, Dorothy, 195
Jefferson Garden Builders, Inc., 72
Jenner, Albert E., 229
Jimmy Green's Tavern, 65-66
Jim's Place, 342
Jinkinson, Earl A., 205, 206, 209, 210
Johnson, Jack, 15, 16, 17
Johnson, Lyndon B., 144, 319
John's Pizza, 327
Joint Civic Committee on Elections, 194
Jones, Roy B., 6, 7
Joyce, Edward, 207
"Juice," 16, 50-60, 78, 159
Justice Department. See U.S. Justice Department
Justin, Jerry F., 267

Kaczminski, Theodore, 75-76
Kahn, Nathan, 229
Kai Kai restaurant, 332
Karns, John Marshall, 193-94, 297
Karnuth, Elmer H., 33
Karras, Alex, 235, 237, 238, 239
Karras, Sol, 238, 239
Katz, Phil, 158, 172, 271
Katz, Stewart, 271
Katzenbach, Nicholas B., 10, 233
Kaufman, Jacob D., 34
Keane, Thomas E., 28, 135, 179-82, 316
Keenan, Frank, 146
Kefauver, Estes, 93, 130, 134
Kefauver Committee, 75, 130, 140, 144, 156, 173, 192, 207, 242, 308, 309, 321-53 passim
Kells, George D., 175-76
Kelly, Edward, 122, 124, 125-26, 134, 138, 171, 184, 187, 200
Kelly, John J., 127
Kenna, Michael "Hinky Dink," 97, 98, 99, 100, 117, 137, 138

Kennedy, John F., 1, 169, 172, 193, 201-2
Kennedy, Robert F.: orders Chicago FBI chief not to testify on surveillance methods, 9; and Louis Romano, 28; gives first order to FBI to investigate a Chicago gangland murder, 31; gives alleged Libonati ultimatum to Mayor Daley, 147-48; mentioned, 150, 154, 158, 161, 248
Kennedy, Rose, 44, 45
Kennelly, Martin H., 126, 130, 135, 176, 184, 242, 245
Kerner, Otto, 172-73, 190, 202
Khrushchev, Nikita, 216
Kilgallen, Dorothy, 12
Kilpatrick, John A., 30-32
Kingsbury Iron and Metal Company, 33
Kinky, 4
Kirkland, Ellis, Hodson, Chaffety & Masters, 106-7
Kizas, Louis W., 317-19
Klarkowski, Stanley, 225
Klein, S. Harvey, 82
Klingbiel, Ray I., 308
Klinkhamer, James, 301
Kluczynski, Thomas E., 228
Kofkin, Oscar, 39
Kohn, Aaron, 245
Kokonas, Nick, 53
Kola's Klub, 48-49
Koniecki, Edward, 289
Konovsky, Erwin J., 267-68
Kool-Vent Awning Co., 339
Korshak, Marshall, 91, 202, 207, 230
Korshak, Sidney, 202, 230
Kreml, Frank, 255
Kries, George, 183
Kringas, Gus, 165-66
Kringas, John P., 165
Kruse, Leslie Earl, 122, 296, 344
Kucharski, Edmund J., 177-78
Kunz, Stanley H., 189
Kupcinet, Irv, 48
Kurtz, Seymour, 311
Kusper, Stanley, 198

L and P Milk Company, 244, 245
LaBarbera, Joseph Anthony, 68, 344-45
Labor racketeering, 19-20, 22-44
Labriola, Paul, 27, 90, 181, 182, 284, 310
LaBuy, Walter J., 72
Ladon, Nathan, 22
Laino, Joseph J., 153-54, 208
Landau, David, 269
Landesman, Irving, 304
Lane, George A., 209
Lang, Harry, 118-19
Lansky, Meyer, 213, 223, 230
Lapiane, Frank, 75
LaPorte, Frank, 3, 38, 88, 211, 253, 345-46
Lardino, Daniel, 26
Lardino, John, 7, 26, 178, 346
LaSalle Hotel, 23
Laskowski, Casimir, 136
Lasky, Morris, 83, 84
Latin Quarter, 90
Lavin, Anna R., 309, 313
Lawndale Enterprises, Inc., 224
Laundry Workers Union, 310
Lederer, Louis, 230
Lee, Edward, 42-43
Lee, Jason, 243-44
Lee, Robert M., 111
Lee, William A., 30
Lee Berco Inc., 90
LeFore Insurance Company, 301
Leibe, Gus, 296
Leibowitz, Samuel, 308-9
Leighton, George N., 9, 305-6, 308
Leonardo, James B., 143, 165
Lester, Ada (Everleigh), 95
Lester, Minna (Everleigh), 95, 100
Levin, Hymie, 138
Levine, Izzy, 129
Lewis, Benjamin F., 168-70, 193, 252
Lewis, John W., Jr., 188
Lewis, Samuel, 158, 159

Libonati, Ronald V., 73, 142-50, 176, 189, 217, 286
Lido Motel, 335
Liebe, Gus, 122, 307
Lieberman, Ernest, 217
Liebling, A. J., 86-87
Lightnin', 1, 111, 180, 216, 217, 221
Lindheimer, Arthur J., 217
Lindheimer, Ben, 217
Linen of the Week, Inc., 39
Lingle, Alfred "Jake," 107-14, 117
Link, Ted, 110-11
Lipsky, Marcus, 245
Lisciandrello, Frank, 307
Lisciandrello, Sam, 65
"Little Apalachin dinner," 65
"Little red notebook," 242-47
Littrell, Dallas O., 160 n
The Living Room, 325, 339
Loan racket. See "Juice"
Local 44, Amalgamated Industrial Union, 33
Local 734, Bakery Wagon Drivers Union, 30
Local 450, Bartenders, Waiters, Waitresses and Miscellaneous Workers Union, 25-26, 29, 323
Local 278, Chicago Bartenders and Beverage Dispensers Union, 23-25
Local 658, Drugstore, Fountain and Luncheonette Employees Union, 26
Local 755, Film and Exhibitors Truck Drivers Union, International Brotherhood of Teamsters, 27
Local 727, Funeral Drivers, Directors, Embalmers and Miscellaneous Union, International Brotherhood of Teamsters, 333
Local 569, Hoisting and Portable Engineers Union, 20
Local 593, Hotel and Restaurant Employees and Bartenders International Union, 26, 89, 346
Local 19, International Longshoremen's Association, 41, 42
Local 309, International Union of Operating Engineers, 212
Local 46, Laundry, Cleaning and Dye House Workers International Union, 19, 342
Local 110, Motion Picture Operators Union, 33-35
Local 703, Produce Drivers Union, International Brotherhood of Teamsters, 38
Local 1248, Retail Clerks International Protective Association Union, 336
Local 777, Taxicab Drivers Union, International Brotherhood of Teamsters, 36-43 passim
Local 286, United Industrial Workers of America, 30
Loesch, Frank J., 115, 128
Loftus, "Buck," 244
Lohman, Joseph D., 268, 278, 286
Lombardi, Joseph, 59
Long, Alma, 35
Lormar Distributing Company, 166, 338
Los Angeles Warehouse Company, 223
Losurdo, Sam, 140
Lownes, Victor, 88, 90
Lucas, Scott, 130, 134
Lucenti, Charles G., 33
Luciano, Lucky, 112, 125
Lueder, Arthur C., 224
Lurie, Harold, 83
Lurie, Irene J., 82, 83
Lynch, Thomas, 119
Lynch, William J., 317

M. C. Clark Company, 205, 209
MSC. See Material Service Corporation
MacDonald, David R., 195
Madden, Arthur, 134
Maddox, Claude, 25-26
Madigan, John, 149
Maggio's Steak House, 338, 341
Mahon, Thomas, 275
Mahoney, Neal, 301
Maine-Idaho-Ohio, 45
Maloy, Tommy, 33-34
Mancin, Albert, 173
Mangano, Lawrence, 125, 173, 181, 182
Mangano, Philip, 19
Manhattan Brewery, 224
Manno, Fred, 172

362

Manno, Nick, 172
Manno, Pat, 78
Manno, Pat, Jr., 78
Manno, Sam, 172
Manno, Thomas, 172
Manny Skar's Sahara, 70, 74
Mantynband, Louis, 224, 230
Maraldo, John, 14
Marblehead Lime Company, 215
Marcie, George, 39
Marcus, Leon, 8, 271
Marcy, Pat, 12, 142, 151, 152, 153, 160, 161, 162-63
Marcy, Paul, 142
Marijuana, 208
Marinelli, Albert, 125
Mario's Pizzeria, 344
Market Introduction Corporation, 80
Marks, Harry, 112
Marks, Willie, 19
Mark Twain Hotel, 337, 345
Marovitz, Abraham Lincoln, 293, 316
Marshall Savings and Loan Association, 74, 75, 76-77
Martin, Hans, 288
Martin, Jim, 61-62, 175
Martin, Richard, 29
Maryland Hotel, 248, 326
Marzullo, Vito, 142, 148, 155, 158, 165, 316
Marzullo, William, 165
Massey, Robert L., 148
Masters, Edgar Lee, 102, 103
Material Service Corporation, 214-21
Matheos, John J., 270, 273
Maurovich, Walter A., 256
Maxwell, W. D., 111, 230
Mayfair Acceptance Corporation, 41, 82
McAvoy, Walter, 191
McCahey, James, 219
McCann, Forbes E., 200
McClellan, John L., 28, 44, 64, 306
McClellan Committee, 22, 28, 31, 36, 37, 39, 40, 41, 44, 63, 227, 249, 295, 321-54 passim
McCluskie, Ben, 304-5
McCluskie, Norma, 304-5
McConnell, Curtis, and McConnell, 209
McConnell, Francis, 209
McCormack, John W., 201
McCormick, John V., 229
McCormick, Robert R., 86, 106, 108, 110, 111, 112
McCormick Place, 35, 42-43
McCulloch, William M., 150
McDermott, John J., 255
McDonald, Michael Cassius, 97, 98, 103, 116
McDonnell, Robert J., 52, 53, 54, 68, 254, 299, 300, 302
McDonough, Joseph, 105
McFetridge, Bill, 258
McGuire, Phyllis, 8, 12, 14
McGurn, Jack, 6, 18, 26, 54, 143
McKenna, Jeremiah, 90
McLane, George B., 23-25
McMullen, Jay, 187
McSwiggin, William H., 112
Meade Electric Company, 209
Meader, George, 149
Meadowmoor Dairy, 17, 158
Meek, Joe, 57
Meister, Harriet, 78
Mendola, Donna, 293
Mendola, Guy, 272-73, 285, 293
Mensik, C. Oran, 72, 73
Mercurio, Sam, 59
Mercury Record Corporation, 40
Merlo, Mike, 100
Merriam, Robert E., 242
Mesi, James, 180-81
Mesi, Philip, 181, 286
Mesi, Sam, 180-81, 346
Messino, William, 58-59, 65, 76, 346-47
Metropolitan Sanitary District, 116, 134, 135, 153, 177, 181, 183, 191, 199-215, 218, 219, 222, 231
Meyers, David S., 280
Michigan Cleaners, 18
Middle West Utilities, 103
Mid-State Jaguar Ltd., 41

Midwest Maintenance Company, 43
Mid-West News, 207
Midwest Triumph Distributors, 41
Mike Fish's restaurant, 322, 351, 352
Mike's Restaurant, 341
Milano's Restaurant, 328, 351
Milk Wagon Drivers Union, 17
Miller, Harry, 119, 127
Miller, Peter L., 191
Mirro, James, 16, 53-54, 60, 65, 254, 347
Mitchell, Donald, 41
Mitchell, Rosie, 21
Mondo, Joe, 174
Monroe Electric Company, 209
Montana, Joey, 34
Moon's Restaurant, 334, 340, 346, 347
Moore, Edward F., 269
Moor's Mud Baths, 327
Moran-Aiello gang, 112, 114, 115, 117
Moran, George "Bugs," 18, 19, 60, 115, 182, 183
Moran, Jack, 275
Moravec, Henry J., 74, 75
Morhouse, L. Judson, 90, 91
Morelli, Fred M., 138, 139
Morris, Joseph, 46, 176
Morrison, Richard, 235-38
Morrison Hotel, 119, 123
Morrissey, F. Emmett, 281, 282, 308
Morton, Arnold, 88, 90, 91
Morton Construction Co., 217
Moschiano, Anthony, 65-68, 182
Moulding-Brownell Company, 220
Mount Prospect Country Club, 80
Movietown Motel, 350
Mulea, Henry T., 238, 239
Munizzo, Tom, 296
Murphy, Tim, 19, 218
Murphy, W. J., 188
Murray, James, 286
Murray, Laverne, 38, 39
Murray, Simon A., 212
Musso, Victor, 185

Nanini, Sam, 218-19, 226, 230
Nanini, William, 219
Napoli, Alexander J., 30, 303, 308, 317
Narcotics traffic, 11, 12, 68-69, and passim
Nash, Dana Horton, 32-33
Nash, Patrick A., 103, 116, 117, 122, 124, 175, 184
Nasser, Arthur, 80
National Cuba Hotel Corporation, 213
National Labor Relations Board, 41, 42
National Lumber Company, 80
National Operating Company, 315
National Service Company, 42
Navarolli, Anthony, 77
Near North Insurance Company, Inc., 185
Neglia, Thomas, 244
Neibert, Betty Jeanne, 21, 22
Neistein, Bernard S., 148, 166, 197
Newberry, Ted, 112-19 passim
Newmark, Ben, 101
New Michigan Hotel, 349
Newport Construction Company, 80
New York World, 109
Nickey's Frozen Pizza, 56
Nicoletti, Charles, 5, 65, 68, 77, 81, 347-48
Nick's restaurants, 332
Nicosia, Charles, 151
Nitti, Frank, 5, 23-25, 34, 118, 119, 122, 202
Nitti, Michael, 81
Nixon, Richard M., 193, 194, 224
Normandy Inn, 152
North Avenue Steak House, 327, 335, 343, 346, 351
Northern Illinois Agrolith Company, 218
Northern States Company, 205, 209
Northern States Construction, 209
North Side Grape Distributors, 350
Nuccio, Dominick, 130-31, 348
Nudleman, Samuel L., 217

Oak Forest Hospital, 200, 201
O'Banion, Dion, 182, 183, 224
O'Brien, John T., 147

363

O'Brien, Lawrence C., 184
O'Brien, Thomas J., 145, 146, 266, 286
Occidental Life Insurance Company, 37
Ochs, Martin, 284
O'Connel, Ruth, 297
O'Connel, Bernard J., 89-90
O'Connor, John, 54
O'Connor, Timothy, 239, 242, 245, 251, 255
Office of Price Administration, 225
Ogilvie, Richard B.: on Giancana's jail stay, 15, 16, 17; challenges voter registration, 196-97, 198; on Sanitary District, 208; and war on crime, 266-76; and Sam DeStefano, 303; mentioned 136, 157, 281
O'Grady, Alderman, 220
O'Hara, Ralph J., 34
O'Hare, Edward J., 185
Ohlin, Carl, 284
O'Leary, James, 98
Olf, Murray H., 145
Oliver, Frank, 308
Olshon, Max, 311, 312-13
O'Malley, Walter R., 246
O'Mara, Michael, 277
Opper, Hal, 41
Orchid Flower Shop, 39
Oser, Fred F., 34

P&S By-Products Company, 83
Pacelli, William V., 143
Pacheco, Louis, 209-10
Pacific Brewing Co., 340
Palmer, Potter, 3
Palmer House, 27, 84
Panczko, Edward "Butch," 282, 283, 284-86, 288-89, 294
Panczko, Joseph "Pops," 282, 283, 284, 286-89, 292, 294-95
Panczko, Paul "Peanuts," 272, 282, 283, 284-85, 290-95, 318
Panos, James, 288
Pantaleo, Frank V., 38, 39, 75
Pantillo, Michael, 125
Panton, Thomas, 24
Paolo Salce, Inc., 40
Papa Milano's Pizza, 337
Pape, Frank, 256-57
Pardo, Sam, 172
Parrillo, Donald, 158-60
Parrillo, William, 158
Parr Finance, 158-59
Parr Loan, 158-59
"The Patch," 332
Paterno, Tony, 244
Patras, Peter, 244
Patrick, Leonard, 122, 130, 169, 348-49
Patronage, 188-89, 191
Payne News Agency, 99
Peacock, Donald, 195
Pearson, Drew, 229, 230
Pease, James, 99
Peoples Gas Light & Coke Company, 103, 106
Pepito's, 325, 326, 330, 337, 338, 339
Perry, Joseph Sam, 310, 311, 313
Personal Business Service, 189
Pesch, Frank, 42
Peterson, Virgil W., 46
Petrone, Patrick, 176
Petrone, Robert, 286
Phelan, Kryan V., 239
Phil's Lounge, 347
Pierce, Ralph, 19, 22, 143, 207, 250, 262, 349
Pigano, James, 80
Pignatello, Joseph, 78, 81
Pike, C. S. Bentley, 310
Pinelli, Anthony R., Sr., 3, 38, 172, 200, 349-50
Pinkerton, Ralph R., 203-4, 205
Plan-It Travel Bureau, 81
Playboy Clubs, 87-92, 325, 329, 330, 338, 340, 351, 354
Police corruption, 127-34, 199, 233-319, and passim
Policy racket, 6-7, 45, 108-10, 170-72
Political corruption, 93-232, and passim
Polito, Joseph, 81 n
Polk, Ralph, 32, 33

Polo, Ron, 53
Pontarelli, Anthony, 212-13
Pontarelli, Michael, 212
Pontone, Dolly, 81
Pope, Joseph A., 7, 285
Pope John XXIII, 200
Porcaro, Frank, 177-79, 201
Posner, Bernard, 22
Posner, Herman, 35
Postl's Health Club, 152, 336, 354
Potenza, Rocco, 5, 65, 253, 350-51
Potts, Ernest D., 129
Poultry Drivers Union, 36
Powell, Paul, 178, 179, 188, 191, 206, 217
Powers, John, 100
Practical Supply Company, 138
Pranno, Rocco Salvatore, 65, 71, 351
Pratico, Louis, 211
Prendergast, John C., 126, 130, 131-32
Preuss, Robert, 90
Prignano, Al, 143
Prio, Ross, 63, 87, 89, 158, 182, 187, 243-51 passim, 309, 351-52
Produce and Florist Drivers Union, 36
Producers Supply and Engineering Company, 215
Prostitution, 95-100, 124, 240, and passim
Prudential Insurance Company, 226
Publix Parking Company, 244
Puffpaff, Robert, 301
Pullman, George, 3
Punchboards, 47-48
Pussycat Lounge, 347

Quinn, Paul, 248-49, 264 n

R. and M. Construction Company, 73
Rado, Harold, 223
Raft, George, 153
Ragen, James, 130
Rago Brothers' Funeral Home, 176
Rainey, John W., 100-1
Recorded Music Service, 40
Reddi-Sales Company, 80
Reddi-Whip, 245
Red Lion Inn, 351
Regal Vending Company, 88
Regan, Thomas J., 294
Regency Hotel, 325, 326, 337, 344, 345
Regular Republican Club of Cook County, 115
"Rehash," 78
Reid, John E., 265
Reinhardt, Bill, 85
Reinhardt, Ruth, 85
Remus, George, 315
Republican Party, 197 and passim
Republican State Central committee, 189
Resinous Products and Chemical Corporation, 223
Retreat Lounge, 350
Rex Hotel, 138
Reynolds, Don B., 227
Ricca, Paul, 3, 23, 24, 34, 35, 38, 51, 139, 143, 146, 260, 271, 352-53
Richards, Judy, 14
Richardson, Frank, 315
Riley Management Corporation, 80
Rim Rock Ranch, 166-67, 338
Rinella, Frank A., 16
Rio, Frank, 143
Rite-Lite Neon Sign Co., 326
Riverwood Country Club, 63, 333
Riviera, Lupe, 67-68
Riviera Lanes, 334
Riviera Lounge, 350
Roasa Nova Tailor Shop, 334
Robert's Lounge, 351
Robson, Edwin A., 308
Rockefeller, Nelson A., 90
Rock Road Construction Company, 218, 219
Roe, Theodore P., 7, 45, 189
Rogers, Walt, 183
Rohm-Haas Corporation, 222
Roma, Tony, 87-89
Romano, Albert Louis, 24 n
Romano, Louis, 24, 25, 26

Romano, Fred A., 244-45
Romano, Sam, 189
Roosevelt, Franklin D., 118, 119-20, 221
Roosevelt, James, 126, 223
Roosevelt Club, 251
Roosevelt Finance Company, 224
Rosanova, Louis, 61, 63
Rosenberg, Alan Robert, 78, 79-80
Rosenberg, Benjamin, 19
Rosenberg, Lawrence, 41, 78, 82
Rosenberg, Mike, 104-5
Rosenberg, Moe, 104-7, 116, 117, 122, 124, 224
Rosenberg Iron & Metal Company, 105
Ross, Don, 41, 42
Ross, Paul C., 185
Rossano, Lawrence, 29-30
Rosenheim, Julius, 112
Rosinia, Michael L., 218
Roth, Edwin C., Sr., 222
Roth-Adams Fuel Co., 222, 329
Royko, Mike, 63, 144, 192
Rugendorf, Leo, 41, 76, 78, 81, 82, 83
Russell, Harry, 172, 207
Russell, William F., 108, 109-10, 113
Russo, Michael, 75-76
Ryan, Daniel J., 302
Ryan, Frank, 217
Ryan, Robert Emmet, 230

S.A.C. Club, 329
S. L. Suth Company, 80
S. L. Suth Jewelry Company, Inc., 80
Safeway Insurance Company, 159
Sahara Inn North, Inc., 74, 76
Sahara Motel Corporation, 74
Sain, Harry L., 175
St. Clair County, 192
St. Louis Star, 110-11
St. Valentine's Day Massacre, 6, 19, 112, 332
Salamoni, Vincent, 195
Salce, Victor P., 40
Salvatore, Rocco, 65, 69, 353
Sands Hotel, 230
Sanitary District. See Metropolitan Sanitary District
Santa Fe Saddle and Gun Club, 65
Santucci, Frank, 53, 304
Sapienza, Sebastian, 181
Saporito, Michael, 310, 311, 312, 314
Saporito, Robert, 310, 311, 312, 313
Savings and Loan, 73
Sbarbaro, John A., 7
Scala, Florence, 157
Scala National Bank, 159
Scalise, George B., 23
Scam, 77-84
Scanlan, John F., 207
Scaramuzzo, Joseph, 65
Scaramuzzo, Louis, 65
Scaramuzzo & Sons, 65
Scariano, Anthony, 192-93
Schaefer, Wallace C., 308
Schafer, Gus, 132
Schatz, George, 229
Scheidt, Burton A., 204, 206, 231
Scherping, John, 269
Schippers, David P., 35, 161
Schnackenberg, E. J., 104
Scholl, Edward T., 219
Schroeder, Carl A., 269
Schulman, Joseph W., 114
Schulman, Morton, 78
Schwartz, Terrell, 195-96
Schwarz, Ulysses S., 229
Scott, James, 301
Scoyk, Grace Van, 269
Seabrook Apartments, 342
Sears, Barnabas, 308
Seavey, Duane S., 280-82
Secret Service, 293
Senate Crime Investigating Committee. See Kefauver
   Committee
Senese, Dominic, 38, 39, 69
Senese, Frank, 38
Serb, Clarence R., 214

Serritella, Daniel A., 110, 139, 143
Serritella, Vince, 258-59
Service Savings and Loan Association, 59
Shallow, Gerald, 269
Shaw, Donald, 276-79
Sheehan, Timothy P., 16
Sheraton Chicago, 84
Sheridan, Paul M., 165
Sherman Hotel, 84, 129, 230
Shiel, Bernard J., 134, 206
Show Tap Lounge, 332
Siciliano, Joseph, 269
Siegel, Bugsy, 213
Siegel, Evelyn V., 82-83
Silvan, Joachim, 81
Silvestri, Anthony Rocco, 16
Silver Domes, 310
Silverstein, Leroy, 78, 81, 82
Simon, Paul, 190-91, 192-93
Simon, Seymour, 258, 267, 316
Simon Meat and Provision Company, 83
Sinatra, Frank, 8, 71
Singapore restaurant, 123
Singapore Steak & Chop House, 322
Siragusa, Charles, 59, 192, 302, 303
Skalley, William, 19
Skar, Mandel, 69-77
Skidmore, William R., 115, 129
Smart, Ted, 203-6, 209-10, 213
Smith, Al, 119
Smith, Cecil Corbett, 299, 300, 301, 302
Smith, Charles C., 178-79, 206
Smith, Elbert S., 72-73
Smith, Fred "Jukebox," 40, 286
Smith, John Austin, 201
Smith, Lee, 197-98
Smith, Lucille, 307
Smith, S. E., 315
Solomon, Al, 78
Sortino, Frank, 298
Sortino, John, 298
Sortino, John, Jr., 298
Sortino, Joseph, 298
Southwest Community Builders Inc., 72, 73
Spadevecchio, Joe, 269
Spano, Anthony, 26, 323
Spataro, Gabriel, 244
Special Investigations Unit, 268, 275
Speren, Pete, 248, 249
Sportsman's Park, 143, 185, 217, 325, 328, 342, 343,
   346
Spranze, Mike, 165
Stacher, Joseph, 223
Standard-Kollsman Industries Inc., 231
Stanton, Danny, 23, 26
Stark, Ralph, 42
Starr, Harry W., 114
Stege, John, 108, 171
Stein, Ben, 42-43
Stelmaszek, Claire, 48-50
Stelmaszek, Raymond, 48-49
Sterile Glass Company, 311
Sterling Drug, 203
Sterling-Harris Ford Agency, 80-81
Stern, Dora Greiver, 228-30
Stevens, Donald, 271
Stevenson, Adlai E., 41, 126-27, 130, 134-35, 139,
   141, 144
Stolkin, Ralph, 230
Store Properties, Inc., 223
Strader, J. Gail, 166
Strak, Peg, 87
Street Laborers' Union, 218
Structural Maintenance Service, Inc., 207, 209
Stuart, William H., 118
Sturch, Eddie, 183, 184-85
Subway Poolroom, 185, 328, 330, 337, 344
Sullivan, Dan, 22
Sumner, Steve, 17, 18, 21
Sunshine Restaurant, 337, 338
Swig, Ben, 223
The Syndicate, 1-92 and passim
Szelog, Butch, 284-85
Szelog, Charles, 284-85

TFX contract, 227, 228
T. J. Cullen jewelry store, 287
Taj Mahal, 75
Talk of the Town, 81
Tam O'Shanter Country Club, 8, 63
Tannenbaum, Saul, 143
Taorima, Eugene, 244
Tarantino, Arthur Charles, 78
Tarr Tobacco Distributing Company, 72
Tarsch, Willie, 125
Tarsitano, Benjamin, 33
Tatro, Joseph A., 315
Taylor, Elizabeth, 149
Taylor and Company, 25
Taylor Liquors, 342
Teamsters Union, 149-50, 343. *See also* Locals
Teitelbaum, Abraham, 26, 27, 28, 90
Tennes, Mont, 99
Teutonico, Frank, 68
Thompson, William Hale, 100, 101, 106, 109, 116, 147, 196, 258
Tisci, Anthony P., 11, 144-45, 149, 150-51, 161
Toman, John, 100
Tomaszek, Stanley, 297
Tom's Steak House, 326, 332
Torello, James Vincent, 60, 61, 65, 353-54
Torrio, Johnny, 100-2, 112, 137
Touhy, John J., 175
Touhy, John P., 175
Touhy, Roger, 122-23, 132
Touhy, William J., 129, 130
Touhy & Sain, 175
Tournabene, Frank, 96
Towne Hotel, 224, 280, 281, 323
Trans-American, 130, 131
Traylor, Melvin A., 221
Triplett, William, 32-33
Troxel, Franklin D., 204
Truax-Traer Coal Company, 222
Truman, Harry S., 126, 225
Turf Club, 323
Turf Lounge, 29
Turner, Harold, 311
Turner, Paul E., 45
The Twenty Incredible Years, 118
Twin Distributing Company, 83
Twin Food Products Company, 83
Twist Lounge, 327, 332, 347
Tyler, Harrison, 42

U.S. Justice Department, 145-47, 148, 150, 151, 155, 161-62, 163, 164, 205-6, 227, 353
Uddo, Giuseppe, 244
Unione Siciliano, 131
Union racketeering. *See* Labor racketeering
United Credits Corporation, 223
United Electric Coal Company, 221-22
United Equity Corporation, 230-31
United Industrial Workers of America, 30
United Societies, 116

Valentino's Restaurant, 83-84, 240, 325, 326, 328, 330, 337, 351
Valley Farm Market, 334
Vallo, Rocky, 129
Van Lent, George, 114
Van Merritt Beer, 340
Verive, Louis J., 76-77
Vernon Farm Products Company, 38
Viaduct Lounge, 296
Vic Damone Pizza Corporation, 55
Villa Venice, 81
Vine, Irving, 21-22
Vitell, Scott, 174
Vogel, Edward, 21, 22, 40, 87, 89, 122, 138, 152, 166, 253, 286, 354
Vogue Credit Jewelers, 81
Von Lengerke & Antoine sporting goods company, 117
Vote frauds. *See* Election scandals

Vydra, Frank, 168
Vydra, George, 167-68
Vydra Produce Company, 167

Wadden, Thomas A., 14
"Wagon Wheel," 8
Wakefield, Lawrence, 44-45
Wall, John, 16
Walsh, Jimmy, 230
Walsh, Maurice, 309
Walton Club, 347, 351
Ward, Daniel P., 157-58, 164, 193, 204-5, 212, 251, 271, 273, 274, 280, 281
Warren, John T., 184
Waterloo, Nick, 180
Webb, Del E., 226
Webb & Knapp, 223
Webster Hotel, 84
Weinberg, James, 27, 90, 181, 310
Weinberg, Robert L., 14
Weiner, Erwin, 43
Weiner, Irving, 83
Weiss, Earl, 139-40
Weiss, George B., 297, 298
Weiss, Hymie, 224
Wentworth, John, 265
Western Cash Register Company, 99
Western Laundry Service, 39
West Side Bloc, 73, 136, 143, 144, 155, 156, 158, 174-75, 176, 180, 184, 187, 191, 192, 241
West Suburban Scavenger Service, 89
Wexler, Morris J., 193
Whales, Johnny, 62
White, William S., 280
Whitener, Basil L., 149
White Pines Country Club, 332-33, 346
Wien, Lawrence A., 226
Wiley, Floyd, 237
Will, Hubert L., 311, 313
William Hale Thompson Republican Club, 115
Williams, Edward Bennett, 14
Williams, Elmer L., 111, 120, 127, 216, 217, 220, 221, 295
Williams, John J., 196
Williams, Richard J., 115
Wilson, Camille, 275
Wilson, Orlando W., 49, 63-64, 170, 199, 208, 246-65 *passim,* 295-96
Winel, Edward W., 78
Winger, Al, 180
Winkler, Gus, 230
Winston, Strawn, Smith and Patterson, 206
Witsman, William, 53, 268, 272, 274-75
Wolcoff, Robert A., 78
Wolfram, Ray, 150
The Woodlawn Organization, 171
Woods, Joe, 176
Wortman, Frank, 151, 172
Wright, Jack, 35, 40

Yaras, David, 60, 61, 62, 65, 122, 123, 354
Yellow Cab Company, 33, 37, 39, 40
Yerkes, Charles T., 3
"Youngbloods," 5, 7, 16

Zagri, Sidney, 150
Zahn, Louis, 269-70, 271, 272
Zahn Drug Company, 268
Zangara, Giuseppe, 118, 120-22
Zapas, Gus, 19, 87
Zeigler, Dennis H., 20
Ziffren, Paul, 222-23, 224-25
Zimmerman, Abraham H., 48
Zimmerman, Arthur, 271
Zimmerman, Frank, 271
Zimmerman process, 203
Zuckerman, Ben, 124-25
Zuta, Jack, 114-15, 118
Zwillman, Abner, 223

366